The Reconciliation of Humanity in Christ

The Reconciliation of Humanity in Christ

The Church's Ministry of Leading and Serving the Globalized World

PETER Y. HONG

☙PICKWICK *Publications* · Eugene, Oregon

THE RECONCILIATION OF HUMANITY IN CHRIST
The Church's Ministry of Leading and Serving the Globalized World

Copyright © 2024 Peter Y. Hong. All rights reserved. Except for brief quotations in critical publications or reviews, no part of this book may be reproduced in any manner without prior written permission from the publisher. Write: Permissions, Wipf and Stock Publishers, 199 W. 8th Ave., Suite 3, Eugene, OR 97401.

Pickwick Publications
An Imprint of Wipf and Stock Publishers
199 W. 8th Ave., Suite 3
Eugene, OR 97401

www.wipfandstock.com

PAPERBACK ISBN: 979-8-3852-1777-9
HARDCOVER ISBN: 979-8-3852-1778-6
EBOOK ISBN: 979-8-3852-1779-3

Cataloguing-in-Publication data:

Names: Hong, Peter Y., author.

Title: The reconciliation of humanity in Christ : the church's ministry of leading and serving the globalized world / Peter Y. Hong.

Description: Eugene, OR : Pickwick Publications, 2024 | Includes bibliographical references.

Identifiers: ISBN 979-8-3852-1777-9 (paperback) | ISBN 979-8-3852-1778-6 (hardcover) | ISBN 979-8-3852-1779-3 (ebook)

Subjects: LCSH: Globalization—Religious aspects—Christianity. | Theology. | Jesus Christ—Person and offices.

Classification: BR115.G59 .H65 2024 (paperback) | BR115.G59 .H65 (ebook)

12/06/24

All Scripture quotations, unless otherwise indicated, are taken from: The Holy Bible, English Standard Version® (ESV®) © 2001 by Crossway, a publishing ministry of Good News Publishers. All rights reserved.

Scripture quotations marked CSB have been taken from the Christian Standard Bible®, Copyright © 2017 by Holman Bible Publishers. Used by permission. Christian Standard Bible® and CSB® are federally registered trademarks of Holman Bible Publishers.

Scripture quotations marked (NASB®) are taken from New American Standard Bible®, Copyright © 1960, 1971, 1977, 1995, 2020 by The Lockman Foundation. Used by permission. All rights reserved. lockman.org

Scripture quotations marked (NIV) are taken from the Holy Bible, New International Version®, NIV®. Copyright © 1973, 1978, 1984, 2011 by Biblica, Inc.™ Used by permission of Zondervan. All rights reserved worldwide. www.zondervan.com The "NIV" and "New International Version" are trademarks registered in the United States Patent and Trademark Office by Biblica, Inc.™

Scripture quotations marked (NLT) are taken from the Holy Bible, New Living Translation, copyright ©1996, 2004, 2015 by Tyndale House Foundation. Used by permission of Tyndale House Publishers, Carol Stream, Illinois 60188. All rights reserved.

Scripture quotations marked (NRSV) are from New Revised Standard Version Bible, copyright © 1989 National Council of the Churches of Christ in the United States of America. Used by permission. All rights reserved worldwide.

A Gift to the Church

Contents

Permissions ix

Illustrations xi

List of Abbreviations xiii

Preface xv

Acknowledgments xvii

Introduction 1

1 The Nature of Globalization 17

2 The Historical Development of Globalization 51

3 The Hegemonic Globalization of the West 102

4 The Role of Religion in Renewing Globalization 132

5 Theological Attitudes toward Globalization 157

6 Theological Engagement with Globalization 204

Conclusion 257

Bibliography 265

Permissions

Figure 1: The Code of Hammurabi, Wikimedia Commons. Photographed by Mbzt, Creative Commons Attribution 3.0 Unported license, https://upload.wikimedia.org/wikipedia/commons/6/64/P1050763_Louvre_code_Hammurabi_face_rwk.JPG

Figure 2: Model of the Processional Way and Ishtar Gate, Adobe Stock. Photographed by Kirk Fisher–stock.adobe.com, Standard License.

Figure 3: Sacred Dragon and Bull Relief on the Ishtar Gate, Wikimedia Commons. Photographed by Osama Shukir Muhammed Amin FRCP(Glasg), Creative Commons, https://upload.wikimedia.org/wikipedia/commons/0/04/Dragon_and_bulls_of_the_the_Ishtar_Gate_of_Babylon%2C_Iraq%2C_colored_glazed_and_molded_bricks%2C_6th_century_BCE._Pergamon_Museum.jpg.

Figure 4: Winged Lion Relief on the Processional Way, Wikimedia Commons. Photographed by Dudva, Creative Commons Attribution-Share Alike 4.0 International license, https://commons.wikimedia.org/wiki/File:Relief_on_the_Ishtar_Gate,_Pergamenmuseum_2.jpg.

Figure 5: Model of a Mesopotamian Ziggurat, Wikimedia Commons. Photographed by Neoclassicism Enthusiast. Creative Commons CC0 1.0 Universal Public Domain Dedication, https://upload.wikimedia.org/wikipedia/commons/a/a9/Model_of_a_Mesopotamian_ziggurat_in_the_Pergamon_Museum_%2801%29.jpg.

Figure 6: The Hellenistic World in 281 BC, Wikimedia Commons. Created by Cattette. Creative Commons Attribution-Share Alike 4.0 International license, https://upload.wikimedia.org/wikipedia/commons/9/94/Seleucid_Empire_alternative_map.jpg.

Table 1: Change in Population, Rate of Urbanization, and Poverty Rate. Reprinted from The Ages of Globalization, by Jeffrey Sachs. Copyright © 2020 Jeffrey D. Sachs. Reprinted with permission of Columbia University Press.

Illustrations

FIGURES

1	The Code of Hammurabi	69
2	Model of the Processional Way and Ishtar Gate	72
3	Sacred Dragon and Bull Relief on the Ishtar Gate	73
4	Winged Lion Relief on the Processional Way	73
5	Model of a Mesopotamian Ziggurat in Babylon	74
6	The Hellenistic World in 281 BC	78

TABLE

1	Change in Population, Rate of Urbanization, and Poverty Rate	97

List of Abbreviations

AAPI	Asian American and Pacific Islander
AfD	Alternative for Germany
AUMF	Authorization for the Use of Military Force
BLM	Black Lives Matter
CRISPR	Clustered Regularly Interspaced Short Palindromic Repeats
ER	*Encyclopedia of Religion.* Edited by Jones Lindsay. 15 vols. 2nd ed. Farmington Hills, MI: Thompson Gale, 2005.
GDT	*Global Dictionary of Theology.* Edited by William A. Dyrness and Veli-Matti Kärkkäinen. Downers Grove, IL: InterVarsity, 2009.
GMT	Greenwich Mean Time
IMF	International Monetary Fund
ISIS	Islamic State of Iraq and Syria
ISIL	Islamic State of Iraq and the Levant
ISS	International Space Station
ka	kilo annum, or a thousand years
LGBTQ+	Lesbian, Gay, Bisexual, Transgender, Queer or Questioning, and more
MORENA	National Regeneration Movement
NASA	National Aeronautics and Space Administration
NATO	The North Atlantic Treaty Organization

OECD	The Organization for Economic Cooperation and Development
UN	United Nations
UNPROFOR	The United Nations Protection Force
UTC	Coordinated Universal Time

Preface

THE IDEA OF WRITING a book about theological engagement with globalization was conceived in the prison where I work as chaplain. After many years of conversing with the diverse inmate population and observing their behaviors in the chapel, I realized that prison is a microcosm of the globalized world in which we live together and share a common space. Many inmates practicing various religions come to the chapel to find a moment of peace and safety. They take turns in using the common space designated for worship, study, and prayer. Since there is no privacy in a prison compound, all inmates see and know how Christians practice their religious beliefs and values. Throughout the prison compound where inmates mingle together, Christians share life with all kinds of secularists and other religious adherents. This situation gives them a wonderful opportunity to share the gospel and help those who are struggling emotionally, physically, and spiritually. Many sincere Christians in prison do their best to live in accordance with God's word and care for others as God commands. Regardless of their differences, all inmates have the common goal of going home and being reunited with their family and friends. I wrote this book to fulfill the goal of educating and equipping Christians who are in prison for the ministry of reconciling all people with God and with each other. I therefore dedicate my book to those who will return to society and complete the church's mission of saving and renewing all peoples, nations, and civilizations of the world. They will be returning to a world in which more and more people are sharing the common space for humanity. They will be returning to a place called the globalized world, and they will know how to minister to all people.

Acknowledgments

I COULD NOT HAVE written this book on my own. First and foremost, I thank Jesus Christ for redeeming my life and allowing me to overcome all the trials I faced during my life. I was able to write about all the things I learned and experienced while living as a Christian. I am especially grateful to Professor Ted Rivera for guiding and assisting me throughout the writing process. I was also able to complete this book because of my family's unwavering love and support. During the time of writing this book, my wife and daughter were always there for me. Their constant prayer and encouragement carried me through all the difficulties. I am also grateful for my parents, parents-in-law, and friends for their prayer and support. Lastly, I want to thank all the editors for assisting me with the editing of my book.

Introduction

THE PROBLEMS OF THEOLOGICAL ENGAGEMENT WITH GLOBALIZATION

THE UBIQUITOUS AND IRRESISTIBLE influence of globalization is changing humanity, both as individuals and society. As important as globalization is, Christians do not appear to be as involved in this process as the rest of society. This book addresses the problems of theological engagement with globalization. The term *globalization* first began to appear in business and sociology literature in the 1980s. The first extended debates about the reality of globalization took place within social sciences in the 1990s. According to global studies expert Manfred Steger, it is variably used in both the popular press and academic literature to describe "a process, a condition, a system, a force, and an age." He adds that "the opinions on globalization have ranged from enthusiastic embrace to blanket condemnation."[1] For most people, globalization speaks to the growing development of increasingly integrated political, economic, technological, and cultural systems, ideas, and products. At the beginning of the new millennium, experts in sociology, economics, and political science turned their focus on the consequences of globalization that have fundamentally changed the world.[2] Anthropologists and historians lagged behind but eventually joined the dialogue. Theologians have in turn responded to the social, ethical, and missional issues raised by the globalized world. However, most Christians remain uninformed and unequipped in regard to the problems of globalization.

---

1. Steger, *Globalization*, 1.

2. According to the Library of Congress catalog, more than five thousand books about globalization were published between 2000 and 2004.

This globalization in turn presents at least three issues of societal importance. The first issue is social justice. The theological responses to this issue have provided several frameworks on how Christians can engage with globalization to steer it toward humanity's flourishing; however, there are many gaps on how Christians can actually influence specific domains of globalization to ameliorate injustice in society.[3] The second issue is religious pluralism and ethics. Christian leaders are now grappling with the question of what it means to be both disciples of Jesus Christ and good citizens in a pluralistic society.[4] There is a need to develop a new framework of how Christians should interact with secularists and adherents of other religions while advancing the gospel and ethics of God's kingdom in a globalized world. The third issue is the church's missional method. Globalization has turned the world into a new mission field in which diverse cultures are coexisting in a highly contested space.[5] Further research is needed to redefine the biblical mandate for the church in the twenty-first century. Considering these issues, comprehensive research is necessary to answer the question of how globalization influences theology and how the church should approach globalization.

The rationale for this book is that the power of true religion becomes evident in the world when all Christians engage with globalization to reconcile humanity with God and with each other in preparation for the consummation of God's kingdom (Eph 1:7–10).[6] God's people are given the ministry of reconciliation—the unity of many peoples, nations, and civilizations with God and each other—through the gospel of Jesus Christ (2 Cor 5:18). In the last century, evangelical Christians in general were focused on reconciliation of individual persons with God while neglecting reconciliation between cultures. Globalization's unitary movements, however, have drastically diminished the possibility of practicing private faith within a Christian subculture. There is now an increasing public consensus for the solidarity of all people to work together for the

---

3. Volf, *Flourishing*; Groody, *Globalization, Spirituality, and Justice*; Waters, *Just Capitalism*; Hunter, *To Change the World*.

4. Netland, *Christianity and Religious Diversity*; Berger, *Many Altars of Modernity*; Küng and Kuschel, *Global Responsibility*; Stackhouse, *Globalization and Grace*; Goudzwaard and Bartholomew, *Beyond the Modern Age*.

5. Myers, *Engaging Globalization*; Grenz, *Renewing the Center*; Franke, *Missional Theology*; Hiebert, "Missionary as Mediator."

6. The term *true religion* refers to right beliefs and practices in accordance with the gospel of Jesus Christ, which would lead all believers to demonstrate God's love, truth, justice, and righteousness in society.

common good of humanity.[7] On the other hand, globalization's fragmentary movements have given rise to separatism and antagonism between different peoples, nations, and civilizations. In the midst of this paradoxical influence of globalization, there exists a creative tension for the church to exploit and reclaim its God-given role of leading and serving the globalized world which is in a state of unrest. The significance of this book is that all Christians can become agents of renewal for globalization by administering God's grace and peace for humanity.

THE INFLUENCE OF GLOBALIZATION ON THEOLOGY

Interconnection of the World

Among social theorists, the highly complex, ambiguous, and controversial phenomenon of globalization is generally referred to as "the historical process by which all the world's people increasingly come to live in a single social unit."[8] These theorists believe that the world has entered the "age of globalization" in which a universal and inclusive society has emerged. Although globalization means different things to different people, it can be described as an all-encompassing civilizational concept that has political, economic, technological, and religious dimensions. It is a "new world order," which is translated from the old Latin phrase *novus ordo seclorum*, conveying that the world is both an arranged society with a reliable order and consists of epochs that bring novelty.[9] Korean theologian Young Sub Song observes that through the rapid changes of globalization, people living in different parts of the world are becoming simultaneously interconnected, interdependent, and interrelated. He says, "As a result of this interconnectivity, globalization is reshaping the ways of thinking, lifestyle, and attitude."[10] Catholic theologian Daniel Groody says, "Globalization is radically changing the way we understand ourselves, others, God, and the environment in which we live in, and

---

7. On December 22, 2005, the General Assembly of the United Nations identified solidarity as one of the fundamental and universal values that should underlie relations between peoples in the twenty-first century. It decided to proclaim December 20 of each year as International Human Solidarity Day.

8. Beyer, "Globalization and Religion," 3497.

9. Stackhouse and Paris, *Religion and the Powers*, 21–22.

10. Song, "Cultural Context of Globalization," 243.

it presents the human community with unparalleled opportunities and possibilities, but also with unprecedented challenges and difficulties, especially in the face of widespread social injustice."[11]

The current world order, which is driven by the spread of liberalism and capitalism, is in a state of crisis.[12] In the age of globalization, more and more people are no longer satisfied with pursuing their own happiness as individuals. They are acutely aware of the inequalities that exist around the world, and they are refusing to accept the status quo of injustice in a globalized world.[13] Indeed, on July 8, 2017, a large and violent protest was organized in Hamburg, Germany, against the G20 Summit under the motto "Solidarity without borders instead of G20." The protesters expressed their disdain toward the world leaders that were responsible for causing the problems of globalization. They also organized an alternative summit with multiple plenaries and workshops during which global problems such as poverty, human exploitation, oppression, war, and environmental destruction were discussed.[14] The result, however, was far from being constructive. Iranian sociologist Simin Fadaee assesses the result of the protests:

> Although the alternative summit or Global Solidarity Summit's main objective was to discuss "strategies to realize a solidarity-oriented world," none of the strategies discussed during the summit were reflected in the protests. Moreover, the alternatives and counter-institutions that have been developed over the years did not find their way into the protests either. The protests captured huge media attention, but it was the disruptive and violent nature of the protests which made headlines rather than the scale, variety and demands of the protests.[15]

---

11. Groody, *Globalization, Spirituality, and Justice*, 29.

12. Fukuyama, *Liberalism and Its Discontents*, 1–18, and 130–41. In response to those who are expressing discontent toward globalization, Fukuyama defends liberalism as the best solution to the problems created by diverse societies. He makes a strong case for keeping an international order that is open, inclusive, and progressive without sacrificing individual autonomy.

13. Piketty, *Time for Socialism*, 19–22. Piketty sees inequality as the main problem of globalization and promotes socialism as the best solution. He believes that social-federalism and transnational parliamentary assemblies will be necessary to regulate international economic relations and design adequate financial, fiscal, and environmental regulations.

14. Global Solidarity Summit, "Alternative to the G20 Summit."

15. Fadaee, "Hamburg G20 Protests," para. 5.

From a biblical perspective, activism or revolution cannot change the world, which has become corrupt by humanity's sin and the existence of evil in society (Rom 5:12; Eph 6:12). Individuals first need to be set free by hearing and believing the gospel of Jesus Christ. Then, they can lead others in reforming society in an orderly manner by applying the ethics of God's kingdom without coercion. Although the ministry of preaching the gospel is the highest priority, Christians cannot remain silent about ideological systems that claim moral superiority while allowing human misery to persist. The world needs the spiritual and moral guidance of the church to address the social ills of humanity. As evangelical theologian Bryant Myers says, "The church and all religions must demand that no economic or political system can be judged to be moral if it tolerates anyone living a life that is not fully human."[16] According to Fergus O'Ferrall, a Methodist lay leader of the Irish Humanities Alliance, "Human flourishing is the end of all social, economic and political activity. If any activity is known to be harmful to the overall well-being of human beings, or any of one person or group in society, then it should be opposed and ended."[17] Hispanic feminist theologian María Pilar Aquino therefore proclaims, "No future is possible without justice for women. No future is feasible without human rights for women. No future is viable without meeting women's basic human needs. No future of feminist Christianity can flourish without a just world."[18] The church can heal and renew globalization by preaching the gospel which would lead all believers to administer God's grace and peace by exercising love, truth, justice, and righteousness in society (Isa 1:17; Amos 5:24; Matt 6:33; Rom 12:9; 1 John 3:18).

The world's interconnection through globalization presses theology to promote social justice for humanity's existence as a single society, and to address how the church should spiritually and morally lead the development of globalization for the common good of humanity. At the moment, however, the church does not seem to have a clear direction in caring for a global society. Thus, the church needs to develop a coherent vision, plan, and strategy to influence the institutions of globalization toward human flourishing.

---

16. Myers, *Engaging Globalization*, 189.
17. O'Ferrall, "Flourishing Society," 1.
18. Hunt and Neu, *New Feminist Christianity*, 41.

Integration of Diverse Cultures

Globalization has now become a universal concept that has replaced the tension between modernity and postmodernity in social theory, giving a novel name for the present age that has successfully integrated postmodernity into the current social order. The "globalized world" is forged by the convergence of unitary and fragmentary powers in society. It is not a homogenous culture of modernity and secularism but an integration of diverse cultures of postmodernity and pluralism. According to sociologist John Tomlinson, "Globalization lies at the heart of modern culture; cultural practices lie at the heart of globalization." He claims that "the politics and economics of globalization yield to a cultural account which takes conceptual precedence."[19] Anglican theologian Richard Bauckham assesses, "Our culture is a fluid mixture of modern and postmodern features, which we misunderstand unless we give full recognition to both."[20] While modernity is marked by its optimism in the economic and technological progress of humanity, postmodernity is characterized by its rejection of a meta-narrative and its celebration of diverse views. The integration of diverse cultures means that the globalized world is no longer a unipolar society driven by the secularized West but is a multipolar society brimming with diverse religious beliefs, values, and commitments of the Majority World.[21] The globalized world is a highly contested society where peoples, nations, and civilizations from developing parts of the world are all contributing to humanity's flourishing with their own cultural heritage.

According to Austrian sociologist Peter Berger, all the movements of modernity, which include economic growth, urbanization, mass migration, general literacy and higher education for increasing numbers, and the new technologies of communication, inevitably lead to pluralism. In a world where diverse views are globalized, people have no choice but to know and associate with those who live a different way of life.[22] Thus, evangelical theologian Harold Netland asks, "How should followers of Jesus Christ respond to the religiously diverse and pluralistic world of the early twenty-first century?" He proposes that new ways of thinking must be crafted because the religious, cultural, and political landscape of

---

19. Tomlinson, *Globalization and Culture*, 1–2.
20. Bauckham, *Bible in the Contemporary World*, xi.
21. Dugin, *Theory of a Multipolar World*, 4–16; Hiro, *After Empire*.
22. Berger, *Many Altars of Modernity*, 15.

many nations today are uncharted territory.²³ In this uncertain pluralistic context, Netland believes that Christians "can be entirely faithful to the biblical witness and still acknowledge that there is some truth, beauty, and goodness in other religions."²⁴ He explains that "neither cultures nor religions are completely self-contained, discrete, hermetically sealed systems that remain intact throughout time."²⁵ Due to the cultural reality of pluralism, Christians can no longer disregard the values of others while upholding their own values in society. Globalization presses the church to collaborate with others for the common good of humanity rather than pursuing cultural warfare to dominate society.

While affirming that all religions are not neutral in their values, Christian philosopher Roy Clouser suggests that Christians must take on a new attitude of love, forbearance, and tolerance with practices and lifestyles that may be at odds with Christianity. He says, "In both practical life and in theorizing we must concentrate on the task of recognizing and uprooting what is unbiblical in our own practices and theories, rather than attacking those of other faith communities." Although painful, this approach of practicing religious life will equip Christians to minister over "the entire spectrum of life for the benefit of all humankind."²⁶ In a highly contested world, it is not possible to teach others about the ethics of God's kingdom when Christians are not living by them in both private life and the public domain. Through globalization, God is sanctifying the church so that believers can exercise biblical love, truth, justice, and righteousness to lead and serve others. God's people can shine as bright lights in the world by living in full obedience to the gospel and being blameless in the eyes of the world (Phil 2:15).

A common theme that runs through the theologians who have engaged with globalization and pluralism is their endorsement of developing a "global ethic" and willingness to interact and cooperate with adherents of other religions. Swiss Catholic theologian Hans Küng was in the forefront of developing a global ethic since the early 1990s. His book *Global Responsibility: In Search of a New World Ethic* begins with the following proclamation: "No survival without a world ethic. No world peace without peace between the religions. No peace between the religions

---

23. Netland, *Christianity and Religious Diversity*, x.
24. Netland, *Christianity and Religious Diversity*, 180.
25. Netland, *Christianity and Religious Diversity*, 37.
26. Clouser, *Myth of Religious Neutrality*, 329.

without dialogue between the religions."²⁷ Küng initiated the project *Weltethos*, which is an attempt to describe what the world's religions have in common and draw up a minimal code of rules of behavior everyone can accept. Centered around the Golden Rule that is evident in most religions, there are four irrevocable directives that emerge: (1) commitment to a culture of non-violence and respect for life, (2) commitment to a culture of solidarity and just economic order, (3) commitment to a culture of tolerance and a life of truthfulness, and (4) commitment to a culture of equal rights and partnership between men and women.²⁸

Theologian and social ethicist Max Stackhouse also stresses the need for Christians to have critical dialogue with adherents of other world religions and philosophies in order to develop social ethic for "a highly pluralistic global civil society."²⁹ He asserts that "public theology is the most important theological development today in terms of its potential capacity to address the issues posed by globalization."³⁰ He believes that through Christian Public Theological Ethics, globalization will become "a form of creational and providential grace coming to a catholic and ecumenical partial fulfillment that points us toward a salvific vision for humanity and the world."³¹ According to Korean theologian Sebastian Kim, public theology draws on the resources, insights, and compassionate values of the Christian faith to contribute to the welfare of society. It has a global perspective because many issues affect countries across borders, such as immigration, climate change, and refugees.³²

The integration of diverse cultures through globalization presses theology to answer the question of what it means to be both disciples of Jesus Christ and good citizens in a pluralistic society. The precedent research has shown that Christians need to work in partnership with all peoples, nations, and civilizations while engaging with globalization for the common good of humanity. However, it is still unclear how the church should interact with secularists and adherents of other religions to advance the ethics of God's kingdom. How can the church cooperate with those who may despise Christians' deeply held religious beliefs, values, and commitments? Küng's idea of drawing up a global ethic, a

---

27. Küng and Kuschel, *Global Responsibility*, xv.
28. Küng and Kuschel, *Global Responsibility*, 24–34.
29. Stackhouse, *Globalization and Grace*, 114–16 and 230–50.
30. Stackhouse, *Globalization and Grace*, 77.
31. Stackhouse, *Globalization and Grace*, 249.
32. Kim, *Theology in the Public Sphere*, 3–26.

minimal code of rules of behavior for the world, seems to diverge from the biblical vision of teaching all nations to live in full obedience to God's holy statutes (Isa 2:3; Matt 28:20). On the other hand, Stackhouse's idea of universalizing Christian Public Theological Ethics seems overly optimistic in a world that is temporal, corrupt, and fragmented (2 Cor 4:18; 2 Tim 3:1–7).

Global Consciousness of Humanity

According to Brazilian liberationist theologian Leonardo Boff, globalization influences all spheres of life, thereby giving rise to humanity's collective consciousness.[33] Spanish sociologist José Casanova explains that the present age of globalization is the age in which people, whether they like it or not, become consciously aware of each other's existence. It is a world with a "global consciousness" in which everything that happens affects everybody else on the globe.[34] Global consciousness of humanity develops as the movements of modernity diffuse age-old struggles between people and creates synergy to build a better future. Thus, in describing globalization, Catholic theologian T. Howland Sanks says that "the subjective aspect is just as important as the objective one."[35] He adds, "Globalization does not simply refer to the objectiveness of increasing interconnectedness. It also refers to cultural and subjective matters. . . . How we think about the world, ourselves, our countries, and the relationship between them is part of what we mean by globalization."[36] As Myers puts it, "Globalization is not just changing the world; it is changing us and the way we view the world. . . . While we tend to remain rooted in our local and national identities . . . we cannot escape developing a global way of viewing, thinking about, and experiencing the world."[37] The formation of global consciousness in the world is leading toward the idea that humanity should be reconciled as a single race. This inclusive perspective influences the church's approach to its evangelistic mission. Rather than a divisive approach of "us against them" that pits people against one another, an inclusive approach of "we are in this together"

33. Boff, *Global Civilization*, 30–33.
34. Casanova, "Globalization and the Growing Church."
35. Sanks, "Globalization and the Church's," 632.
36. Sanks, "Globalization and the Church's," 637.
37. Myers, *Engaging Globalization*, 38.

becomes necessary in order to overcome misogyny, xenophobia, racism, gender identity conflicts, class conflicts, ethno-religious conflicts, and other problems that are persistent in the globalized world.[38]

Among many problems of globalization, humanity's sin of hatred against others has manifested itself through racism. Globalization has weakened national borders and allowed an influx of other ethnic peoples into traditional communities, upending the age-old way of living in separation from others. Consequently, it has stirred up the fundamental problem of racial and ethnic division that persists in the world. According to anthropologist and paleobiologist Nina Jablonski, "race" and "ethnicity" have been and continue to be used as ways to describe human diversity. Race is understood by most people as a mixture of physical, behavioral, and cultural attributes. Ethnicity recognizes differences between people mostly on the basis of language and shared culture.[39] She explains that David Hume and Immanuel Kant's writings on the superiority of European whites, the inferiority of African blacks, and the immutability of racial hierarchies had potent effects on the views of government leaders and business interests in Europe and the United States from the mid- and late eighteenth century onward.[40] For a long time, many Christians in Western society have followed the secular philosophers in perpetuating a racist attitude and ethnic discrimination against those who were not "white."

In the globalized world, people are now consciously awakening to the fact that diverse ethnicities of humankind originated from a single race. The formation of global consciousness was bolstered with the completion of the Human Genome Project in 2003.[41] It has confirmed that humans are 99.9 percent identical at the DNA level and there is no genetic basis for different races. The American Society of Human Genetics explains:

---

38. Hunt and Neu, *New Feminist Christianity*, 56–59; Kim, *Embracing the Other*, 31–58; Macedo and Gounari, *Globalization of Racism*.

39. Jablonski, "Skin Color and Race," 438.

40. Jablonski, "Skin Color and Race," 441.

41. National Human Genome Research Institute, "Human Genome Project." In April 2003, the International Human Genome Sequencing Consortium announced that it had generated an essentially complete human genome sequence; it accounted for 90 percent of the human genome and fewer than 400 gaps. On March 31, 2022, the Telomere-to-Telomere (T2T) consortium announced that it had filled in the remaining gaps and produced the first truly complete human genome sequence.

> The science of genetics demonstrates that humans cannot be divided into biologically distinct subcategories. Although there are clear observable correlations between variation in the human genome and how individuals identify by race, the study of human genetics challenges the traditional concept of different races of humans as biologically separate and distinct.[42]

As a result, in 2014, more than 130 leading population geneticists condemned the idea that genetic differences account for the economic, political, social, and behavioral diversity around the world.[43] Since then, however, new discoveries have shattered old assumptions. According to paleogeneticist David Reich, massive technological innovations have revolutionized the study of ancient DNA and transformed the understanding of the lineage of modern humans. The new genetic data shows that mixture and displacement of humans have occurred over thousands and tens of thousands of years, and that people's assumptions of the nature of human populations in the past were wrong. The genome revolution has now revealed that humanity has an uncertain ancestry that is a mixture of many peoples, including archaic hominins. Old stereotypes about identity are being replaced by "a new basis for identity."[44] For Reich, the genome revolution has given humanity "a way to come to grips with who we are—a way to hold in our mind the extraordinary human diversity that exists today and has existed in our past."[45]

The origin of humanity's true ancestry is still buried in history. Scripture says that God created Adam's race and Eve became the "mother of all living" (Gen 3:20). However, much of humanity, including the church, has struggled to overcome the racist attitude and ethnic discrimination that have been pervasive throughout history.[46] The church's missional method needs to be realigned with the eschatological vision of all things holding together in Christ to glorify God on the earth (Col 1:17). Evangelical missiologist Paul Hiebert assesses that the new context of globalization requires missionaries to take on the new role of a mediator by building bridges between different cultures.[47] Racial and ethnic

---

42. American Society of Human Genetics Perspective, "ASHG Denounces Attempts," 636.
43. Prontzos, "Concept of 'Race.'"
44. Reich, *Who We Are*, 259–67.
45. Reich, *Who We Are*, 272.
46. Caselli and Coleman, "Theory of Ethnic Conflict," 162.
47. Hiebert, "Missionary as Mediator," 297–99.

conflicts can be ameliorated in society when all Christians take on the role of a mediator by preaching the gospel and pursuing the ministry of reconciliation for humanity. In this book, the term *World Christians* refers to all believers that take on the role of a mediator to preach the gospel and unite humanity as one in Christ. All God's children are called to be peacemakers (Matt 5:9).

The formation of global consciousness presses theology to enhance the church's missional method by redefining the biblical mandate for God's people in the twenty-first century. Two thousand years ago, when people were separated by the barriers of distance, language, and culture, Jesus commanded the church to go into the ends of the earth and make disciples of all nations. Today, however, Christians are living in an age in which the previous barriers of separation are coming down. All nations are coming to Christians living in the West in droves through free trade, mass migration, and digital connection. Many are coming from the least developed countries that are highly traditional and religious, but they are refusing to assimilate by following the rules and order of Western society. No one knows how this intercultural dynamic will determine the final outcome of globalization. While humanity remains in a state of uncertainty and anxiety, World Christians can administer God's grace and peace for all nations. The task of theology is, therefore, to educate and equip the church for the ministry of reconciliation that aims to unite humanity with God and with each other through the gospel of Jesus Christ (2 Cor 5:18–19).

THE THEOLOGICAL CHALLENGE OF GLOBALIZATION FOR THE CHURCH

Christians' theological engagement with globalization first requires its interpretation. Sanks says that for theologians, our growing awareness and analysis of globalization is "part of the ongoing reading of the signs of the times."[48] As David Fraser states, "Theological response grows out of an understanding of how God is related to history, especially the history of the last two hundred years."[49] In studying globalization, however, theologians should not remain merely as observers or interpreters of our time but should respond with world transforming action and encourage others

---

48. Sanks, "Globalization and the Church's," 651.
49. Fraser, "Globalization," 339.

to do the same. According to evangelical theologian Kevin Vanhoozer, theology should become *lived* knowledge of the church, *sapientia* ("wisdom" in Latin), rather than abstract theoretical knowledge of academia.[50] He proposes a theological method that relies not only on exegetical skill but also on imaginative insight.[51] An interpretation of globalization that results from a theological engagement should lead to decisive action by all Christians, which can influence other people to do the same.

According to German Catholic theologian Johannes Metz, for Christians, the world should be seen as coming into being "historically as a result of the heavenly promises of God, a process for which believers have an essential responsibility."[52] He explains that in Christ, human beings should no longer understand themselves as trapped within an eternal cosmos but should view themselves as "liberated agents of change," capable of transforming both nature and history.[53] Vestiges of the Greek cosmocentric thought-form exist today in modern Christianity, especially in "metaphysical theology," which includes scholastic and neo-scholastic theologies. This metaphysical theology develops privatistic understanding of religious experience.[54] He further explains that "modern theology," which includes transcendental, existential, and personalist theologies, has fallen under the influence of modernity's view of human beings as private individuals; therefore, it has a tendency to privatize the Christian message. Against Christianity's misguided appropriation of the Greek consciousness and the modern consciousness, Metz emphasizes that the Christian anthropocentric form of consciousness is present when it becomes clear that humanity is allowed to make use of the world as a materialistic resource for mankind's God-given freedom.[55] He writes, "The 'creation' of God is mediated everywhere by the 'work' of man."[56] Thus, Metz insists that the social and political life of Christians must not become secondary appendages to their private life. By speaking about the Christian anthropocentric form of consciousness, he is implying that Christians should lead and serve all people by developing a new kind of awareness that can benefit humanity. Today, the church can appropriate

50. Vanhoozer, *Drama of Doctrine*, 50.
51. Vanhoozer, *Drama of Doctrine*, 285.
52. Metz, *Theology of the World*, 53.
53. Metz, *Theology of the World*, 68.
54. Metz, *Theology of the World*, 22.
55. Metz, *Theology of the World*, 54.
56. Metz, *Theology of the World*, 61.

his claim to mean that the most important challenge for the church is to turn from its apathy in the face of people's suffering while preaching the gospel. All Christians must lead and serve humanity by administering Christ's grace and peace in the world. Having the same attitude of Christ's humility, Christians are called to be like-minded, have the same love, and be one in spirit and purpose so that one day every tongue will confess Jesus Christ is Lord (Phil 2:1–11). Theology's progression from interpretation to world transforming action requires the church to be interdisciplinary, biblical, and dialogical in its response to globalization.

THE THEOLOGICAL METHOD FOR ENGAGING WITH GLOBALIZATION

In engaging with globalization, Christians must consider its three characteristics that are difficult to respond to theologically. The theological method of this study aims to overcome those difficulties. First, globalization is an enormously complex and multidimensional process encompassing the historical development of human beings, economics, governance, technology, culture, and religion. Christians might possess certain knowledge that derives from Scripture and religious experience, but they do not know everything about the world. Theological response consequently requires an interdisciplinary method that incorporates vast knowledge shared by diverse experts of globalization. Solving the problems of globalization requires interaction and cooperation between God's redeemed people and the people of this world. Interdisciplinary theology seeks to renew humanity's pursuit of a comprehensive understanding of reality while acknowledging that all things in the world must unite with Jesus Christ. The scope of this study is wide with the goal of developing a universal and coherent theological response to the problems of globalization.

The second characteristic of globalization is that its nature, meaning, and outcomes are ambiguous. From a secular perspective, no one oversees globalization, and it is unclear how it arose, what purpose it serves, and where it will ultimately lead humanity. As Jens-Uwe Wunderlich and Meera Warrier observe, "There is little consensus on what globalization actually is, what drives it, whether it is a qualitatively new phenomenon, and whether it is a primarily beneficial or damaging process."[57] They

---

57. Wunderlich and Warrier, *Dictionary of Globalization*, 1.

further add, "Even though the term globalization is used liberally in political rhetoric and in the press, its meaning is somehow assumed to be intuitively known; it is rarely spelt out."[58] From a biblical perspective, however, God is in control of globalization. Scripture provides a clear purpose and meaning for humanity's existence. The ambiguity of globalization is the consequence of its detachment from biblical input which alone can provide the common vision for humanity. Stackhouse contends that globalizing forces cannot be understood apart from grasping the ways in which they are derived from biblical and Christian religious grounds.[59] Thus, the theological response must provide a clear biblical understanding of how the power of God's word is working through globalization for humanity's salvation and flourishing. Biblical response to globalization exegetes Scripture by both the historical-grammatical method and the allegorical method.

Third, globalization is a highly contested concept, and its interpretation often results from one's ideological disposition or religious identity. According to Nayef Al-Rodhan and Gérard Stoudmann, "this term brings with it a multitude of hidden agendas. An individual's political ideology, geographic location, social status, cultural background, and ethnic and religious affiliation provide the background that determines how globalization is interpreted."[60] Rather than promoting harmony and peace, a theological response to such a controversial subject can lead to inciting further division and disturbance in society. Throughout history, the church's dogmatic stance on controversial issues has caused division, strife, persecution, and war. Considering the highly controversial nature of globalization, a theological response must be dialogical rather than dogmatic. The dialogical method engages with theologians, philosophers, social scientists, anthropologists, geopolitical experts, economists, journalists, and religious adherents of the world representing diverse views. This study attempts to expound the gospel for humanity's salvation by conversing with those who care about the world and the final outcome of globalization. Although opinions on social, political, and economic issues vary widely, the theological method of this study attempts to highlight the views that are held by the majority of the world and those who suffer by the negative effects of globalization. The purpose of this book

58. Wunderlich and Warrier, *Dictionary of Globalization*, 1.

59. Stackhouse, *Globalization and Grace*, 32.

60. Al-Rodhan and Stoudmann, "Definitions of Globalization," 3. This study lists 114 definitions offered by the experts from various background.

is to educate and equip Christians for understanding the basic problems that are hindering the development of globalization so that the church can begin to hold constructive dialogue with secularists and other religious adherents from diverse cultures.

OVERVIEW

The first chapter interprets the nature of globalization by defining its terms and concepts. The second chapter explores the historical development of globalization. The third chapter gives an examination of the hegemonic globalization of the West that has perpetuated social injustice. The fourth chapter considers the role of religion in renewing globalization. The fifth chapter analyzes different theological attitudes toward globalization. The sixth chapter acknowledges the cultural realities that are emerging through globalization and engages with the theological issues raised by a globalized world. The conclusion gives a synthesis of the entire study.

1

The Nature of Globalization

ALTHOUGH GLOBALIZATION IS KNOWN for defying a universal definition, it generally refers to the global integration of all the domains of human life that are differentiated by social scientists including politics, economics, technology, culture, and religion. When anyone engages with globalization, one of the great challenges is the difficulty of pinning down its elusive definition and describing its ambiguous nature. Social scientists have debated if it is an old or new phenomenon, and have not yet reached a consensus.[1] Since Scripture claims "there is nothing new under the sun" (Eccl 1:9), this study will draw the working definition of globalization from a biblical perspective: Globalization is the divinely ordained process of creation, multiplication, dispersion, separation, redemption, integration, and sanctification of humanity in preparation for the consummation of God's kingdom. God's plan and purpose of globalization is humanity's salvation and renewal in Christ. As coheirs with Christ, the church is given the mandate to rule the globalized world by serving all people. This biblical understanding of globalization competes against the contemporary conception of globalization. Chapter 1 interprets the nature of globalization to set the stage for the remainder of the study. The first section assesses the contemporary understanding of globalization as a false religious belief system. The second section expounds on the relationship between globalization and religion. The final section gives the biblical narrative of globalization.

---

1. Lecler, "What Makes Globalization," 355–57.

THE CONTEMPORARY CONCEPTION OF GLOBALIZATION

The contemporary conception of globalization derives from the fusion of the political doctrine of liberalism, the economic doctrine of *laissez-faire* capitalism, and the scientific doctrine of technological progress. Its proponents believe that rational, enlightened individuals who can harness the benefits of a liberal democracy, an unregulated free market, and advanced technology will lead humanity into a new age of justice, freedom, security, and prosperity. Today, globalization is largely influenced and shaped by those who believe in the power of humanity to save itself from poverty, war, disease, and environmental disaster without God's power of salvation through Jesus Christ.

Among many views, British political scientist David Held's definition is helpful in gaining an initial understanding of the contemporary conception of globalization. He writes, "Globalization, at its simplest, refers to a shift or transformation in the scale of human organization that links distant communities and expands the reach of power relations across the world's regions."[2] In other words, it is the process of decentralization of state power that is happening across the world and affecting all the domains of human life.[3] The result is that states can no longer control the direction and outcome of the globalized world. Globalization has simply shrunk the world, giving an astonishing level of power and resources to individual actors who can leverage freedom, the market, and technology to diminish a state's sovereignty. Swedish author Johan Norberg believes that the advancement of "the individual freedoms, open economy, and technological progress" in an interconnected world is allowing all humanity to be related to each other and flourish together as a global society.[4] On the other hand, German political scientist Lena Partzsch suggests that the shift of power from state to non-state actors "implies a new concentration of power on very few individuals with respective resources."[5]

---

2. Held, *Global Covenant*, 1.

3. The term *state power* refers to the capacity of a state to regulate behaviors and enforce order within its territory. It includes the extroverted concept of power in international relations and the introverted concept of power within a society.

4. Norberg, *Progress*, 5.

5. Partzsch, "Powerful Individuals," 5–13.

According to evangelical ethicist Brent Waters, we are transitioning from a world order that was built on nation-states to market-states. In the twentieth century, during the years of the Long War (1914–90), nation-states arose to promote national interests and the welfare of citizens. Globalization has changed this trend. Waters explains that "the market-state is oriented toward promoting opportunities for individual citizens rather than their collective welfare."[6] It has led the globalized world to be driven and shaped by corporations that seek maximum profit to enrich individual investors. Evangelical ethicist William Walker explains how this transition promises to fulfill liberal dreams:

> This view of globalization also rests on the tenets of liberalism, namely, that the promises of modernity will continue to be fulfilled: that the growth of the market, profits, democracy, and personal freedoms are all inevitable byproducts of rational and self-interested progress. It is suggested that the increase of these things is a sign of humanity's flourishing and innovation, successfully harnessed for building a better future and global society.[7]

The great flaw of such a conception of globalization is that it fails to resolve the animosity between humans caused by the uneven use of power and resources. Held explains, "For not only does the awareness of growing interconnectedness create new forms of understanding, it also fuels deep animosities and conflicts. Since a substantial proportion of the world's population is largely excluded from the benefits of globalization, it can be a deeply divisive phenomenon."[8] For those who have gained capital from globalization, their feats are truly incredible. In 2002, South African business magnate and investor Elon Musk founded SpaceX, which is a private space exploration company that cooperates with the US National Aeronautics and Space Administration (NASA). The private company has developed, among its innovative projects, Falcon 9, which is the first orbital class rocket that is reusable. Musk's SpaceX is also developing a giant rocket called Starship to take people to Mars in the future.[9] A powerful individual is single-handedly leading humanity into the age of space tourism. Taking advantage of this opportunity,

---

6. Waters, *Just Capitalism*, 66.
7. Walker, *Theology of the Drug War*, 18.
8. Held, *Global Covenant*, 1.
9. Chang, "SpaceX Wins."

Japanese billionaire Yusaku Maezawa purchased a ticket to become the first civilian passenger to go on a lunar Starship mission by the end of 2023. Although this plan was eventually canceled, he was able to go on a twelve-day journey to the International Space Station (ISS) in 2021. He shared the video clips of his orbital experiences via YouTube. The current market prices for Space Adventures flights to the ISS range from $50 million to $60 million.[10] Opinions are divided on an economic system that enables a handful of individuals to venture into building a space exploration company or go on a space tour while approximately a billion people who never had a chance to tap into the benefits of globalization are suffering in poverty and hunger.

American political philosopher Michael Sandel asks a simple but profound question for humanity: "What's the right thing to do?" In order to achieve justice, Sandel proposes that people ought to engage publicly and politically in proper moral discussion about what is good for a society and then should start enacting those policies that will bring about both the good and a feeling of solidarity within the community.[11] From a theological perspective, Myers is critical of the thin and unsatisfactory anthropology undergirding the contemporary conception of globalization. He says, "Human beings are more than rational, value-maximizing, economic beings," and adds that "the greatest failure of the secular materialist underpinning of globalization is that it ignores the relational nature of human beings." Myers asserts that in a sinful world with significant inequalities of wealth and power, globalization's pursuit of the "total good" is not likely to be the same as the "common good."[12]

The contemporary conception of globalization is a religious belief system that claims humanity can save itself and rule over the world on its own without any help from God. In resisting the gospel, its proponents believe that political freedom, economic liberalization, and a scientific revolution would give enormous power and resources to individuals to achieve incredible feats for humanity's progress. Liberalism, the ideological belief system that triumphed over fascism and communism at the end of the twentieth century, has now morphed into what is commonly referred to as neoliberalism, global capitalism, market fundamentalism, or globalism. The Nobel prize-winning economist Joseph Stiglitz describes this unwavering belief in the market as "the prevailing religion of the

---

10. Wattles, "First Space Station Tourism."
11. Sandel, *Justice*, 260–69.
12. Myers, *Engaging Globalization*, 209.

West."[13] According to politics and international relations scholar Luca Mavelli, neoliberalism is not merely an ideological belief, but a religious one: "The power of neoliberalism stems from being a rationality of government that continuously evokes religious meanings and significations. Neoliberalism displaces and redraws the boundary between secular and religious, and appropriates an aura of sacredness while concealing itself behind an authoritative secular rational façade."[14]

The economic policies of neoliberalism are ruthlessly implemented and driven by technocracy, which is a government that is controlled or influenced by experts in science and/or with technical expertise in an area.[15] For example, the International Monetary Fund (IMF) enforced its austerity measures in response to the European sovereign debt crisis that began in 2009. Ordinary people of Greece, Ireland, and Latvia suffered in ensuing years due to the "savage budget cuts" devised by the technocrats. Unemployment, job insecurity, income reduction, poverty, and the increase of mental disorders were among the most serious consequences of the crisis in socioeconomic life.[16] Singaporean globalization specialist Parag Khanna explains, "Technocracy, simply put, is an approach to governance in which policy decisions are administered by independent public servants, not political appointees." He argues that in order for the Unites States to effectively address global problems such as the COVID-19 pandemic, its democratic sentiment needs to marry data analysis in order to come up with solutions that serve the entire population.[17] Those who adhere to a comprehensive, data-driven scientific system to govern the society are referred to as the global elite, globalists, or technocrats. Technocrats are individuals with technical training and occupations who perceive many important societal problems as being solvable and often propose technology-focused solutions. For example, French President Emmanuel Macron is viewed to be the ultimate technocrat "because of his attitude to politics and his desire to rule France 'like Jupiter' free of dirty politics and substituting left and right for what works and getting things done."[18]

13. Stiglitz, "Moving beyond Market Fundamentalism," 345.
14. Mavelli, "Neoliberalism as Religion," 57–76.
15. Gallo, "Three Varieties," 556.
16. Ifanti et al., "Financial Crisis," 8–12.
17. Khanna, "America's 'Deep State.'"
18. Esmark, *New Technocracy*, 54.

In 2004, Samuel Huntington famously introduced them as "Davos Men" or "gold-collar workers," the emerging class that is empowered by the new notion of global connectedness. He wrote, "It includes academics, international civil servants and executives in global companies, as well as successful high-technology entrepreneurs.... Estimated to number about 20 million in 2000, of whom 40 percent were American, this elite is expected to double in size by 2010."[19] Believing in the power of humanity, they view themselves as cosmopolitans who are not subservient to a particular religious or political authority. Thus, they have forsaken any traditional identity that is rooted in community or nation of origin. Together, they foster global citizenship, arguing that people should direct their allegiance to the worldwide community of human beings.[20] Adhering to the false religion of globalization, the global elite believe that enlightened individuals can save humanity from all the problems that exist in the world. How did this false religious belief system rise to dominate the course of globalization in the twenty-first century?

The Objective Aspect of Globalization

This study will first take a descriptive approach to understand the contemporary conception of globalization. The word *global* paved the way for the rise of the word *globalization* and its conception. In the English language, the meaning of global as "relating to, or involving the entire world" is relatively new. For a long time, it only meant "a round body, a sphere, or a ball."[21] Global differs slightly from the word *worldwide* by adding the nuance of interconnection. It gives the idea that the world is not only big in scope, but united as one. Wunderlich and Warrier note, "Today, the term 'global' summons up the planet as a physical entity, but also hints at something more than just the sum of its parts. It suggests a transformation of the spatial content of social relations, as it evokes something over and above just the territorial."[22] The word *global*, as in relating to the whole world, came into usage only by the end of the nineteenth century as the physical discovery and mapping of the whole world was

---

19. Huntington, "Dead Souls," 5.
20. Huntington, "Dead Souls," 6.
21. Wunderlich and Warrier, *Dictionary of Globalization*, 4.
22. Wunderlich and Warrier, *Dictionary of Globalization*, 5.

completed.²³ The development of modern cartography became possible through a variety of technological advancements, allowing different map projections that showed the world more precisely than before. According to geographer Benjamin Hennig, "Graphic displays have a long history in translating the complexity of our environment, with maps being the most fundamental image that we have in our minds when we reflect on the spaces that we are living in. Maps and visualizations literally shape our view of the world."²⁴ As people began to see the whole world as one, they came to understand globalization objectively as the forces or processes that unite the world as one.

British sociologist Anthony Giddens defines globalization as "the intensification of worldwide social relations which link distant localities in such a way that local happenings are shaped by events occurring many miles away and vice versa."²⁵ He explains that globalization is the consequence of modernity marked by the separation of time and space. What he labels "time-space distanciation" is the conditions under which time and space are organized to connect one's presence and absence.²⁶ This stretching of time and space means that in a globalized world, one's location becomes increasingly irrelevant to one's ability to interact with other parts across the globe. In pre-modern times, people were bound by the time and space of their locality. "When" was intimately connected with "where," and each locality had used its own time measurement that was not relevant to other measurements of time. The distance of the relationship between time and space began to "stretch" as new networks of railways, steamships, and telegraph communications brought distant localities into unprecedented proximity.²⁷ Thus, the concept of universal time began to emerge.

As railway systems developed in the nineteenth century, the differing local solar times used in each town and city made it nearly impossible to coordinate departures, arrivals, and general railway operations without a synchronized time. By 1848, most railways in Great Britain came to use the time set at the Royal Observatory in Greenwich. The Greenwich Mean Time (GMT) was slowly adopted by all the towns and cities, culminating with the installation of the Great Clock of Westminster in 1862,

23. Wunderlich and Warrier, *Dictionary of Globalization*, 4.
24. Hennig, "Remapping Geography," 74.
25. Giddens, *Consequences of Modernity*, 64.
26. Giddens, *Consequences of Modernity*, 14.
27. Giddens, *Consequences of Modernity*, 17.

which is commonly known as Big Ben. The significance of this monumental landmark lies in its unprecedented level of accuracy and massive size that signaled the uniformity of time separated from space. According to the clock expert Mark Frank, size and accuracy are conflicting parameters in clock design. This predicament was overcome by implementing Edmund Denison's gravity escapement design, which is considered one of the great advances in the science of horology. Frank notes that "it was soon adopted as the standard for the best tower clocks, as well as domestic clocks where there was a need for exceptional accuracy as in observatories or time standard master clocks."[28] The new technology that allowed the display of accurate time in public made it possible to standardize time across the nation. With the Statutes (Definition of Time) Act of 1880, the standard time was first legalized throughout Great Britain. The United States followed with the Standard Time Act of 1918.

Coinciding with the emergence of universal time, humanity entered the period that historians commonly describe as the first golden age of globalization. This period from 1870 to 1914, the beginning of World War I, was marked by mass migration, global trade, and foreign investment.[29] The British Empire began to see the need to coordinate social and commercial events in accordance with the time that was relevant to all people in all places. Historian Vanessa Ogle says that early advocates for uniformity believed a standardized system of time would act as a "kind of lubricant for this globalizing world, and would facilitate the flow of goods, people, and ideas."[30] Promoters of uniform time also called for the adoption of the Gregorian calendar as the universal calendar that would replace the numerous religious and cultural calendars used throughout the world.[31] These changes were resisted around the globe into the 1940s, up until World War II. By then, the world was too interconnected, and people saw the need to use a universal time that mattered to every nation across the globe. A worldwide time zone system based on the GMT was adopted by most major countries. In 1972, the Coordinated Universal Time (UTC), also known as Z or Zulu Time, became the new standard for keeping the world's civil time.

People around the globe came to understand that space exists in places where they themselves are not present. Giddens says that the

---

28. Frank, "Brief History."
29. Zinkina et al., *Big History of Globalization*, 195 and 221.
30. Ogle, *Global Transformation of Time*, 75–98.
31. Ogle, *Global Transformation of Time*, 177.

"emptying of time" was the preconditioning for the "emptying of space." He explains that the development of empty space may be understood in terms of the separation of space from place. The term *place* refers to the locale of the physical settings of social activity as situated geographically. In pre-modern societies, human activity only happened in a specific place. He says that modernity increasingly tears space away from place by fostering relations between those who are absent from face-to-face interaction. The dislocation of space from place meant that "locales are thoroughly penetrated by and shaped in terms of social influences quite distant from them."[32]

Giddens explains why the separation of time and space is critical to the development of globalization. First, it allows the process of "disembedding," which he defines as "the 'lifting out' of social relations from local contexts of interaction and their restructuring across indefinite spans of time-space." This means that it opens up manifold possibilities of change in a globalized society by "breaking free from the restraints of local habits and practices." Second, this separation allows the development of rationalized organizations that promote globalization and raises up modern organizations, including states, that are able to connect the local and the global in ways which would have been unthinkable before. Third, the separation of time and space allows the conception of history as the "systematic appropriation of the past to help shape the future." A standardized dating system that is universally acknowledged enables an appropriation of a unitary past and forms a world-historical framework for humanity's experience and action in a globalized world.[33]

During the 1960s, the conception of globalization began to solidify. By then, air travel, the radio, and the color television became a part of a normal human experience. People saw, heard, and experienced global events in real time. At this time, the main event that drew humanity's attention was one man's adventure in space. On April 12, 1961, at 6:07 a.m. UTC, Vostock 1 spacecraft atop an R-7 rocket designed by Sergei Korolev was secretly launched from Baiknonur Cosmodrome in southern Kazakhstan. Aboard was Russian cosmonaut (космонавт) Yuri Gagarin, who became the first man to orbit the Earth once in 108 minutes (from the blast-off until his feet touched back down onto the Earth) at a maximum altitude of 187 miles (301 km). He traveled at 18,000 miles per

---

32. Giddens, *Consequences of Modernity*, 18–19.
33. Giddens, *Consequences of Modernity*, 20–22.

hour, ten times faster than a rifle bullet. Crossing a sunset and a sunrise over oceans and continents, he witnessed a beautiful aura of the Earth and a rainbow rising from the planet's surface. Gagarin came back not just as a national hero, but as an international celebrity.[34] Prime Minister Jawaharlal Nehru of India praised the Soviet Union for "a great victory of man over the forces of nature" and urged that it be "considered as a victory for peace."[35] Japanese newspaper *Yomiuri Shimbun* urged that "both the United States and the Soviet Union should use their new knowledge and techniques for the good of mankind."[36]

Challenged by his country's bitter rival, President John F. Kennedy declared that the United States of America would land a man on the Moon before the end of the decade. Building the Saturn V rocket under the Apollo program was an extremely difficult project. On January 27, 1967, the world was grieved by the tragic deaths of the first three Apollo 1 astronauts: Virgil I. "Gus" Grissom, Edward H. White, and Roger B. Chaffee. Their spacecraft was lit on a flash fire during a ground test on the launch pad. The United States overcame the setback and reaped the fruit of its intense labor. On December 24, 1968, a billion people around the globe tuned in to watch the crew of Apollo 8 making the first lunar orbit. While broadcasting to the largest public audience that had ever listened to a human voice, astronauts William Anders, James Lovell, and Frank Borman appropriately took turns in reading the account of God's creation of the world from the first ten verses of the Bible: "In the beginning God created the heaven and the earth. . . . And God called the dry land Earth; and the gathering together of the waters called he Seas; and God saw that it was good." After a short pause, Borman spoke more personally: "And from the crew of Apollo 8, we close with good night, good luck, a Merry Christmas and God bless all of you—all of you on the good Earth."[37] From tens of thousands of miles away, humanity had a glimpse of God's perspective, and saw the world without political boundaries. The Earth appeared simply as one: interconnected, complete, and good.

The Earth is still the only known planet where life exists in the entire universe. Out in the deep darkness, Lovell famously remarked, "The vast loneliness is awe-inspiring, and it makes you realize just what you have back there on Earth. The Earth from here is a grand oasis to the

---

34. Walker, *Beyond*.
35. *New York Times*, "Man in Space."
36. *New York Times*, "At Home and Abroad."
37. Benson and Faherty, *Moonport*, 458.

big vastness of space."[38] Reflecting back, Anders remarks that the iconic photo of Earthrise taken by the Apollo 8 crew was instrumental in recognizing the Earth as humanity's only home, a fragile and beautiful planet that needs to be taken care of by all people instead of them shooting at each other and threatening with nuclear war.[39] According to NASA's Kurt Debus, the impact of this global event defied quantitative measurement. The Kennedy Space Center had received over five thousand telegrams, phone calls, and letters from all over the world. Debus reported, "They came from men, women, the elderly, the young, the black, the yellow, the Christian, the Jew, the Moslem, the Heads of the State, the laborer, the engineer and the underprivileged."[40]

Although NASA had started the Apollo program with the geopolitical motive of beating the Soviet Union in space, it inadvertently produced a global event that united the world. On July 16, 1969, when Apollo 11 landed on the Moon, the whole world celebrated together as Neil Armstrong put his left foot on the lunar surface and said, "That's one small step for man, one giant leap for mankind."[41] No one heard the "a" in "a man" at the time. Although Armstrong had intended to say "a man," he later explained that he misspoke in the excitement of the moment.[42] Regardless of his intention, the whole world identified with Armstrong's step on the Moon as theirs. It was a rare moment in history when one human being represented all of humanity. This was the greatest moment of unity in human history. As historian Chris Dixon says, "The grainy black-and-white TV image of Neil Armstrong setting foot on the Moon represented a transcendent, unifying moment. This was not just an American triumph, but a sign that all peoples, regardless of nation, race, or faith, were inhabitants of the same precarious planet."[43] All over the world, people celebrated by shouting, "We did it!"

By the mid-1980s, even though the world was in a state of division due to the Cold War, globalization became recognized as a significant concept in academic circles. When the Berlin Wall fell in 1989, it was widely believed that Western liberal democracy and capitalism had triumphed over all other ideologies in history. Believing that freedom,

38. NASA Earth Observatory, "All of You."
39. Sample, "Earthrise."
40. Benson and Faherty, *Moonport*, 458.
41. Launius, *Apollo's Legacy*, 116.
42. Launius, *Apollo's Legacy*, 116.
43. Maguire, "How the Moon Landing," para. 20.

equality, and prosperity could finally become universal, many people had a positive outlook for the future of humanity. By the end of the twentieth century, the World Wide Web became the new symbol of an interconnected world. The Information Age came into full swing as people all over the world used the Internet to share an unprecedented amount of knowledge. The distance between time and space has now been stretched as far as it could be. By the turn of the millennium, the debate over the reality of globalization was settled, and virtually all experts agreed that the world was fundamentally transformed. Globalization naturally came into the public's conscience as academic disciplines and media commentators expounded on the reality of living in a single society that was becoming simultaneously interconnected, interdependent, and interrelated.

For the last two decades, according to Manfred Steger and Paul James, the main narrative of globalization theory has been developed on the belief that there are three distinct groups who have different frameworks to interpreting globalization: the hyperglobalists, the skeptics, and the transformationalists. These three intellectual streams are understood as to have come in "waves" or "phases" of globalization theory.[44] The first wave came from the hyperglobalists who insist that globalization is a new epoch of human history defined by the emergence of a single global market of capitalism. The global age transcends the old world order established by traditional nation-states and borders, and eradicates local cultures. They believe that the rise of a global civilization is a positive phenomenon because it is characterized by economic growth, a high level of prosperity, and the spread of democracy.[45] Commonly known as neoliberalism, this view is the dominant narrative driven by the corporate and political elites.[46]

The second wave came from the skeptics who argue that globalization is the great myth of our time. It is an ideological construction that was created to justify and legitimize the restructuring of international economic order. Rather than building up a truly integrated global economy, powerful national governments are simply regionalizing by organizing economic activity into three major financial and trading blocs: Europe, Asia-Pacific, and North America.[47] The skeptics believe that globalization has come in many waves throughout history and there

---

44. Steger and James, *Globalization Matters*, 53.
45. Held and McGrew, *Global Transformations Reader*, 2–5.
46. Robinson, *Latin America and Global Capitalism*, 18.
47. Held and McGrew, *Global Transformations Reader*, 5–7.

is nothing special about the contemporary one. The migration of people, the expansion of trade, financial and cultural flows worldwide, and international cooperation have all been seen before.[48]

Finally, the third wave came from the transformationalists who believe that globalization is an unprecedented force, leading all states and societies to profound change as they adapt to a more interconnected but highly uncertain world. It is shaking and transforming state power and world politics. In contrast to the optimistic view of the hyperglobalists, the existence of a single global system is not taken as evidence of the arrival of a single world society. Rather, globalization is seen to be causing both integration and fragmentation, and the final outcome is indeterminate.[49]

The Subjective Aspect of Globalization

For those who study globalization, it becomes evident that the descriptive approach falls short of providing a satisfactory understanding. People simply do not agree where globalization is headed and what it should accomplish for humanity. The globalized world consists of not only integrating forces but also fragmenting ones. This study will therefore turn to its subjective aspect to explain why the contemporary conception of globalization has not yet led to human solidarity despite all the positive trajectories of modernity. The subjective aspect of globalization speaks of humanity's emotional reaction to cultural facts and changes; this feature is based on people's spiritual and moral outlook on the issues and events in a global society.

In the previous section, Giddens implies that globalization is a dialectical process between the local and global, but he does not explain how the local and global faces of globalization are affected.[50] Filling this gap, sociologist Roland Robertson sees cultural factors as central to human societies and claims that culture plays an important role in the globalization process. Accordingly, Robertson further defines globalization as "the compression of the world and the intensification of the consciousness of

---

48. Lecler, "What Makes Globalization," 356.
49. Held and McGrew, *Global Transformations Reader*, 7–9.
50. Dialectical process is a synthesis or integration of two opposite phenomena or ideas.

the world as a whole."[51] In other words, globalization does not merely refer to a process of interconnection between different parts of the world, but it is also an integration of culture that instills global consciousness. Robertson popularized the term *glocalization* to describe the simultaneous occurrence of both universalizing and particularizing tendencies in contemporary social, political, and economic systems. He argues that globalization drives the paradoxical context where the local and the global coexist.[52] He explains, "The question of global integration is a complex one, whereas the issue of globewide interdependence is much more simple. Whether globalization is leading or will lead to much greater integration of the world cannot be answered straightforwardly, for there are indications for both greater fragmentation and greater global unification."[53] Robertson therefore suggests that no single political ideology, economic system, or cultural and religious way of life will dominate the globalized world. Globalization is an uncertain process without a clear outcome for humanity.

One of the most distinct and complex characteristics of the contemporary globalization is cultural homogenization and diversification. Romain Lecler believes that reducing globalization to transnational movements and exchanges prevents us from understanding the specificity of our contemporary globalization.[54] He says that the scale of cultural exchanges and the circulation of cultural goods have led to the rise of a single world culture and global cultural homogenization, which is being resisted by those who wish to protect their traditional culture in the world.[55] Those living in the Global South generally resent "McDonaldization," globalization's ubiquitous and irresistible power of influence that erodes local culture by crushing difference and variety.[56] The Global South refers to the less-developed countries in the world, including countries in Africa, Latin America, and the developing regions of Asia and the Middle East. The Global North refers to the developed countries of North America, Europe, Asia, and Oceania.[57]

---

51. Robertson, *Globalization*, 144.
52. Robertson, *Globalization*, 182–88.
53. Robertson, "Globalization and the Future," 54.
54. Lecler, "What Makes Globalization," 352.
55. Lecler, "What Makes Globalization," 369–70.
56. Robertson, "Globalization and the Future," 56.
57. The terms *Global North* and *Global South* are dynamic terms that do not consider geographic locations. The north-south divide does not mean a division along

From a Nigerian perspective, Ogechukwi Ugbam, Benjamin Chukwu, and Ann Ogbo observe that Africans generally complain how much globalization is impoverishing the continent, how it is negatively impacting on their political process, and how they are totally at the mercy of the process of globalization. Against this notion, the three of them reason that globalization, as a double-edged sword, has both positively and negatively impacted Nigerian cultures, and there is not enough evidence to believe that its net effect is negative.[58] They assert that Nigerians should overcome their inferiority complex in the process of globalization:

> The truth is that with respect to globalization and culture, our faith and our future is in our hands. Culture is perhaps the aspect of globalization for which people have the power to resist or moderate the process of globalization because we as intelligent human beings have the capacity to discern right and wrong. Unless we accept a foreign culture, no force can impose it on us. . . . Our target should be to continually improve our culture and not to maintain it in its pristine state. Nobody can lay claim to globalization.[59]

From a Swedish perspective, Norberg also acknowledges that developments of globalization are moving toward a common objective, but that objective is not the predominance of a particular culture as the critics of globalization portray. Instead, pluralism is allowing all people to have the freedom to choose from a host of different paths and destinations that were not previously available to them.[60] He claims, "When markets broaden and become international, this globalization increases the prospects of even very narrow cultural manifestations surviving and flourishing."[61]

Globalization is the sum of particular processes made by all peoples, nations, and civilizations. Thus, cultural diversity in the world is a significant factor in determining the final outcome of globalization. Australian sociologist Malcolm Waters emphasizes globalization as an uncontrolled

---

the equator, but the line dividing the richest and the poorest countries on this planet. Alternative terms for the Global South are the Less-Developed World, Developing Countries, Majority World, Non-Western World, Poor World, the South, Third World, Two-Thirds World, and Undeveloped World.

58. Ugbam et al., "Effects of Globalization," 65–69.
59. Ugbam et al., "Effects of Globalization," 69.
60. Norberg, *In Defense of Global Capitalism*, 280–81.
61. Norberg, *In Defense of Global Capitalism*, 281.

and unintentional process in the post-colonial context that has developed in the condition of postmodernity. It is multi-centered rather than dominated by a single center.[62] Indian anthropologist Arjun Appadurai also argues that cross-cultural exchange spreads diversity and revitalizes the world's cultures. He defines the new global cultural economy as "a complex, overlapping, disjunctive order, which cannot any longer be understood in terms of existing center-periphery models."[63] In postmodernity, cultural experiences are the results of "the infinitely varied mutual contests of sameness and difference."[64] Globalization has produced plural modernities that may resemble the Western variety but, nonetheless, remain distinct. The pluralistic world attests to the subjective side of human nature, which should not be seen as a negative characteristic. The world does not consist of only absolutes. Without subjectivity in life, all cultures would look, sound, taste, and feel the same. The subjective aspect of globalization unites humanity by making nations realize that no civilization can become great by itself.

In the previous section, the three dominant frameworks of globalization argued by hyperglobalists, skeptics, and transformationalists were described. Steger and James appreciate the benefits of the descriptive approach, but they see less value for the development of global theory that can break the deadlock of the debate.[65] They identify the subjective aspect of globalization as the lacking element in the study of globalization:

> By comparison, the subjective dimensions of globalization have not received the level of attention that has been paid to the objective aspects of global interchange. This is especially true for the study of the thickening of people's consciousness of the world as an interconnected place. These subjective aspects include meanings, ideas, discourses, moods, sensibilities, identities, and understandings that arise in tandem with material processes of space-time compression.[66]

They argue that "subjective dynamics of globalization matter just as much as global trade flows, investment transfers, or the transnational movement of goods, technologies, and people."[67] Thus, globalization should

62. Waters, *Globalization*, 7.
63. Appadurai, *Modernity at Large*, 32.
64. Appadurai, *Modernity at Large*, 43.
65. Steger and James, *Globalization Matters*, 57.
66. Steger and James, *Globalization Matters*, 78.
67. Steger and James, *Globalization Matters*, 79.

be viewed as cultural practices, meaning-making processes of human history that have real material consequences. In other words, the main driver of globalization is in all those things that make up human civilization, culture, or society. Globalization is simply what humanity as a whole wants the world to become, thereby producing the material fruits of people's values. It conforms to the character, ethos, and desire of the present age, allowing diverse peoples and nations to have an open dialogue to determine humanity's future together. The conclusions drawn from this dialogue are constantly changing people's attitudes and values, ultimately building a consensus toward human solidarity.

Globalization's subjectivity ultimately brings forth a pluralistic society. Berger defines pluralism not as an ideology but as "a social situation in which people with different ethnicities, worldviews, and moralities live together peacefully and interact with each other amicably."[68] He rejects the so-called secularization theory—the belief that modernization and rationalization invariably lead to a decline of religious influence in a society. Instead of believing that we are living in a secular age as argued by Canadian philosopher Charles Taylor, Berger believes that we live in a pluralist age.[69] Pluralism, which has occurred before in history, has now become globalized. What makes globalized pluralism uniquely modern is that it involves the coexistence of the secular discourse with all the religious discourses. The full dynamic of pluralism is unleashed when people pursue sustained conversation for an extended time and cover a wide range of subjects. When people keep on talking with each other, they eventually influence each other. Based on this observation, Berger makes two proposals: first, "cognitive contamination relativizes," and second, "pluralism produces cognitive contamination as an ongoing condition."[70] In other words, he explains, "Pluralism relativizes and thereby undermines many of the certainties by which human beings used to live."[71] In a globalized world, fundamentalism inevitably rises to restore certainty, which has become a rare thing in society. Pluralism therefore poses a vitally intractable political problem. On the one hand, fundamentalism fractures a society by causing either constant conflict or totalitarian

---

68. Berger, *Many Altars of Modernity*, 1.

69. Taylor, *Secular Age*, 1. Taylor writes, "Churches are now separate from political structures. . . . Religion or its absence is largely a private matter. The political society is seen as that of believers (of all stripes) and non-believers alike."

70. Berger, *Many Altars of Modernity*, 2.

71. Berger, *Many Altars of Modernity*, 9.

coercion. On the other hand, relativism undermines the moral consensus on which a society is built.[72]

In the twenty-first century, the globalized world has finally imploded with the political problem of pluralism. In contrast to secularists who believe that religion should be driven out of the public square, Berger believes that the problem can only be solved by the involvement of religious people in politics with their religious commitments. Although people can mitigate the political conflict of globalization by pursuing peaceful relationships with others at the personal level, they cannot resolve the problem without a renewal of religious freedom as the foundation of the political and constitutional order. Thus, Berger asserts, "Pluralism must be politically managed."[73] He proposes in the theory of pluralism that the individual and the political components of this phenomenon should be linked together.[74]

Pluralism, while resisting both relativism and universalism, invites religion into the public sphere. According to political theorist William Connolly, "Deep pluralism . . . reinstates the link between practice and belief that had been artificially severed by secularism; and it also overturns the impossible counsel to bracket your faith when you participate in politics."[75] He explains that pluralism is not the same as cultural relativism, which is known as "absolute tolerance," or "the abandonment of all standards."[76] The contemporary conception of globalization adheres to the philosophical doctrine of cultural relativism, which is the idea that the values, knowledge, and behavior of people must be understood within their own cultural context. Cultural relativism is based on the belief that there is no specific ground rule for what is good or evil. Thus, any judgment on what is true or wrong depends on the society's rules, culture, and belief system. Any opinion on morality or ethics is dependent on a person's cultural perspective. Connolly explains that the problem with cultural relativists is that they support the culture that is dominant in a particular place.[77] Pluralists are, by contrast, "unlikely to define culture through its concentric dimension alone, the definition of culture that

---

72. Berger, *Many Altars of Modernity*, 15.
73. Berger, *Many Altars of Modernity*, 78.
74. Berger, *Many Altars of Modernity*, 79.
75. Connolly, *Pluralism*, 64.
76. Connolly, *Pluralism*, 40.
77. Connolly, *Pluralism*, 41.

allows both relativism and universalism in their simple forms to be."[78] He adds, "Pluralists are attentive both to established connections that exceed the concentric image of culture and to emergent eccentric flows that surge against the grain of the concentric dimension of being."[79] Connolly envisions a world in which cultural antagonisms between secularists and adherents of religion can be transmuted by debates marked by agnostic respect between the partisans. He concludes, "The idea is not to rise either to one ecumenical faith or to a practice of reason located entirely above faith, but to forge a positive ethos of public engagement between alternative faiths."[80] Despite great difficulties ahead, Connolly believes that the contemporary needs require humanity to put away pessimism and pursue a new political path toward resolution.

The contemporary conception of globalization leads to a world in which no ethical position can be considered universal. Without moral objectivity, this conception has struggled to create meaning for humanity's existence. Rather than building an inclusive society with a common purpose to save itself from racism, poverty, war, disease, and environmental disaster, globalization has intensified these global problems during the twenty-first century. Unable to unite people to take decisive action, it could not end the problem of extreme poverty. It could not stop the widening disparity between the rich and the poor. It could not prevent the economic crises in many countries, including the global financial crisis in 2008 that affected all. It could not negotiate peace settlements or prevent wars in Afghanistan, Iraq, Palestine, Myanmar, Libya, Syria, Yemen, and Ukraine. It could not solve the migration crises. It could not respond to the COVID-19 pandemic in an effective and cooperative manner. While acknowledging the catastrophic impacts of global warming, the nation-states of the world could not unite and work together in slowing down climate change. For all these reasons and more, social unrest has been steadily rising around the globe. According to a recent report, the average level of global peacefulness deteriorated in eleven out of the last fourteen years.[81] Unless it establishes universal ethics, globalization perpetuates human conflict and violence. Devoid of spiritual and moral foundation, globalization has given birth to a new kind of totalitarianism that aims to manage and control global society under the doctrines of liberalism,

78. Connolly, *Pluralism*, 41.
79. Connolly, *Pluralism*, 42.
80. Connolly, *Pluralism*, 48.
81. Institute for Economics and Peace, "Global Peace Index 2022."

laissez-faire capitalism, and technological progress. This technocratic scheme by the global elite aims to remove the influence of religion in a globalized world. The contemporary conception of globalization has become the false religion that is misleading humanity.

From a theological perspective, Stackhouse affirms, "Never before in human history has a civilization been formed and sustained without a religious core."[82] Human civilization is built on the three pillars of economics, politics, and religion. Among the three, religion possesses the unique power of uniting society by giving the spiritual meaning of human existence and a moral outlook on life. Secularists are mistaken in their belief that economics, politics, and science and technology can replace the role of religion in a global society. They do not understand how globalization's subjective aspects are driving its paradoxical development. Outside the West, the globalized world is shaped by religious fervor. The vast majority of people living in the world are still religious. The following is an estimate of the world population by religion for 2020: About 85 percent of the world's people identify with a religion. The most popular religion is Christianity, with an estimated 2.38 billion adherents worldwide. Islam is the second-largest religion, adhered to by more than 1.91 billion people. It is expected to either match or surpass Christianity by 2050. Hinduism is third with 1.16 billion adherents. Buddhism is fourth with 507 million adherents. Judaism is fifth with 14.6 million adherents. Other religions belong to two umbrella categories with 491 million adherents. The first is "folk religions," which consist of traditional African religions, Chinese folk religions, and both Native American and Australian aboriginal religions. The second is "other religions," a catch-all that includes smaller belief systems such as Shintoism, Daoism, Sikhism, and Jainism. Finally, a significant number of people—nearly 1.2 billion worldwide—remain nonreligious or have atheist beliefs.[83] In the twenty-first century, globalization is being influenced and shaped by all people, including religious adherents of many kinds.

---

82. Stackhouse and Paris, *Religion and the Powers*, 25.

83. World Population Review, "Religion by Country 2024." Although this report lists Judaism as the fifth largest religion, other reports list Sikhism as the fifth largest religion with approximately 26 million followers (over 24 million of them are in India).

THE RELATIONSHIP BETWEEN GLOBALIZATION AND RELIGION

What then is globalization's relationship to religion? Can it be interpreted in a way that can explain what God is doing in the world, which was created in order to display his "invisible qualities—his eternal power and divine nature" (Rom 1:20)? According to Korean theologian Sang Hyun Lee, "God is conceived as inherently and continuously creative as well as truly actual and absolutely sufficient."[84] He draws his "dispositional reconception of the divine being" from the philosophical theology of Jonathan Edwards. Lee says, "Edwards departed from the traditional Western metaphysics of substance and form and replaced it with a strikingly modern conception of reality as a dynamic network of dispositional forces and habits."[85] Lee contends that the main implication of this reconception of the nature and meaning of the world is that "the creation is viewed as God's external exercise of God's own dispositional essence, an exercise that brings about the extension or repetition in time and space of God's internal fullness."[86] Thus, time (history) returns to the eternal (the Origin) as well as moves toward a goal yet to be achieved (the new creation).[87] Lee adds, "Further, what is to be repeated in time is the infinite being of the Origin, God. Therefore, the duration of such a repetition can only be everlasting."[88]

God's dispositional essence is revealed in the world through globalization when God exercises his "steadfast love, justice, and righteousness in the earth" (Jer 9:24). God will do so eternally in the new heaven and earth (Rev 21:1–8). The external exercise of God's internal fullness in the world has been made possible by humanity's religious devotion and practice. Since the earliest days of civilization, "men began to call on the name of the LORD" (Gen 4:26). In this study, the working definition of the term *religion* means the devotion of one's life to the Lord of creation. This understanding is based on Heb 1:1–14, which explains that Jesus Christ is the radiance of the glory of God and the exact imprint of God's nature. He is called the Word of God. All creation is upheld by the word of his power. He does not change even though the rest of creation will perish

---

84. Lee, *Philosophical Theology*, 211.
85. Lee, *Philosophical Theology*, 4.
86. Lee, *Philosophical Theology*, 211.
87. Lee, *Philosophical Theology*, 211.
88. Lee, *Philosophical Theology*, 211.

and be changed at his command. Before Christ came, religious people have always displayed a glimpse of God's invisible qualities by organizing public worship and mobilizing the adherents to serve the needs of the poor and downtrodden in society. Cornelius, a Roman centurion, was a religious man who gave alms generously to the poor and prayed regularly to God before knowing Jesus Christ (Acts 10:1–2).

For the early Christians, the term *religion* meant a life of godliness, distinguished from the "self-made religion and asceticism and severity to the body" of the pagan world (1 Tim 4:8; Col 2:23). Historian Wilfred Smith notes that prior to the Christian takeover of the Latin term *religio*, the term referred to "multitudinous congeries of religious practices" relating to a "diversity of gods, places and occasions."[89] Diverse religions in the Roman Empire were initially not construed as rivals. However, when the Christian church claimed to practice a religion that is "pure and undefiled before God" (Jas 1:27) and distinguished itself from the corrupt religions, the concept of true religion entered the conscience of the public. From the Renaissance and continuing to the present time, religion "came to center stage in Christian discussions of how to live the gospel truly and how to relate the gospel to what others are doing."[90] From eternity, God chose his children "to be holy and blameless in his sight" so that they can fill the whole world with his glory (Gen 1:27–28; Eph 1:4–5). Those who were devoted to true religion have been fulfilling God's eternal purpose by teaching sound doctrines and doing acts of mercy (1 Tim 6:3–4; Jas 1:22). By preaching the gospel and exercising God's steadfast love, truth, justice, and righteousness for the poor and downtrodden in this global society, Christians have shown God's internal fullness to the world.

According to Canadian sociologist Peter Beyer, "religion and globalization are historically, conceptually, and institutionally related. . . . In concept and institutional form, socially religion is a contingent expression of the historical process of globalization, above all during modern centuries."[91] Disagreeing with the notion that globalization is a modern economic phenomenon, Indian journalist Nayan Chanda argues, "Essentially, the basic motivations that propelled humans to connect with others—the urge to profit by trading, the drive to spread religious belief, the desire to exploit new lands and the ambition to dominate others by armed might—all had been assembled by 6000 BCE to start the process

---

89. Obenchain, "Study of Religion," 64.
90. Obenchain, "Study of Religion," 64–65.
91. Beyer, *Religion in the Context*, 1.

we now call globalization."⁹² The relationship between globalization and religion is far older than the current economic system and distinct from the popular understanding of what globalization entails. Croatian Protestant theologian Miroslav Volf believes that religions and globalization have interacted throughout history and suggests what their relationship should be in the future:

> Globalization is *within* religions and world religions are *within* globalization. . . . More than anything else, with the possible exception of technological innovation, globalization and the great religions are shaping our lives—from the public policies of political leaders and the economic decisions of industry bosses, investors, and ordinary employees, through the content of the curricula in our colleges and universities, all the way to the inner longings of our hearts.⁹³

Thus, Volf argues that "a vision of flourishing found in the quarreling family of world religions is essential to individual thriving and global common good."⁹⁴ The term *world religions* primarily refer to Buddhism, Confucianism, Hinduism, Judaism, Christianity, and Islam. Volf believes that "globalization and religion, as well as religions among themselves, need not clash violently but have internal resources to interact constructively and contribute to each other's betterment."⁹⁵

Among competing religions, Christianity teaches that humanity's main problem is sin and Christ is the solution. According to Christian apologist Timothy Keller, "there is a profound and fundamental difference between the way that other religions tell us to seek salvation and the way described in the gospel of Jesus. All other major faiths have founders who are teachers that show the way to salvation. Only Jesus claimed to actually *be* the way of salvation himself."⁹⁶ He died on the cross to save humanity from the power of sin and death; and therefore, anyone who believes in him can receive the free gift of eternal life. Rather than having us achieve salvation through moral effort, Jesus offered salvation to those who remain in him by his grace. In a pluralistic society, Christians can spread this message while working with all people to make this world

---

92. Chanda, *Bound Together*, 23.
93. Volf, *Flourishing*, 2.
94. Volf, *Flourishing*, 2.
95. Volf, *Flourishing*, 206.
96. Keller, *Reason for God*, 180.

into a better place to live. God loves the world, and he wants all people to know his Son and be saved in him.

South African church historian Retief Müller asserts, "Christianity was a globalising religion from the beginning." He adds that "the seeds of globalisation were planted early on in the history of Christianity."[97] Scripture attests to the fact that Christianity has been the driving force of globalization from its inception. Jesus could not have been more explicit in his globalizing intention when he commissioned his disciples to "go into all the world and proclaim the gospel to the whole creation" (Mark 16:15) and "make disciples of all nations" (Matt 28:19). The globalizing vision of Christ for spreading the gospel throughout the entire world becomes possible through the sanctification of believers in the truth, and their complete unity in God's word. Thus, Jesus prayed for all who would believe in him in the following manner:

> Sanctify them in the truth; your word is truth. As you sent me into the world, so I have sent them into the world. And for their sake I consecrate myself, that they also may be sanctified in truth. I do not ask for these only, but also for those who will believe in me through their word, that they may all be one, just as you, Father, are in me, and I in you, that they also may be in us, so that the world may believe that you have sent me. (John 17:17–21)

Globalizing the truth or God's word entails sending out the disciples of Christ into the world. All Christians are to be sanctified in the truth and united as one for the purpose of evangelizing the world, which would result in the salvation of humanity. The Jewish disciples at first could not comprehend Christ's globalizing mission that included the redemption of the gentiles. Peter later understood the impartial and inclusive nature of the gospel when the Holy Spirit came upon the household of Cornelius (Acts 10:45). It became clear that God has mercy on all who fear him, regardless of their ethnicity. Paul became the first apostle to make a concerted effort to evangelize the gentiles in other parts of the world. He aspired to globalize the gospel as Christ had intended by preaching it "where Christ was not known" (Rom 15:20). The mystery of Christ was revealed to him: the gentiles are fellow heirs and partakers of the promise in Christ along with the Jews (Eph 3:4–6). The reconciliation between Israel and God through the blood of Christ broke down the wall of

---

97. Müller, "Christianity and Globalisation," 2.

division, leading to the unthinkable reconciliation between the Jews and the gentiles (Eph 2:13–16). After two thousand years of globalizing the world through the gospel, much of the world has received God's promise of salvation. Out of 7,360 total languages in the world, Scripture is now written in 3,658 languages: The entire Scripture has been translated into 736 languages, the New Testament has been translated into an additional 1,658 languages, and Bible portions or stories are available in 1,264 other languages.[98] Wherever the gospel has spread, globalization has come with it, and wherever globalization has reached, the gospel also has reached.

When the relationship between religion and globalization is acknowledged in the public sphere, the biblical understanding of globalization can be introduced. Then, through theological engagement, the church can provide God's plan and purpose of globalization, which is unknown to society. The biblical narrative of globalization can never be told fully, and its meaning can only remain hidden, when religion is driven out of public education and discussion. World Christians must be able to bring God's word into a dialogue with others who are interpreting globalization (2 Tim 3:16–17; 1 Pet 3:15). This study now proceeds to interpret globalization from a biblical perspective for the purpose of having the church engage with its complex issues.

THE BIBLICAL NARRATIVE OF GLOBALIZATION

From a biblical perspective, globalization is defined as the historical process of the creation, multiplication, dispersion, separation, redemption, integration, and sanctification of humanity in preparation for the consummation of God's kingdom. There are two important Scriptures that speak on the theme of "God's purpose being fulfilled in time." In the Old Testament, Eccl 3:1–8 speaks poetically about all human activities that take place in time to fulfill God's purpose:

> To everything there is a season, and a time for every purpose under heaven:
> a time to be born and a time to die,
> a time to plant and a time to uproot,
> a time to kill and a time to heal,
> a time to break down and a time to build,
> a time to weep and a time to laugh,

98. Wycliffe Global Alliance, "2023 Global Scripture Access."

> a time to mourn and a time to dance,
> a time to cast away stones and a time to gather stones together,
> a time to embrace and a time to refrain from embracing,
> a time to search and a time to count as lost,
> a time to keep and a time to discard,
> a time to tear and a time to mend,
> a time to be silent and a time to speak,
> a time to love and a time to hate,
> a time for war and a time for peace.

In the New Testament, Eph 1:7–10 speaks logically concerning the redemption of humanity and the unity of all things in Christ that will take effect at the fullness of time:

> In him we have redemption through his blood, the forgiveness of sins, in accordance with the riches of God's grace that he lavished on us. With all wisdom and understanding, he made known to us the mystery of his will according to his good pleasure, which he purposed in Christ, to be put into effect when the times reach their fulfillment—to bring unity to all things in heaven and on earth under Christ. (NIV)

Globalization is a biblical concept pertaining to all human activities that take place in time. This concept has a purpose and meaning that is determined by God and carried out by mankind. Scripture describes this interplay as God's command and man's obedience. Globalization is a historical process that is moving toward the fulfillment of humanity's destiny as coheirs with Christ. Even though Adam and the rest of mankind rebelled against God's word and became slaves to sin and evil, God's grace has been poured out through globalization for the redemption of humanity and the unity of all things in Christ.

The historical process of globalization is metaphorically described as "a time to cast away stones and a time to gather stones together" (Eccl 3:5). Stones represent God's people that went astray and were scattered in the world as diverse nations. Throughout the ages, human civilizations were divided by geography, political borders, and differing cultures and languages. Remaining divided, the nations learned to hate and war against one another. In the fullness of time, however, God is calling his redeemed people to come out from the wickedness of this world and be renewed as a holy nation in Christ (Rev 18:4). According to Scripture, all believers of the gospel are called to become a new kind of nation that is without any division. For this purpose, they would become "living stones" that are gathered and linked together in Christ who is the cornerstone, thereby becoming the spiritual house or the temple of God's presence (1 Pet 2:5). God's permanent dwelling place in creation is called the New Jerusalem, a city filled with his holy presence. It is literally heaven on earth, the perfect merging of the two. Rather than expecting an apocalyptic destruction of the sinful world, Christians should hope for a renewal of the globalized world by the power of God's salvation. The church has received all σοφία (sophia), "wisdom," and φρόνησις (phronésis), "insight," to know God's plan of redemption in Christ (Eph 1:8). God's people are given the wisdom and insight to help the people of this world to know Jesus Christ and to receive his grace and peace. The power of God for humanity's salvation is being revealed in the present time through his word that remains in the heart of all believers.

Creation

The biblical narrative of globalization begins with God's act of creation through Christ and for Christ (Gen 1:1; Col 1:16). God created all things by his will (Rev 4:11). God created his people, his sons and daughters who are called by his name, for his כָּבוֹד (kabowd), "glory" (Isa 43:6–7). The word *kabowd* means "abundance, riches, splendor, honor, and glory." Thus, humanity's flourishing in creation is a direct testament of God's glory given to Christ. God created אָדָם (adam), "man or mankind" in his image and created them as male and female to represent him on the earth together (Gen 1:27). Mankind was commanded to populate the earth and subdue it and רָדָה (radah), "to have dominion," over creation (Gen 1:28–29). The word *radah* denotes that both man and woman were given the authority and power to act as God's agents in and over the earth. Everything God made was very good, preparing the foundation for the coming of Christ into the world (Gen 1:31). The first man, Adam, who was made of dust became a living being to give birth to the human race so that the second man, Jesus, who is spiritual, could come afterward to give the gift of eternal life (1 Cor 15:45–49). God's plan and purpose for creation would remain as a mystery until the revelation of Jesus Christ through the preaching of the gospel. God has made all believers into a kingdom of priests to rule over this world so that the splendor of all creation will belong to Christ forever (Rev 1:6, 22:5). Metaphorically speaking, God created mankind to be united with Christ as his bride (Rev 21:2), and

God's children are called "a chosen race, a royal priesthood, a holy nation, a people for his own possession" (1 Pet 2:9). God's plan for mankind is that they become a temple and city in which Christ would dwell and shine his glory to all creation (Ezek 43:4–7; Rev 21:3). Thus, God's desire for all people is to be completely united as one in Christ and see the glory that God has given him (John 17:20–24).

Multiplication

God commanded mankind to multiply and fill the earth (Gen 1:28). This command indicates God's desire to have many children who can rule over the earth in righteousness. When Adam and Eve chose to eat from the tree of the knowledge of good and evil, they rebelled against God's eternal plan and purpose. As a result, mankind became Satan's agents of corruption and destruction on the earth. Beginning with Cain's murder of Abel, wickedness and violence became widespread over the earth, and as mankind's population multiplied, their corruption filled the earth. When men and women produced children, the strong ones became mighty warriors of old, men of renown. They were called the *Nephilim*, the tyrants or oppressors who drove society into wickedness and violence. Following their leaders, all the people became evil to the extreme; therefore, God made the judgment to exterminate all flesh. The entire human race was destroyed by the flood except for Noah who was אִישׁ צַדִּיק (*ish tsaddiq*), "a righteous man," blameless in his generation (Gen 6:1–9). The word *tsaddiq* means "just, righteous, and blameless." It denotes the character of God's children who are ready to rule the earth. Noah's three sons, Shem, Ham, and Japheth, bore sons and daughters to repopulate the earth. As he did with Adam, God blessed Noah and his sons: "Be fruitful and multiply and fill the earth" (Gen 9:1). God also warned against the sin of murder: "Whoever sheds man's lifeblood, his lifeblood will be shed by man" (Gen 9:5–6). God made a covenant with Noah, who now represented the new Adam or mankind, and said that "there will never again be a flood to destroy the earth" (Gen 9:11). This covenant affirmed God's plan to save mankind from sin, corruption, and evil and enable them to live in righteousness. God's purpose in creating and multiplying mankind was not for their destruction but for the great harvest of his righteous children (Matt 9:35–38).

Dispersion

After the great flood, the population of mankind had one language using the same vocabulary. As the people began to multiply and migrate from the east, they settled in the land of Shinar. When they developed the technology of making bricks, they decided to build together a city with a tower that reached the skies. Their collective aim was to make a name for themselves so that they would not be dispersed over the face of the whole earth (Gen 11:1–4). This settlement was another act of rebellion against God's plan for humanity. God judged the people's project to be contrary to his will and outside the boundary set for mankind. Thus, God frustrated the people's plan by confusing their language so that they could not understand the words they spoke to each other. In accordance with God's decree, the people were dispersed into every corner of the earth so that they would become many גּוֹיִם (*goyim*), "nations" (Gen 11:5–8). The people migrated far away from each other and developed into diverse ethnic groups with various cultures throughout the world. Out of the three sons of Noah, all the nations came into existence and spread over all the earth (Gen 10:1–32). God had dispersed humanity so that he would receive glory through many forms of culture. Psalm 86:9 declares, "All the nations you have made shall come and worship before you, O Lord, and shall glorify your name." Thus, the apostles were given the mission to "bring about the obedience of faith for the sake of his name among all the nations" (Rom 1:5). The dispersion of humanity allowed both the good and the evil elements of culture to spread over the earth. This culminated with the spread of Hellenistic Greek culture and the ensuing rise of the Roman Empire. The domination of the gentiles prepared the world for the coming of the Messiah who would deliver the nations from sin, corruption, and evil. When the nations are saved by the gospel, God's children, who are "the kings of the earth," will bring the nations' glory and honor into the city of God (Rev 21:24–26). With wisdom and understanding, God's children are called to build a house that is filled with "precious and beautiful treasures" (Prov 24:3–4 CSB). This house will be the new heaven and earth that will display all of humanity's achievements and triumphs accomplished by the power of Christ.

Separation

By dispersing mankind, God prepared the ground for separating the Jews from the gentiles. The religious and cultural tradition of Israel was separated from the other nations for the birth of the Messiah. Through this separation, the Jews preserved the character of God's holiness, the absolute moral purity of God. In keeping with his covenant with Abraham, Isaac, and Jacob, God chose the small nation of Israel out of many great nations on the earth "to be a people for his treasured possession" (Deut 7:6–8). The name of the Lord was proclaimed to Israel as "the faithful God who keeps covenant and steadfast love with those who love him and keep his commandments, to a thousand generations" (Deut 7:9). David was anointed as the king of Israel to establish a holy nation that would keep the covenant with God and testify to his steadfast love. God also made a covenant with David, promising to establish the throne of his kingdom forever (2 Sam 7:13). He was persecuted throughout his life by his enemies, but God ultimately vindicated him for his righteousness (2 Sam 22:1–51). Although David established the kingdom of Israel upon God's statutes and ordinances, the Israelites' constant failure to keep the covenant with God resulted in the destruction of Jerusalem and their exile to Babylon. In response to Israel's unfaithfulness, God would make a new covenant with his people, promising to restore שָׁלוֹם (*shalom*), "welfare, prosperity, completeness, and peace," in their land, rebuild the city on its hill, renew their hearts to obey his law, and return the people from their captivity (Jer 29:11, 30:18, 31:31–34, 32:44). God declared, "For I am the LORD your God, the Holy One of Israel, your Savior" (Isa 43:3). Isaiah prophesied concerning the coming of the Messiah: "For to us a child is born, to us a son is given; and the government shall be upon his shoulder, and his name shall be called Wonderful Counselor, Mighty God, Everlasting Father, Prince of Peace" (Isa 9:6). The Messiah will reign from the throne of David to establish his kingdom by upholding justice and righteousness for eternity (Isa 9:7). He will fill the earth with the knowledge of God's salvation and gather his people out of the nations (Isa 11:1–16).

Redemption

Christ was born to become the Redeemer and Savior of humanity. In a broad sense of the word, redemption simply refers to the salvation or deliverance of Israel by God's hand of power (Exod 6:6; Luke 2:38). Within the biblical narrative of globalization, redemption refers to the means by which the salvation of humanity is achieved, namely the sacrifice Christ made as the ransom. His entire life was an act of lowering himself to become a δοῦλος (*doulos*), "bond-slave," to redeem all mankind from its bondage to and the consequence of sin and death (Phil 2:5–8). In order to serve others and give his life as a "ransom for many" (Mark 10:45), Christ lived in obedience to God's command and died on the cross. In the Old Testament, redemption involves deliverance from bondage based on the payment of a price by a redeemer. The principal Hebrew words used for the concept of redemption are פָּדַע (*padah*) and גָּאַל (*gaal*). The first word, *padah*, means "to ransom." It is a legal term concerning the substitution required for the person or animal that is being delivered: "Every firstborn of a donkey you shall redeem with a lamb. . . . Every firstborn of man among your sons you shall redeem" (Exod 13:13). God redeemed Israel from the house of slavery in Egypt and the oppression of Pharaoh when a year-old male lamb without defect was slaughtered for each household during the Passover feast (Exod 12:5; Deut 7:8). The sacrificial lamb represented Christ who died as a ransom to set humanity free from the oppression of Satan in this world. The second word, *gaal*, means "to redeem or act as kinsman": "If your brother becomes poor and sells part of his property, then his nearest redeemer shall come and redeem what his brother has sold" (Lev 25:25). In the book of Ruth, as a type of Christ, Boaz acted as the kinsman redeemer for Elimelek's family (Naomi and Ruth) by fulfilling the law. He first allowed a nearer kinsman to act as the redeemer. When the man refused to act, Boaz then purchased a parcel of land for Naomi and married Ruth to produce a son for Elimelek's family line (Ruth 4:4). He fulfilled the law by restoring the lost fortune of his brother's family that had become poor. In the same way, Christ fulfilled the righteous requirements of God's law through his life and paid the price to redeem broken humanity by his death on the cross. As a result, everyone who believes in him can be healed of the consequence of sin, and their fortunes can be restored to have life abundantly (John 10:10). Christ's redemption of humanity brings forth eternal life, which is a life of abundance in God's kingdom (John 3:16, 10:10).

Integration

In the long course of history, many peoples, nations, and civilizations rose and fell in different parts of the world. Although mankind has made impressive cultural achievements and societal advances, they have also experienced cultural regressions and societal collapses due to their captivity to sin. In ancient times, Sodom and Gomorrah were notoriously sinful cities, which led to their annihilation by sulfur and fire (Gen 19:24). At a later time, God pronounced his judgment against the gentile nations as a result of their wickedness (Ezek 25–32). Israel was no exception. When the people of Israel sinned repeatedly even after the prophets had warned them, Jerusalem was razed, and God's people were exiled to Babylon. In the οἰκονομία (*oikonomia*), "stewardship, dispensation, or administration" of the fullness of time (Eph 1:10), however, God has called all his people from every part of the world to be saved and integrated into God's temple, which is Christ's dwelling place on the earth (Rev 18:4). The biblical concept of integration refers to the time in which God's plan and purpose for humanity will be fulfilled when all creation, including wayward family members, will be brought under God's rule. They will be joined together and built up into a temple. The new temple of God is referred to as οἶκος πνευματικὸς εἰς ἱεράτευμα ἅγιον, "a spiritual house for a holy priesthood" (1 Pet 2:5). This expression denotes humanity's integration as a household or family. The new temple is not a physical structure but a spiritual entity, the body of Christ consisting of both Jews and gentiles. Isaiah prophesied that when "the mountain of the house of the Lord" is established as the highest mountain, many nations shall come near to God's dwelling place and learn to live peacefully with one another (Isa 2:2–4). This prophecy is spoken in a metaphor, using the familiar imagery of Zion to represent all God's people who would be saved by the gospel. Jesus explains that when believers are shining their light by doing good works before others, people of this world would recognize them as "the city on a hill" and give glory to God (Matt 5:14–16). Both Isaiah's prophecy and Jesus's teaching affirm that much of humanity will be saved and integrated into the New Jerusalem. Thus, all believers must live in the power of God to proclaim the gospel and do good works that are universally recognized as contributing to human flourishing.

Sanctification

The biblical narrative of globalization ends with the sanctification of humanity and the recreation of the world at the coming of Christ. Sanctification refers to the power of God's salvation that is working in the lives of believers. When individuals are saved by believing in the gospel, they become God's children who are sanctified by the Holy Spirit to lead and serve all nations, which are corrupted by sin. Sanctification entails denying oneself and following Christ while losing one's life for the good of others (Matt 16:24–25). It is the process of developing one's spiritual and moral life, putting to death the misdeeds of the body and learning to live by the Spirit (Rom 8:13–14). The sacrificial and obedient life in the Spirit prepares God's children to become coheirs of the new world with Christ (Rom 8:17; 2 Tim 2:12). Sanctification or a life of godliness becomes possible through divine power. God's grace and peace are multiplied in the knowledge of God and Jesus Christ (2 Pet 1:2–3). The power of God's salvation fills the world through "the church, which is the body of Christ, the fullness of him who fills everything in every way" (Eph 1:17–23 NIV). In other words, humanity is sanctified through the church when all Christians engage with the world and administer God's grace and peace in every dimension of life. As a result, humanity can be reconciled with God and with each other by the ministry of the church in the globalized world (Titus 2:11–12). The power of God's salvation does not only have a personal effect of saving individuals, but it also has a societal effect of healing and renewing the population at large. Sanctification of humanity means that households, communities, cities, and states can repent en masse and be set free from the curse of sin that permeates this world (Acts 2:38–47). The power of God's salvation that sanctifies humanity and renews the world is "far above all rule and authority and power and dominion" in both this age and the age to come (Eph 1:21).

The globalized world is renewed by the active engagement of God's righteous children who are living in the power of God's salvation. In Scripture, the sanctification of humanity is metaphorically depicted as a spiritual warfare of conquering or overcoming evil. In the Old Testament, God foresaw the renewal of the land of Canaan for Israel's inheritance. Obeying God's command to be bold and courageous, Joshua led Israel to war against the kings of Canaan and conquered the land that was occupied by those who were evil. Joshua's warfare was a typological event that foreshadowed the spiritual warfare of Christians in this world

(Joshua 10–11). In the New Testament, God foresaw the renewal of the world, namely the Roman Empire, for the church's inheritance. Under the lordship of Christ, the believers resisted the corruption of gentile culture and exercised God's love, truth, justice, and righteousness in society (Acts 2:41–47). The nature of spiritual warfare is described in the letters to the seven churches (Rev 2–3). Jesus promises to give all the eternal blessings to those who are spiritually victorious, including the authority to reign with him. He said, "To the one who is victorious and keeps my works to the end, I will give authority over the nations" (Rev 2:26). In fact, the word νικῶν (*nīkôn*) means "conqueror, overcomer, or victorious one." Also, with the outpouring of the Holy Spirit on Pentecost, God has given his power for the church to preach the gospel and to overcome the corruption and evil of this world. The proclamation of God's word and the active engagement of God's people in the world work together in sanctifying humanity. Therefore, Christian ministry involves rescuing the people that are held in the captivity of sin and reconciling them with God's holiness. Globalization is complete when humanity is sanctified and becomes fully ready for the consummation of God's kingdom. God's children, then, consisting of the new humanity, should become blameless at the end of time for the coming of Christ (1 Thess 5:23). Being united with Christ, the new humanity will reign over the new creation (Rev 21:1–2). Upon the completion of globalization, all God's children consisting of sanctified humanity will shine as lights over all the earth forever.

2

The Historical Development of Globalization

Now that the nature of globalization has been interpreted, its historical development toward the unity of humanity will be explored in the light of God's word. According to Bauckham, Scripture suggests that "human society and history have an inherent orientation toward the global that stems from the fundamental unity of the human race and its limitation to a common home on the earth."[1] Humanity, which became separated by language, distance, and culture, is becoming reconciled through the power of Christ that is demonstrated through the ministry of the church. Globalization is not the inevitable and universal progress of humanity, but rather, it is God's redemptive plan and purpose for humanity. God is reconciling the world to himself by the preaching of the gospel and the outpouring of the Holy Spirit on all flesh (Joel 2:28–29). Those who know and follow Jesus Christ are becoming the divine structure that can bring renewal to the corrupt structures of this world. This chapter aims to explain how God's decree of uniting humanity has unfolded throughout the historical development of globalization. The first section discusses the rise of complex and fragile structures in society that can be renewed by the divine structure of Christ. The second section examines the political, economic, technological, cultural, and religious innovations and institutions that have linked diverse societies together. The final section surveys the development of economic integration in the modern era.

---

1. Bauckham, *Bible in the Contemporary World*, 66.

COMPLEX AND FRAGILE STRUCTURES IN SOCIETY

The Word of God is calling his people to turn away from the sinful project of building a globalized world without his holy presence (Rev 18–19). Humanity's repentance toward the biblical understanding of globalization begins by acknowledging that Jesus Christ is the creator, redeemer, and sanctifier of the world. The globalized world is the most complex society that humanity has ever built, and yet, it is the most fragile civilization. According to Myers, the globalized world comprises "complex adaptive social systems." He explains, "Civilizations, societies, and cultures are made up of self-aware people who do not have to follow rules in the way that atoms and molecules must in mechanical systems."[2] These systems develop counterintuitively, and they are inherently unpredictable.[3] Thus, Scripture affirms that no social system or structure can be sustained permanently without God's involvement. Psalm 127:1 says, "Unless the Lord builds the house, those who build it labor in vain. Unless the Lord watches over the city, the watchman stays awake in vain." Knowing that God is the sustainer of all things, kings of the earth must build and rule the globalized world in meekness (Matt 5:5). Christ's redemption of humanity gives his people the opportunity to serve the world as kingly priests (Rev 5:9–10).

In Scripture, the king of Babylon represents depraved humanity that is in rebellion against God's authority (Isa 14:12–14). The prophet Daniel was given the divine understanding that King Nebuchadnezzar might enjoy longevity and prosperity of his reign if he would break off from his sinful and wicked ways; therefore, the king was exhorted to practice righteousness and show mercy to the oppressed in his kingdom (Dan 4:27). When the king ignored Daniel's wisdom and insight and boasted about making Babylon great as a royal residence by his mighty power, God removed him from his office and made him live in the wild with beasts for "seven periods of time." At the end of that time, Nebuchadnezzar's reason returned to him, and he blessed the Most High, finally acknowledging God's eternal power over his creation. After his repentance, Nebuchadnezzar's majesty and splendor were restored and his kingdom was returned to him with even more greatness (Dan 4:29–37). This biblical account teaches the foundational lesson drawn from the historical development of globalization: the collective endeavor of humanity in building the

---

2. Myers, *Engaging Globalization*, 26.
3. Myers, *Engaging Globalization*, 26.

world great cannot succeed without submitting to the reign of Christ and the administration of his grace and peace for all people. Scripture affirms the supremacy of Christ in creation:

> He is the image of the invisible God, the firstborn of all creation. For by him all things were created, in heaven and on earth, visible and invisible, whether thrones or dominions or rulers or authorities—all things were created through him and for him. And he is before all things, and in him all things hold together. (Col 1:15–17)

Christ is the divine structure, "the chief cornerstone" in God's building project of the new creation (Isa 28:16; Matt 21:42–44). Through the progression of history, God has allowed humanity to build complex structures in society. In time, all the works of humanity will be joined together as the globalized world and ultimately unite with the divine structure of Christ. Even though societal structures in the world are weak and flawed because of sin, the globalized world can be renewed as the New Jerusalem by connecting to the divine structure of Christ (Rev 21:10–27). In accordance with God's decree, the old creation under the curse of sin will be replaced by the new creation at the coming of Christ. The fundamental problem of globalization is rooted in the unwarranted desire of humanity, which rebels against God's sovereignty and wisdom over creation, to forge its own destiny and build the world by its own power. Anthropologist and geneticist Spencer Wells expresses this attitude among secularists:

> Since our ancestors came down from the trees, we have used our intellect to explore outward and extrapolate into the future. Over the past few thousand years, we have changed our world—and our place in it—for ever. With the development of agriculture, and the cultural chain reaction it ignited, we gained the power to choose our own evolutionary trajectory. With this power, though, came increased responsibility. One responsibility that we neglect at our peril is that of self-discovery.[4]

Secularists believe that scientific knowledge and technological revolution are the keys that can unlock the power of humanity to determine its own future. Humanity is now at the cusp of controlling its genome, which is the entire set of genetic instructions in the nucleus of every cell. Launched in the late 1980s in the United States, the Human Genome

4. Wells, *Journey of Man*, 196.

Project has been an ambitious attempt by international groups of researchers to map and sequence the approximately 3 billion nucleotides in the human genome.[5] The goal of the project was to identify the precise function of each of the 80,000 to 100,000 genes that human beings were thought to possess.[6] In 2003, a reference human genome was essentially sequenced from a conglomerate of more than sixty people's DNA. In 2022, a fully complete human genome became available, further improving biomedical studies.[7] Geneticist Ting Wang clarifies that while having a complete genome reference is an important achievement, "the human genome" of a single individual still does not exist.[8] With the possession of this newfound knowledge, scientists have developed CRISPR (Clustered Regularly Interspaced Short Palindromic Repeats), the revolutionary gene editing technology that can correct DNA sequencing errors to treat and prevent genetic disorders. Fyodor Urnov, a professor of molecular and cell biology at the University of California in Berkeley, explains that approximately 400 million people worldwide are suffering with one of the 7,000 diseases caused by mutations in single genes. He says, "In medicine, CRISPR gene editing allows physicians to directly fix typos in the patients' DNA. And so much substantive progress has been made in the field of genetic medicine that it's clear scientists have now delivered on a remarkable dream: word-processor-like control over DNA."[9]

This application of CRISPR has been dubbed as "playing God," expressing the ethical and moral concerns raised by the public and academics.[10] Its seemingly super-human act brings up many questions that science alone cannot answer. Optimism about the potential health benefits of DNA sequencing is invariably matched by concern about new, pernicious kinds of discrimination. Ethical issues in the public arena are wide-ranging and include privacy, international competition for supremacy, loss of human value and human dignity, stigmatization and

---

5. A nucleotide is the basic building block of nucleic acids (RNA and DNA). A nucleotide consists of a sugar molecule (either ribose in RNA or deoxyribose in DNA) attached to a phosphate group and a nitrogen-containing base. The bases used in DNA are adenine (A), cytosine (C), guanine (G), and thymine (T).

6. Kovacs, "Human Genome Project," 1.

7. Green, "Human Genome Sequence."

8. Saey, "We Finally Have."

9. Urnov, "We Can Cure Disease," para. 7.

10. Locke, "Promise of CRISPR," 27–30.

ostracism, the rights of the unborn, and revival of eugenics.[11] Moral and ethical questions make it extremely difficult for humanity to determine what is the right way to use the information it has gained. Gyula Kovacs therefore ponders, "It remains for history to decide whether the mapping of the human genome is among the greatest human achievements of all time or one of mankind's greatest follies."[12] With the availability of the genome editor CRISPR, it is inevitable that scientists will attempt to create genetically engineered babies. In 2019, Chinese biophysicist He Jiankui was jailed for violating medical regulations; he had secretly altered the DNA of human embryos and implanted them into two women who gave birth to three babies. Many scientists believe that transplanting edited embryos with the technology available today is reckless due to CRISPR's shortcomings.[13] Once the technology is perfected, however, scientists will certainly proceed to create healthy and perfect human beings that will replace handicapped and imperfect ones. Given the choice, no parent would want to have their own babies with rare diseases.

The globalized world is built on the belief that humanity has the power to create the meaning of life for itself and advance as a species by relying solely on natural science. The theory of naturalism relates scientific method to philosophy by affirming that all beings and events in the universe are natural. According to theoretical physicist and naturalist Sean Carroll, naturalism comes down to three things: (1) There is only one world, the natural world; (2) The world evolves according to unbroken patterns, the laws of nature; (3) The only reliable way of learning about the world is by observing it.[14] Rejecting the ontological story of creation told by Scripture, Carroll asserts, "Purpose and meaning in life arise through fundamentally human acts of creation rather than being derived from anything outside ourselves."[15] He claims, "The universe is not a miracle. It simply is, unguided and unsustained, manifesting the patterns of nature with scrupulous regularity. . . . We are the miracle, we human beings. . . . Our emergence has brought meaning and mattering into the world."[16]

11. Kovacs, "Human Genome Project," 3–5.
12. Kovacs, "Human Genome Project," 6.
13. Cohen, "As Creator of 'CRISPR Babies.'"
14. Carroll, *Big Picture*, 20.
15. Carroll, *Big Picture*, 11.
16. Carroll, *Big Picture*, 431.

Resisting God's sovereignty, secularists believe that nature, including humans and society, can be controlled by technology. Thus, they aim to take control of globalization by using new technologies. Secular Jewish historian Yuval Harari asserts, "New technologies kill old gods and give birth to new gods."[17] He explains that religions that lose touch with the technological realities of the day forfeit their ability even to understand the questions being asked in society. Those questions are:

> What will happen to the job market once artificial intelligence outperforms humans in most cognitive tasks? What will be the political impact of a massive new class of economically useless people? What will happen to relationships, families, and pension funds when nanotechnology and regenerative medicine turn eighty into the new fifty? What will happen to human society when biotechnology enables us to have designer babies, and to open unprecedented gaps between the rich and poor?[18]

Harari claims that religion has hardly made any significant discoveries, inventions, or creation in the last century. Religious scriptures are no longer a source of creativity.[19] Thus, he predicts that "in the twenty-first century, humans will try to attain immortality, bliss and divinity. This forecast . . . simply reflects the traditional ideals of liberal humanism."[20] He further predicts that humans will be driven by Dataism, which is the emerging ideological or religious belief in information flow as the supreme value, and believes that the evolving computer algorithm will know humans best and make decisions that are beyond human capacity.[21]

Turning away from this false religious belief and accepting God's assessment of the world, which is revealed in Scripture, can lead to humanity's flourishing as God intended. The biblical account of God's creation affirms that the world is good, although it has fallen into corruption by sin. The whole creation's bondage to decay correlates with the spiritual problem of humanity (Rom 8:20–24). God's desire is to save and heal the world that is broken by sin and evil so that it can be built to last forever in his righteousness. This is an essential understanding of globalization which both Christians and secularists have often failed to grasp properly.

---

17. Harari, *Homo Deus*, 270.
18. Harari, *Homo Deus*, 271.
19. Harari, *Homo Deus*, 277.
20. Harari, *Homo Deus*, 278–79.
21. Harari, *Homo Deus*, 392–402.

Misunderstanding God's creation account leads to the abandonment of this world into further corruption or the false hope of building a utopia without the gospel of Jesus Christ. Myers emphasizes God's work of grace in human history:

> Since our great disobedience, God has been carrying out a work of grace that will ultimately redeem and restore God's creation and us, if we choose, to God's original intent. God is actively working in human history today. This biblical truth about God is a direct challenge to the contemporary conception of globalization and its underlying theology of secular humanism.[22]

The world consists of both physical and spiritual dimensions; however, secularists do not acknowledge the existence of the God who created the cosmos, which they understand as an orderly or harmonious universe. In their inquiry of the cosmos, scientists have developed theories that are independent of any association with religion, resulting in the denial of any religious claim on the reality of nature. The denial of God's involvement in creation has led to many Christians opposing the principles of continuity and evolution in natural processes. However, God's people must realize that the warfare model against science does not resolve any problem.[23] The dichotomy between science and religion can be resolved by recognizing that the two domains are inseparable in a globalized world. Society cannot progress in accordance with God's plan and purpose without the contribution of both natural science and theology. German theologian Wolfhart Pannenberg makes a critical assertion that scientific descriptions of knowledge are provisional versions of objective reality; therefore, theology can make important contributions to science. According to his view, science seeks to understand aspects or parts of reality while theology seeks to understand not particularities but the totality of reality.[24] Through globalization, scientific discoveries will become fully coherent at the end of history when understood in the light of the biblical knowledge of God. Taiwanese theologian Shao Kai Tseng explains, "[Francis] Bacon insisted that the discipline of natural science consists of the activity of the redeemed mind performed by the process of sanctification. One who is born again in Christ seeks to exclude conceptual idols and seek the manifest glory of God in creation through the light

---

22. Myers, *Engaging Globalization*, 17.
23. Orji, *Science-Theology Rapprochement*, 53–56.
24. Orji, *Science-Theology Rapprochement*, 51–52.

of Scripture."[25] Until the coming of Christ, the two domains of natural science and theology work in tandem to bring forth a coherent understanding of the meaning of human life and the existence of the world.

According to a team of Russian historians led by Julia Zinkina, "The universal history that is emerging within modern scientific scholarship (itself a product of globalization) begins with the idea of the Big Bang.... We do not yet understand how or why it happened, but we have a remarkably detailed understanding of *what* happened."[26] They believe that an astonishing concentration of energy appeared, squashed, at first, into an almost infinitely small amount of space. The primordial atom expanded very fast within the first second of its existence. Then, its expansion slowed and continued at a more constant pace. As the universe expanded, it cooled to the temperatures measured today in the outer layers of stars. The consensus among scientists, astronomers, and cosmologists is that this improbable sequence of events generated the astonishing variety and beauty of today's universe. Christian astrophysicist Hugh Ross explains that the Big Bang is a misnomer. Rather than being an explosion, it "represents an immensely powerful yet carefully planned and controlled release of matter, energy, space, and time within the strict confines of very carefully fine-tuned physical constants and laws which govern their behavior and interactions."[27] From the moment he created the heaven and the earth, "the Spirit of God was hovering over the face of the waters" (Gen 1:2). God is intimately involved in every aspect of the universe, creation, and natural science.

Without the ability to observe the beginning of the cosmos, secularists have no way of knowing how or why the universe exists. Secularists and Christians can therefore agree that the Big Bang model does not claim to know how or why the universe was created but, rather, claims to know how it evolved. The scientific account of how the universe dramatically changed since its infancy gives Christians the first important insight into how they should engage with globalization. Zinkina explains how the history of the universe reflects the same kind of intricate process that made the complex and fragile structures of the globalized world:

> We are beginning to see how, over 13.8 billion years, the simple forces and entities that emerged within the Big Bang began

25. Tseng, "Theological Foundations," para. 13.
26. Zinkina et al., *Big History of Globalization*, 2.
27. Ross, "Beginner's—and Expert's—Guide," 2–3.

to connect, according to strict rules. And as they connected, they formed entirely new entities with new emergent properties that could, in turn, create new synergies with other entities and forces. And this, of course, is exactly what we observe in studying globalization—the forging of new connections that form new structures with new properties, the evolution of those structures, their occasional break-down or re-arrangement, and eventually the emergence of staggeringly complex and possibly fragile structures of structures, such as those that make up today's globally connected world.[28]

This observation helps all people to conceive the historical development of globalization as God's act of slowly renewing the world in his time. In other words, God does not simply create a perfect world from the beginning, but he also works in the manner of a potter who molds the clay with his hand many times over and over (Jer 18:6; Isa 64:8). Complex and fragile structures in society are built by humanity, but they are perfected in the course of time by God. He allows diverse cultures to rise and integrate with one another and finally become united with the divine structure of Christ. Throughout history, God has used all peoples, nations, and civilizations to take part in building the world with new innovations and contributing toward the advancement of globalization. The next section will examine how diverse societies have become interlinked over time to forge the globalized world.

THE INTERACTION OF DIVERSE SOCIETIES ACROSS THE WORLD

The historical development of globalization can be divided into several ages. In each stage of its growth, revolutionary changes were introduced to accelerate humanity's advancement as a complex society that is globally connected. Among many experts, economist Jeffrey Sachs gives the widest interpretation by affirming that humanity has always been globalized.[29] He says, "Globalization signifies the interlinkages of diverse societies across large geographical areas. These interlinkages are technological, economic, institutional, cultural, and geopolitical. They include interactions of societies across the world through trade, finance, enterprise,

---

28. Zinkina et al., *Big History of Globalization*, 2–3.
29. Sachs, *Ages of Globalization*, 1.

migration, culture, empire, and war."[30] Sachs highlights globalization's changing character throughout seven distinct ages in its history:

1. The Paleolithic Age (70,000 BC to 10,000 BC) when humans were foragers, hunting and gathering in a nomadic setting. Long-distance interactions were by migration in small groups. They carried with them their tools, know-how, and emerging cultures.

2. The Neolithic Age (10,000 BC to 3000 BC) when farming first began and villages were formed. The range of human interaction widened from the clan to the village and to politics and trade between villages.

3. The Equestrian Age (3000 BC to 1000 BC) when the domestication of the horse enabled rapid, long-distance overland transport and communications. The effective use of calvary gave rise to powerful militaries. In politics, the horse hastened the arrival of the state by enabling the reach of public administration and coercive force across much greater distances.

4. The Classical Age (1000 BC to AD 1500) when large land-based empires first emerged and embarked on vast territorial expansions, which succeeded as the result of advantages in both military and political governance. The major empires were spurred by new religious and philosophical outlooks.

5. The Ocean Age (1500 to 1800) when empires became transoceanic or global for the first time, with temperate-zone imperial powers of Europe conquering and colonizing tropical regions of Africa, the Americas, and Asia. Revolutionary changes in global trade ensued, including the rise of multinational corporations. Politics also became global in scale for the first time.

6. The Industrial Age (1800 to 2000) when the industrial revolution brought waves of technological advances and a powerful new alliance of science and technology. The use of fossil fuels made the invention of the steam engine and the internal combustion engine possible. Industrial production soared. The global population soared, too, as the result of massive increases in food production. It gave rise to the first global hegemon, Great Britain, and later, the United States.

---

30. Sachs, *Ages of Globalization*, 2.

7. The Digital Age (2000 to the present) when the global transmission of data is pervasive: computational power has multiplied billionfold, and information technologies are disrupting every aspect of the world economy, society, and geopolitics. An era of hegemonic power is giving way to a multipolar world in which several regional powers coexist.[31]

Sachs emphasizes that the changes of globalization have often come quickly and violently. Thus, he proposes, "In the twenty-first century, we need to change peacefully and wisely; in the nuclear age, there may be no second chances in the event of global war. By studying the history of globalization, we can arrive at an informed understanding of globalization in the twenty-first century and how to manage it successfully."[32] This overview of the ages of globalization demonstrates that humanity has come a long way in building the world as it stands today. Humanity has finally entered the critical stage of history in which all people from diverse civilizations will have to work together to solve the problems of globalization. New innovations and institutions are required for humanity to be united in working together toward its flourishing in the twenty-first century. According to Sachs, there are three great issues that must be resolved in our time. First, humanity needs to build a world of shared prosperity, social inclusion, and environmental sustainability. Second, humanity needs to move on from the Anglo-American age and organize global governance in a truly multipolar world. Third, humanity needs to pursue global peace by establishing a model of human understanding and ethics.[33]

However, Sachs believes that there is one obstacle that prevents humanity from achieving global peace. He observes, "The challenge of globalization from the earliest days of humanity has been the lack of consensus."[34] In order to solve this age-old problem, he has taken up Pope Francis's advice to explore the possibilities and limits of consensus. Gathering with religious leaders and adherents of the world's major faiths as well as secular philosophers over two years, Sachs recently co-led a multifaith effort to find the common basis for global action for sustainable development. The faith leaders and ethicists identified three moral

---

31. Sachs, *Ages of Globalization*, 3–5.
32. Sachs, *Ages of Globalization*, 1.
33. Sachs, *Ages of Globalization*, 31.
34. Sachs, *Ages of Globalization*, 211.

precepts common to all of the world's faiths. The first is the Golden Rule, the principle of reciprocity: Do not do unto others what you would not have them do to you. The second is the preferential option for the poor—giving due attention to the poorest members of society. The third is the protection of creation—the physical Earth.[35]

Human Civilization

Among many creatures, only humans possess the unique ability to build civilizations. The Paleolithic Age set the course for humankind to develop linguistic, ethnic, and cultural diversity for globalization. This is the period that is least understood and most overlooked by both secularists and Christians. The perspectives from both sides will be discussed in this section to find a common ground for building human civilization.

From a secular perspective, it is believed that a great acceleration of cognitive and cultural development occurred roughly 50,000 years ago, the transition period between the Middle Paleolithic and the Upper Paleolithic Period. The anthropological evidence suggests that humanity made advances in art, language, and religious practices.[36] The question of whence the first modern humans—*Homo sapiens* ("wise humans" in Latin)—originated, how they left Africa, and where they went is still not settled. The wealth of new paleoanthropological, archaeological, and genetic evidence has cast doubt on the conventional narrative and timeline of human migration based on the "Out of Africa" theory. For half a century, anthropologists had theorized that *Homo sapiens* evolved in Africa around 200 ka (kilo annum, a thousand years) and migrated to other continents about 60 ka, replacing archaic human populations including Neanderthals. In 2017, however, the oldest known modern human fossil dating about 315 ka was found at Jebel Irhoud in Morocco. Before this discovery, the oldest specimen, which was found in southern Ethiopia, was dated to about 195 ka (or 230 ka). In 2015, excavations at a cave in China's Hunan province yielded the fossil teeth of modern humans dating between 120 ka and 80 ka, confirming that *Homo sapiens* migrated to Asia far earlier than was previously known. Sophisticated stone tools created by flint knapping, known as "Levallois core assemblage," dating between 100 ka to 47 ka were found in southern Arabia. Similar tools

---

35. Sachs, *Ages of Globalization*, 211–12.
36. Sachs, *Ages of Globalization*, 37.

dating between 80 ka to 48 ka were also found in northern India. Together, they suggest that tool-using humans moved through the world on a much earlier timeline than the previous estimates.

In recent years, the technology of genome sequencing has changed everything that was once believed about the origin of humanity. Swedish paleogeneticist Svante Pääbo was the first to successfully retrieve and sequence bits of ancient DNA from a Neanderthal in 1997. Then, his team sequenced a complete Neanderthal genome in 2009 and a Denisovan in 2010. Based on the new study of ancient DNA, it is now argued that multiple migrations out of Africa began as early as 180 ka, leading to interbreeding with archaic humans—Neanderthals in Eurasia and Denisovans in Asia and Oceania.[37] According to Reich, the new evidence for many lineages and admixtures has shaken the confidence in an unquestioned assumption that Africa has been the epicenter of all major events in human evolution.[38] He states, "The genetic data show that many groups of archaic humans populated Eurasia and that some of these interbred with modern humans. This forces us to question why the direction of migration would have always been out of Africa and into Eurasia, and whether it could sometimes have been the other way around."[39] The updated theory posits that modern humans have migrated and mixed with one another as well as with archaic humans many times over before they finally settled into a place and established themselves as the ethnic groups that are recognized today. Reich concludes, "The centrality of mixture in the history of our species, as revealed in just the last few years by the genome revolution, means that we are all interconnected and that we will all keep connecting with one another in the future."[40]

The exact place and time of the emergence of *Homo sapiens* remain obscure because the fossil record is scarce and the chronological age of many key specimens remains uncertain. The tale of humanity's origin is further muddled by Chinese fossils discovered over the past four decades, which cast doubt over the linear progression from African *Homo erectus*

---

37. Sachs, *Ages of Globalization*, 34.
38. Reich, *Who We Are*, 67–68.
39. Reich, *Who We Are*, 71. The latest data from ancient DNA indicates that non-African humans have 2 percent of their genomes from Neanderthals. New Guinean humans have 3 to 6 percent of their genomes from Denisovans. Thus, in total, 5 to 8 percent of New Guinean ancestry comes from archaic humans.
40. Reich, *Who We Are*, 273.

to modern humans.[41] They show that, roughly between roughly 900,000 and 125,000 years ago, east Asia was teeming with hominins endowed with features that would place them somewhere between *Homo erectus* and *Homo sapiens*. All experts believe that recovering more fossils from all parts of Asia and sharing their data can contribute to a better understanding of human history. However, the proper interpretation of those data remains problematic. As Chinese paleoanthropologist Xinzhi Wu says, "Many Western scientists tend to see Asian fossils and artefacts through the prism of what was happening in Africa and Europe." He further explains that those other continents have historically drawn more attention in studies of human evolution because of the antiquity of the fossil finds there and because they are closer to major paleoanthropology research institutions. "But it's increasingly clear that many Asian materials cannot fit into the traditional narrative of human evolution."[42] Most Chinese paleontologists believe in the "Multiregional Evolution" theory. This alternate model suggests that the first hominins that left Africa established a source population of modern humans in the Middle East, where the climate was favorable. This move gave rise to many transitional species that spread to Europe, East Asia, and Africa. Modern humans then evolved in Africa. Yet, not many experts in the West are convinced by this proposition. "Fossil interpretations are notoriously problematic," remarks Pääbo.[43]

There is a third view that can unite humanity for globalization. In contrast to the uncertain and competing evolutionary models that struggle to understand the ancient fossil evidence, Scripture gives a simple and definitive picture of humanity's origin. After creating the fish, birds, and livestock, God then created the first man from the dust of the earth and breathed the breath of life into his nostrils. God gave the man the linguistic and cultural task of naming all the animals, which would have required a high level of intelligence and creativity. When God saw that the man needed a helper, he created the first woman with the rib taken out of the man, signifying that the two are to be united as one flesh. Being together, Adam and Eve began to explore nature and build human civilization on earth (Gen 2:4–25). Many Christians have traditionally believed that this biblical narrative is a literal and accurate description of

---

41. *Homo erectus* means "upright man." It is an extinct species of archaic human from the Pleistocene, with its earliest occurrence about 2 million years ago. It made crude stone tools and had a brain about two-thirds the size of modern humans.

42. Qiu, "How China Is Rewriting," 22–25.

43. Qiu, "How China Is Rewriting," 25.

God's creative act in history. It tells the timeless story of God's creation of humanity and the beginning of globalization. Scripture establishes the foundational truth that all humans are made in God's image when he breathed the breath of life into Adam's nostrils and made him a living being (Gen 2:7). God's breath of life is his Spirit, which dwells within a human being to give consciousness. There is nothing natural about the process of God's breath entering a human being. God created humans who can have communion with him spiritually and represent him in a physical world that they would rule over. God created humans with the capability to master conceptual language and innovate culture. God created the first man and woman as mutual partners to rule over nature and build human civilization.

Ethnic Diversity

During the Neolithic Age, the agricultural revolution allowed nomads to settle down in different parts of the world. The invention of agriculture occurred independently in several locations across the settled parts of the world. It involved a process of learning how to plant selectively the seeds of plants, mainly grasses, for the cultivation of crops. The perplexing archeological and anthropological discovery is that hunters and gatherers seem to have had better nutrition, fewer diseases, more varied diets, less strenuous labor, and longer lives than contemporaneous farmers. Scholars have assumed that because farming can support a far larger population per unit area, people eventually left a life of foraging for a more arduous life.[44]

The diffusion of early agriculture by geography occurred because specific crops have distinctive ecological ranges. Five early agricultural regions in Eurasia that made fundamental and lasting contributions to human civilization are ancient Egypt, Mesopotamia, the Indus Valley, the Yellow River, and the Yangtze River. These civilizations rose and advanced around 5000 to 3000 BC. They were based on alluvial farming. They used domesticated animals for food, transport, and traction, and invented forms of writing that became the precursors of modern scripts. Most of Eurasia's population has lived in a subtropical band of latitude and in a climate zone that historians have named "the lucky latitudes." This is the area from twenty-five degrees north to forty-five degrees north in Eurasia.

44. Sachs, *Ages of Globalization*, 41–44.

They are called lucky because they have been home to humanity's greatest technological and economic progress. The long east-west extent of Eurasia's lucky latitudes offered a vast area of the subtropical climate zone, allowing both innovation and diffusion. It gave rise to early civilizations and the proto-states that would emerge in the next age of globalization.[45]

Sachs emphasizes the importance of the major civilizations that developed in the lucky latitudes, but he overlooks the importance of other civilizations that developed outside the "perfect environment." God's purpose for human civilization extended beyond the confines of ideal landscapes and climates. In Scripture, God commanded humankind to multiply and fill the whole earth. From a human perspective, the lucky latitudes seemed to be the best environment to build their civilization. People therefore resisted God's will to extend their civilization far and wide and settled in the land of Shinar, the southern region of Mesopotamia. In response to their resolve to remain together as a single, unified civilization, God separated people by languages and dispersed them over the face of all the earth. An overview of the earth's terrestrial domain reveals at least nine different ecological zones, each displaying a specific combination of geology, topography, and climate. Out of these different geological environments, people emerged with a wide array of languages, ethnicities, and cultures. Each civilization learned to use the natural resources that were available to them and developed distinct cultural traits based on its environment. Currently, there is no consensus as to how many ethnic groups exist in the world today. The definition of the term *ethnic group* is changing constantly, and it is understood differently by various people. According to one study, the linguistic, ethnic, and cultural fractionalization of humanity has produced around 650 distinct ethnic groups in 190 countries around the world at the turn of the millennium.[46] Measured for evangelistic purposes, the Joshua Project estimates that there are about 17,400 ethnic peoples in the world (by country) separated by language and dialect, ethnicity, religion, caste, and culture.[47]

In nature, diversity is deemed beautiful when there is coherence and harmony rather than division and conflict. Since the diversity and intricacy of nature is pleasing to all observers, it can be deduced that the diversity of human language, ethnicity, and culture reflects God's creativity. The final outcome of his creation project is to see every tribe, language,

---

45. Sachs, *Ages of Globalization*, 46–52.
46. Alesina et al., "Fractionalization," 6.
47. Joshua Project, "How Many People Groups"

people, and nation come together in worship (Rev 5:9–10). God's glory shines when diverse nations come together in Christ to build a harmonious and peaceful world. Furthermore, God wants to see his people glorify him by flourishing over all the earth. The first sign of the Holy Spirit's presence and power among God's people who were saved from sin and evil was complete unity in worship. On the day of Pentecost, the Holy Spirit came upon the believers who gathered to pray together; and they began to "speak in other tongues" as the Spirit enabled them (Acts 2:4–12). People of different ethnicities who witnessed the event were amazed and perplexed when they heard the believers praising God in their own language. God's intention to save all flesh and unite humanity as one body in Christ was clearly displayed in public. This great revelation was confirmed when the apostle Peter reported that the household of Cornelius had received the Holy Spirit just as the Jews did upon hearing the gospel (Acts 11:15). The apostle Paul therefore wrote that "all Gentiles are called to the obedience of faith" (Rom 1:5).

Religious Belief System

The Equestrian Age gave rise to the first religious civilizations, preparing humanity to grow in the knowledge of God by receiving his word. The period from 3000 to 1000 BC was transformative for the major civilizations in the Fertile Crescent, including Egypt, the Levant, and Mesopotamia. Eurasia, which is the largest contiguous land area on the Earth, became home to most of humanity. During this period, three profound technological breakthroughs were most decisive: the domestication of the horse, the breakthroughs in metallurgy that included the use of copper, bronze, and iron, and the development of writing systems. These Eurasian civilizations built the first cities, establishing methods of public administration and tax collection. They also created new philosophies and religions that would profoundly influence Judaism and Christianity.[48]

All human civilizations are founded on religious belief systems. Throughout history, religion was foundational in establishing a society's social cohesion and orderly government. French historian Jean Bottéro explains that the religious belief system of ancient Mesopotamia has the oldest body of recorded literature of any religious tradition, dating from the fourth millennium BC to the birth of Christ. The Mesopotamians' entire

---

48. Sachs, *Ages of Globalization*, 51–68.

existence was infused by their religiosity. Their religion was polytheistic, and they worshiped over 2,100 different deities associated with a specific state such as Sumer, Akkad, and Assyria or a specific city such as Nineveh, Ur, and Babylon.[49] Bottéro explains that the history of the civilization of the land began with the encounter and the intermixing of two populations, the Sumerians and the Akkadians. Their long symbiosis produced the ancient Mesopotamian civilization whose religion had a profound influence on Western civilization. Logical and religious structures of Near Eastern and Mesopotamian cultures served as precursors to those of the West.[50]

The Sumerians were the first to introduce comprehensive legal codes to maintain order in society. The Code of Hammurabi (written ca. 1754 BC), a collection of 282 rules, established standards for commercial interactions and set fines and punishments to meet the requirements of justice. The primary copy of the text was inscribed on a basalt stele that is two and one quarter meters tall. At its top, the basalt stele shows the royal lawgiver Hammurabi standing before the sun god Shamash, the divine guardian of justice (see fig. 1). Below these images are about 4,130 lines of cuneiform text: one-fifth contains a prologue and epilogue in poetic style, while the remaining four-fifths contain the laws. In the prologue, Hammurabi claims to have been granted his rule by the gods to prevent the strong from oppressing the weak. The artifact implies that the king's authority to administer justice was based on his relationship with his god.[51]

Another significant archeological example of Mesopotamian religious belief system is the Uruk Vase (ca. 3200–3000 BC), which was found in the temple complex of the Sumerian goddess Inanna in the ruins of the city Uruk. The subject matter of the vase is the presentation of offerings to the goddess Inanna. It is a ritual enactment representing the Sacred Marriage, which is the union of a god or a goddess and a mortal, usually the ruler or a member of the ruling family. The bottom register displays naturalistic components of life, including water and plants, such as date palm, barley, and wheat. On the upper portion of the lowest register, alternating rams and ewes march in a single file. The middle register depicts men carrying baskets of food as offerings. Then, the top register depicts the goddess Inanna, represented by two reed bundles, accepting a votive offer through a priestess.[52]

49. Bottéro, *Religion in Ancient Mesopotamia*, 1–11.
50. Bottéro et al., *Ancestor of the West*, 51.
51. Bottéro, *Religion in Ancient Mesopotamia*, 156–84.
52. Bourke, *Middle East*, 67.

THE HISTORICAL DEVELOPMENT OF GLOBALIZATION 69

Figure 1. The Code of Hammurabi in the Louvre Museum of Paris.

Under the leadership of kings who claimed their authority to rule through religious belief system, the ancient people of Mesopotamia developed the first great civilization of humanity. The Semitic-speaking Akkadians, led by their renowned founder Sargon, succeeded in uniting all the Sumerian city-states under his rule. The ancient empire of Mesopotamia reached its political peak between the twenty-fourth and twenty-second centuries BC. Although the Mesopotamian civilization had developed its logical and religious structures that ordered its society, it did not yet receive God's promise to deliver humanity from its bondage to sin and evil. People had put their faith in their heroes, mortal kings that represented false gods. Around 2000 BC, according to Scripture, God called Abraham to come out from his homeland and start a journey to become "the father of a multitude of nations" (Gen 17:5). Detailed in Gen 12–25, Abraham was commanded to leave behind the sociopolitical organization and the religious belief system of his forefathers so that he can discover a new one for humanity. The significant part played by the patriarch in redemptive history is the receiving of divine promise:

> I will make you into a great nation and I will bless you;
> I will make your name great, and you will be a blessing.
> I will bless those who bless you, and whoever curses you I will curse;
> and all peoples on earth will be blessed through you.
> (Gen 12:2–3 NIV)

Abraham was originally from the city of Ur in Mesopotamia, which was most likely in southern Chaldea. He married Sarah and migrated from Mesopotamia to Haran and then later to Canaan and Egypt. His journey was a long and dramatic one of faith and encountered many different cultures, customs, and people groups along the Fertile Crescent from Mesopotamia to Egypt. Abraham and Sarah also miraculously had their son Isaac in their old age. When Abraham obeyed God's command to sacrifice his only son on the altar, God saw his faith and credited it to him as righteousness (Rom 4:3). Not only did God stop Abraham from proceeding with the sacrifice, but he also promised that all the nations of the earth will be blessed through Abraham's offspring (Gen 22:18). Abraham's faith and act of obedience in response to God's promise opened the way for Christ to be born through his lineage. What follows is the epic story of how God raised up Israel as a holy nation and prepared the world for the birth, death, and resurrection of Christ.

Western Civilization

The Classical Age, the period between 1000 BC and AD 1500, gave rise to the strongest and largest civilizations that would eventually shape the world. Many of the world's major religions including Judaism, Christianity, Islam, Buddhism, and Hinduism were formed during this time. The prominent philosophies of life were taught by Plato and Aristotle, Confucius, the Buddha, and other sages. It was in this age that the four kingdoms of Daniel's vision in Scripture rose in succession: the Babylonian Empire, the Achaemenian Persian Empire, the Hellenistic Greek Empire, and the Roman Empire. The rise and fall of these four kingdoms gave birth to Western civilization.

The Babylonian Empire became the most renowned civilization for its scientific, religious, and engineering feats. The range of its scholarship was extensive, but it became famous for the astronomical sciences that included astrology. With great accuracy and technical sophistication, Babylonians made night-sky observations and interpreted the movements of planets and stars in terms of human and terrestrial implications. Their mixture of divination and astronomy ultimately established a Western, astrological tradition of relying on horoscopes in making daily decisions. Greek astronomy was later built from Babylonian data collections stretching back to the early second millennium BC.[53] Astrology was absorbed and transformed by Greek geometric and kinetic models, which added the aspects, or angles of separation between planets and points, and emphasized the importance of the *horoscopos* or Ascendent, the degree of the zodiacal sign rising on the eastern horizon. By the second century, the most famous and influential work in astrology was formulated by Ptolemy in his *Tetrabiblos*.[54] From ordinary citizens to those who hold the highest positions in public office, reliance on astrology became widespread in the West. According to Christine Smallwood, "Western astrology had its origins in ancient Mesopotamia, and spread throughout Egypt, Greece, the Roman Empire, and the Islamic world. Astrology helped people decide when to plant crops and go to war, and was used to predict a person's fate and interpret his character."[55] The former US president Ronald Reagan made almost every major move and decision by consulting with his astrologer Joan Quigley. Those decisions included the timing of his reelection announcement, military actions in Grenada and Libya, and disarmament negotiations with Mikhail Gorbachev. Likewise, the former French president François Mitterrand consulted his astrologer Elisabeth Teissier in making all his important decisions between 1989 and 1994. Today, around a third of Americans read the horoscope daily, finding perceived insight and comfort in the twelve astrological signs of the zodiac. In France, four out of ten people now believe in astrology, and nearly 70 percent of French youth between the ages of eighteen to twenty-four believe in astrology.[56]

King Nebuchadnezzar II (reigned 605–562 BC) transformed Babylonia from a local power into a world empire. His destruction of Jerusalem, its temple, and the deportation of its people to Babylon brought Judah's independent monarchy to an end (587 BC). Under his direction, the Babylonians were able to build complex and large-scale structures with their great riches. Archeological excavations testify to the biblical account of Nebuchadnezzar's achievements and glory. The city of Babylon

53. Bourke, *Middle East*, 203–7.
54. Curry, "Astrology," 24.
55. Smallwood, "Astrology in the Age," para. 8.
56. Wilkins, "Revival of the Occult."

sprawled over three square miles, which was enclosed within eleven miles of fortified walls. At its heart lay the palace and temple district, protected by another triple-layered wall. A channel was dug out around this area so that the Euphrates River flowed in to protect it as a moat. The north entrance to its official quarter was the magnificent Ishtar Gate that measured over thirty-eight feet (eleven and a half meters) high. It was a double gate, with the second gate measuring more than fifty feet (fifteen meters) high (see fig. 2). It was built with blue-glazed bricks emblazoned with sacred dragon and bull friezes, symbolic representations of the deities that protected Babylon (see fig. 3). Through the gatehouse was the Processional Way, which is a brick-paved corridor over half a mile (800 meters) long with walls over fifty feet (fifteen meters) tall on each side. The walls were adorned with 120 winged lion friezes, symbolizing Nebuchadnezzar's pride, power, and reign (see fig. 4). The Processional Way led to the temple of Marduk called *Esagila* ("temple whose top is lofty" in Sumerian), which sat on the top of a massive ziggurat (see fig. 5). Historians attest that the most significant thing about Nebuchadnezzar was his religious devotion.[57] According to Scripture, after many years of living in great pride, he turned from his wrong way and confessed, "Now I, Nebuchadnezzar, praise, exalt, and glorify the King of heaven, because all His works are true and His ways are just. He is able to humble those who walk in pride" (Dan 4:37).

Figure 2. Model of the Processional Way and the Ishtar Gate, in the Pergamon Museum of Berlin.

57. Bourke, *Middle East*, 208–9.

THE HISTORICAL DEVELOPMENT OF GLOBALIZATION 73

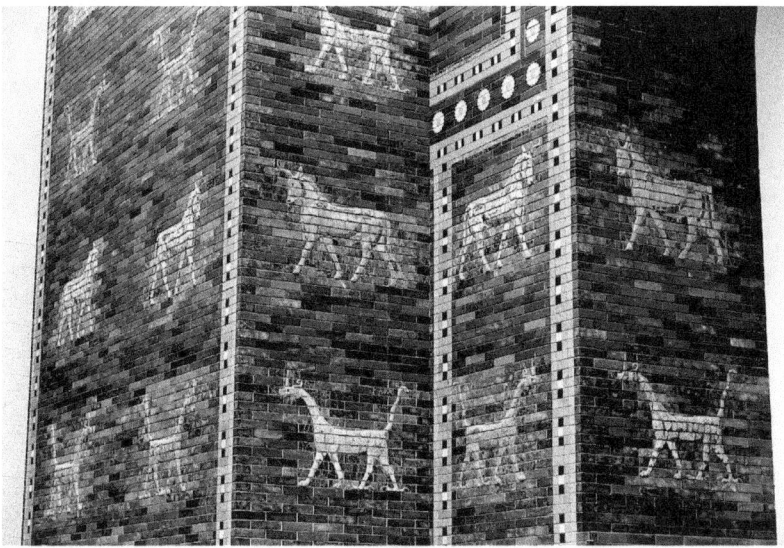

Figure 3. Sacred Dragon and Bull Relief on the Ishtar Gate of Babylon, in the Pergamon Museum of Berlin.

Figure 4. Winged Lion Relief on the Processional Way, in the Pergamon Museum of Berlin.

Figure 5. Model of a Mesopotamian Ziggurat in Babylon, in the Pergamon Museum of Berlin.

The Achaemenian Persian Empire dominated land stretching from India to Egypt, from Iran to the Balkans. It survived and thrived in a dangerous region for some two hundred years due to its superior administrative structure of governance. After the fall of Nineveh (612 BC), three major powers dominated the Middle East: the Babylonians, the Lydians in western Anatolia, and the Medes in northern Iran. As Scripture foretold, King Cyrus (reigned 550–529 BC) greatly expanded the kingdom's territory by conquering these powers (Isa 45:1–3). In the first year of his reign, Cyrus declared an edict that allowed the Jews to return to Jerusalem and rebuild their temple (Ezra 6:3–5). In the years after the conquest of Babylonia, Cyrus gained a truly international empire. Aria, Parthia, Sogdinan, and Margiana fell to him on the eastern front. Near the Jaxartes River, he founded a city called Cyropolis which marked the northeastern border. In the west, Cilicia, Syria, and Palestine came under his rule. Later, King Darius (reigned 522–486 BC) effectively controlled this vast empire by dividing it into twenty provinces called satrapies, with each governed by a satrap. Each satrapy was assessed for its wealth and taxed accordingly in the form of an annual tribute that had to be paid to the central administration. Royal secretaries and military personnel who were directly responsible to the king were critical components of satrapal administration. Darius also built the Royal Road, which connected Susa to Sardi, to facilitate rapid communication and intelligence gathering throughout the empire; royal messengers were effective in weeding out any rebellious officials.[58]

The remarkable expansion of the Achaemenian Persian Empire came to a historic clash against Greece. The Persian-Greek Wars began when Persia attacked mainland Greece in 490 BC. The wars resulted in a decisive victory for Western civilization in 449 BC. Just after the end of those wars, Athens and Sparta engaged in the Peloponnesian Wars from 431 to 404 BC, which led to the demise of the Athenian Republic. It marked the end of the Golden Age of Athens, a city which inspired the West by its democratic institutions, scholarship, the arts, and civil participations. Although Athens was completely devastated and never regained its pre-war prosperity, it still produced Plato and Aristotle, who would shape Western philosophy. When Alexander became the king of Macedonia in 334 BC, he captured Egypt and the Achaemenian Persian Empire and continued his conquest east to the Indus River. After his sudden death in 323 BC, the Greco-Macedonian Empire was divided by his generals and followers, who launched a complex series of wars of succession. The ensuing successor states continued to spread Greek colonization, trade, culture, and philosophy throughout the lands that Alexander conquered.[59]

The consequence of Alexander's conquest was that Hellenistic Greek culture became a world culture by blending with Egyptian, Persian, and Indian influences. Dutch philosopher Herman Dooyeweerd explains that when Alexander's empire spread, certain eastern religious motives began to mingle with the Greek religious motives that were rooted in the worship of the Olympian gods in Athens.[60] Most ancient Greeks recognized the twelve major Olympian gods and goddesses—Zeus, Hera, Poseidon, Demeter, Athena, Ares, Aphrodite, Apollo, Artemis, Hephaestus, Hermes, and either Hestia or Dionysus. Dooyeweerd also says, "Alexander made use of the Asiastic belief in the divine ancestry of monarchs in order to legitimize and give divine sanction to the Greco-Macedonian world empire."[61] He explains that the worship of Alexander as Dionysus (god of wine, fertility, and religious ecstasy) became the foundation of the religious *imperium* (absolute power) idea, which became the driving

58. Bourke, *Middle East*, 232–35.
59. Bourke, *Middle East*, 248–71.
60. Dooyeweerd, *Roots of Western Culture*, 22.
61. Dooyeweerd, *Roots of Western Culture*, 22.

force behind the Roman conquest of the world.[62] Wine was a religious focus in the cult of Dionysus and was his earthly incarnation. Wine could ease suffering, bring joy, and inspire divine madness. Festivals of Dionysus included the performance of sacred dramas enacting his myths, the initial driving force behind the development of theater in Western culture. Alexander's self-deification became a rational policy that was repeated by Hellenistic kings, Roman emperors, and other rulers.

Among its competitors, the Seleucid Empire (312–63 BC) rose as a major center of the Hellenistic world (see fig. 6). It was officially founded when Seleucus I established himself in Babylon as the head of an empire comprising most of the Iranian, Central Asian, and Indian possessions of Alexander. The Seleucid Empire embraced a wide variety of cultures, and over the course of its existence numerous elements of syncretism between the Greek, Levantine, and Mesopotamian cultures occurred. At its height, the empire consisted of territory that covered Anatolia (Asia minor), Persia, the Levant, and what are now modern-day Iraq, Kuwait, Afghanistan, and parts of Turkmenistan. Between 305 and 303 BC, Seleucus engaged in a war against Emperor Chandragupta Maurya of the Maurya Empire. The war ended in a settlement resulting in the annexation of the Indus Valley region and part of Afghanistan to the Mauryan Empire, with Chandragupta securing control over the areas that he had sought, and a marriage alliance between the two powers. In consequence of their arrangement, Seleucus received five hundred war elephants from Chandragupta, a military asset that would play a decisive role in his victory against the Hellenistic kings at the Battle of Ipsus in 301 BC. In addition to this treaty, Seleucus dispatched two Greek ambassadors, Megasthenes and, later, Deimakos, to the Mauryan court at Pataliputra. Thus, the Hellenistic world of the West and the Mauryan Empire of the East began to maintain diplomatic ties. The Khyber Pass, which exists on the modern-day boundary of Pakistan and Afghanistan, became a strategically important point of trade and interaction between the West and India.[63]

As the Hellenistic world expanded, its religion spread to the Near East. Greek temples were to be found everywhere—in Phoenicia, Syria, and even in distant Iran. Social contact with the indigenous peoples gave the Macedonians and Greeks access to the most diverse religions of the Near East—the cult of Mithra in Iran, Marduk and Ishtar in Babylonia,

---

62. Dooyeweerd, *Roots of Western Culture*, 22.
63. Bourke, *Middle East*, 272–73.

Astarte and Hadad in Syria and Phoenicia, the Magna Mater in Anatolia, and many others. The people of the West assimilated many of these foreign gods as their own, and Greek religiosity became syncretized as the Hellenistic civilization spread. In this process, the "royal cult" was organized during the second generation of Seleucids by Antiochus I (reigned 281-261 BC). Emulating Alexander, the rulers adopted cult names, such as Soter, Theos, and Epiphanes. Clearly, this cult was intended to be a unifying influence on the various peoples and nations of the kingdom.[64]

Daniel 11 foretold the epic struggle between the kingdom of the North (the Seleucid Empire of Syria) and the kingdom of the South (the Ptolemaic Empire of Egypt). Their political and military intrigues culminated with the domination of Antiochus IV Epiphanes (reigned 175-164 BC), the most notorious and brutal king of the North who oppressed the Jewish people, suppressed the Jewish religion, and magnified himself above all gods (Dan 11:36).[65] He declared that "all should be one people and that all should give up their particular customs" (1 Macc 1:41-42 NRSV). His reign brought forth a time of great tribulation against the Jews that would reveal those who were righteous and wicked (Dan 12:1). Historians note that the reign of Antiochus is significant for his confrontation with Rome and his involvement with Jerusalem during his campaigns against Egypt.[66] After defeating Ptolemy VI at Pelusium in 169 BC and taking control of Egypt, except Alexandria, Antiochus plundered the temple in Jerusalem on his return to Syria. Yet his second invasion of Egypt was not successful because of Rome's intervention, forcing him to retreat. Being enraged, he began his suppression of "the holy covenant" and sponsored the construction of a pagan altar in the temple that was referred to as the Abomination of Desolation by the Jews (Dan 11:30-31).

---

64. *New Encyclopædia Britannica*, s.v. "Greco-Roman Civilization," 289-93.

65. Steinmann, *Daniel*, 536-46. Most critical scholars as well as a few evangelical scholars interpret 11:36-45 as applying to Antiochus. The traditional Christian interpretation understands 11:36-45 as applying to an eschatological king, which in NT terms is the Antichrist or "the man of lawlessness" (2 Thess 2:3-12).

66. Bourke, *Middle East*, 272-75.

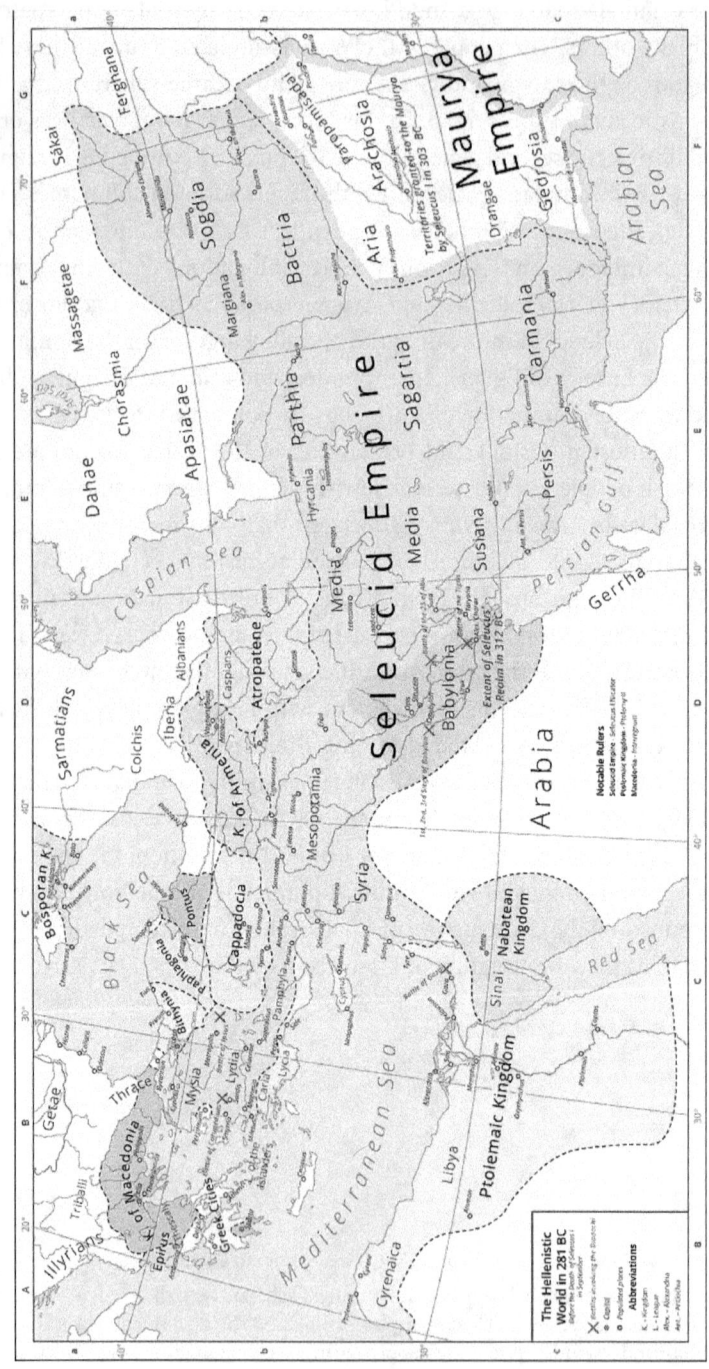

Figure 6. The Hellenistic World in 281 BC.

Nevertheless, not all Jews reacted negatively to Antiochus's effort to eradicate the Jewish culture and religion. Some saw it as a way of better integrating Jewish society within the Hellenistic world; however, there was a group of people that opposed all compromise with Greek culture and religion. In 167 BC, a group of Jewish fighters, a priestly family called Hasmoneans who were led by Judas Maccabeus, stood up against Antiochus and against Hellenistic influence on Jewish life. These fighters were called the Maccabees, and they led the rebellion that led to the recapture of Jerusalem and the temple and the restoration of worship in accordance with the law of Moses. Their righteous actions, which was foretold by the prophet Daniel (Dan 11:32), are chronicled in the apocryphal books of 1 and 2 Maccabees.[67] After the gentiles had desecrated the temple, the Maccabees rededicated the temple on December 24 of 164 BC. This was the first Hanukkah (dedication), which became a Jewish festival commemorating this rededication (John 10:22). Had Antiochus's policy succeeded, Judaism would have ceased to exist, and Christianity would never have had the climate from which it would later emerge. After this family resisted the cultural and religious suppression by the gentiles, the Hasmonean Dynasty was established to rule Judea from 141 to 37 BC. It lasted until Herod the Great displaced the last ruler. During his reign, Herod rebuilt and greatly enlarged the temple to please the Jews, but Christ came to reveal himself as the true temple of God's kingdom (John 2:19). According to God's decree, Judaism fulfilled its role of preparing the world for the birth, death, and resurrection of Christ. It was in this context that the fourth kingdom of Daniel's vision came into fulfillment (Dan 7:7).

While the remnants of the Hellenistic Greek Empire were in decline, a new civilization of the Romans rose to power. Rome originated as a small community of farmers and tradesmen on the Tiber River in the center of the Italian peninsula as early as the tenth century BC. In time, it became a terrifying kingdom of legions that subdued all the neighboring nations. The Roman Republic completed its conquest of Greece in 146 BC, yet it remained heavily dependent on Greek science, philosophy, and religion. Dooyeweerd explains that the Roman Republic was a network of towns ruled by local clans and by provinces that were administered by military commanders. During this time, the religious motive of power and law thoroughly pervaded the old folk law (*ius civile*) of Roman tribalism. This common law was applicable exclusively to the citizens of Rome.

---

67. For an excellent introductory study of the Maccabean revolt as a biblical revolution, see Harrington, *Maccabean Revolt*.

With the head of the clan serving as its priest, the family deified and worshiped its ancestors. Unlike the modern nuclear family, each *familia* was a community of family, an economic unit, a miniature state, and a community of worship. The household heads were mutually equal as bearers of power; no one had jurisdiction over the other.[68]

When Rome became an empire, its interlinked society consisting of many nations was now in need of a universal law that could apply to both citizens and foreigners. The development of a universal law common to all free people presented the Roman legislators with a deeply religious problem. They had no foundation to build a universal law for the empire. Thus, they relied on the Stoics' philosophical doctrine of an absolute natural law (*ius naturale*) that reached back to a prehistoric golden age, an age without slavery or war and without distinction between Greeks and barbarians. Over time, because of the pervasive power and control of the Roman Empire, the universal law (*ius gentium*) became, for practical purposes, the law observed by all nations. The Roman Empire provided its citizens not only with the military glory and material luxury of *Pax Romania* but also with the stability and certitude of its legal system. The Roman Empire's discovery of the universal law was, according to Dooyeweerd, a gift of God's common grace to Western culture.[69] The direct effect of the Roman law was the West's conception of and claim to universality, which manifested itself after Constantine the Great adopted Christianity as the Roman state religion in AD 380. Anthony Pagden remarks:

> After the triumph of Christianity, ancient Greek and Roman notions of exclusivity were further enforced by Christians' insistence upon the uniqueness both of the Gospels and of the Church as a source of moral and scientific authority. Custom, in Lactantius's words, had been "made congruent with religion." Christianity was thought of as spatially coextensive with the Roman Empire. The world, the *orbis terrarum*, thus became, in terms of the translation effected by Pope Leo the Great in the fifth century, the *orbis Christianus* or, as it would be called in the European vernaculars, "Christendom."[70]

The apostle Paul's Epistle of Romans, which expounds the gospel most clearly in judicial terms, was written for all people to understand God's purpose and plan of reconciling humanity in Christ. It explains

---

68. Dooyeweerd, *Roots of Western Culture*, 23–25.
69. Dooyeweerd, *Roots of Western Culture*, 26–27.
70. Pagden, *Idea of Europe*, 43.

how God has been faithful to his promises to the patriarchs of Israel by uniting Jews and gentiles in Christ, and how this good news calls the new family to live together as one, to the glory of God. This new understanding of God's word began to spread throughout the Roman Empire, paving the way for the rise of a new kind of civilization, which adopted a new religion called Christianity. Throughout the Middle Ages, the Roman Catholic Church continued to pursue universal claims, not only in spiritual matters but also in political and legal matters. By the tenth century, the religious, cultural, economic, and political society known as Christendom had come into being in Western civilization.

Islamic Civilization

The Classical Age saw the spectacular rise of Islam (الإسلام) as a new religion in the Arabian desert. A succession of vast, Islamic empires rose rapidly on a massive scale. Within a century, the Islamic realm extended from the Atlantic coast of Iberia, across North Africa, the Arabian Peninsula, and the Levant, into Persia, and beyond to the Indus River. The prophet Muhammad (ca. AD 570–632) was born in Mecca and became the founder of Islam, which means "submission to the will of God" in Arabic. Muslims believe that he was a prophet divinely inspired to preach the *Qur'an* (ٱلْقُرْآن), which means "recitation." Standing against the polytheistic beliefs of the Arab people, he claimed there was only one true God: Allah.[71] According to Ja'far ibn Abī Ṭālib, one of the early companions of the prophet, the teachings of Muhammad delivered his followers from the depravity of Meccan society at the time. Many Muslims fled the severe persecution in Mecca and migrated to Abyssinia (today's Ethiopia). In seeking the protection of the Negus, the ruler of Abyssinia, Ja'far made the following speech:

> O King, we were an uncivilized people, worshipping idols, eating corpses, committing abominations, breaking natural ties, treating guests badly, and our strong devoured our weak. Thus we were until God sent us an apostle whose lineage, truth, trustworthiness, and clemency we know. He summoned us to acknowledge God's unity and to worship him and to renounce the stones and images which we and our fathers formerly worshipped. He commanded us to speak the truth, be faithful to our engagements, mindful of the ties of kinship and kindly hospitality, and

71. Esposito, *Oxford History of Islam*, 1–62.

to refrain from crimes and bloodshed. He forbade us to commit abominations and to speak lies, and to devour the property of orphans, to vilify chaste women. He commanded us to worship God alone and not to associate anything with Him, and he gave us orders about prayer, almsgiving, and fasting. We confessed his truth and believed in him, and we followed him in what he had brought from God, and we worshipped God alone without associating aught with Him.[72]

During the ten years between his arrival in Medina and his death in 632, Muhammad laid the foundation for the ideal Islamic state. A core of committed Muslims was established, and a community life was ordered according to the requirements of the new religion. In addition to general moral injunctions, the institutional requirements of the religion became known as the five pillars of Islam. They are the profession of faith (*shahada*), prayer (*salat*), almsgiving (*zakat*), fasting (*sawm*), and pilgrimage (*hajj*). After Muhammad's death in 632, his immediate successors called "caliphs" inherited an expanding but loose-knit social fabric. They administered the growing Islamic sphere of influence from the city of Medina. By 640, the Arab army captured the whole of Byzantine Syria. The first powerful Islamic Caliphate of the Umayyads was then founded in 661, with the capital in Damascus.[73]

By the eighth century, the Islamic Empire covered an area larger in expanse than either the Roman Empire at its height or all the land conquered and ruled by Alexander the Great. For a period stretching over seven hundred years, the international language of science was Arabic. In spite of these things, two important events prevented the Arabs from extending their conquest into Europe. On the western front, they were defeated by the Franks in the Battle of Tours (732) in today's France. On the eastern front, the Arab siege of Constantinople (717–718) was the most determined effort by the caliphs to conquer the Byzantine Empire. They were, however, defeated by Emperor Leo III, preventing the Islamization of the region. Still, Islam extended far beyond their conquered territories. Arab merchants and seafarers brought Islam to Indian Ocean settlements and subsequently, it took hold in parts of India, China, and Southeast Asia.

When the Umayyad Caliphate became overextended and experienced revolt, it was overturned by the Abbasid Caliphate in 750. During the reign of Abbasid caliph Harun al-Rashid (786–809), the Islamic

---

72. Ibn Ishaq, *Life of Muhammad*, 151–52.
73. Sachs, *Ages of Globalization*, 86–87.

Golden Age began. It was a period of scientific, economic, and cultural flourishing that lasted until the thirteenth century. The Islamic civilization opened its doors to new ideas from the East and the West. Being firmly rooted in the teachings of the Qur'an, the confident Muslims took these ideas and remolded them in a uniquely Islamic mold. Out of this mixing came Islamic art, architecture, astronomy, chemistry, mathematics, medicine, music, philosophy, and ethics. Harun established the legendary library *Bayt al-Hikma*, the "House of Wisdom," in Baghdad in present-day Iraq and ruled from this city until he moved his court and government to Raqqa in present-day Syria. By the ninth century, Baghdad had become the largest city in the world with a population of one million. It also became the center of the civilized world, attracting the very best of Arab and Persian philosophers and scientists for several centuries to come.[74]

One of Baghdad's most famous rulers was Abu Ja'far al-Ma'mun (786–833). This enigmatic caliph became the greatest patron of science among the Islamic rulers and the person responsible for initiating the world's most impressive period of scholarship and learning since Ancient Greece. Under Ma'mun's patronage and the spirit of openness that he fostered toward other religions and cultures, many scholars from all over the empire gravitated toward Baghdad. One of the scholars employed in the House of Wisdom was al-Kindi (801–873), simply known as "the philosopher of the Arabs" to this day. He is regarded as the first of the Abbasid polymaths and is mostly famous for being the first to introduce the philosophy of Aristotle to the Arabic-speaking world. His work fused Aristotelian philosophy with Islamic theology, thereby creating an intellectual platform for debates between philosophers and theologians that would continue for hundreds of years. Another scholar named Muhammad ibn Musa al-Khwarizmi (780–850) worked in the House of Wisdom as a mathematician, geographer, and astronomer. He is known as the most important scientist in the period between 800 and 850. Together with Kindi, he was instrumental in introducing the Arabs to the Hindu decimal numerals that are used today. Khwarizmi's greatest legacy is his extraordinary book on algebra. The word *algebra* is derived from the title of his book: *Kitab al-Jebr*, "The Book of Completion," in which he lays out for the first time the rules and steps of solving algebraic equations.[75]

---

74. Esposito, *Oxford History of Islam*, 159–70.
75. Al-Khalili, *House of Wisdom*, 67–171.

Chinese Civilization

During the rise of the Roman Empire in the West, China was becoming established as a great civilization on the eastern edge of Eurasia. The emperor Qin Shi Huang, who is known for his burial with the Terracotta Army, first united China in 221 BC. The Qin Dynasty was short-lived, but it was followed by the Han Dynasty, which lasted four hundred years from 206 BC to AD 220. The Han Dynasty established boundaries that remain the core of the Chinese state today, and it excelled in the development of homegrown technologies. A partial list of spectacular breakthroughs includes papermaking, navigation (the rudder), mathematics (negative numbers, the solution of equations), flood control, the waterwheel, metallurgy (wrought iron), and the seismometer. The empire invented an administrative model that would endure throughout China's history: a centralized national government ruling over a hierarchy of provinces, counties, districts, and villages. Confucianism was also codified as the state ideology. Moreover, the stability and productivity of the Han Empire had relatively allowed its population to reach an estimated 60 million people around AD 1. At the time, the Roman Empire reached around 45 million people. Thus, the Han and Roman Empires together accounted for about one half of the world's population.[76]

Chinese literature is among the most creative and interesting in the world, a vast subject that spans thousands of years. Much of the serious literature was composed using a formal written language that is called Classical Chinese. According to Taiping Chang, "Chinese scholars traditionally have considered the Han *fu*-rhapsody, Tang *shi*-poetry, Song *ci*-song lyrics, and Yuan *qu*-drama, as the highest literary achievements of their respective dynasties."[77] However, Chinese literature embraces a far wider range of writing than these four genres, and it has developed into a treasure trove that offers rich information about Chinese society, thought, customs, and social and political movements.[78] For the people of East Asia, the fourteenth-century historical novel called *San Guo Yan Yi* (三國演義) has had a lasting influence in shaping their culture and society. The novel's title can be translated as "Three Kingdoms Performing *Yi*." For Chinese people, the concept of *Yi* (righteousness or duty) is essential in building a harmonious society. This essential concept also

---

76. Sachs, *Ages of Globalization*, 80–82.
77. Chang, "Three Millennia of Writings," para. 1.
78. Chang, "Three Millennia of Writings."

encompasses honor, benevolence, loyalty, selflessness, and brotherhood. In reference to the literary work, Moss Roberts says that "one can look at the novel as a consummation of many Chinese traditions and as a gateway to those traditions."[79] The novel is set in the turbulent years toward the end of the Han Dynasty and the beginning of the Three Kingdoms period in Chinese history. The story romanticizes and dramatizes the lives of feudal lords and their retainers, who tried to either replace the dwindling Han Dynasty or restore it. While the novel follows the lives of nearly a thousand dramatic characters who are historical figures or are fictional, its focus is mainly on the three power blocs that emerged from the remnants of the Han Dynasty. They would eventually form the three states of Cao Wei, Shu Han, and Eastern Wu. Taking place over a period of almost one hundred years, the novel deals with the stories, personal and military battles, intrigues, and struggles of these states to achieve dominance. From the beginning to the end, the novel is interweaved with more than two hundred poems, heightening the emotional response of the reader. One of those poems is "Lin Jiang Xian" (The Immortals by the River), which was written by Yang Shen during the Ming Dynasty and later included as the opening words of the novel:

滾滾長江東逝水	The mighty Yangtze River flows ever eastward,
浪花淘盡英雄	Its waves scouring away countless heroes.
是非成敗轉頭空	Right and wrong, success and failure, it does not seem to matter.
青山依舊在	Green mountains are always present;
幾度夕陽紅	How many times has the setting sun been red?
白髮漁樵江渚上	The white-haired fishermen and woodcutters work on the shoals,
慣看秋月春風	Accustomed as they are to gazing at the autumn moon and the spring breezes.
一壺濁酒喜相逢	A jug of wine to drink in their happy meeting,
古今多少事	Things from past and present,
都付笑談中	Are all talked and laughed on with each other.[80]

Since ancient times, the philosophical concept of harmony has been put forward and interpreted, and the Chinese nation has pursued it as a vital value. According to Wang Zhongwu, a sociology professor at Shandong University, "The practice of fine traditional Chinese values has indicated

---

79. Luo, *Three Kingdoms*, ix.
80. The ancient poem "Lin Jiang Xian" is translated by the author of this book.

that a harmonious society can be achieved."[81] The former Chinese premier Wen Jiabao explains, "'Harmony without uniformity' is a great idea put forth by ancient Chinese thinkers. It means harmony without sameness and difference without conflict. Harmony entails coexistence and co-prosperity, while difference conduces to mutual complementation and mutual support."[82] In East Asia, the intersection of Confucianism, Daoism, and Buddhism has produced stable and moral societies with sophisticated cultures in China, Korea, Japan, and Vietnam, as well as other territories. According to Goossaert and Palmer, although Chinese religion does not have a unified formal theology, all communities and religious specialists share common cosmological notions. This cosmology dictates that the material and spiritual realms are not separate.[83]

The Tang Dynasty (618–907) came almost four hundred years after the demise of the Han Dynasty and the ensuing period of fragmentation. It is generally regarded as a golden age in Chinese civilization and the beginning of its first cosmopolitan age. It created the largest Chinese empire before the eighteenth century and became a centralized empire with a postal system and an extensive network of roads and canals, which radiated from the capital to the far west and northeast. Chang'an (today's Xi'an) became the new capital with a population of nearly one million people. The city became a political and ritual center for over a thousand years. Chinese cultural achievements in the arts, literature, and history were extraordinary in the Tang era, to the extent that it is traditionally considered the greatest age for Chinese poetry. Two of China's most famous poets, Li Bai and Du Fu, belonged to this age, and contributed with other poets, such as Wang Wei, to the monumental *Three Hundred Tang Poems*. Many famous painters such as Han Gan, Zhang Xuan, and Zhou Fang were active, and Chinese court music flourished with instruments such as the pipa (the Chinese lute).[84]

In AD 645, a Buddhist monk named Xuanzang, who had left China and spent more than sixteen years traveling and studying in India returned to Chang'an. Turning down the emperor's invitation to become his prime minister, Xuanzang unpacked his cargoes containing Buddhist sutras, sacred texts, figurines, statues, and antiquities. He then began his massive translation project comparable to that of Greek into Arabic and

81. Xinhua, "Cultural China," para. 18.
82. *Harvard Gazette*, "Remarks of Chinese Premier," para. 44.
83. Goossaert and Palmer, *Religious Question*, 20–27.
84. Wood, *Story of China*, 125.

Persian in the Islamic caliphate or Greek into Latin during Europe's three renaissances between the eighth and fifteenth century. Historian Michael Wood notes, "The next few decades saw the coming into being of what has been called the 'Buddhist cosmopolis' of Central Asia, India, China, Korea and Japan. In that time many hundreds of monks travelled between these countries, along with countless more merchants and diplomats."[85] He adds, "Reflecting on the previous thousand years or more of Chinese history, Xuanzang saw that the ancients had built the Chinese state on the foundations of a Confucian ethos whose ideology was key to an ordered cosmos, while Daoism had given them the spiritual dimension of a traditional religion, and that these two twin pillars had served the country well."[86] In addition to these uniquely Chinese traditions, he now established Buddhism, which was a transnational, universal religion. It opened China to the wider world intellectually, as well as in its spiritual life, directly questioning the previously assumed centrality of Chinese culture and her unique civilizing mission.[87]

China experienced another golden age during the Song Dynasty (960–1279). A newly unified and peaceful China entered a period of stunning technological innovation, population growth, and economic prosperity. The Song Dynasty is characterized by the excellence of governance based on Confucian Rule. The Song society was transformed and managed by a new elite class of scholar-officials that were recruited through a competitive civil service examination system.[88] According to historian Dieter Kuhn, this movement—often labeled Neo-Confucianism in the West—aimed primarily to establish a social and political order. He writes:

> Previous dynasties had relied on the great families, aristocratic officials, scholars, and military men. It was only during the Song empire that thinking and writing, government and administrative action, were brought down to a common denominator.... During the Song Dynasty, a new self-consciousness and self-esteem took shape among the people who identified themselves as descendants of the Han Chinese. The social system they invented during the Song empire became the paradigm for what Chinese and Westerners of the twentieth century would refer to as "traditional China."[89]

85. Wood, *Story of China*, 141.
86. Wood, *Story of China*, 142.
87. Wood, *Story of China*, 142.
88. Kuhn, *Age of Confucian Rule*, 276–82.
89. Kuhn, *Age of Confucian Rule*, 1.

Under the workings of a rationalistic Confucian philosophy and state ideology, the Chinese civilization brought major advances in navigation, shipbuilding, and metallurgy; invented gunpowder, explosives, artillery, the movable-type printing press, and paper currency; introduced institutions of banking, insurance, and joint-stock enterprises; and vastly improved mechanized means of production. The increase of agricultural productivity supported the Song population so that it doubled to around 120 million, resulting in a massive increase in the urban population. The Song society's economic growth, resembling the advanced features of modern capitalism, propelled China into becoming the richest civilization in the world during the early part of the eleventh century.[90]

Indian Civilization

India became a great civilization of the East that rose alongside the Hellenistic world of the West. The Indus Valley Civilization flourished in the northern region of the Indian subcontinent from ca. 3300 BC to ca. 1300 BC. It was founded on the religious belief that *Brahman*, or Supreme Consciousness, pervades the entire universe. The roots of Indian culture were first recorded during the Vedic period (ca. 1500–500 BC) in today's states of Haryana and Punjab. The name Vedic derives from the most ancient Hindu literature, the *Veda* (वेद), which means "knowledge." Believed to have been directly revealed to seers among the early Aryans in India, and preserved by oral tradition, the four chief collections are the Rig Veda, Sama Veda, Yajur Veda, and Atharva Veda. Alexander the Great crossed the Indus River in 326 BC and he exchanged ideas with the Brahmins, the highest-ranking priests in India's *varnas* (castes).[91] The Mauryan Empire (ca. 324–187 BC) came into being when Chandragupta Maurya stepped into the vacuum created by Alexander's departure from the western borders of India. Chandragupta subjugated the border states, recruited an army, overthrew the Nanda power in Magadha (present-day eastern India), and crowned himself as king. In his rise to power, he was advised by his chief minister Kautilya (also known as Chanakya), who wrote the *Arthashastra*, a treatise about kingship and governance. The name of the work comes from the Sanskrit word *Artha* (अर्थ), which translates as "meaning, sense, goal, purpose, or profit." The goal of the

---

90. Sachs, *Ages of Globalization*, 90.
91. Singh, *History of Ancient*, 94–131.

THE HISTORICAL DEVELOPMENT OF GLOBALIZATION   89

work was a comprehensive understanding of statecraft which would enable a monarch to rule effectively. The title, therefore, has been variously translated as *The Science of Politics*, *The Science of Political Economy*, and *The Science of Material Gain*.[92] *Artha* is understood in Hinduism as one of the four fundamental aims of human beings; it denotes "wealth, property, economic success, fame, and social influence." The second aim is *Dharma* (righteousness, responsibility, order, harmony, or moral values). The third aim is *Kama* (desire, pleasure, the aesthetic enjoyment of life, or love), and the fourth aim is *Moksha* (liberation, release, self-actualization, or eternal union with God). Together, they make up the *Purushartha*, which means the "purpose of human being" or the "object of human pursuit."[93]

The accession of Chandragupta Maurya (ca. 325–321 BC) is significant in Indian history because it inaugurated the first Indian empire and established the religious principles of *dharma* (धर्म) throughout the land. *Dharma* is a key concept with multiple meanings in Indian religions, such as Hinduism, Buddhism, Jainism, Sikhism, and others. The concept of *dharma* was already in use in the historical Vedic religion, and its meaning and conceptual scope have evolved over several millennia.[94] Although there is no direct single-word translation for *dharma*, it is commonly translated as "righteousness" or "religious and moral duties" governing individual conduct. The Mauryan Dynasty ruled almost the entire subcontinent under a centralized, imperial system. In his ruthlessness, Chandragupta enslaved his subjects and executed any opposing enemy. His son Bindusara succeeded him and followed the path of conquest and oppression. However, when Aśoka became the third ruler in 272 BC, he had a change of heart under the influence of the Buddhist sage Upagupta. Aśoka repented of his ambition and cruelty and became a ruler of piety and peace. He then began to issue a large number of edicts, which were inscribed to many parts of the empire. In one of his edicts, Aśoka described the first major event in his reign, which was a campaign against Kalinga in 260 BC. A hundred thousand fell in battle, and many more died from famine and disease. The suffering that resulted caused him to reevaluate the notion of conquest by violence, and gradually, he was drawn to Buddhism. He began to express the idea and practice of *dharma* in his edicts: nonviolence, tolerance of all sects and opinions,

92. Singh, *History of Ancient*, 320–67.
93. Flood, *Introduction to Hinduism*, 17; Brown, *India*, 29–37.
94. Dhand, "Dharma of Ethics," 351.

obedience to parents, respect for the Brahmins and other religious teachers and priests, liberality toward friends, humane treatment of servants, and generosity toward all. Aśoka's own activities under the impact of *dharma* included attention to the welfare of his subjects, the building of roads and rest houses, the planting of medicinal herbs, the setting up of centers to cater to the sick, a ban on animal sacrifices, and the curtailing of killing animals for food. He also instituted a body of officials known as the *dharma-mahamattas* who served the dual function of propagating the *dharma* and keeping him in touch with public opinion. They were also sent as Buddhist missionaries to the neighboring kingdoms.[95]

The Gupta period (ca. AD 320–540) is known as the Golden Age of India. It was a period during which the norms of Indian literature, art, architecture, and philosophy were established. It was an age of material prosperity in most areas, particularly among the urban elite, and it was a period of reemerging Hinduism. Orthodox Brahmanism was encouraged by the royal families, acquiring a locality and an institution in the form of the temple. Temples were richly endowed with wealth and land, and the large endowments could accommodate the universities of higher learning, primarily for priests. Hindu philosophy became classified into six major schools: Nyāya, Vaiśeṣika, Sāṅkhya, Yoga, Pūrvamīmāṃsā, and Vedānta. While the monasteries and temples were centers of formal learning, the guilds were centers of technical knowledge. During the Gupta period, Sanskrit literary masterpieces emerged. The plays and poems of Kālidāsa are believed to have been written during this time. Impressive achievements were also made in the fields of mathematics, astronomy, medicine (surgery), and chemistry. Aryabhata was an astronomer and the earliest Indian mathematician. He is known for his two works: *Aryabhatiya* and *Aryabhatasiddhanta*. In a section called *Ganita* (Mathematics), he named the first ten decimal places and gave algorithms for obtaining square and cubic roots by using the decimal number system. He also treated geometric measurements by using 62,832/20,000 (3.1416) for π and developed properties of similar right-angled triangles and of two intersecting circles. He even calculated the solar year to 365.3586 . . . days and states that the earth was spherical and rotated on its axis. Additionally, Aryabhata had a profound influence on the development of Islamic astronomy.[96]

---

95. *New Encyclopædia Britannica*, s.v. "India," 36–38.
96. *New Encyclopædia Britannica*, s.v. "India," 45.

Of the many gods in Hindu pantheon, three are held universally supreme: Brahman, the Creator; Vishnu, the Preserver; and Shiva, the Destroyer. During the seventh century, a new form of Vaishnavism (worship of Vishnu) and Shaivism (worship of Shiva) based on the *bhakti* cult began to flourish in the Tamil region of southern India. *Bhakti*, which means "attachment" or "devotion to," is a movement emphasizing the mutual intense emotional attachment and love of a devotee toward a personal god and of the god for the devotee. It sought to bring religious reforms to all strata of society by adopting the method of devotion to achieve salvation. Drawing on earlier Tamil secular traditions of erotic poetry as well as royal traditions, *bhakti* poets applied to the god what would usually be said of an absent lover or of a king. The *bhakti* cult competed with Jainism and Buddhism, both of which suffered a decline. *Bhakti* spread to other major states such as Karnataka and Maharashtra and would finally extend to eastern and northern India in the fifteenth century, reaching its zenith between the fifteenth and the seventeenth centuries. One of the major themes of *bhakti* is that of *avatar*: a god manifesting himself on earth in some form in order to benefit humankind in times of trouble. In the Vaishnavite tradition, Krishna (the eighth avatar of Vishnu) is often worshiped as the supreme god. In the Shaivite tradition, Shiva ("the auspicious one" in Sanskrit) is the supreme god who re-creates, protects, and destroys the universe. Hindus believe that destruction is only the necessary prelude to creation in this universe of endless cycles of repetition, where all things are in a constant and endless process of being destroyed and being reborn.[97]

Hinduism became not only a religion but also an integral identity of the majority of people in India. Many Hindus believe that Brahman is formless and infinite and can appear in many forms; therefore, there are variety of ways in which all human beings can connect with the divine. Others believe that the divine is in one form, specifically in Krishna or Vishnu. The Hindu tradition generally accepts ascetic life, emphasizes yoga, and encourages an individual to discover and be one with Shiva within. While Shiva is revered broadly, Hinduism itself is a complex religion and a way of life, with a diversity of ideas on spirituality and traditions. Hinduism's uniqueness is that it rejects nothing. As a result, it has never been supplanted in India by other religions but has instead absorbed them all.[98]

97. *New Encyclopædia Britannica*, s.v. "India," 45; Brown, *India*, 10.
98. *New Encyclopædia Britannica*, s.v. "India," 45–46; Brown, *India*, 9–11.

This section has only highlighted some of the important achievements by humanity that are not well-known to people in the West. There are, of course, many other civilizations in history that cannot be covered here. The argument made here is that humanity's great achievements were made possible by the interlinkages of innovations and institutions from diverse cultures throughout history. Globalization has allowed humanity to grow, mix, and develop so that it could enter the modern era in which economies of the world would converge together.

ECONOMIC INTEGRATION IN THE MODERN ERA

The world has finally entered the period that gave birth to global capitalism, which unfolded in three stages: the Ocean Age, the Industrial Age, and the Digital Age. In 1500, the Ocean Age began when the Old World and the New World were connected through the invention of the caravel and the voyages of Christopher Columbus from Spain to the Americas and Vasco da Gama's voyages from Portugal to India. During this age, empires became transoceanic for the first time, with empires of Europe conquering and colonizing tropical regions in Africa, the Americas, and Asia. Revolutionary changes in global exchange followed, including the rise of multinational corporations, transoceanic trade, and the mass movement of millions of people across the oceans, including slaves. In 1800, the Industrial Age began with the tapping of fossil fuels, made possible by the invention of the internal steam engine by James Watts at the University of Glasgow in Scotland and the internal combustion engine by various people. The Industrial Age gave rise to the first global hegemon, Great Britain, and later, the United States. In 2000, the Digital Age began with the development of digital technologies, including computers, the Internet, mobile phones, and artificial intelligence. These developments led to the digital revolution driven by the Tech Giants, including Alphabet (Google), Apple, Microsoft, Amazon, and Meta (Facebook), and this period became the age in which contemporary globalization began to dominate the world.[99]

In the fifteenth century, Europe was badly struggling from the impacts of the Black Death and the perpetual wars between its countries. Meanwhile, China, India, and the Arab nations were far ahead of Europe in economic, cultural, and technological achievements. However,

---

99. Sachs, *Ages of Globalization*, 95–194.

between the fifteenth and eighteenth centuries, China receded from the position of being the leading civilization while Europe experienced a cultural renaissance, scientific revolution, and religious reformation. A major turning point for Europe during this period was the Treaty of Westphalia in 1658, which ended the Thirty Years' War and established the sovereignty of each nation-state. From the ashes of feudalism, the European nation-states emerged in the form of absolute monarchies, united under one religion, and practicing a new economic theory. The mercantilist economic system that arose forged a unified relationship between government and its people by superseding feudalism and developing a merchant class that bridged the gap between the peasant and ruling classes. In this system, merchants and government worked together to foster international trade, the generation of wealth, and national power.[100]

Mercantilism was the foundation from which global capitalism was born. Myers explains that human beings had not yet learned how to create wealth; therefore, they resorted to exploiting and extracting wealth from other nations or colonies. By taking advantage of weaker nations and colonies, the European nations effectively reduced the trade deficit and created a surplus.[101] The Portuguese, Spanish, Dutch, British, and French Empires competed in colonizing Africa, Asia, and the Americas to extract their wealth. An example of this was the British East India Company, which defeated the princes of India with 260,000 mercenaries. It then plundered India's riches as the British government protected the company's interests. Most of the Parliament members were its stock owners. Another example was the Dutch East India Company, which became the wealthiest commercial operation in the world with 50,000 employees worldwide and a private fleet of 200 ships. With the support of the Dutch government, it established headquarters in many different countries. The company also had a monopoly over the spice trade for two decades, and it had semi-governmental powers in that it was able to begin wars, prosecute convicts, negotiate treaties, and establish colonies. In return, the company gave its shareholders a 40 percent annual dividend.[102] Sachs describes the insatiable greed of the empire builders during this time:

> The remarkable scramble by the European powers for riches, glory, and colonies in the New World and Asia, and the

---

100. Myers, *Engaging Globalization*, 74–78.
101. Myers, *Engaging Globalization*, 75.
102. Freiden, "Modern Capitalist World Economy," 17–22.

> privatization of wealth-seeking via the new joint-stock companies, ushered in a new ethos of greed. It was one thing to exploit the native populations and grab their land; it was another to create an ethos that justified such actions. The Christian virtues of temperance and charity had long preached self-control over the passions for wealth and glory. A new morality was needed to justify the remarkable efforts toward conquest and the subjugation of whole populations. Over time, the justification was the idea that conquest was a God-given right, even a responsibility, to bring civilization to the heathens. Success, moreover, was a sign of God's favor and providence.... The age of global empire was also an age of monumental cruelty, with ruthless greed built into the emerging capitalist order.[103]

He further explains that the history of the New World involved three distinct groups. The first were the indigenous peoples of the Americas, who were stricken by Old World diseases and conquest; the second were the European conquerors and settlers; and the third were the African slaves who were brought by the millions to work the mines and plantations of the New World.[104] Sachs describes the evil network of trade that became established:

> With the slave plantations in the Americas arose the infamous three-way trade pattern commonly known as the "triangular trade." The slave colonies of the Americas imported slaves and exported slave-made products—sugar, cotton, and tobacco—to Europe. Europe imported the commodities and exported manufactured goods, including textiles, weapons, and metals, to Africa. And African chieftains exported slaves to European slave traders in return for Europe's manufactured goods. The colonization of the Americas and the expanded trade with Asia also unleashed a new frenzy of consumerism in Europe, marked by soaring demand for spices from Asia and Africa.[105]

Such an evil network of trade exists today in various forms, including transnational sex trafficking and the dark web. For Christians to gain credibility in their involvement with renewing globalization, the church must first understand that there is something intrinsically evil about the global system of trade that humanity has built. To this day, it is still driven

---

103. Sachs, *Ages of Globalization*, 114.
104. Sachs, *Ages of Globalization*, 116.
105. Sachs, *Ages of Globalization*, 120.

by human greed, which disregards those who are vulnerable in society.[106] Since most humans have a propensity toward greed, the global system of trade aims to maximize financial profit by taking advantage of this innate human weakness. As a result, those who aim to make a financial profit through this system have fallen into the temptation of making unjust gain.[107] Corruption has now become an undeniable problem in the age of globalization. In his exposition of capitalism and globalization, leading Serbian economist Branko Milanović gives a comprehensive review of the liberal meritocratic capitalism of America and the political capitalism of China, which seem to be in competition with each other.[108] He explains that incentives for corruption are inherent in both systems, "and there is nothing one can do, short of changing the system of values, to affect it."[109] He unabashedly suggests that "we should become used to increased corruption and treat it as a logical (almost normal) source of income in the age of globalization."[110] Because greed leads to corruption, Jesus warned, "Be on your guard against all kinds of greed; life does not consist in an abundance of possessions" (Luke 12:15). Paul also warned, "Those who want to be rich, however, fall into temptation and become ensnared by many foolish and harmful desires that plunge them into ruin and destruction" (1 Tim 6:9).

Christians in Europe and America who lived during the first stage of global capitalism saw the evils of globalization, but they were powerless in resisting those who perpetrated great injustice and allowed unspeakable cruelty against humanity to prevail. Why were the religious people who understood the Bible and spoke about God's love for humanity unable to instruct the kings and merchants to turn away from developing the structure of evil in society? The global system of trade has not only benefited the nations so that they grow rich, but it has destroyed the lives of an untold number of people. Scripture gives a plain warning to the kings and merchants of this world regarding their fornication with Babylon the Great and commands God's people to not take part in this partnership

---

106. Volf, *Flourishing*, 46–47.

107. Socialists have historically asserted that capitalism is built on greed. This assertion is now challenged by many thinkers among Marxist socialists. They believe that capitalists are not motivated by greed but by market pressures. For a full explanation of this view and the basic structure of capitalism, see Chibber, *Confronting Capitalism*, 5–50.

108. Milanović, *Capitalism, Alone*, 12–128.

109. Milanović, *Capitalism, Alone*, 173.

110. Milanović, *Capitalism, Alone*, 175.

with the evil structure, which gives material riches and luxury: "Come out of her, my people, so that you will not share in her sins, so that you will not receive any of her plagues; for her sins are piled up to heaven, and God has remembered her crimes" (Rev 18:1–8). Babylon the Great is a metaphorical description of a corrupt political and economic scheme from which the great temptation of the riches and pleasures of this world emanates. Sachs gives the following assessment of the first stage of global capitalism:

> In total, an estimated 14 million Africans were carried as slaves during this period. This was truly a grim and horrific stage of global capitalism. The cruelty that accompanied the development of the modern world economy must not be forgotten, because that cruelty shows up in other ways today; human trafficking is one of the greatest examples, which also continues in the form of bonded labor and child labor as part of global supply chains. Humanity is not done with the horrific abuse of others in pursuit of greed and profit.[111]

The British Empire came out on top of this brutal competition and became the largest empire in history, positioning itself to usher in the second stage of global capitalism. The Industrial Age marks the time in which a good portion of humanity finally broke the chains of poverty and made significant progress toward living in material abundance without laboring in pain. Around 1800, the world was still mostly poor and rural. About 84 percent of the world's population barely survived through farming. Then, in two hundred years, the population and urbanization grew exponentially as the rate of poverty greatly diminished (see table 1 below). This phenomenon started in Britain and soon spread to other countries that implemented industrialization and the free market capitalism system. Sachs explains that only Britain offered an extraordinary combination of favorable conditions that allowed the industrial revolution to take off. In the past, other nations such as China's Song Dynasty and Holland had some of the elements needed to industrialize, but they did not have all of them. Sachs suggests that all the favorable conditions for self-sustaining industrialization came together in Britain by chance. Just as he believes that life on the Earth emerged from a unique confluence of circumstances, so he believes that somehow all the pieces came together to allow self-sustaining economic growth in Britain.[112]

---

111. Sachs, *Ages of Globalization*, 120.
112. Sachs, *Ages of Globalization*, 129–37.

Table 1. Change in Population, Rate of Urbanization, and Poverty Rate[113]

World	Around 1800	Around 2000
Population	1 billion	6 billion
Rate of urbanization	7.3%	46.8%
Extreme poverty rate	84%	25%
Life expectancy at birth	29	66

It is astonishing that three-quarters of humanity came out of the shackles of poverty and misery through industrialization and the free market capitalism system that began in Britain. From a Christian perspective, Myers explains that when the nations finally learned how to create wealth through free market capitalism, colonialism was no longer the main source for their growth. Myers attributes this outcome to the transformation of Britain:

> What happened in nineteenth-century Britain is the story of remarkable convergence of the idea and practice of political freedom and the rule of law coupled with the emergence of technological innovation and a fundamental change in Christian theology. These coalesced into a new family of conceptual formulations that led to Adam Smith's proposal for a political economy and the market system.[114]

Politics, economics, technology, and religion converged together into a powerful system that was ready for the beginning of a new kind of globalization. In this second stage of global capitalism, Britain would lead the way in creating enormous wealth by using its citizens' labor and production and the free market capitalism system that was no longer bound by cultural tradition or authoritarian command. Other nations in the West, including the United States, soon followed Britain's lead.[115]

Historians commonly refer to the period from 1870 to the beginning of World War I as the first golden age of globalization. A truly global market for capital emerged during this time. According to Zinkina, the most important manifestations of this wave of globalization can be found in the dramatic intensification of global flows of capital, goods, and migrants. She explains, "The global networks of the late nineteenth

---

113. Sachs, *Ages of Globalization*, 120.
114. Myers, *Engaging Globalization*, 80.
115. Myers, *Engaging Globalization*, 81.

and early twentieth centuries encompassed previously unimaginable amounts of capital and goods, as well as enormous numbers of people."[116] After the discovery of America's silver mines, a free silver market became the chief globalizing factor. Then, the nations of the world attempted to create an international regulatory system for managing global flows of precious metals. The most famous and popular international monetary system was the gold standard.[117] According to the estimates provided by Simon Kuznets, in the early nineteenth century, the volume of global exports equaled just 1 or 2 percent of global economic production. By 1850, this proportion had increased to 5 percent and further on to 10 percent by 1880. From 1880 to 1913, the growth of this indicator somewhat slowed down but still continued, reaching 12 percent by World War I. This means that, all in all, the proportion of global exports in global economic production increased by an order of magnitude over the course of less than a century. In absolute figures, the dynamics of the volume of global exports was even more astonishing—it increased by nearly 200 times between 1800 and 1913.[118]

In the United States, this period was led by the great American entrepreneurs commonly known as the titans of industry. Cornelius Vanderbilt constructed railroads that connected the massive landscape of America; John D. Rockefeller provided kerosine oil that lighted every household; Andrew Carnegie produced steel on a massive scale for constructing longer bridges and high-rise buildings; and J. Pierpont Morgan financed businesses and even the government. America's highly innovative, competitive, effective, and yet controversial business practices driven by unrestrained greed, pride, and ambition laid the foundation for the best and the worst of today's global capitalism.[119]

The first global market was built not only by innovation and competition but also by the exploitation of weaker nations in the world, especially in Asia. The European nations' incursions into China and India—two countries that represented more than 60 percent of the world's population—led to these two nations' long decline and humiliation. The British Empire's forced opium trade with China caused wars and devastations, killing tens of millions of people throughout the nineteenth century. The British Empire also kept India's famed textiles out of the British

---

116. Zinkina et al., *Big History of Globalization*, 221.
117. Zinkina et al., *Big History of Globalization*, 196.
118. Zinkina et al., *Big History of Globalization*, 202–4.
119. Tedlow, "What Titans Can Teach," 70–79.

market during the eighteenth century, driving millions of spinners and weavers into poverty in the nineteenth century. Sachs gives the following assessment of British policy:

> From 1858 until India's independence, British policy aimed to turn India into a supplier of raw materials for the British market rather than a competitor of British industry producing finished textiles. The British ruthlessly governed the countryside, standing idle in the face of multiple famines that reflected the combination of nature and Britain's neglect of Indian lives. . . . Around the time of independence, India's illiteracy rate stood at 80–85 percent, and its life expectancy during 1950–55 averaged 37 years.[120]

Under British rule, the word *India* was made synonymous to poverty, hunger, and disease. The economic policies of the British deliberately kept India out of the industrial revolution. In essence, India was impoverished first by plunder and tyranny and then by unfair trade practices and later by economic exploitation. Dylan Sullivan and Jason Hickel give the following assessment of British brutality:

> [It is now estimated] that some 50 million excess deaths occurred under the aegis of British colonialism during the period from 1891 to 1920. . . . While the precise number of deaths is sensitive to the assumptions we make about baseline mortality, it is clear that somewhere in the vicinity of 100 million people died prematurely at the height of British colonialism. This is among the largest policy-induced mortality crises in human history. It is larger than the combined number of deaths that occurred during all the famines in the Soviet Union, Maoist China, North Korea, Pol Pot's Cambodia, and Mengistu's Ethiopia.[121]

Only Japan avoided subjugation to European rule and embarked on a period of seemingly peaceful and successful industrialization. The Meiji Restoration of 1868 sought to respond to the Western challenge by modernizing Japan. The country's feudal structure under the Tokugawa shogunate was overturned, and the feudal lands were converted into prefectures under the control of a new centralized government. The Iwakura Mission was launched, allowing Japanese diplomats to travel around the world and establish new diplomatic relations with Europe and the United States. Nishi Amane was Japan's main political advisor, who carefully

120. Sachs, *Ages of Globalization*, 149.
121. Sullivan and Hickel, "How British Colonialism Killed," paras. 4 and 6.

studied the structure of the Western system that made modernization possible. The problem was that the more Japan learned about the Western legal order described by Hugo Grotius, the more it began to emulate the Western nations' behavior of aggression. After Japan modernized and became a major international power, it came to see poorly defended Korea as "a dagger pointed at the heart of Japan."[122] Korea was a threat not because of its strength but because it was a weak tributary country to China that could easily fall prey to aggressive Western nations. In order to defend its borders, Japan believed that it had to attack China to wrest control of Korea away from China. Japan first defeated China in the First Sino-Japanese War of 1894–95. When Japan did not receive diplomatic assurances that Russia would not interfere in Korea, it also attacked Russia and triumphed in the Russo-Japanese War of 1904–5. Becoming the new regional power, Japan annexed Korea from 1910 to 1945. These series of events ultimately led to the tragedy of World War II and became the source of great tension in Japan's relationship with Korea, China, and Russia today.[123]

Myers views that globalization accelerated in two phases, and it was greatly disrupted in between by war, economic depression, and political revolution:

1. Globalization I (the first phase) accelerated from 1800 to 1914.
2. Globalization was disrupted by World War I, the Great Depression, the Russian Revolution, World War II, and the Cold War.
3. Globalization II (the second phase) accelerated from 1989 to the present.[124]

After the demise of fascism and communism, Western liberal democracy and capitalism became widely accepted as the ideology that would ensure justice, freedom, security, and prosperity for the world. When World War II came to an end, Britain first pursued social welfare democracy in which the state was to manage or direct its economy. Most of Europe and the United States followed its lead. When the limits of a mixed economy became obvious by the end of the 1970s, the administrations of Margaret Thatcher and Ronald Reagan in the West aggressively promoted a worldwide *laissez-faire* economic policy, which is an extreme

---

122. Hathaway and Shapiro, *Internationalists*, 151.
123. Hathaway and Shapiro, *Internationalists*, 151–60.
124. Myers, *Engaging Globalization*, 86–103.

THE HISTORICAL DEVELOPMENT OF GLOBALIZATION 101

form of free market capitalism that opposes any form of government intervention.[125] Myers sees the end of the Cold War as the beginning of the present form of economic integration, which has become controversial. He explains how this new expression of globalization came about:

> In the aftermath of the Great Depression, three things came together to create a new expression of globalization. First, the adoption of the key elements of the neoliberal model of capitalism and the market system began to spread rapidly over much of the world. The modern economies of Europe, the United States, and Japan were joined by the Asian Tigers, China, India, Indonesia, Brazil, and South Africa. Second, the digital revolution in technology exploded onto the scene. Third, the international economic institutions created after World War II—the World Banks, International Monetary Fund, and eventually the World Trade Organization—were reinvented to support the spread of neoliberal economic orthodoxy (the Washington Consensus) and thus to help eradicate poverty. The current period of very fast economic growth and a more closely connected world is called Globalization II.[126]

Much debate has ensued between those who promote or resist the contemporary conception of globalization, namely neoliberalism. Before Christians can engage with globalization, the church must have a clear understanding of both the benefits and perils of the powerful structure that rules the world today. This great controversy of globalization in the Digital Age will be carefully examined in the next chapter.

---

125. Myers, *Engaging Globalization*, 98–100.
126. Myers, *Engaging Globalization*, 99–100. The Asian Tigers refers to the high-growth economies of Hong Kong, South Korea, Taiwan, and Singapore.

3

The Hegemonic Globalization of the West

SINCE THE WORLD IS under the effects of sin, humanity's efforts to build a global society inevitably produces injustice. In response to this predicament, the Word of God calls his people to believe in him so that they can become his kingly priests who would love others, speak the truth, and do righteousness and justice. Psalm 89:14 proclaims, "Righteousness and justice are the foundation of your throne; Mercy and truth go before you" (NASB). God's justice and mercy flow into the world through the church's involvement with all domains of globalization. After the fall of fascism and communism, it was widely believed that the world would converge under the ideology of Western liberal democracy and capitalism. The West, led by the United States, established a globalization system that aims to integrate all the economies of sovereign states. Hegemonic globalization, however, did not lead to a just, free, secure, and prosperous world in which all people could flourish together. Instead of uniting the human race, globalization's fragmentary movements have given rise to separatism and antagonism between different peoples, nations, and civilizations. During the first two decades of the twenty-first century, globalization has imploded by the growing forces of fundamentalism, nationalism, and racism. This chapter argues that without restructuring globalization by engagement of the church with God's wisdom and insight, globalization cannot be salvaged. The first section examines the rise and fall of the globalization system, which was built to dominate the world. The second section explains the reasons for defiance against the globalization system.

The third section surveys the ethical failure of the globalization system and explores the forces of fundamentalism, nationalism, and racism, which keep the world fragmented. The final section ends with a discussion concerning the establishment of global governance.

THE RISE OF THE GLOBALIZATION SYSTEM

Globalization can take place in many spheres of life, making its meaning notoriously ambiguous; but it became widely known as economic integration among nation-states. According to Robertson, economistic conceptions of globalization quickly arose in the 1990s and overtook a much more comprehensive conception that was elaborated by sociology of religion and religious studies in the late 1970s and early 1980s. An economistic view reduces life to the economic-material factors. Along with the prevalence of economistic conceptions of human life, the view that the world is being swept by homogenizing forces also became widespread. These two powerful ideas were combined to establish the cultural dominance of the West, which is characterized by a materialistic outlook in life. The Western culture of materialism consists of the belief and attitude that physical well-being and worldly possessions constitute the greatest good and highest value in life. During the post–Cold War period, globalization was driven by neoliberalism and its policies to produce immense economic growth in the world. Economists that promoted neoliberalism played a key role in determining the popular understanding of globalization by gaining pivotal political offices and/or influence in many countries.[1] As a result, the growth of the global-market economy became the highest priority for much of the world.

At the turn of the millennium, there was widespread optimism that the world was becoming a global village. The song "We Are the World: U.S.A. for Africa," which became a worldwide phenomenon in 1985, became the popular slogan for global interconnectedness and oneness. According to literary scholar Sue-Im Lee, the term *global village* has become "the dominant term for expressing a global coexistence altered by transnational commerce, migration, and culture."[2] The global village reflects the utopian ideal of secularism, built by an economistic view of globalization. Almost all economists were in agreement that globalization

---

1. Robertson, "Globalization and the Future," 56–57.
2. Lee, "We Are Not the World," 502.

is an inevitable and unstoppable force that can only bring progress for all humanity. World politicians followed the advice of economists and pursued the ideology of neoliberalism. Also, under the influence of economists, globalization became typically understood as the removal of trade barriers. Known as "free trade," this practice often meant that industry would move from rich countries, where labor was expensive, to poor countries, where labor was cheaper. People in rich countries would either have to accept lower wages to compete or lose their jobs. This would not be a problem since the unemployed could get new, higher-skilled jobs with proper training. Meanwhile, the goods they formerly produced would now be imported and consumers could buy them at a cheaper price. In a global village, capital can freely move across national borders, people can dream and live wherever they want to grow their enterprise, and a new homogenizing culture that transcends traditional boundaries would ensure humanity's flourishing.[3]

With his bestselling book *The Lexus and the Olive Tree* (1999), American economic journalist Thomas Friedman became the most popular interpreter of globalization for the public. At the turn of the millennium, most people did not yet understand how the world was changing. Friedman accomplished the difficult task of effectively expounding globalization by doing two things at once: first, by looking at the world through a multi-lens perspective; second, by conveying that complexity through simple stories, not grand theories.[4] He explained that after the fall of the Berlin Wall, globalization became the dominant international system, which replaced the Cold War system "with its own unique logic, rules, pressures and incentives."[5] Globalization contrasts sharply with the Cold War's overarching feature of division. Friedman defined globalization as the world integration of finance markets, nation-states, and technologies within free market capitalism on a scale never seen before. Individual nations have no choice but to sacrifice their economic sovereignty to global institutions, a situation he has termed the "Golden Straitjacket."[6] This prosperous and homogenizing globalization system is a dynamic ongoing process. It is a world of constant change where

---

3. Saval, "Globalisation."
4. Friedman, *Lexus and the Olive Tree*, 19.
5. Friedman, *Lexus and the Olive Tree*, 7.
6. Friedman, *Lexus and the Olive Tree*, 104.

innovation replaces tradition. The human drive for enrichment (the Lexus) confronts the human need for identity and community (the olive tree).[7]

One of the important themes Friedman expounded was the worldwide perception that globalization is forcing everyone to become American. He claimed unapologetically that globalization basically means Americanization. He agreed with historian Joseph Nye Jr. that America has orchestrated the present globalization system since World War II to create an open international economy to forestall another depression and to balance Soviet power and contain communism. Now that America has become the lone "hyperpower," only America can dictate the terms of globalization. Friedman declared:

> With the end of the Cold War, globalization is globalizing Anglo-American style capitalism and the Golden Straitjacket. It is globalizing American culture and cultural icons. It is globalizing the best of America and the worst of America. It is globalizing the American Revolution and it is globalizing the American gas station....[8]

> We Americans are the apostles of the Fast World, the enemies of tradition, the prophets of the free market and the high priests of high tech.... We want the world to follow our lead and become democratic, capitalistic, with a Web site in every pot, a Pepsi on every lip, Microsoft Windows in every computer and most of all—most of all—with everyone, everywhere, pumping their own gas.[9]

According to Friedman, the hegemony of the globalization system would universalize American democracy, capitalism, business practices, and culture, thereby allowing all nations of the world to take part in the global village. There was no need for America to go to war and conquer other nations, for they all want to be like America. The prime example of America's innovative business model was a company called Enron. It had already set up an online marketplace where companies all over the world could sell and buy various commodities such as natural gas, electricity, and coal. Enron had now discovered the immense potential of the bandwidth market. It was making big plans to be the first mover and

---

7. Friedman, *Lexus and the Olive Tree*, 42.
8. Friedman, *Lexus and the Olive Tree*, 380.
9. Friedman, *Lexus and the Olive Tree*, 384.

destroy its competitors with a strong market position. Friedman believed Enron's daring move into the bandwidth market would have geopolitical implications; he was certain that the Europeans would learn a lesson from the American way of doing business in the globalization system. Moving fast and keeping up with the speed of change was paramount in a winner-take-all system, so the European values of careful planning and minimizing the social cost must be put aside.[10] In August of 2000, Enron's shares skyrocketed to an all-time high of $90.56. The stage was set for the United States of America to lead the twenty-first century through the globalization system.

DEFIANCE AGAINST THE GLOBALIZATION SYSTEM

It is commonly known that the twentieth century was an American century. America's triumphs and accomplishments far surpassed those of other nations. The twenty-first century, however, has been a disastrous one for America. Only a year after the publication of Friedman's exuberant exposition on globalization and his claim that there was no need for America to go to war against any country, an unimaginable tragedy struck. On September 11, 2001, the Muslim terrorist network known as al-Qaeda destroyed the Twin Towers of New York's World Trade Center, the symbol of globalization and America's unmatched economic power and prosperity. They also attacked the Pentagon, which serves as a symbol of American military power. These unthinkable attacks involving the use of commercial airplanes signified that the Islamists led by Osama bin Laden were determined to fight against the hegemonic globalization of the West at all costs.[11] In al-Qaeda's "Declaration of War" in 1996, bin Laden specifically condemned the US military presence in Saudi Arabia, criticized the international sanctions on Iraq, and opposed the US support for Israel. In his next major statement in 1998, bin Laden claimed that the United States had made "a clear declaration of war on God, his messenger, and Muslims" through its policies in the Islamic world,

---

10. Friedman, *Lexus and the Olive Tree*, 387–88.

11. Because the term *fundamentalism* originated from Christianity and carries negative connotations and because its use in the Islamic context emphasizes the religious roots of the phenomenon while neglecting the nationalistic and social grievances that underlie it, many scholars prefer to use "Islamists" or "Islamist movements" instead of Islamic fundamentalists.

making defensive jihad the duty of all Muslims.[12] Bin Laden was most interested in "resisting western domination and combating regimes that fail to rule according to Islamic law."[13] His ideological and religious belief of global Islamism was in direct confrontation with the ideological and religious belief of global capitalism. He fought against the claim that the West, led by America, can globalize the world as it pleases. By using sophisticated technology and a multinational network, bin Laden and al-Qaeda defied the hegemony of the globalization system.

When the first plane crashed into the north tower of the World Trade Center, Miroslav Volf was just a few blocks away at the United Nations and finishing a talk on the theme of reconciliation. Just as he was making the point that religion can bring people together, he looked up and watched the flames and smoke representing the evil and hate perpetrated by those who claimed to be religious. Reflecting on the tragic moment, Volf says that he was proven wrong on the spot. Religion did not stop the hatred and violence in the world, but rather, brought them in the most vicious manner. Since the time of the tragedy, Volf has been at the forefront of researching and teaching how world religions can find a way to guide globalization onto a peaceful path. He has expounded on the theme of reconciliation—the reconciliation of humanity to God and the reconciliation of peoples and individuals to one another.[14]

After the attack on September 11, America wanted to bring the Muslim terrorists to justice. America therefore made its fateful decision of going to war against al-Qaeda and the Taliban in Afghanistan, and later, against Iraq. Most American politicians and most American people, including evangelical Christians, supported the decision to send the troops to find and destroy the terrorist network. The California representative Barbara Lee was the only member of Congress to cast the no vote on the Authorization for the Use of Military Force (AUMF) that the House approved 420 to 1. Lee explained that she voted no not because she opposed military action but because she believed that the AUMF, as written, granted the president overly broad powers to wage war at a time when the facts regarding the situation were not yet clear.[15] Responding to an angry public that saw her as a traitor, she wrote about a better way to respond to terrorism:

12. Sozek, "Osama bin Laden's Global Islamism," 42.
13. Commins, *Wahhabi Mission*, 185.
14. Volf, "After the Grave."
15. Lee, "Why I Opposed."

> It [AUMF] was a blank check to the president to attack anyone involved in the Sept. 11 events—anywhere, in any country, without regard to our nation's long-term foreign policy, economic and national security interests, and without time limit. . . . We must respond, but the character of that response will determine for us and for our children the world that they will inherit. I do not dispute the president's intent to rid the world of terrorism—but we have many means to reach that goal, and measures that spawn further acts of terror or that do not address the sources of hatred do not increase our security.[16]

No one in Congress or the Bush administration tried to understand Lee's valuable insight by having a dialogue. While they ignored the voice of a lone African American congresswoman, the dominant narrative at the time was that Islamic fundamentalism was the central motivating force driving the terrorism against America. The simple, grand solution was to transform Arab societies by implementing Western political institutions and social norms as the ultimate antidote to the virus of Islamic extremism.[17] Only by creating Western-style democracies in the Muslim world could America defeat terrorism once and for all. This goal created the long-term military occupation of Iraq and Afghanistan. In hindsight, according to historian Melvyn Leffler, America's plan was the most consequential US foreign policy decision in the twenty-first century, which tarnished its standing in the world.[18] He explains, "The war in Iraq demoralized the American people, intensified their partisan divisions, and shattered trust in their government. Abroad, it alienated key allies, aroused widespread anti-Americanism, and devastated its moral authority."[19] Political scientist Bessma Momani says, "The Iraq War left behind five-million Iraqi orphans, took more than 100,000 Iraqi lives, forced four- to five-million Iraqis to flee their homes and communities, displaced ancient Iraqi minority groups, and devastated much of Iraq's infrastructure and economy."[20] All in all, it has brought immense human suffering to the world without achieving its ultimate goal of defeating

---

16. Lee, "Why I Opposed," para. 5.
17. Pape, "It's the Occupation."
18. Leffler, *Confronting Saddam Hussein*, xvii.
19. Leffler, *Confronting Saddam Hussein*, xvii.
20. Momani, "Human Cost of the Iraq War," para. 2. For a detailed Iraq mortality study, see Hagopian et al., "Mortality in Iraq."

terrorism.[21] Journalist David Frum, who was a speechwriter for President Bush, had once supported the war against Iraq. Today, he makes a sobering judgment:

> Inside the Bush administration, we thought we were ready to remake Iraq for the better—but we were not. We were ignorant, arrogant, and unprepared, and we unleashed human suffering that did no good for anyone: not for Americans, not for Iraqis, not for the region. Almost two decades later, the damage to America's standing in the world from the Iraq War has still not been repaired, let alone that war's economic and human costs to the United States and the Middle East.[22]

The 9/11 tragedy was followed by thirty-seven terrorist acts on US soil, including the Boston marathon bombing in 2013 and the Orlando nightclub shooting in 2016. While fourteen of those terrorist acts did not have fatalities, twenty-three attacks resulted in 151 total deaths.[23] Political scientist Robert Pape believes that the reason for the rise of suicide terrorism in the twenty-first century is mainly due to America's occupation in Muslim countries. In 2000, before the occupations of Iraq and Afghanistan, there were suicide attacks around the world, but only one was directed against Americans. However, in the twelve-month period before October of 2010, there were 300 suicide attacks, and over 270 were anti-American. He gives the following summary of America's actions that continue to stir up hatred and violence from the terrorists:

> In the decade since 9/11, the United States has conquered and occupied two large Muslim countries (Afghanistan and Iraq), compelled a huge Muslim army to root out a terrorist sanctuary (Pakistan), deployed thousands of Special Forces troops to numerous Muslim countries (Yemen, Somalia, Sudan, etc.), imprisoned hundreds of Muslims without recourse, and waged a massive war of ideas involving Muslim clerics to denounce violence and new institutions to bring Western norms to Muslim countries.[24]

The war in Iraq brought forth another terrifying entity no one had foreseen. A new terrorist network known as the Islamic State of Iraq and

21. For alternate views that justify America's decision to go to war against Iraq, see Mellow, "Iraq: Morally Justified Resort," 293–310; French, "In Defense of the Iraq War."
22. Frum, "Take It From," para. 9.
23. Ilich, "United States after 9/11."
24. Pape, "It's the Occupation," para. 2.

the Levant (ISIL), also known as the Islamic State of Iraq and Syria (ISIS), gained global prominence in early 2014 when it drove Iraqi government forces out of key cities in its Western Iraq offensive and also captured the historic city of Mosul with its 1.5 million inhabitants. As a caliphate, ISIS claimed religious, political, and military authority over all Muslims worldwide. It ruled the captured cities with unimaginable cruelty including beatings, beheadings, and mutilations. When it captured the city of Sinjar and the surrounding countryside, thousands of people, particularly men and boys, were executed while thousands more, especially women and girls, were abducted and raped as sex slaves by ISIS fighters. Yezidis were a non-Muslim, religious, and ethnic minority in northern Iraq who were viciously targeted and persecuted by ISIS for their beliefs.[25] In Syria, ISIS took control of the major city of Raqqa. Without understanding the nature of ISIS and dismissing it as an offshoot of al-Qaeda, America became mired in the Syrian civil war from 2015 to 2018. Out of a population of about 18 million people, as many as 500,000 Syrians died due to violence during the war. Over 6 million were internally displaced, and 5 million fled the country as refugees.[26] These tragedies could have been avoided if America had been more careful and wiser in its response to the 9/11 terrorist attack.[27]

On April 14, 2021, President Joe Biden announced his plan to withdraw the US military from Afghanistan. On August 10, US intelligence warned that the Afghan government in Kabul would collapse in thirty-nine to ninety days; however, the Taliban entered Kabul only five days later to take over the country. On August 31, America withdrew all its military presence from Afghanistan, marking the end of an era that attempted to install Western liberal democracy in the Middle East. The human cost of the war was staggering: 2,448 US military members have died; 3,846 US contractors have died; 1,144 allied service members have died; 66,000 Afghan national military members and police have died; 47,245 Afghan civilians have died; 51,191 Taliban and other opposition fighters have died; 444 aid workers have died; and 72 journalists have died. The financial cost of the war is estimated at more than two trillion

---

25. Cetorelli and Ashraph, *ISIS's Attack*.

26. For a graphic review of the human suffering in Syria, see Taylor, "Six Million Displaced."

27. For an assessment of US military involvement in Syria, see Bridgeman and Rosen, "Still at War."

dollars. The interest to be paid by 2050 is estimated at 6.5 trillion dollars.[28] On September 11, 2021, America solemnly reflected on the tragedy that led to the longest war in its history. After twenty years of fighting against the terrorist network, America's plan to change the Middle East for good came to an end. Although the American people had suffered greatly by the terrorists, America's response to the tragedy has caused millions of ordinary people in Afghanistan, Iraq, and Syria to suffer unimaginable level of violence for a very long time. The evil powers in those countries were not eliminated by American military power.[29] The Muslim terrorists had defied the globalization system. There must be another way to establish justice, freedom, security, and prosperity for all people in the Middle East, America, and the rest of the world.

THE ETHICAL FAILURE OF THE GLOBALIZATION SYSTEM

A major financial scandal soon followed the 9/11 tragedy. Enron's corrupt business practices became fully exposed in a stunning fashion. From the outside, Enron had received Fortune 500's award as the most innovative company for six years in a row. From the inside, however, they were mired in massive debt that they tried to hide from investors. The Enron corporation and its management resorted to an unethical scheme and malpractice. It created a special economic vehicle to hide the massive debt from its external stakeholders, namely creditors and investors. In October of 2001, Enron reported a $618 million loss and a $1.2 billion-value write-off, causing its stock to drop from $90.56 to $38.84. In November of 2001, Enron admitted that it had been inflating its income by around $586 million since 1997. In December of 2001, Enron filed for bankruptcy, and its stock closed at $0.26. In January of 2002, Enron was suspended from the New York Stock Exchange, and Enron's accounting firm Arthur Andersen was convicted of obstructing justice. Enron's shareholders lost $74 billion in the four years leading up to its bankruptcy, and its employees lost $1.2 billion in pension benefits.

Enron's demise was only a preview of what was to come. It was soon exposed that the entire financial industry on Wall Street was corrupt. By

---

28. Knickmeyer, "Costs of the Afghanistan War."

29. For detailed accounts of America's achievements and failures in Iraq and Afghanistan, see Bolger, *Why We Lost*; Malkasian, *American War in Afghanistan*.

August of 2007, the dominoes of corrupt financial institutions began to fall. It became apparent that the financial markets could not solve the subprime crisis and that the problems were reverberating well beyond the US borders. In October of 2007, the Swiss bank UBS became the first major bank to announce losses—$3.4 billion—from subprime-related investments. In March of 2008, the global investment bank Bear Stearns, a pillar of Wall Street that dated to 1923, collapsed and was acquired by JPMorgan Chase. Then, the collapse of the venerable Wall Street bank Lehman Brothers in September of 2008 marked the largest bankruptcy in US history.[30] Due to the interconnectedness of the global economy, it was assessed that the US banks that caused the financial meltdown with bad investments had to be bailed out in order to prevent a financial devastation of the entire world. Brazilian journalist Glenn Greenwald notes that the Obama administration failed to arrest or prosecute "any senior Wall Street banker for the systemic fraud that precipitated the 2008 financial crisis: a crisis from which millions of people around the world are still suffering."[31]

Meanwhile, Europeans had accepted the hegemony of the globalization system and played by its logic, rules, pressures, and incentives. Deutsche Bank, founded in 1870, was the most typical, most representative, and most prestigious German bank. Its original mission was largely trade finance, helping to promote the German export machine. It was built on the traditional long-term relationship between major companies, banks, and politicians of Germany, which brought relatively low profits. In the era of the globalization system, however, Deutsche Bank turned away from its past and tried to become a global investment bank. It pursued financial globalization more aggressively than other competing banks by using extreme leverage. Instead of funding itself through retail deposits, it used short-term borrowing from other institutions to buy high-yielding securities, which it held for short-term gain and without the long-term control that had characterized the traditional system. After the 2008 US subprime mortgage crisis, it was found that Deutsche Bank was most responsible for buying up the poorly secured mortgages from US home buyers, wrapping them up in highly complex financial products, and selling them on to other banks as secure investment products.

---

30. Singh, "2007–2008 Financial Crisis."
31. Greenwald, "Untouchables," para. 1.

In 2017, the bank settled with the US authorities by paying $7.2 billion due to its sale and pooling of toxic mortgage securities.[32]

The globalization system also changed the business practice of Germany's successful auto industry. Germany was by far the largest vehicle exporter in the world. Europe's economic powerhouse exported an impressive $245.4 billion worth of automobiles in 2011. Volkswagen was the symbol of superior German engineering. In 2015, however, Volkswagen was found guilty in an emissions cheating scandal. The US Environmental Protection Agency had found that Volkswagen had intentionally programmed turbocharged direct injection (TDI) diesel engines to activate their emissions controls only during laboratory emissions testing. This caused the vehicles' nitrogen oxide output to meet the standards during regulatory testing, whereas the vehicles emitted up to forty times more nitrogen oxide in actuality. After the company lost 46 percent of its value within two months, or $42.5 billion, it was estimated that their scheme had resulted in the costliest business scandal ever. Volkswagen paid $15 billion in fines as part of a civil settlement in the United States.[33] The humiliation of Deutsche Bank and Volkswagen has pushed the German people to reflect on the relationship between their inherited national identity and the present-day economic reality of globalization. The common theme in these two scandals is that the traditional way of doing business in Germany succumbed to the globalization system, which demanded innovation and high profit even at the cost of ethical failure.

THE FALL OF THE GLOBALIZATION SYSTEM

Although globalization has brought forth great economic gains for the world in aggregate, it is now acknowledged that there have been significant losses. Globalization has produced winners and losers, and it has caused irreversible economic and political damage in society. Since globalization does not properly compensate those who lost, the disparity between the rich and poor has become wider than ever. Many people around the world, those who are politically on the left and those on the right, have one thing in common: they believe that the globalization system is rigged against the ordinary people. The gains that were made under it have not led to the fostering of prosperity for all. Rather, the

---

32. James, "Deutsche Bank Isn't."
33. United States Environmental Protection Agency, "Volkswagen Clean Air Act."

system is organized to siphon the gains from innovation upward, such that the fortunes of the world's billionaires now grow at more than double the pace of everyone else's and the top 10 percent of humanity has come to hold 90 percent of the planet's wealth.[34]

In the United States, according to a recent study, the top 10 percent of earners today earns more than twice as much before taxes as a similarly situated person in 1980. The study also shows that the top 1 percent of earners today earns more than triple what the 1 percent earned in 1980. By contrast, the average pretax income of the bottom half of adults has stagnated at about $16,000 per adult since 1980, while the average national income per adult grew by 60 percent to $64,500 in 2014. Over the same time span, the bottom half of Americans saw their average pretax income rise from $16,000 to $16,200. This means that approximately 117 million people have been "completely shut off from economic growth since the 1970s."[35] By 2016, ordinary Americans were fed up with the globalization system, which took away their jobs and stagnated their income for almost five decades. In the United States, the backlash against globalization led to the rise of populism and the ordinary people's rebellion against the elite.

ProPublica has obtained a vast trove of the Internal Revenue Service data on the tax returns of thousands of the nation's wealthiest people. Its recent report shows that America's twenty-five wealthiest individuals pay little to no income tax compared to their massive wealth. For example, Jeff Bezos, Elon Musk, Michael Bloomberg, and George Soros paid no federal income tax in recent years. The report also provided an unprecedented look inside the financial lives of America's financial titans, including Warren Buffett, Bill Gates, Rupert Murdoch, and Mark Zuckerberg. The report has exposed the myth of the American tax system: that everyone pays their fair share and that the richest Americans pay the most. The report has conclusively proven that the wealthiest elites legally pay income taxes that are only a tiny fraction of their fortunes. For example, Warren Buffet paid 0.10 percent, Jeff Bezos paid 0.98 percent, Michael Bloomberg paid 1.30 percent, and Elon Musk paid 3.27 percent. In recent years, the median American household earned about $70,000 annually and paid 14 percent in federal taxes. Moreover, the highest income tax rate of 37 percent is now required from couples that

---

34. Roberts and Lamp, *Six Faces of Globalization*, 3–19.
35. Piketty et al., "Distributional National Accounts," 553.

are earning above $628,300. The report has proven that the wealthiest people are effectively sidestepping the system that is designed to tax them at a higher rate for the common good. In 2018, the tax collected from the top twenty-five wage earners was $1.9 billion, while the ordinary wage earners paid $143 billion.[36]

According to the elite insider Anand Giridharadas, this startling reality of the globalization system has sunk in with the voting public, which resulted in "embracing populist movements on the left and right, bringing socialism and nationalism into the center of political life in a way that once seemed unthinkable.... There is a spreading recognition, on both sides of the ideological divide, that the system is broken and has to change."[37] He explains that today's elites are conflicted between social concern and predation. They want to help the society while continuing to amass their wealth by means of predatory business practices. They are among the more socially concerned elites in history. At the same time, however, they are also among the more predatory in history. Giridharadas says, "By refusing to risk its way of life, by rejecting the idea that the powerful might have to sacrifice for the common good, it clings to a set of social arrangements that allow it to monopolize progress and then give symbolic scraps to the forsaken."[38] He explains how the elites with a social conscience perpetuate social injustice:

> In an age defined by a chasm between those who have power and those who don't, elites have spread the idea that people must be helped, but only in market-friendly ways that do not upset fundamental power equations. The society should be changed in ways that do not change the underlying economic system that has allowed the winners to win and fostered many of the problems they seek to solve.[39]

The elites, according to Mexican economist and diplomat Ángel Gurría, have found myriad ways to "change things on the surface so that in practice nothing changes at all."[40] The essence of the problem of globalization, according to Giridharadas, is this: "The people with the most

---

36. Eisinger et al., "Secret IRS Files."
37. Giridharadas, *Winners Take All*, 5.
38. Giridharadas, *Winners Take All*, 7.
39. Giridharadas, *Winners Take All*, 8.
40. Giridharadas, *Winners Take All*, 9.

to lose from genuine social change have placed themselves in charge of social change, often with the passive assent of those most in need of it."[41]

FORCES OF FRAGMENTATION

The narrative that the world is becoming more and more integrated by the homogenizing forces of globalization underestimates the growing forces of fragmentation that are in the world today. The twenty-first century has witnessed the continual rise of fundamentalism, nationalism, and racism, which has left the people in this world divided against one another. These forces rise from globalization's attempt to universalize secular Western culture and unite the world by suppressing old traditions and the values of local cultures, which are founded upon religion.

Fundamentalism

Fundamentalism is a form of a religion, especially Islam or Protestant Christianity, that upholds belief in the strict, literal interpretation of scripture. It is a religious reaction against secularizing aspects of modernity. Fundamentalism's rejection of globalization is the natural reaction to the secular Western culture's outright disregard for the traditions and values of local cultures. Myers observes that "large groups of people resist moving forward into globalization on religious and cultural grounds. Growing fundamentalist movements—Muslim, Christian, Jewish, Hindu, and Buddhist—reject both the processes and the outcomes of globalization as they understand them. They want to go back to a purer, more righteous way of living in the world."[42] There are between 2.5 and 3.5 billion people described as religious exclusivists, and the number is expected to grow in the future. Volf observes, "Significantly, people with a vibrant, numerically growing, and publicly assertive religion, the sort of religion that makes most difference politically, are predominantly religious exclusivists."[43]

According to Islamic scholar Jamal Khwaja, the predicament of traditional Muslims all over the modernized world is that their religious tradition stands for the unity of religion and state, while secularism stands for the separation of religion and state. The Islamic tradition is that Islam

---

41. Giridharadas, *Winners Take All*, 9.
42. Myers, *Engaging Globalization*, 58.
43. Volf, *Flourishing*, 143.

is not merely a spiritual discipline but is *Shariah*—a complete way of life. Shariah encompasses much more than the conventional understanding of law.[44] While Shariah provides the legal framework for the foundation and function of a society, it also details moral, ethical, social, and political codes of conduct for Muslims at an individual and collective level. Though not inspired like the Qur'an, Shariah is deemed as all-embracing and sacrosanct. It relies on scholarly consensus, legal analogy, and interpretive reasoning in deciding rulings. Hence, there are areas of Shariah that the scholars unanimously agree on due to clearly defined evidence and also areas where disagreements exist.[45]

Muslims in general hold that a sovereign secular democratic state is bound to fall headlong into "Satanic" politics and the amoral pursuit of power. In other words, they equate the separation of religion from politics with immoral politics. They honestly tend to hold that the secular approach to politics destroys or erodes true Islam, which they believe is a seamless and complete map of conduct according to divine guidance.[46] Muslims living in the West, however, accept that Islamic law cannot be exported to countries without a Muslim majority. American Sufi journalist Stephen Schwartz says that the call for introduction of Shariah in non-Muslim countries is a new and radical concept, without any support from Islamic legal traditions. A small group of powerful fundamentalists, associated with the Egyptian theologian Yusuf al-Qaradawi and the Swiss Muslim author Tariq Ramadan, have developed a new concept, "Shariah for Muslim minorities living in the West," or "parallel Shariah." Their intention is to erect a separate legal system in the Western countries that would have jurisdiction over Muslims, backed by the authority of the non-Muslim state. The Shariah debate in Western Europe has been badly complicated by the incompetent intervention of non-Muslim politicians, who, in their desire to appear tolerant, have offered opinions in favor of the introduction of Shariah into their countries.[47]

According to Swedish environmentalist Helena Norberg-Hodge, despite mainstream media's narrow and misplaced focus on the Islamic world in reporting on religious extremism, no part of the world is spared from religious and ethnic conflict. She explains, "There has been violence between Sinhalese and Tamils in Sri Lanka, Buddhists and Hindus in

44. Khwaja, *Call of Modernity*, 50.
45. Khwaja, *Call of Modernity*, 51.
46. Khwaja, *Call of Modernity*, 51.
47. Schwartz, "Shariah in the West," 256.

Bhutan, Hindus and Sikhs in Punjab, Eritreans and Ethiopians in the Horn of Africa, the Hutu and the Tutsi in Rwanda, ethnic Russians and Ukrainians in the former Soviet Union, and many more. The fact is that fanaticism, fundamentalism, and ethnic conflict have been growing for many decades—and not just in the Islamic world." "The problem is particularly acute in the Global South, where people from many different ethnic backgrounds are pulled into cities where they are cut off from their communities and cultural moorings and face ruthless competition for jobs and the basic necessities of life."[48]

The conflict arises from the complex interrelated effects of globalization on individuals and communities worldwide. Throughout the world, globalized "development" generally entails an influx of external investments that are then used to build up an energy and transport infrastructure. This new infrastructure then shifts the locus of economic and political life from a multitude of villages and towns to a handful of large urban centers. This is what happened in Ladakh. For more than six hundred years, "Buddhists and Muslims lived side by side in Ladakh with no recorded instance of group conflict. They helped one another at harvest time, attended one another's religious festivals, and sometimes intermarried." Since 1975, however, "tensions between Buddhists and Muslims escalated rapidly, and by 1989 they were bombing each other's homes."[49] Norberg-Hodge does not think that the West's attempt to solve these problems have been successful:

> Tragically, the primary "solutions" to the problem of terrorism have involved smart bombs, drone attacks, and wall-to-wall surveillance programs. At the same time, governments continue to undermine cultural identity through policies promoting a worldwide monoculture for the benefit of global corporations and banks. Such policies will only breed further desperation and fanaticism among people who already feel betrayed and disenfranchised. Encouraging instead a deeper dialogue between people in the Global North and the Global South, while shifting our economic policies to support local and national economies, would set us on the path toward a more harmonious world.[50]

---

48. Norberg-Hodge, "How Globalization Fuels Terrorism," paras. 2 and 24.
49. Norberg-Hodge, "How Globalization Fuels Terrorism," para. 7.
50. Norberg-Hodge, "How Globalization Fuels Terrorism," para. 38.

Nationalism

Nationalism is an ideology that emphasizes loyalty, devotion, or allegiance to a nation or nation-state and holds that such obligations outweigh other individual or group interests. However, globalization diminishes the sovereignty of nation-state and promotes the market-state. Nationalism has been on the rise due to people's fear of losing their agency, identity, and homelands. Protectionist, populist politicians have gained favor in many parts of the world. The nationalists have decried the globalists' multinational institutions, which no longer serve a purpose. They have attacked the liberal elites as sellouts who care more about foreigners than their fellow citizens. The Brexit referendum in 2016 was largely a consequence of the erosion of national sovereignty and the EU's failure to deal with the refugee influx and the eurozone debt crisis.[51] Since 2015, about 2 million refugees seeking asylum have come into the EU. Even more significant is the projection that some 200 million Africans will migrate to Europe by 2050. The EU's current population is about 450 million. The picture of Europe overrun by foreigners of different colors and religions is making a significant number of native Europeans feel that they are losing their identities and countries.

In the 2016 US presidential election, American voters also rebelled against globalization. They elected Donald Trump, an unexpected political outsider who single-handedly defeated the establishments of the Republican Party and the Democratic Party establishments. His win signified that the majority of ordinary Americans have turned to populism, no longer supporting either the center-right or the center-left of the political establishment. During his campaign, Trump railed against the globalist elites, who stifled the economic mobility of the working-class and showed disdain for them. He promised to "Make America Great Again" by building a wall to protect the country's borders from illegal migrants, by raising tariffs on imports, and by bringing manufacturing jobs back from China and Mexico. Hungarian geopolitical expert George Friedman explains that those who assert that fascism is rising in Europe and America are misrepresenting a very real phenomenon. He says:

> Nationalism is the core of the Enlightenment's notion of liberal democracy. It asserts that the multinational dynasties that ruled autocratically denied basic human rights. Among these was the

---

51. Carl, "CSI Brexit 4."

right to national self-determination and the right of citizens to decide what was in the national interest.... Liberal democracy does not dictate whether a nation should be a member in a multinational organization, adopt free trade policies or protectionism, or welcome or exclude immigrants.... What we are seeing is the rise of the nation-state against the will of multinational organizations and agreements.[52]

In Germany's 2017 election, the Alternative for Germany (AfD) party entered the federal parliament for the first time with 12.6 percent of votes. The AfD stood against Chancellor Angela Merkel's welcoming policy toward refugees who were particularly from the Arab world. In the 2021 election, the party received 10.3 percent of votes. In France's 2017 election, Marine Le Pen received 33.9 percent of votes compared to Emmanuel Macron's 66.1 percent. Her campaign prioritized the national interests of France and an exit from the eurozone, emphasizing her party's traditional concerns about security, immigration, and national sovereignty. In Italy's 2022 election, Giorgia Meloni of the Brothers of Italy (FdI) party claimed victory, becoming the country's first female prime minister. The country has also chosen its most right-wing government since World War II. During her campaign, Meloni forcefully declared, "I am Giorgia. I'm a woman. I'm a mother. I'm Italian. I'm Christian. And you're not going to take that away from me."[53] In her speech at the National Conservatism Conference, Meloni said, "Our main enemy today is the globalist drift of those who view identity and all its forms to be an evil to overcome. And constantly ask to shift real power away from the people to supranational entities headed by supposedly enlightened elites."[54] In another speech, "she brought the crowd to its feet when she shouted, 'Yes to the natural family, no to LGBT lobbies! Yes to sexual identity, no to the ideology of gender! Yes to the universality of the cross, no to Islamic violence! Yes to secure frontiers, no to massive migration!'" While the secular media interprets that Meloni's rhetoric is turning Italy toward fascism, the conservative media's narrative is that her deeply personal experience with God will protect Italy from Islamization.[55]

In recent years, nationalism has become an important means by which Latin Americans have attempted to shield themselves against the

52. Friedman, "Nationalism Is Rising," paras. 2, 7–8.
53. Poggioli, "Giorgia Meloni," para. 4.
54. Meloni, "God, Homeland, Family," para. 2.
55. O'Connell, "Giorgia Meloni Is a Christian," 14–15.

negative aspects of globalization. Latin American nationalism is relatively weak compared to that of other regions because its population is incredibly diverse in terms of race, religion, and ethnicity and is split by some of the world's deepest chasms between social classes.[56] In Brazil's 2018 election, however, Jair Bolsonaro was elected as the president, his motto being "Brazil above everything, God above all." "He promised to combat the 'ideology of gender' teaching in schools, 'respect our Judeo-Christian tradition,' and 'prepare children for the job market, not political militancy.'"[57] In Mexico's 2018 election, Andrés Manuel López Obrador (commonly known as AMLO) was elected as the Mexican president. His party, the National Regeneration Movement (MORENA), declares itself an anti-neoliberal and populist party. Supporters have praised him for promoting institutional renewal after decades of high inequality and corruption and for refocusing the country's neoliberal consensus toward improving the state of the working class.[58]

Racism

Racism is prejudice or discrimination against or antagonism toward people based on their race or ethnicity, typically one that is a minority or marginalized. Racism does not necessarily derive from nationalism, although there can be intersection between the two, and is far more prevalent in modern society than people are willing to admit.[59] According to Dutch researcher Ineke van der Valk, "The most important and most far reaching forms of social inequality today are related to group relations based on gender, class, and ethnic background. . . . Historically, specific mechanisms of group dominance have produced and reproduced these forms of social inequality. Racism is a typical expression of group dominance."[60] Modernity's political and social efforts to eradicate racism in order to build up a cohesive global village has proven to be a failure in the leading Western countries.

In the United States, according to the Pew Research Center's report, "four-in-ten Latinos say they have experienced discrimination [in 2018],

56. Siekmeier, "Nationalism and Globalization," 68–69.
57. Fisch et al., "Brazil's Bolsonaro Assumes Presidency," para. 9.
58. Romero, "López Obrador Takes On."
59. For a review of current scholarship around racism and nationalism, see Rutland, "Racism and Nationalism," 629–42.
60. Van der Valk, "Racism, a Threat," 48.

such as being criticized for speaking Spanish or being told to go back to their home country."[61] Also, in 2018, a white supremacist attacked the Tree of Life Synagogue in Pittsburgh, murdering eleven people and wounding six. It was the deadliest attack against the Jewish community in the United States.[62] The COVID-19 pandemic has also fueled violent racist attacks against Asian Americans. A total of 9,081 racially motivated attacks against Asians was reported between March 19, 2020, and June 30, 2021. The incidents included verbal harassment, shunning, physical assault, civil rights violations, and online harassment.[63] Sixty-five-year-old Vilma Kari became one of those victims when she was suddenly attacked by a stranger on her way to church in midtown Manhattan. "'You don't belong here, you Asian,' he said, cursing and beating her so violently that the elderly woman was left with serious pelvic injuries." A nationwide survey of more than 1,000 respondents found that about one in five had experienced a hate incident in 2021.[64]

In the wake of George Floyd's death on May 25, 2020, Black Lives Matter (BLM) became a global movement against racial injustice and police brutality toward black people by organizing demonstrations in cities across the world. The BLM movement was launched in 2013 by the activists Patrisse Cullors, Alicia Garza, and Opal Tometi after the man who killed Trayvon Martin, a seventeen-year-old African American boy, in Florida the previous year was acquitted on murder charges. In 2016, Tometi delivered a speech before the UN General Assembly and issued a statement emphasizing an "urgent need to engage the international community about the most pressing human rights crises of our day."[65] She also stated in an interview, "We see these rallies in solidarity emerging all across the globe, and I have friends texting me with their images in France and the Netherlands and Costa Rica, and people are showing me that they are showing up in solidarity."[66] Over the past several years, BLM activists have forged meaningful alliances with activists and human rights campaigners all over the world. They have a global network of dozens of chapters, which is expected to grow exponentially in the coming

---

61. Lopez et al., "More Latinos Have Serious Concerns," para. 1.
62. Selk et al., "They Showed His Photo."
63. Stop AAPI Hate, "2023 Impact Report."
64. Yeung, "She Was Attacked," paras. 2 and 22.
65. Blain, "Civil Rights International," 177.
66. Blain, "Civil Rights International," 181.

years.[67] The popularity of BLM has rapidly shifted over time. Whereas public opinion on BLM was net negative in 2018, it grew increasingly popular throughout 2019 and 2020.[68] A June 2020 Pew Research Center poll found that 67 percent of American adults expressed either *strong* or *some support* for the BLM movement. However, a later poll conducted in September 2020 showed that overall support had dropped to 55 percent. Additionally, the share of those who *strongly* support the movement dropped from 38 percent to 29 percent.[69]

Many evangelical Christians are critical of the BLM movement. While many of them have publicly condemned racism, they see BLM as Marxist, radical, anti-American, and anti-Christian. Some churches and seminaries have publicly warned Christians against supporting BLM, highlighting that the movement stands against the nuclear family, promotes homosexual and transgender ideologies, and is an admittedly Marxist organization.[70] Southern Evangelical Seminary and Bible College released a statement that includes the following:

> SES, along with fellow Evangelical ministries such as the Billy Graham Evangelical Association and the American Family Association, have grave, fundamental disagreements with their moral, cultural, and political agenda. . . . Thus, it seems prudent for Christians to seek to avoid even the appearance of evil and find other ways to express their justifiable outrage at racial injustice.[71]

American evangelical pastor Tony Evans gives a more nuanced understanding of BLM in the light of its recent ties with critical race theory, which attacks systemic racism. He explains that critical race theory is not concerned with an individual's racism, but it is only concerned about racism infiltrating the structures and the systems of society and how those structures continue to have negative effects on minorities.[72] Evans then explains BLM's controversial connection to critical race theory:

---

67. Blain, "Civil Rights International," 181.
68. Cohn and Quealy, "How Public Opinion."
69. Thomas and Horowitz, "Support for Black Lives Matter."
70. Klett, "Evangelical Seminary Condemns"; Addison, "Stated Goals of Black Lives Matter."
71. Southern Evangelical Seminary and Bible College, "Racism and Social Justice," paras. 4 and 6.
72. Evans, "Kingdom Race Theology."

> BLM is two things, not one. It is an emphasis and an entity. It is a movement and an organization. The movement said the lives of black people matter, in the same way that white evangelicals would say the lives of the unborn matter. Out of the movement, or concurrent and concomitant with the movement, is an entity that says black lives matter, but they both use the same name.[73]

He clarifies that apart from a movement, there is an entity that wants to "dissolve the black nuclear family" and "promote transgender rights." He says, "There is a movement and an entity that is using the same name." It has, therefore, created a situation in which "if you agree with the movement, you can be accused of agreeing with the entity."[74] Evans's analysis is the most accurate way to understand the BLM movement. Understanding the complex situation, Christians must clearly stand against systemic or structural racism. Evans also offers an excellent definition of systemic racism:

> Systemic racism is the presence or secular resultant effects of racist practices and processes embedded in and shaping the social, political, economic, legal, educational, infrastructural, medical systems and policies of a society initially established and perpetuated by the government. These then overlap and interconnect in such a way as to give an unjust advantage of resources, rights, mindsets, and privileges for a majority number of one race while denying or limiting it to a majority number of another race or ethnicities.[75]

Over the years, evangelical Christians have struggled to address systemic racism directly and effectively. Eliza Griswold documents one person's struggle: For thirty years, Brenda Salter McNeil was "one of the most prominent figures in the racial-reconciliation movement" working with white evangelical Christians. As a black evangelical leader, "she explicitly avoided talking about aspects of structural racism, such as the racial wealth gap or the high death rate of Black mothers during childbirth; she sought to insure that her sermons were rooted in the Bible and not, as she saw it, in politics. . . . Her workshops focused on inspiring personal stories but left listeners with few practical tools to root out racism in their communities." In 2014, after visiting the activists of the BLM movement to discuss what role the church should take in addressing

---

73. Evans, "Kingdom Race Theology," 46:36.
74. Evans, "Kingdom Race Theology," 46:36.
75. Evans, "Kingdom Race Theology," 46:36.

police brutality against people of color, Salter McNeil changed her approach to the social issue of racism completely. She heard from the young activists that "the church's failure to address systemic racial injustice in the United States rendered American Christian leaders like Salter McNeil part of the problem. In addition, they took issue with what they saw as the church's culture of homophobia and misogyny." They resented the church's hypocrisy and treatment of LGBTQ people. After listening to the angry activists, Salter McNeil realized that they viewed Christians "as not simply irrelevant but on the wrong side of justice." The next day, she reluctantly took part in a street protest with the activists. When she witnessed a young white protester with spiky hair putting himself in physical danger by climbing a fence put up by the police, she feared for his safety and knelt down to pray. The other faith leaders at the protest also knelt nearby. Some of the young activists, who expressed disgust at the church for not taking any meaningful stand for black lives, also did the same. In that moment, Salter McNeil "felt the nearness of God in a way that she never had from the pulpit or on stage." Since then, she has joined the social justice movement to address systemic racism directly by speaking out against US policies that she sees as racist.[76] This personal account merely highlights the church's constant struggle of addressing racism, which has allowed social activists to take the lead in eradicating racism in the United States.

In Europe, France is an ethnically diverse country, and yet, racism persists through *laïcité* (loosely translated as secularism) and the principle of race-neutrality or colorblindness in public policy. The percentage of non-white citizens is roughly 5 percent, far less than in the United States, although France does not track the race of its residents. In contrast to most other developed countries, none of France's public policies are directed at specific racial or ethnic groups. France simply expects other races to adopt and integrate into French culture. In other words, France avoids dealing with the problem of racial discrimination by choosing to remain in denial. Thus, French Muslims continue to struggle with unemployment, social immobility, and systemic racism in spite of the French government's calls for integration which runs into deep-seated racism at every turn.

The outcome of the French approach has been disastrous. On January 7, 2015, there was a horrific terrorist attack and mass shootings at the

---

76. Griswold, "How Black Lives Matter."

Paris offices of the satirical newspaper *Charlie Hebdo* that killed twelve people. The attack began three days of bloodshed in Paris and marked the onset of a wave of Muslim terrorist violence that killed scores more. Homegrown militants, Algerian French brothers Chérif and Saïd Kouachi sought to avenge their prophet Muhammad. Many Muslims found the *Charlie Hebdo* drawings particularly offensive not just because they depicted their prophet, but because they did so in a way that some critics said perpetuated racist, bigoted stereotypes of Muslims. Rather than trying to address this racism, many French people identified with the principle of free speech and displayed solidarity by marching with the slogan "Je suis Charlie" (I am Charlie).[77] The French natives expect and demand Muslims adjust their religious and cultural ideals to the French principle of freedom of speech. However, they themselves insist on having the right, without facing any social consequence, to display offensive images in public that will insult Muslims.

More than 250 people have been killed in France due to Muslim terrorist violence since the attacks, which exposed France's struggle to counter the threat of militants brought up in the country and foreign jihadists.[78] One attack was particularly gruesome and tragic. On October 16, 2020, a public middle-school teacher named Samuel Paty showed *Charlie Hebdo*'s caricatures of the Muslim prophet Muhammad to his students during a class about free speech. Abdoullakh Anzorov, an eighteen-year-old refugee from Chechnya, beheaded Paty with a butcher knife as the teacher made his way home.[79] After a series of high-profile terrorist attacks by Muslim extremists in France, the country has now found itself in a heated debate over its cherished value of free speech. A controversial new bill proposed by President Emmanuel Macron targeting "Islamic separatism" was met with fierce opposition. Cailey Griffin explains the purpose of the bill:

> Broadly speaking, the bill is meant to reinforce France's lay tradition by discouraging behavior seeking to impose religious viewpoints in the public sphere. First, the bill expands the "neutrality principle" forbidding not only civil servants but "all private contractors of public services" from sharing political opinions or even wearing physical representations of their religion, according to Al Jazeera. The bill also allows French

---

77. Dodman, "Year Charlie Hebdo."
78. Salaün, "Charlie Hebdo Attackers Killed."
79. Makooi, "'Violence Shook Me Profoundly.'"

authorities to temporarily shut down places of worship to stop preachers from spreading hatred. Lastly, French associations with specific religious ties that receive any "foreign funds will have to provide a strict accounting," as reported by the *New York Times*.[80]

France has pursued after *laïcité* and the principle of race-neutrality, but it has fallen short of building a society that produces equality for all. Vanessa Bee reports that France is at a cultural crossroads:

> For more than a century, the country's social and political life has been built around one particular idea: a secularism and universalism that places citizenship above all individual traits and identities. The French call this laïcité. . . . But a rising generation of thinkers and activists, many of them French people of color, are challenging the notion that ignoring race, religion, and colonial history can actually produce equality for all. Now, a wave of terrorist attacks is pushing these issues into the public square and fueling a fierce culture war.[81]

According to Cathie Lloyd, French colonialism was shaped by a variety of political, economic, and cultural factors, and the most prominent among these was the *mission civilisatrice* (civilizing mission), which promoted the advancement of French civilization, cultural norms, and political ideals in colonized nations and was furthered by colonial officials and Catholic missionaries. French colonialism was not simply an expansion of French governance but was an active effort to assimilate colonized peoples into a French way of being. Simultaneously, the mission was used to mask the basic political and economic motivations of colonialism.[82]

Sociologist and race theorist Howard Winant observes that race has always operated as an organizing factor in society.[83] Race and racism continue to exist as dark matter in the modern epoch. He asserts, "Despite the best efforts of both politicians and social scientists to render race invisible, it keeps exerting significant sociopolitical 'gravity': in the economy, in global politics, and in an increasingly internationally networked culture as well."[84] Racism does not seem to be going away despite the fact that much effort was made by global institutions such as the

80. Griffin, "France's Islamist Separatism Bill," paras. 4–5.
81. Deconstructed, "France and the Myth," paras. 3, 5.
82. Lloyd, "Race and Ethnicity," 34–52.
83. Winant, "Dark Matter," 313–24.
84. Winant, "Dark Matter," 324.

United Nations. In fact, the UN itself has been dealing with racism within the organization. A recent survey of over 688 UN staffers in Geneva has revealed that "more than one in three staff have personally experienced racial discrimination and/or have witnessed others facing racial discrimination in the workplace. And two-thirds of those who experienced racism did so on the basis of nationality."[85] In a separate survey by the UN Staff Union in New York, 59 percent of the respondents said, "They don't feel [that] the UN effectively addresses racial justice in the workplace, while every second respondent noted they don't feel comfortable talking about racial discrimination at work."[86] In the United Nations' online survey on racism, the staffers were asked to identify themselves as "black, brown, white, mixed/multi-racial, and any other." Prisca Chaoui of the UN acknowledged that the findings of the survey confirm that racism exists within the United Nations.[87]

This chapter has so far demonstrated that the hegemonic globalization of the West has underestimated the divisive forces of fundamentalism, nationalism, and racism. The antagonism and separatism that exist in response to the homogenizing forces of globalization cannot be resolved by universalizing secular Western culture. Furthermore, humanity's efforts to build a global society cannot succeed without receiving God's grace and peace, which can unite diverse cultures as one in Christ.

GLOBAL GOVERNANCE

The main problem of the hegemonic globalization of the West is the loss of national sovereignty and democratic policies. In illustrating the fundamental problem of globalization, Turkish economist Dani Rodrik presents a menu of options for reconstructing the world economy: the Political Trilemma of the World Economy.[88] He uses this triangular diagram to explain that there is a fundamental tension between national democracy and global markets. He theorizes that to manage the tension of globalization, nation-states can choose any two items from the menu. The three available items are hyperglobalization (a fully integrated economic system), national sovereignty, and democratic policies. Rodrik

---

85. Deen, "Widespread Racism," para. 4.
86. Deen, "Widespread Racism," para. 6.
87. Deen, "Widespread Racism."
88. Rodrik, *Globalization Paradox*, 200.

explains that it is not possible to choose all three at once in a completely globalized world: "If we want hyperglobalization and democracy, we need to give up on the nation-state. If we must keep the nation-state and want hyperglobalization too, then we must forget about democracy. And if we want to combine democracy with the nation-state, then it is bye-bye deep globalization."[89]

The first option is choosing hyperglobalization and nation-state. This option means that a fully globalized world economy becomes possible when nation-states focus exclusively on economic globalization and on becoming attractive to international investors and traders. This option is called the "Golden Straitjacket" because then nation-states can no longer make economic policies based on the democratic will of their citizens; otherwise, they would not be allowed to benefit from a world economy that is fully integrated. Since the 1980s, governments had no choice but to pursue policies that built market confidence and attracted trade and capital inflows at the expense of social insurance for ordinary people. The globalization system demanded free trade at the expense of democratic policies. In order to prosper together, the world had to choose technological innovations led by the United States over the local culture's traditional ways and values.[90]

The second option is choosing nation-states and democratic politics. This option indicates that nation-states can limit globalization in order to maintain national sovereignty and democratic legitimacy. This option becomes possible by the renewal of the "Bretton Woods compromise." The original Bretton Woods Agreement between forty-four countries was implemented with the creation of the International Monetary Fund and the World Bank at the 1944 Bretton Woods Conference and the signing of the General Agreement on Tariffs and Trade (GATT) in 1947. All the countries in the Bretton Woods Conference agreed to a fixed peg to the US dollar with diversions of only 1 percent allowed. Countries were required to monitor and maintain their currency pegs, which they achieved primarily by using their currency to buy or sell US dollars as needed. The Bretton Woods compromise therefore minimized the exchange rate volatility of international currency, which helped international trade relations. Increased stability in foreign currency exchange rates was also a factor in the successful support of international loans and grants from

89. Rodrik, *Globalization Paradox*, 200.
90. Rodrik, *Globalization Paradox*, 200–202.

the World Bank. In 1971, however, President Richard Nixon devalued the US dollar relative to gold in order to address the country's inflation problem and to discourage foreign governments from redeeming more and more dollars for gold. By 1973, the Bretton Woods compromise had collapsed, making way for the globalization system.[91]

The third option is choosing hyperglobalization and democratic politics. This option conveys that nation-states would lose national sovereignty by pursuing globalization and democracy. This kind of world becomes possible via "global governance." Robust global institutions with regulatory and standard-setting powers would align legal and political jurisdictions with the reach of markets and remove the transaction costs associated with national borders. Politics would relocate to a global level and become, for example, a form of global federalism—the US model expanded on a global scale. Alternate forms of global governance built around new mechanisms of accountability and representation are also possible. National governments would not disappear, but their powers would be severely circumscribed by supranational rulemaking and enforcing bodies empowered (and constrained) by democratic legitimacy. The European Union is a regional example of this option.[92]

The fundamental problem of globalization is that the world cannot have hyperglobalization, democratic policies, and national sovereignty at the same time. As Rodrik demonstrates through these combinations for reconstructing the world economy, only two items from the political trilemma menu can be chosen by nation-states. In democratic societies, people cherish democracy and national sovereignty. Yet, during the 1990s and 2000s, world politicians at large had chosen hyperglobalization and national sovereignty. They had chosen the way of Golden Straitjacket, which meant that they had to follow the strict rules of globalization. Their decision led them to sign many trade agreements that allowed capital to flow freely worldwide. This unstable and incoherent state of affairs has been the main cause of social and political turmoil around the globe. In conclusion, Rodrik says that when his students are presented with the trilemma and asked to pick the two items, most of them choose hyperglobalization and democratic policies via global governance.[93] Rodrik himself does not believe it is a viable solution and proposes a renewed

---

91. Rodrik, *Globalization Paradox*, 204–5.
92. Rodrik, *Globalization Paradox*, 202–4.
93. Rodrik, *Globalization Paradox*, 200–206.

Bretton Woods compromise that can lead to improved capitalism and "sane globalization."[94]

According to Robert Gorman, "*global governance* is a term that has gained favor over the past two decades among students and practitioners of international relations and international organizations when referring to the structures of cooperation that exist among nations to advance their mutual interest and to resolve problems and issues in their international relations."[95] In this sense, it is without controversy. In another sense, however, the term *global governance* refers to the political dimension of globalization. Global governance advocates tend to prefer both a transnational regulation of markets and the creation of new human rights norms marked by increased centralization. Gorman says:

> It seeks to establish an entirely secular order in which activities such as education, health care, economic development, and justice are fashioned by global experts rather than by the leaders in their natural local and national contexts. Rules by experts, by global bureaucrats, is regarded as the ideal. These experts in turn share a common outlook on the world. They are secularists who are at best suspicious of but often outright hostile to religion and traditional culture as influences on civilizations. They are bureaucrats or advocates of bureaucracy who believe that government by experts rather than by elected officials is the only way to advance a progressive agenda of modernization.[96]

Globalization has now brought the issue of global governance to the forefront, necessitating a discussion on religious pluralism and ethics. The world can no longer avoid the theological question of how to determine universal ethics that can uphold the common good of humanity.

---

94. Rodrik, *Globalization Paradox*, 207–84.
95. Gorman, *What's Wrong with Global Governance?*, 2.
96. Gorman, *What's Wrong with Global Governance?*, 4.

4

The Role of Religion in Renewing Globalization

GLOBALIZATION HAS FALLEN BECAUSE it lacks the spiritual and moral foundation that comes from deeply held religious beliefs, values, and commitments. The failure of hegemonic globalization driven by the West allows humanity to discover a new future that is based on religious pluralism and ethics. From a biblical perspective, the globalized world must be renewed under the reign of Christ and through the ministry of the church. The religion that preaches the gospel and exercises God's love, truth, justice, and righteousness in society has the power to establish the ethics of God's kingdom for human flourishing. In a world of pluralism, however, Christians must learn to lead and serve the globalized world while respecting other cultures and religions. This chapter considers the role of religion in renewing globalization and what it means to be both disciples of Jesus Christ and good citizens in a pluralistic society. The first section claims that the church must respond to globalization and the cultural changes it brings to society by engaging with its development. The second section asserts that the church must maintain a public dialogue with others to cultivate mutual understanding while preaching the gospel. The third section argues that the creative tension resulting from pluralism enables the development of a theological framework for addressing the problems of globalization. The fourth section discusses how theology can integrate universal Christian beliefs and values with local cultures in the globalization process. The fifth section explains how Christians can understand the problems of globalization with empathy.

The final section addresses how the church should interact with secularists and adherents of other religions in developing the ethics of God's kingdom, which can lead to human solidarity.

CHRISTIAN RESPONSE TO GLOBALIZATION AND CULTURAL CHANGES

Globalization inevitably brings forth cultural changes throughout every society, challenging established traditions and ways of life. People easily recognize the benefits of globalization brought on by what lies beyond one's traditional boundary: ease of worldwide communication and travel, cross-cultural exchanges, better products at lower prices, collaboration and shared resources, spread of knowledge and technology, open-mindedness and tolerance, and a higher standard of living across the board. However, there remains a great concern as to what all these changes will amount to. As Nigerian social scientist Kabiru Ibrahim Yankuzo observes, "Globalization is like an uncontrollable wildfire that has started and nobody knows where it is taking us. What is evident is that no person, family, religion and society are immune to it."[1] His main concern is the loss of African cultural heritage due to economic, political, and cultural globalization led by the West.[2] Fernando López-Alves and Diane Johnson explain how the developing countries in Latin America feel about the uncertainty of globalization:

> Uncertainty results when the outcome of a situation is not known or fixed, just as the direction and effects of twisting winds are unpredictable. The whirlwind analogy applies to those who aim to construct a theory of globalization, but it also reflects the day-to-day experience—within the framework of different social, institutional, and political contexts—of all those caught up in the global process. Particularly in the developing world, this experience produces uncertainty in the minds and lives of people who see globalization as a force that they cannot control.[3]

In the emergence of a new kind of global society that transcends all borders and cultures, an increasing number of people are now recognizing

---

1. Yankuzo, "Impact of Globalization," 44.
2. Yankuzo, "Impact of Globalization," 44–48.
3. López-Alves and Johnson, *Globalization and Uncertainty*, 2.

the crucial societal role of religion, which can restore meaning and identity to individuals, community, and nation. Journalist Ian Johnson has traveled throughout China to converse with ordinary people and observe how religion has become the antidote in a society transformed by a materialistic outlook of life:

> Hundreds of millions of Chinese are consumed with doubt about their society and turning to religion and faith for answers that they do not find in the radically secular world constructed around them. They wonder what more there is to life than materialism and what makes a good life. As one person I interviewed for this book told me, "We thought we were unhappy because we were poor. But now a lot of us aren't poor anymore, and yet we're still unhappy. We realize there's something missing and that's a spiritual life."[4]

Religion has the spiritual and moral power of giving meaning to individuals and uniting society for a common purpose. Thus, the role of religion cannot remain confined to the private sphere as secularism demands. Since the 1980s, according to Casanova, religious traditions around the world have made their way out of the private sphere and into the public sphere, causing the "deprivatization" of religion in contemporary life. He explains, "By deprivatization I mean the fact that religious traditions throughout the world are refusing to accept the marginal and privatized role which theories of modernity as well as theories of secularization had reserved for them."[5] Religion always transcends any privatistic reality and serves to integrate the individual into an intersubjective, public, and communal world.[6] Many scholars across various disciplines agree that the world is currently experiencing a worldwide religious resurgence.[7] Contrary to the widespread belief in the West that religion belongs to the past, 84 percent of the global population identifies with a religious group.[8] Christians must realize that the age of modernity is passing away just as the age of Christendom has passed away. Humanity has now entered the age of globalization, in which diverse cultures and religions are contending for legitimacy and contributing to the formation of universal ethics. The world has become a pluralistic society in which

---

4. Johnson, *Souls of China*, 18.
5. Casanova, *Public Religions*, 5.
6. Casanova, *Public Religions*, 216.
7. Dawson, "Religious Resurgence," 201–21.
8. Sherwood, "Religion."

people cannot easily dismiss the values of others while accepting their own values uncritically.

There are three ways Christians can respond to the reality of globalization and the cultural changes it brings to society. The first way is to create a totalitarian system that brings uniformity of religion for its society. The second way is to resort to sectarianism by detaching from the larger society and remaining in a protective subculture. The third way is to engage with pluralism and to enter into open dialogue with the alternatives that exist beyond one's own traditional belief system.[9] In a pluralistic world, creating a totalitarian Christian society is neither possible nor desirable. Engaging with a pluralistic society involves the risk of falling prey to relativism, which is the doctrine that knowledge, truth, and morality, rather than being objective and absolute, exist in relation to culture, society, or historical context. While withdrawing from pluralism is seemingly the safest choice, this approach has the devastating consequence of the Christian faith becoming irrelevant in a globalized world. Despite possessing the gospel of salvation for humanity, evangelical Christians have largely chosen to remain sectarian, and their contribution to the development of globalization has been sparse.

From a theological and missiological perspective, globalization calls forth a Christian response: interpretation of its nature and engagement with its development. However, Christians have devoted little energy to understanding globalization and biblically assessing its benefits and perils. As Romanian theologian Marcel Măcelaru says, "Consistent theological responses to, and interactions with, [globalization] are scarce and varied. As such, systematic reflection on this topic has become necessary."[10] Myers asks, "If globalization is universally understood as a significant stage of civilization, why should Christians remain disengaged?" He attributes the present situation to the fact that globalization as a topic is vast and complicated, involving economics, technology, and politics. Contemporary Christians also tend to focus on spiritual issues and leave worldly matters in the hands of the materialists and the secular humanists.[11] Spirituality and morality, however, cannot be separated from the mundane things that matter in the physical world. Nigerian theologian Bulus Galadima believes there can be honest engagement with the challenges of globalization without falling into relativism: "In order for this

9. Berger, *Many Altars of Modernity*, 34–50.
10. Măcelaru, "Theology Encounters Globalization," 67.
11. Myers, *Engaging Globalization*, 5.

last possibility to happen, we must identify the core of the Gospel. The seeming facile nature of this task is deceptive. It requires tact, creativity, and especially the enablement of the Holy Spirit."[12] A Christian response to globalization must be infused with sensitivity toward cultural changes and creativity of theological engagement. The church can learn about the problems arising from globalization by conversing with diverse peoples, nations, and civilizations. If the church is led by the Holy Spirit in the process of engaging with globalization, it can withstand the onslaught of totalitarianism, liberalism, and relativism.

PUBLIC DIALOGUE FOR MUTUAL UNDERSTANDING

God loves the world, and he wants to see humanity flourish by repenting from its sin. Christians can help the world solve its problems by providing a spiritual and moral foundation; however, they tend to prioritize religious beliefs, values, and commitments over people who stand in opposition to the gospel. This false priority has been the main cause of the church's antagonism against secularists and adherents of other religions. While preaching the gospel, the church tends to condemn the sinful world. In contrast to this attitude, Scripture reveals God does not want the world to perish in sin because of his love (John 3:16). The world was made for Christ; therefore, it is precious to God. The church must realize that without the world, its eternal inheritance in Christ does not exist. When the people of this world and their society perish in sin, it is a great loss for the church. Thus, God's eternal decree is to redeem this world through the death of his Son and renew it by the reconciling ministry of his church. God will not simply destroy the world and create something new out of nothing; rather, he wants to redeem and renew the wonderful work of his creation. Thus, the ministry of the church in a globalized world is twofold: it must understand the problems of the world by engaging with all people in dialogue, and it must invite all people into God's kingdom by communicating the gospel of repentance without condemning them (Acts 3:17–23). While preaching the gospel, Christians must identify with the problems of globalization and demonstrate empathy toward humanity's predicament. When Christians depart from the public square where people are gathered to discuss the problems plaguing

---

12. Galadima, "Religion and the Future," 201.

society, the church loses the power to reconcile humanity with God and with each other.

Jesus demonstrated the ministry of reconciliation when he publicly engaged with the Samaritan woman at the well (John 4:7–26). As a Jewish man, he crossed the social boundaries of ethnicity and gender by initiating a dialogue. As a teacher of the law, he started an unusual conversation with a woman who, having had five husbands and was now living with another man, was living a sinful life. He offered her the "living water," wanting to satisfy the longing of her heart and solve the root of all her problems. When she brought up the issue of the differing religious beliefs between the Jews and Samaritans, Jesus replied, "Believe me, woman, a time is coming when you will worship the Father neither on this mountain nor in Jerusalem. You Samaritans worship what you do not know; we worship what we do know, for salvation is from the Jews." Then, he clarified the essence of true religion, saying "But the hour is coming, and is now here, when the true worshipers will worship the Father in spirit and truth, for the Father is seeking such people to worship him." Through this interaction, the Samaritan woman understood there is a true way of worship that is acceptable to God. She discovered the spiritual and moral resource for living a new life by knowing Jesus as the Christ. She met the Savior who knew everything she did in her life and did not give up on her. Allegorically speaking, the Samaritan woman represents the sinful world. Today, Jesus is sending the church to reach out to the world, which is mired in the false religion of globalization and its ethical failure. The world longs to become a global village where all people can live together in harmony, but it remains divided without knowing Jesus as the Christ and the ethics of God's kingdom.

Public dialogue paves the way toward mutual understanding and solidarity between diverse peoples, nations, and civilizations in a globalized world. According to German philosopher Jürgen Habermas's social theory, communicative action is cooperative action undertaken by individuals based upon mutual deliberation and argumentation. It serves to transmit cultural knowledge and renew it, and this process makes it possible to achieve mutual understanding. As the communicative action progresses, it can coordinate toward solidarity and social integration.[13] Reflecting on Habermas's theory of communicative action, theologian

---

13. Tracy, "Public Theology, Hope," 232–35.

David Tracy makes the following diagnosis against the homogenous aspect of globalization:

> In Western societies, the entire life-world, including the public realm, has been subject to an "internal colonization" as the systems of late-capitalist economics, political bureaucratic administration, and modern global technologies have increasingly (but not completely) colonized the life-world; hence, the "citizen," who, by definition, must be involved in communicative action, can become a mere "producer," a "client," and a "consumer."[14]

To understand our cultural situation, Tracy says that one must expand the cultural horizons of contemporary discussion beyond Western centeredness and the Western sense of its own pluralism. In short, it has become necessary to allow for global polycentrism. There are multiple centers now, of which the West is merely one. Tracy warns that, above all, one must avoid much of the media and modernity's central temptation: the drive to systematize, to render a totalizing system that makes everything simply more of the same.[15]

While the West easily recognizes the evils of other cultures and ideologies, it refuses to observe the totalizing nature of Western culture and the ideology of liberal democracy. It admires itself as the supreme civilization, ensuring freedom and justice for all individuals. Even for those who recognize its problems, Western liberal democracy is perceived as a useful form of government that rose above all others. It is also believed that all alternatives are worse; therefore, there is no option but to bear the shortcomings of liberal democracy. This attitude of complacency is no longer acceptable as Western liberal democracy has now revealed its propensity toward totalitarianism. It has turned decisively against Christians and their traditional beliefs and values by enshrining abortion, same-sex marriage, transgenderism, and euthanasia into law. Those who speak up against these laws are publicly shamed and ostracized. American political theorist Patrick Deneen argues liberalism has failed to keep its promises to secure human liberty and dignity: "Ideology fails for two reasons—first, because it is based on falsehood about human nature, and hence can't help but fail; and second, because as those falsehoods become more evident, the gap grows between what the ideology claims and the lived experience of human beings under its domain until the regime

---

14. Tracy, "Public Theology, Hope," 237.
15. Tracy, "Public Theology, Hope," 252.

loses legitimacy."[16] Realizing that liberalism has exhausted itself, Deneen argues that Christianity is no longer compatible with liberal democracy. Other Christian thinkers believe that it is still salvageable, and that retreating from liberal democracy will not solve any of the problems facing humanity.[17] It seems Christian thinkers are struggling to find the solution, and the future of humanity remains uncertain.

According to Polish philosopher Ryszard Legutko, totalitarianism manifests itself not only in communist societies but also in liberal democratic societies. He says "[both ideologies are] fueled by the idea of modernization. In both systems a cult of technology translates itself into acceptance of social engineering as a proper approach to reforming society, changing human behavior, and solving existing social problems."[18] Both regimes also clearly distance themselves from the past. Both embrace the idea of progress with all its consequences, believing in the power of *technê* (art, craft, technique, or skill). Both use the favorite expressions of condemnation pointing to the old: "superstition," "medieval," "backward," and "anachronistic." Both use the favorite adulatory term "modern." Both systems generate a sense of liberation from the old bonds. Both hate religion, social morality, and traditions. Having the brand of the new is always preferable, while alignment with the old is always suspect. Both ideologies have pity on those who continue to be attached to long-outdated rules and succumb to the bondage of unreasonable restraints.[19]

Christians must realize that the role of religion is not merely to promote Western culture but all the cultures in the world that are being renewed by the gospel. Secularism, while claiming to be tolerant of other beliefs and values, is a totalizing ideology that must separate religion from political, economic, technological, and cultural aspects of life. When Christians submit to secularism and avoid engaging with globalization, they lose the power to influence society. On the other hand, pluralism allows Christians to have a dialogue with secularists and other religious adherents, thereby clearing the path to discovering truth and justice in society. Pluralism allows all religions that seek truth and justice to have a voice in public discussion. As Louise Hickman asserts, a religion that is committed to the Platonic ideals of the Good, the Truth,

16. Deneen, *Why Liberalism Failed*, 6.
17. Miller et al., "Is Christianity Compatible."
18. Legutko, *Demon in Democracy*, 7.
19. Legutko, *Demon in Democracy*, 8.

and the Beautiful has the potential to resolve the most urgent problems of the age described as a "post-truth world."[20] It is now believed that the world has become a place in which objective facts are less influential in shaping public opinion than appeals to emotion and personal belief. From a biblical perspective, the world is lost in a vast sea of knowledge because it has rejected Christ, who claims to be "the way, the truth, and the life" (John 14:16). The future of a globalized world needs to be based on religious pluralism, which would allow Christians to have a voice in the public square. Dialogue between Christians, other religious adherents, and secularists can lead to mutual understanding and solidarity in search of truth and justice.

CREATIVE TENSION OF A PLURALISTIC SOCIETY

Globalization is a complex phenomenon that has produced a paradoxical result of both the convergence and divergence of many cultures worldwide. It is an emerging and ongoing reality that has taken the West by surprise with its heterogenizing outcomes. The paradoxical nature of globalization allows various cultures to legitimize and strengthen their uniqueness all over the world. The process of revitalizing local culture can bring about solidarity, rather than further disintegration, throughout humanity. The strengthening of cultural diversity in the globalization process can overcome the totalizing effects of homogenization by providing a "creative tension" for humanity to discover a new way to conceive universal ethics for its reconciliation. According to Song, "The focal problem of current global processes seems to be the tension between cultural homogenization and cultural heterogenization. The globalization process is rapidly reshaping the paradoxical context around the world and the paradoxical context of globalization provides a creative tension between homogenous and heterogeneous force of culture."[21]

From an African Christian perspective, theologian Jehu Hanciles from Sierra Leone rejects the notion that the processes of globalization perpetuate structures of Western hegemony. Although contemporary globalization has been the most powerful transformative process of our time, it nevertheless has deep historical roots and denotes a complex reality that is still evolving. While America's economic dominance is a

---

20. Hickman, "Good, the True," 9.
21. Song, "Cultural Context of Globalization," 250.

tremendous global force, it is no more immune to the disruptions caused by evolving global structures than those of other industrial nations.[22] He states that "the processes of globalization are multidirectional, inherently paradoxical, and incorporate movement and countermovement."[23] This dynamic allows for "globalization from below," which refers to non-Western cultural movements with a global reach that includes the West. Hanciles argues that the migration of African Christians carries within it the seeds of renewal for the whole church. These Christians have the potential to reshape the church-state and religious and cultural relations on a global scale.[24]

Although recognizing the dangers of globalization against Islamic culture, sociologist Abu Sadat Nurullah recommends fellow Muslims to use the potentials of globalization to strengthen and retain the absolute Islamic cultural trait prescribed by Allah. He argues:

> Globalisation poses a challenge to Islamic culture and identity because globalisation promotes the transmission of information through the media and this has resulted in the dominance and hegemony of Western culture over the rest of the world. This poses a challenge to Islamic ways of life, values, and principles. However, as globalisation is inevitable, Muslims should take the benefits and opportunities provided by globalisation in spreading and demonstrating the unique traits of Islamic cultural identity around the world through various means.[25]

Indian author Meera Nanda explains that India is experiencing a rising tide of popular Hinduism, including government financing of Hinduism despite the nation's secular characteristic. She demonstrates that neoliberal globalization has created an institutional matrix that is enabling Hindu nationalism to embed itself deeper into the civil society, the state, and the business sector. Far from eroding the public presence and political power of religion, neoliberalism and globalization have revitalized Hinduism in India. The new, largely Hindu middle classes are successfully blending their religiosity with growing appetites for wealth and profits. Nanda provides the following synopsis of the revitalization of religion in India:

---

22. Hanciles, *Beyond Christendom*, 2–3.
23. Hanciles, *Beyond Christendom*, 3.
24. Hanciles, *Beyond Christendom*, 374–81.
25. Nurullah, "Globalisation as a Challenge," 45.

India today is teeming with millions of educated, relatively well-to-do men and women who enthusiastically participate in global networks of science and technology. The Indian economy is betting its fortunes, at least in part, on advanced research in biotechnology and the drug industry, whose very existence is a testament to a thoroughly materialistic understanding of the natural world. And yet, a vast majority of these middle-class beneficiaries of modern science and technology continue to believe in supernatural powers supposedly embodied in idols, divine men and women, stars and planets, rivers, trees, and sacred animals. By all indications, they treat supernatural beings and powers with utmost earnestness and reverence and go to great lengths to please them in the hope of achieving their desires. Hindus are not the only ones who are becoming more religious—data shows that all the many religious communities of India are showing signs of growing religiosity.[26]

When powerful forces of modernism and postmodernism clash, this exposes certain problems of globalization due to its lack of spiritual and moral foundation. The creative tension between homogenous and heterogenous cultural forces provides a space for Christians to develop a theological framework for addressing the answers sought by diverse peoples, nations, and civilizations in the age of globalization. True religion unites humanity to work together toward resolving global issues such as hate, racism, misogyny, discrimination, poverty, environmental disaster, violence, and war. Universal ethics can be developed only when Christians lead and serve the world by living in accordance with God's word. The power of true religion becomes evident in the world when all Christians spread the gospel and engage with globalization to reconcile humanity with God and with each other. The power to unite humanity through the gospel and the ethics of God's kingdom cannot be unleashed in global society while religion remains confined to people's private life.

The modern world that drove religion from the public sphere has produced polarizing ideologies that redefine and replace values across the entire spectrum of life. Multiplicity and fragmentation of knowledge have been the consequences of modernity's pursuit of certainty. French philosopher Jean-François Lyotard asserts that the grand narratives of modernity have not delivered on their promises and have lost all credibility.[27] The modern ideologies that failed to deliver on the promise of

---

26. Nanda, *God Market*, 61–62.
27. Lyotard, *Postmodern Explained*, 19.

certainty were fascism, communism, socialism, liberalism, capitalism, and neoliberalism. The fall of globalization marks the end of modernity's pursuit of certainty. By contrast, postmodernity values holistic knowledge and pluralism and celebrates the unique beliefs of local cultures. It has ushered in a new age of heterogeneity and numerous narratives. Traditional Christianity, which became dependent on modernity and rationalism, has struggled to remain relevant in a pluralistic society that rejects the authority of Scripture and its claims to truth.

Dan Stiver asserts that, rather than seeing postmodernism as the enemy of the gospel, theology can use the demise of modernism to its advantage. The world has turned away from the trend of pessimism and turned toward the hope of an inclusive world. Postmodernity's interpretative or hermeneutical turn means that all knowledge is rooted in hermeneutical acts of judgment that cannot conclusively be proven or demonstrated. Linguistic turn is the realization that knowledge is always mediated through language. Since hard-and-fast foundations are not available, argumentation proceeds dialogically. Consensus is worked out by dialogue and conversation, not by knockdown arguments. When theology is open to a dialogue, it finds its place in the public arena; it engages the conflict of interpretations with the realization that others, too, have plausible perspectives that cannot be easily dismissed.[28] Bauckham, however, reminds the church that postmodernism is not the wholly supportive ally of Christianity. Its tendency toward the radical fragmentation of life and its deconstructive critique of any claims to universal truth are challenges to Christian theology.[29] Christians must recognize that in a globalized world, all ideologies and their grand narratives are being discredited, thereby giving rise to creative tension for the church to exploit. Humanity is now in a spiritual and moral crisis, desperately seeking the true meaning of life and the ethics to live by. The time has come for the church, especially Christians in the Majority World, to demonstrate that reconciliation of humanity is possible in Christ.

---

28. Stiver, *Theology after Ricoeur*, 11–14.
29. Bauckham, *Bible in the Contemporary World*, xi.

INTEGRATION OF UNIVERSAL CHRISTIAN BELIEFS AND VALUES WITH LOCAL CULTURES

Theology has the potential to reconcile humanity with God and with each other. Christians can develop the ethics of God's kingdom and help all people live together in a globalized world; however, Christians cannot effectively lead and serve the world until they first possess a theology that unites all believers as one in Christ. The church's beliefs and values can become global by integrating the contribution of local cultures and theologies. Theologians Craig Ott and Harold Netland propose a development of "globalizing theology" that aims to "expand the discipline of theological inquiry beyond local-contextual theologies, on the one hand, and rigidly defined systematic theology, on the other, to theological inquiry that is truly global in nature and scope."[30] First, World Christians must recognize the danger of contextual theologies emphasizing the local over the universal and thereby remaining partial. Globalizing theology can bring local theologies into conversation with one another on mutual concerns. Second, systematic theology must also be recognized for being influenced by contextual and historical factors, and for its danger of imposing philosophical systems on the biblical text.[31] As Ott and Netland explain, "The globalizing of theology seeks to expand theology's horizons through the use of new forms of argumentation, alternate cognitive styles, and new idiomatic expressions. It may help theologians become more aware of unreflected presuppositions that they have taken for granted but that are not shared by Christians everywhere."[32] One important task of theology is to discover what the "global church can learn from one another regarding the encounter of Christianity and non-Christian religions and various worldviews."[33] In the globalizing process, globalizing theology integrates universal Christian beliefs and values with local cultures. In return, it welcomes all local cultures into the kingdom of God that can be positively related to God. In this way, according to Song, "Globalizing theology urges the non-Western theologians to find the God-given heritage of indigenous spiritual and cultural treasures."[34]

---

30. Ott and Netland, *Globalizing Theology*, 314.
31. Ott and Netland, *Globalizing Theology*, 312–13.
32. Ott and Netland, *Globalizing Theology*, 314.
33. Ott and Netland, *Globalizing Theology*, 327.
34. Song, "Cultural Context of Globalization," 260.

The potential value of African, Asian, and Latin American culture and theology for the West is tremendous. Since the church in the West is in decline, it is imperative that Western Christians show humility and listen to theology from the Global South, where the majority of Christians now live and practice their faith. According to Marilyn Gardner, who grew up in Pakistan and lived in the Kurdish region of Iraq, Christians in the Global South know what it is to suffer, whether as a result of religious persecution or socioeconomic difficulty. The Global South also knows what it is to live without safety, security, and physical comforts, which are a Western illusion. Finally, the Global South knows what it is to live in collective community, which is a biblical ideal. Christians are called to live not for themselves, but out of responsibility and love for each other. Gardner adds, "Western Christians are great at being in community with people they like, people who agree with them politically, spiritually, and materially—but when disagreement enters, we are quick to absolve ourselves of the same community we spoke so highly of."[35]

For many people living in the West, the existence of evil in the world is a significant problem. Western theologians and philosophers often wonder why good and powerful God allows the presence of evil in this world. Since the problem of evil is an unresolved theological issue, Christians find it difficult to deal with the realities of sickness, natural disasters, death, and other sufferings and tragedies in their personal life. Christians generally believe their life should be healthy, safe, and secure, and they often fall into a crisis when these expectations are not met. According to Ghanaian theologian James Nkansah-Obrempong, most African cultures do not crumble so easily at the presence of evil and suffering in the world. When they face suffering and tragedy of evil, they still recognize God's presence, his providential care and love. They experience God's deliverance and protection from evil. For Africans, even if life does not turn out the way they want, God is still the most powerful reality. Instead of allowing the problem of evil to draw them away from God, they instead affirm the reality of God's care for them.[36]

In advocating for African theology, Ghanaian theologian Kwame Bediako does not think African theology ought to be transplanted into the West. He speaks of African theology and Western theology as "overlapping circles, sharing in their overlaps certain common elements and

---

35. Gardiner, "Led by the Global South."
36. Nkansah-Obrempong, "Problem of Evil," 301.

features, which, therefore, give them a 'family' air."[37] Christians in Africa and the West are a family, contending for their faith in very different places. Many Christians have forgotten that theology once moved from Africa to Europe and Asia, shaping the development of what is now called Western theology. As church historian Thomas Oden argues, "Africa played a decisive role in the formation of Christian culture."[38] The greatest center of early Christianity was an Afro-Asiatic city, Alexandria. This is where the great early theologians of the church were centered: Athanasius, Clement, Cyril, Tertullian, and Origen. Some of the greatest intellectual contributors to the modern understanding of Christianity, including the Trinity and the divinity of Christ, came from the African fathers of faith. These church fathers and others were greatly involved in theological disputes of the time, and their proposed solutions were used to resolve them at major councils including Nicaea and Constantinople.[39] Saint Anthony the Great, the father of monks, was born in Egypt in AD 251. Upon hearing the gospel, he immediately put it into action. Distributing to the poor all he had, he fled from all the turmoil of the world, departing to the desert to live an ascetic life. He became one of the Desert Fathers and influenced Christian monasticism, which later spread in the West.

The church first began in Asia and then spread to northern Africa. Under the direction of the Holy Spirit, the apostle Paul went first to the cities of Asia Minor (modern Turkey) to preach the gospel. The seven churches of Rev 2–3, namely, Ephesus, Smyrna, Pergamum, Thyatira, Sardis, Philadelphia, and Laodicea, were all in Asia Minor. These Christians endured the greatest persecutions, sowing the seed of the gospel with their blood. The gospel then spread in Europe. During the medieval age, for one thousand years, God allowed the gospel to transform European society and bring forth the Christendom. As a result, from the sixteenth century to the mid-twentieth century, Western theology had trained and produced almost all the missionaries who evangelized many parts of the world. Through Western missionaries, the gospel once again reached Africa; this time, the power of God's salvation penetrated deep throughout the continent.

Mary Mitchell Slessor was a Scottish Presbyterian missionary to Nigeria. She is most famous for having stopped the common practice

---

37. Bediako, "African Theology as a Challenge," 53.
38. Oden, *How Africa Shaped*, 9.
39. Oden, *How Africa Shaped*, 33–59.

of infanticide of twins in Okoyong, an area of Cross River State, Nigeria. When she first arrived at Calabar in West Africa in 1876, she learned Efik, the local language, and began to preach the gospel and serve the locals. Calabar was an established mission station where the missionaries, with the help of King Eyo Honesty II and other local personalities, had already made much progress in establishing Christian values. Persevering together, they had eradicated the practice of killing newborn twins and their mother. Realizing she would make little impact if she remained in the comfort zone of Calabar, Slessor boldly chose to take charge of a new station at Okoyong, an area where male missionaries had previously been killed. There, she found all the horrors of heathenism, witchcraft, the poison ordeal, twin murder, and hard drinking. She gained the trust and acceptance of the locals and was able to spread the gospel and establish the ethics of God's kingdom. For the last four decades of her life, Slessor suffered intermittent fevers from the malaria she contracted in Calabar. Her health weakened, but she refused to return to Scotland. She led and served the African people until she could no longer walk, and she died in Africa in 1915.[40] Through the faith and sacrifice of many Western missionaries, the gospel has now saved many peoples, nations, and civilizations worldwide. Their prayer and work have produced enormous result and engendered numerous non-Western missionaries. Today, as sociologist Kerby Goff reports, "Almost half of the 425,000 foreign missionaries in the world are non-Western, according to the World Christian Database. There are Brazilians serving in India, Chinese serving in Central Asia, Nigerians planting megachurches in Europe, and even Texas, and Koreans serving everywhere. To ignore this reality is to miss one of the great transformations of missions in the modern age."[41]

In 1865, Robert Jermain Thomas, a Welshman who was trained in a Western theological school, became the first Protestant missionary to Korea. During his first visit to the country, Thomas quickly learned to speak Korean and wore a Korean hat to cover his Welsh heritage. At the time, tensions between Koreans and foreigners were at an all-time high. In 1866, Thomas returned a second time, boarding a trade ship called the General Sherman, which made it to the city of Pyongyang. When locals attacked and burned the ship, Thomas was captured by hostile troops on shore. He is said to have kneeled and given his executioner a Bible

---

40. Imbua, "Robbing Others to Pay," 139–58.
41. Goff, "GlobalPlus," paras. 9–10.

before being killed.[42] According to one account, Thomas jumped from the ship and handed out Bibles to an angry crowd while shouting "Yesu, Yesu" (Jesus in Korean). Although the details of his martyrdom are buried in history, what is certain is that Koreans began to read the Bible for the first time and became Christians through the ministry of Western missionaries.

In 1907, forty years after Thomas's martyrdom, Pyongyang experienced one of the greatest revivals in history. Presbyterian missionary William Blair preached to thousands of Korean men, telling them to turn away from their hatred of Japanese people, with whom they had a long history of ethnic conflict. Many repented from their collective sin along with personal sin with weeping, confession, and prayer, and the church of Pyongyang experienced its own Pentecost of fire from heaven. The city became known as the "Jerusalem of the East." Many of those Christians later escaped to the south during the Korean War (1950–53), while others remained in the north and faced persecution. Today, one third of South Koreans claim to be Christians, surpassing the traditional religion of Buddhism. South Korea is now the second largest missionary-sending country after the United States.[43] Western theology was instrumental in training the missionaries who brought the Bible and preached the gospel to a hermit kingdom mired in perpetual poverty, thereby liberating many people from the caste system of a society built on Confucianism.

Through globalization, South Korea has emerged from the ashes of the Korean War and transformed itself into one of the world's largest economies. As well as a global exporter of everything from Samsung smart phones to LG appliances to Hyundai and Kia cars, it has become a global soft power, exporting pop culture and entertainment worldwide. Furthermore, it now boasts one of the highest life expectancies in the world.[44] Despite its huge success, it has acquired new problems that old Korea did not have. The first issue is lack of care for the elderly. Filial piety—caring for one's parents both emotionally and physically—has been largely considered as one of the most important traditional values in Korea. A recent study showed that "fewer Koreans believe that grown-up children should be responsible emotionally and financially to care for

---

42. Kim and Kim, *History of Korean Christianity*, 44–48.

43. Kim and Kim, *History of Korean Christianity*, 93–99; Lee, "Korean Pentecost," 73–83.

44. Kim, *Korean Culture and Society*, 3–5.

their aging parents."⁴⁵ Another study revealed that 48.6 percent of South Korea's elderly citizens aged over sixty-five were living in poverty (defined as earning 50 percent or less of median household income) in 2011.⁴⁶ The second issue is the rising suicide rate, which has risen drastically in the past two decades. As Youna Kim reports, "Korea has the highest suicide rate (29.1 per 100,000 persons) among the OECD countries, outpacing Hungary and Japan, and this rate is more than twice the OECD average of 12.5 per 100,000 persons (OECD 2016)." She explains, "The sudden rise of suicides since the late 1990s is viewed as a by-product of Korea's rapid industrialization, educational competition, and familial expectations and social pressures to succeed in this hyper-competitive society."⁴⁷ The third issue is the falling birth rate. In 2022, South Korea's birth rate fell to 0.81 births per woman, down from 0.84 the previous year. Following six consecutive years of decline, it is the world's lowest fertility rate.⁴⁸ Despite its economic and cultural development, according to the Better Life Index published by the Organization for Economic Cooperation and Development, South Korea now ranks as one of the unhappiest countries among the developed countries in the world.⁴⁹

South Korean society perfectly demonstrates the benefits and perils of globalization. Within just a few decades, it has emerged from perpetual poverty and advanced as a modern society by following the political and economic model of the United States. The problem, however, is that while embracing modernity and pursuing its promise of material riches and comforts, South Korean people have abandoned their old traditions and values without discernment. They have forgotten how to live in a collective community by taking care of others, especially their own parents. Korea will now have to turn to the Majority World to rediscover and reclaim parts of its cultural heritage that aligns with the teachings of Christ. According to Reverend Syngman Rhee, who served as the moderator of the General Assembly of the Presbyterian Church (USA), new

45. Lee, "Fewer Koreans Feel Responsible," para. 1.
46. McCurry, "South Korea's Inequality Paradox."
47. Kim, *Korean Culture and Society*, 10. The Organization for Economic Cooperation and Development (OECD) is an intergovernmental organization with thirty-eight member countries that are committed to democracy and market-based economy. It is a forum providing a platform to compare policy experiences, seek answers to common problems, identify good practices, and coordinate domestic and international policies of its members.
48. Mao, "South Korea Records."
49. Choi, "S. Korea among Unhappiest Countries."

insights over the past century reveal that third world churches have much to offer the church in the more developed world. In the midst of human suffering, they have received the gift of faith to overcome their tribulations through the power and inspiration of the Holy Spirit.[50] Under the teachings of the Western missionaries, Korea has learned how to be saved as individuals, grow as disciples, and go out as missionaries. Despite their population having grown to a total of 17,000 Protestant churches and 3,000 Catholic churches, Korean Christians must accept that their society has not been renewed by the gospel. By chasing the benefits of globalization, South Korea has become a highly competitive society in nearly every aspect. From kindergartners to housewives, people of all ages, genders, and social status center their lives around building a competitive edge to become rich. However, despite unparalleled economic success, poverty is far from being eradicated. Living in a society that leaves little sympathy for individuals who are not financially successful, those who become losers in globalization are left behind to suffer in social isolation.[51]

Korea became divided at the end of World War II in 1945, due to many factors beyond its control. Although South Korea has benefited from the Western political and economic system, following the path of rigid and hostile ideological battle against North Korea ultimately prevented the reunification of Korea. As the first generation of Korean Christians, the first Korean president, Syngman Rhee, and the independence movement depended heavily on the United States to solve Korea's problem. Their prayers, political lobbying, and social activism did not bring the outcome they had hoped for.[52] It is now up to the new generation of Christians and peacemakers to depend on God and find a way to reconcile the divided country. Kim explains the problem of the Korean church's historical response:

> The Christian attitude toward the Communist North and the Korean War was that the war was the result of the Communist aggression and this need to be responded with decisive force and vigour, on the one hand, and with prayer and mission toward the people of North Korea, on the other. This response was particularly common since many of the senior leadership of the churches in the South were those who had escaped from persecution by the communist regime in the North during the war

---

50. AIB Spiritual Journey, "Rev. Dr. Syngman Rhee."
51. Jo and Walker, "Social Isolation and Poverty," 175–87.
52. Fields, *Foreign Friends*, 169–74.

and also because, on this issue, the conservative sections of the Christian church and the military-backed government shared same attitude toward the communist government in the North. They believed regime change was the ultimate solution for peace and stability, and co-existence with communist North was not an option. So, in this understanding, the evangelisation of North Korea was understood as prior to unification.[53]

This rigid and hostile attitude toward North Korea did not achieve anything significant. For North and South Koreans to be reconciled as one nation, they will need the help of Christians from the Majority World to develop a new attitude that can heal the deep wounds caused by societal injustice. The ethical failure of globalization is an opportunity for Korean Christians to turn to Jesus Christ and his uncompromising ethics for building a free and just society. Kim emphasizes that an important step was taken when the Korean National Council of Churches declared 1995 as the year of Jubilee. It was "the proclamation of the liberation of the Korean people from the bondage of ideological hegemony, and from political systems which hinder the formation of a common community."[54] When the communists in North Korea recognize that South Korea is sincerely working toward building a just world, they will abandon their false ideology. If North and South Koreans can be reconciled as one in Christ and become a free, just, and prosperous country, they will bear a powerful testimony for the rest of the world, which remains in division and hatred. The reunification of Korea and the flourishing of its renewed society can become a precious cultural treasure the Korean people can give to the world.

According to theologian Timothy Tennent, "Despite the growth of Majority World Christianity and the corresponding decline in the vitality of Western Christianity, there remains the view that Western theological writings and reflection somehow represent normative, universal Christian reflection whereas non-Western theology is more localized, ad hoc, and contextual."[55] There is, however, no single systematic theology that can be upheld as universally adequate for all Christians. Tennent explains: "The basic problem is that Western systematic theologies are still written with a Christendom mind-set, assuming the absence of rival theistic claims as well as rival sacred texts. They tend to be overly preoccupied

---

53. Kim, "Future Shape of Christianity," 76.
54. Kim, "Future Shape of Christianity," 77.
55. Tennent, *Theology in the Context*, 11.

with philosophical objections to the Christian message, rather than with religious objections based on sacred texts or major social traditions that contract the claims of Scripture."[56] Tennent also warns against the fragmentation of theology by embracing the notion that globalization and diversity within the church mean that all local people should have their own indigenous theology, such as India's *dalit* theology and Korea's *minjung* theology.[57] This approach perpetuates the idea that indigenous theologies are ancillary subsets of Western theology. He further adds that "every authentic theology must not only celebrate the insights of its own particularity, but also reflect a universalizing quality that expresses the catholicity shared by all Christians everywhere."[58]

Globalizing theology must go a step beyond the method of contextualization, harmonizing and unifying what each culture has discovered for God's glory without weakening the essential elements of the gospel. Theology in the age of globalization must find a way to turn from the homogenizing tendencies of the West and learn to use the force of cultural diversity, which can fill what is lacking in the evangelization of the entire world. Today, at least five billion people remain as unevangelized, and it may be that the present formulation of theology is limiting the potential of the gospel to save more people, especially those in the Arab nations.

ETHICS OF GOD'S KINGDOM FOR HUMANITY

Providing the ethics of God's kingdom to the world involves introducing Jesus Christ as the Savior and Lord who loves sinners and demands the whole life of those who believe in him. Christian ethics is not about following a list of rules; rather, it is an issue of heart. A new conscience of spirituality and morality is implanted on the hearts of those who believe the gospel of Jesus Christ and become God's children (Jer 31:33). They are led by the Spirit of God to live in a way that is pleasing to God (Rom 8:2–14). Jesus affirmed that all the demands of the law are met by loving God and one's neighbor (Matt 22:37–40). The purpose of theology is to help the ordinary people of this world understand the gospel so they can give their whole life to God as a living sacrifice. To lead humanity toward

---

56. Tennent, *Theology in the Context*, 257.
57. Tennent, *Theology in the Context*, 263.
58. Tennent, *Theology in the Context*, 264.

knowing Christ, Christians must take the path of engagement that responds to the issues raised by the globalized world with empathy.

In the age of globalization, the only viable way for the church to understand the cultural changes arising from diverse peoples, nations, and civilizations is through dialogue, which allows all voices to be heard and evaluated by those who participate in the public sphere. For Christians, the purpose of engaging in dialogue with others is to reveal God's love and truth to the unbelieving world. As previously mentioned, this is seemingly an uncertain process that naturally leads toward cultural or moral relativism. The other options are totalitarianism and sectarianism, both of which this study rejects as possible solutions. When Christians pursue dialogue with others while possessing full conviction of biblical truth and sincere compassion for all people, there is no need to fear the final outcome of globalization.

According to Stanford philosophers John Perry and Ken Taylor, the primary philosophical problem of our age is understanding what constitutes "global justice."[59] What new principles of justice will help the world manage distinctively twenty-first-century problems, such as environmental preservation, while enabling poorer nations to improve their standards of living? Closely related to the problem of global justice, the world is desperately seeking a new basis for shared values that will bring its people together rather than tear them apart. Another pressing issue is finding a new basis for "social identification." In a world in which distant and powerful forces—not answerable to local communities—shape so much of our lives, how can we sustain local communities with which we identify? Is this the time to abandon the idea of local community and embrace the concept of "global citizenship"? There is also a great need to find new models of collective decision making and collective rationality. This problem became all too evident in the recent global pandemic as nations, communities, and individuals made wide-ranging responses to mitigate the spread of COVID-19. Solving the problems of the twenty-first century will require coordinated rational action on a massive scale. The philosophers admit that we have no models of "collective rationality," no idea of the institutional, social, political, and economic structures that will allow us to overcome these challenges.

---

59. This paragraph highlights the dialogue between the philosophers at Stanford University, their guests, and the listeners in a radio program. Philosophy Talk, "Move Over Letterman."

Without a judge to determine the right course of action, the world is conflicted between virtue and freedom. According to philosopher Michael Sandel, "The conviction that justice involves virtue as well as choice runs deep. Thinking about justice seems inescapably to engage us in thinking about the best way to live."[60] Christians believe that in Christ, humanity has both freedom and virtue to live in the world as God's agents by demonstrating his love, truth, justice, and righteousness. In response to the problems raised by globalization, Christians must reflect on God's promise to give humanity a new future. Isaiah 2:2–4 prophetically describes how the nations will climb the highest of the mountains and come together into Jerusalem to discover the ethics of God's kingdom:

> It shall come to pass in the latter days that the mountain of the house of the LORD shall be established as the highest of the mountains, and shall be lifted up above the hills; and all the nations shall flow to it, and many peoples shall come, and say: "Come, let us go up to the mountain of the LORD, to the house of the God of Jacob, that he may teach us his ways and that we may walk in his paths." For out of Zion shall go the law, and the word of the LORD from Jerusalem. He shall judge between the nations, and shall decide disputes for many peoples. . . . Nation shall not lift up sword against nation, neither shall they learn war anymore.

"The mountain of the house the LORD," "Zion," and "Jerusalem" can be interpreted as the true religion among many religions. When nations seek love, truth, justice, and righteousness, they will become ready to hear the gospel and learn to live in accordance with the ethics of God's kingdom. God's people who already believe in Jesus as the Savior and live in obedience to his word are the ones who know the truth; therefore, they will judge the world with him (1 Cor 6:2).

CHRISTIAN ENGAGEMENT WITH GLOBALIZATION

God's truth revealed in Scripture can provide the definitive answers that humanity needs to resolve the issues of globalization. How then should Christians interact with secularists and other religious adherents in a pluralistic society? Paul exemplified how the gospel can be preached while

---

60. Sandel, *Justice*, 10.

respecting the traditions, beliefs, and values of others (Acts 17:22–31). Christians must have full conviction in their salvation by knowing and trusting Jesus Christ. They must believe in God's promise to give his wisdom and insight to his children who are called to be the lights in this world. On the other hand, they must also realize that God has revealed certain aspects of his truth to all humanity; therefore, Christians can also learn about the world from others. Christians must work toward bringing all the knowledge of this world under the lordship of Jesus Christ. The church's constructive engagement with globalization should lead the people of this world to believe the gospel and prepare their spiritual and moral life for the consummation of God's kingdom on earth. Theologians should enter their respective public spheres of influence to offer biblical insights that are lacking in the current state of understanding globalization. To introduce the ethics of God's kingdom in a globalized world, theologians must enter into dialogue with various academic disciplines, as well as other religious traditions.

The Cape Town Commitment is a statement of shared biblical convictions produced by the Third Lausanne Congress of World Evangelization held at Cape Town, South Africa, in October 2010. Over 4,000 Christian leaders from 198 countries gathered to discuss critical issues of the time as they related to the church and evangelization. In seeking a fresh way for Christians to be faithful to the biblical message but also respectful and sensitive to others, Netland draws the following five principles based on the Commitment:

1. *Bearing witness to the gospel of Jesus Christ among religious others is not optional, but rather is obligatory for the Christian church.* Thus, The Cape Town Commitment begins by stating, "We remain committed to the task of bearing worldwide witness to Jesus Christ and all his teaching."

2. *Christians are to bear witness to the gospel in accordance with God's love.* The Cape Town Commitment eloquently says, "The mission of God flows from the love of God. The mission of God's people flows from our love for God and for all that God loves."

3. *Christian witness must be respectful of others and be conducted with humility and moral integrity.* The Cape Town Commitment distinguishes evangelism from proselytizing and calls for humble and respectful witness that is "scrupulously ethical."

4. *Christian witness should include appropriate forms of interreligious dialogue.* Thus, The Cape Town Commitment calls for "the proper place for dialogue with people of other faiths," a dialogue that "combines confidence in the uniqueness of Christ and the truth of the gospel with respectful listening to others."

5. *Christians are to reject violence and the abuse of power in witness.* Christians must give careful attention to the perceived and real relationship between witness and power. Physical violence is surely unacceptable, yet the abuse of power can also include psychological, social, economic, or political forms of manipulation or coercion. Religious violence and abuse of power often are found in cases of ethnic conflict, when religious identity becomes enmeshed with ethnicity. The Cape Town Commitment confesses past Christian involvement in such conflicts.[61]

In the twenty-first century, applying these principles in engaging with globalization can enable Christians to become peacemakers in the world. The prescription of the principles can lead to ending violent conflicts occurring between Christians and Muslims, especially in Africa and Asia.[62] Rather than simply aiming to outgrow Islam through competitive evangelism, Christians can learn to live together with Muslims within the same continent, country, city, and community. In Europe and North America, Christians need to pursue constructive dialogue with secularists and diverse religious adherents. In Latin America, Protestants and Catholics can learn to ameliorate their social and political conflict.[63] The role of religion in renewing globalization is to preach the gospel and promote God's kingdom to grow and permeate throughout society. Christians can help all people to know Christ and lead them in developing the ethics of God's kingdom, which would unite humanity as one in Christ. At the coming of Christ, the religion that accomplishes human solidarity will be recognized universally as the true religion.

---

61. Netland, *Christianity and Religious Diversity*, 234–42.

62. Griswold, *Tenth Parallel*. Investigative journalist Griswold has spent seven years traveling between the equator and the tenth parallel in Africa and Asia, and reports the violent religious conflicts in Nigeria, Sudan, Somalia, Indonesia, Malaysia, and The Philippines.

63. Pew Research Center, "Christianity and Conflict."

5

Theological Attitudes toward Globalization

THE CHURCH EXHIBITS FOUR prevalent theological attitudes toward the cultural realities arising from globalization:[1] (1) avoidance, (2) condemnation and resistance, (3) control and domination, and (4) engagement. This chapter surveys these theological attitudes and explains how Christians from various theological circles have identified with each of them. It demonstrates that these attitudes are drawn from diverse interpretations of Scripture, which are rooted in one's traditions and values. In addition, the chapter argues that the renewal of globalization requires the church to administer God's grace and peace with the attitude of engagement, which is characterized by mercy and love. All Christians can influence globalization by engaging with its cultural realities through dialogue and empathy. As Christians become involved in solving worldly problems as Christ's witnesses, unbelievers can readily recognize the reign of Christ and accept God's work of creating, redeeming, and sanctifying the world. If the church lacks the attitude of engagement regarding the problems of globalization, its theology will stagnate and become powerless in administering God's grace and peace in the world.

---

1. Cultural realities are manifestation of the common beliefs and values of a particular culture.

AVOIDANCE

Among Christians, the attitude of avoidance is the most widespread response to globalization. According to Myers, "with the exception of some within the Christian academy who think we need to resist globalization, the larger Christian community seems to be ignoring globalization or fearing it."[2] Ignorance of globalization results from deep trust in liberal governments and their agencies; those who have this trust believe democratically elected leaders and public officials are making good decisions that will benefit humanity. Fear and apathy go hand in hand: apathy toward globalization results from the fear of facing the newly emerging cultural realities and addressing the colossal challenges that accompany them. Among the various theological circles, evangelical Christians in the United States generally seem to have avoided addressing the challenges of globalization at the turn of the millennium. Throughout the 1990s and 2000s, most Christians in evangelical churches and academies were not interested in knowing about the cultural realities that were unfolding in the world at the time. Although globalization was well underway by the turn of the millennium, theological students and faculty members within various schools of the evangelical tradition seemingly were neither informed nor concerned about the controversies that globalization was causing in society.

The tribulations of globalization first became evident in the southeastern corner of Europe, in the Balkans. The Yugoslav Wars began after Slovenia seceded from the federation of Yugoslavia on June 25, 1991. Against the trend of globalization, which aimed for nations to become economically integrated, there emerged a rash of violent ethnic and religious conflicts throughout the state. Since World War II, Yugoslavia had enjoyed relative prosperity under the communist regime of Josip Broz Tito; however, from September 1989 to June 1991, Yugoslavia regressed from its status as the most progressive socialist country in Europe and gradually underwent a process of disintegration.[3] According to Karen Talbot, "Yugoslavia was a victim of the worldwide process of capital restructuring and profit maximization."[4] She explains that the economic destabilization of Yugoslavia began in the 1980s with IMF and World Bank structural adjustment programs (SAPs). After striving to comply with the

---

2. Myers, *Engaging Globalization*, 4.
3. Hayden, "Yugoslavia's Collapse," 1377.
4. Talbot, "Real Reasons for War," 99.

market reforms imposed by the IMF and World Bank, the Yugoslav government resisted those reforms, including the drive to privatize all public enterprises. Workers protested the reforms through mass strikes, and President Borisav Jović, who headed the government from 1990 to 1991, opposed the devastating austerity measures due to the economic havoc they were wreaking on the people. Among others, Slobodan Milošević, who was the president of the Republic of Serbia at the time, backed Jović in that stance.[5] According to Talbot, this was the "unpardonable sin" that led to further destabilization and the dismemberment of Yugoslavia. In response to this "stubbornness" by Yugoslavia, the US Congress passed the 1991 Foreign Operations Appropriations Law 101–513, abruptly cutting off all aid, credits, and loans to Yugoslavia. It also demanded separate elections in each of the six republics comprising Yugoslavia.[6] Severe sanctions were implemented for seven years as Yugoslavia was declared a "terrorist state," along with Cuba, Iraq, North Korea, Iran, the Sudan, and Syria.[7]

The West, led by the United States, had a compelling justification for condemning Yugoslavia. In 1992, the Bosnian Serbs (or the Bosnian Orthodox Christians) were accused of conducting ethnic cleansing against the Bosnian Muslims. The Serbian Chetniks—a resistance movement against Nazi Germany during World War II—were led by General Ratko Mladić to retaliate against the Croatian Ustaše, which was a rival resistance movement that blended fascism, Roman Catholicism, and nationalism. The Croatian Ustaše promoted ethnic Muslims as a constituent people of Croatia alongside Catholics while Serbian Chetniks viewed them as historical enemies of Orthodox Christians.[8] The bitter rivalry between these two nationalist movements resulted in the genocide of the Bosnian Muslims after the Bosnian Serbs were incited to violence by the rhetoric and political action of Milošević. The genocide was first uncovered by a few journalists working in the field, but Western government officials were slow to acknowledge the problem and unwilling to act in response to the humanitarian crisis.[9] Making political calculations, both the European and American governmental leaders were hesitant to take

---

5. Talbot, "Real Reasons for War," 103–4.
6. Talbot, "Real Reasons for War," 104.
7. Talbot, "Real Reasons for War," 107.
8. Elzarka, "Role of Religion," 32.
9. Halberstam, *War in Time of Peace*, 128–31.

the lead in solving the colossal problem of ethnic and religious hatred, which was inflamed by globalization.[10]

The United Nations Protection Force (UNPROFOR) were largely ineffective in limiting the violence by implementing the policy of being impartial peacekeepers, demonstrating the weaknesses and indecisiveness of the member nations.[11] At Strebrenica, a Bosnian village near the eastern border with Serbia under the protection of the UN troops, more than 7,000 Muslim men of all ages were executed in cold blood.[12] Meanwhile, American Christians largely remained detached from the humanitarian crisis caused by the ethnic and religious conflicts of Yugoslavia. With the failure of UNPROFOR and without any meaningful action taken by Christians, the United States finally established a policy to intervene. The US government, led by the Clinton administration, decided to respond with massive high-technology bombing, simply known as "carpet bombing."[13] On August 30, 1995, the North Atlantic Treaty Organization (NATO) launched Operation Deliberate Force, which became the heaviest bombing in NATO history. Overall, 1,026 bombs were dropped in Bosnia and Herzegovina; nonetheless, collateral damage to civilians was kept to a minimum. On March 24, 1999, Operation Allied Force carried out another aerial bombing campaign under the name of peacekeeping promotion. NATO's justification for the campaign was to bring down Milošević and end his brutalities in Kosovo, which impeded on Albanian self-determination.[14] This time, however, the bombs were dropped in Serbia and Montenegro, with no effort to minimize the collateral damage to civilians.

The tragedy that unfolded in NATO's military campaign speaks for itself. For seventy-eight days, the people of Serbia suffered incessant bombing that destroyed 25,000 houses and apartment buildings; 19 hospitals; 69 schools; 176 cultural monuments, roads, railway tracks, bridges, industrial plants, and private businesses; as well as numerous barracks and military installations. Approximately 500 civilians were killed and around 6,000 wounded as the result of NATO's indiscriminate operation.[15] This was the first time NATO had used military force with-

10. Halberstam, *War in Time of Peace*, 133–34.
11. Halberstam, *War in Time of Peace*, 125–26.
12. Daalder, "Decision to Intervene."
13. Halberstam, *War in Time of Peace*, 294–331.
14. Bobinac, "Disintegration of Yugoslavia," 10.
15. Zivanovic and Haxhiaj, "78 Days of Fear"; Voon, "Pointing the Finger," 1085; Hudson and Bowman, *After Yugoslavia*, 30.

out the consent of the UN Security Council, triggering debates over the legitimacy of the intervention. Political scientist Michael Mandelbaum describes NATO's war against Yugoslavia as "a perfect failure," concluding that the Balkans emerged from the war considerably worse off than they had been before, and that the effects of the war damaged the West's relationship with Russia and China.[16] The optimistic belief that the world would become prosperous and peaceful thanks to the governmental agencies and non-governmental organizations of the West had taken a major hit.[17] By the end of the Yugoslav Wars, over 140,000 people were killed, and 4 million others were displaced across the region. The country that was arbitrarily made up in 1918 by the winners of World War I had disintegrated into six separate republics. The tribulation of globalization was just getting started: other wars in Afghanistan, Iraq, Libya, Syria, Yemen, Ukraine, and Palestine would follow.

Meanwhile, most evangelical Christians in the United States were preoccupied with the ministry of preaching the gospel and making disciples in accordance with biblical commands and theological trainings (Rom 1:16; Matt 28:19). There was hardly any interest in the international affairs of the world, namely, how globalization was shaping the economic and geopolitical future. Globalization meant that diverse peoples, nations, and civilizations were being driven to live together in a single society, igniting ethnic and religious conflicts worldwide. Many evangelical theologians, students, and ministers at the time did not see the need to invest substantial time and energy in worldly issues that were unrelated to the objectives of evangelistic ministry or studies. Indeed, the core of evangelical attitudes toward globalization was based on Scripture's exhortation to look forward to the "city that is to come" (Heb 13:14). For many, the New Jerusalem was understood as the city that is to come in the millennial kingdom or the afterlife in heaven. Many believed that Jesus would resolve all the conflicts in the world upon his return. As a result, evangelical Christians in large measure did not see the need to comprehend and engage with the cultural realities that were emerging in the world.

The experts who were closely following social science, economics, and geopolitics knew the world was entering into a new era. In 1981, US President Ronald Reagan signaled the change toward neoliberal policies

---

16. Mandelbaum, "Perfect Failure," 2.

17. For an extensive study on the problems of humanitarian intervention for resolving genocide and ethnic cleansing, see Kuperman, "Moral Hazard," 49–80.

in his inaugural address by declaring that "government is not the solution to our problem, government is the problem." UK Prime Minister Margaret Thatcher, expressing her unwavering commitment to a future based solely on the market, used the slogan "There Is No Alternative." Together, these powerful conservative leaders of the West were claiming that unregulated free market capitalism would alleviate the problems of this world. They promoted an integrated economic system that would come to be known as neoliberalism—global capitalism unrestricted by government regulation of sovereign nation-states. A vast majority of evangelical Christians chose to follow Reagan's idealistic vision of the world, in which the United States would become the preeminent leader of spreading individual liberty and democratic government, thus fostering globalization. As Justin Garrison explains, "Reagan held that the United States had a unique, moral responsibility to advance the global growth of democracy and freedom and that America had a long tradition of pursuing such a foreign policy."[18] Aligning with Reagan's vision, the post-Cold War era was expected to be "the end of history," in which Western liberal democracy and capitalism would triumph as the final ideology of humanity. Many evangelical Christians believed the US government was doing its utmost to achieve and maintain world peace, and that it was their duty to save the lost souls until the return of Christ.

Throughout the 1980s and 1990s, protectionist measures used by the nation-states were brought down by new international trade agreements. In response, there was significant civil society mobilization against globalization, culminating in a violent protest against the World Trade Organization Ministerial Conference at Seattle in 1999. The protesters were angry about the increased unemployment among US workers caused by cheap labor from China, the outsourcing of polluting activities to poor countries, unsafe imports ranging from food to toys, poor working conditions in other countries, and global capitalism in general.[19] At the time, however, evangelical Christians showed little interest in the problems of globalization, and discussion of these issues among members of the local church and academia was scarce. The lack of interest in the social, political, and economic issues of globalization among evangelical Christians was rooted in ignorance.

---

18. Garrison, "Covenant with All Mankind," 36.
19. Smith, "Dark Side of Globalization."

Christians who ignore the problems of globalization believe that they are following the Scripture, which says "set your minds on things that are above, not on things that are on earth" (Col 3:2). From early on, Christian ascetics had disengaged their life from this world in search of the heavenly realm. Francis Schaeffer describes this problem as the "nature and grace" dichotomy. It means that the realm of grace belonged to God the Creator, pertaining to heaven and heavenly things, whereas the realm of nature belonged to the created, relating to earth and earthly things. In pursuit of the realm of grace, most evangelicals in the twentieth century separated themselves from engagement with the realm of nature.[20] Schaeffer argues that Christians must not only live in the realm of grace and remain satisfied by one's salvation but also have compassion for the secular people, who are in despair for lacking meaning in life. In the age of modernity, secular humanists have disallowed people in the modern world from hearing any communication from "the God who is there."[21] Schaeffer's most important contribution to the evangelical church was his constant reminder that Christians must not ignore secular people's deep anguish of losing their spiritual and moral sense. He was one of the few voices exhorting evangelical Christians to engage with secular culture by observing its cultural indicators in this world.

The term *apathy* comes from the Greek word *apatheia*, which is made up of two words: *a*, meaning "without," and *pathos*, meaning "suffering." German feminist theologian Dorothee Soelle defines apathy as "a social condition in which people are so dominated by the goal of avoiding suffering that it becomes a goal to avoid human relationships and contacts altogether."[22] Due to the fear of dealing with the enormously complicated problems of the world, Christian engagement with globalization remains almost non-existent in many churches. Myers suggests three broad reasons why most Christians fear globalization. First, globalization as a topic seems too big and complicated for Christians, too involved with economics, technology, and politics. Second, Christians have socially accepted their relegation to the private realm of spiritual things, leaving the world of economics, politics, and technology to the West's materialists and secular humanism. Third, having lost confidence

---

20. Schaeffer, *Complete Works*, 1:209.
21. Schaeffer, *Complete Works*, 1:47. Schaeffer's expression "the God who is there" captures his apologetic theme that a personal God is present in this world, and he communicates to people through verbal proposition.
22. Soelle, *Suffering*, 36.

while living in a post-Christian world, Christians are unsure if they have anything to offer at the public table when it comes to assessing and engaging with globalization.[23]

This attitude of avoidance stems from Christian authorities that do not see the need to train their ministers and leaders in engaging with contemporary culture. Brian McLaren explains that his generation of Christian leadership did not recognize the cultural shift of the mid-1990s, while young Generation X Christians were grappling with the reality of living in postmodern culture. In other words, the older generation of Christian leaders were ignoring the complex issues of postmodernity, whereas their younger counterparts were saying, "This is our world, and this is the future. And the Christian faith and our individual churches, we've got to engage with and deal with it."[24] According to Stanley Grenz, "Postmoderns look beyond reason to nonrational ways of knowing, conferring heightened status on the emotions and intuition."[25] He explains that postmodern people view the world holistically. Rejecting the Enlightenment ideal of the dispassionate, autonomous, rational individual, they instead embrace a wider realm of nature (the ecosystem) and community (the social dimension of existence).[26] Grenz adds, "They believe that truth consists in the ground rules that facilitate personal well-being in community and the well-being of the community as a whole."[27] In other words, individuals are embedded in community, and there is no contradiction between individual and collective human needs. The problems of globalization have uncovered the flaws of liberal and individualistic society that evangelical Christians often ignore, including the degradation of the environment and the marginalization of the poor.

Evangelicalism in the twentieth century was built on the pillars of rationalism and the correspondence theory of truth, not just on Scripture.[28] Conservative theologians consequently oppose postmoderns

---

23. Myers, *Engaging Globalization*, 5.

24. McLaren, "Brian McLaren Extended Interview," para. 6. McLaren explains his experience of pastoring the new converts in his church who did not grow up in a church environment. For the first time in his life, he heard from them about the issues of life that were different from those who grew up in a fundamentalist church environment.

25. Grenz, *Primer on Postmodernism*, 14.

26. Grenz, *Primer on Postmodernism*, 14.

27. Grenz, *Primer on Postmodernism*, 14.

28. Stanley, *Global Diffusion of Evangelicalism*, 121–39. Stanley explains the legacy of the Enlightenment on evangelical apologetics by surveying the works of Cornelius Van Til, Edward J. Carnell, Carl F. H. Henry, and Francis A. Schaeffer.

who reject the certainty of truth and the existence of universal truth. Although defending the biblical truth is an important issue, Christians must realize that contemporary culture has changed to embrace a holistic worldview. To many people, the welfare of their community now matters more than the doctrines that can save individual souls. This cultural shift means people now value a holistic gospel that includes evangelism and social responsibility.[29] Rational presentation of the gospel with correct theological doctrine is often insufficient to convert unbelievers to Christianity. Many people in the world now care about the planet Earth and the marginalized people, both of which have become vulnerable to predatory economic practices of large corporations with a global impact. Millennials and Generation Z adults in particular want to see that Christians care about the environment and the underprivileged.[30]

Christians have fallen behind in adjusting to the new cultural realities of globalization. According to Indian theologian J. Paul Rajashekar, although new curriculums have been introduced and improvements made, some significant issues still need to be addressed for theological education in North America to be responsive to global realities.[31] In 2005, Catholic theologian Robert Schreiter identified four global flows: liberation, feminism, ecology, and human rights. These four flows, in his view, are important universal concerns that transcend geographical and cultural boundaries. In addition to this list, Rajashekar identifies inter-religious/intercultural engagement as another important theme that has emerged in a globalized world.[32] In Africa and Asia, religious conflicts between Christians and Muslims have turned violent. In Myanmar, the Buddhists and Muslims have faced genocide. The Muslims in Pakistan and Hindus in India have been on the brink of war, with both countries possessing nuclear weapons. The bombings and killings between the Jews and the Palestinians have no end in sight. From a secular perspective, the Borgen Project identifies the most pressing problems of today as follows: (1) poverty, (2) religious conflicts and war, (3) political polarization, (4) government accountability, (5) education, (6) food and water, (7) health in developing nations, (8) credit access, (9) discrimination, and (10) physical fitness (obesity).[33]

29. Ferris, "Gen Z, Let's Prioritize."
30. Meehan, "Next Generation"; Tyson et al., "Gen Z, Millennials Stand Out."
31. Rajashekar, "Theological Education."
32. Rajashekar, "Theological Education."
33. Singh, "Top 10 Biggest Issues."

Poverty is closely related to the global problems of drugs and violence. One of the most urgent problems with which evangelical churches in the United States have not engaged is the Mexican drug war. The Council on Foreign Relations reports on this issue as follows:

> Mexican drug cartels are leading suppliers of cocaine, heroin, methamphetamine, and other illicit narcotics to the United States.... Mexican authorities have been waging a deadly battle against drug cartels for more than a decade, but with limited success. Thousands of Mexicans—including politicians, students, and journalists—die in the conflict every year. The country has seen more than 431,000 homicides since 2006, when the government declared war on the cartels. The United States has partnered closely with its southern neighbor in this fight, providing Mexico with billions of dollars to modernize its security forces, reform its judicial system, and fund development projects aimed at curbing migration at Mexico's southern border. Washington has also sought to stem the flow of illegal drugs into the United States by bolstering security and monitoring operations along its border with Mexico.[34]

Despite these efforts by the governments, the situation had not improved on either side of the border. In his book *The Dope: The Real History of the Mexican Drug Trade* (2021), historian Benjamin Smith documents a century of drug war investigations and arrests. He uncovers the origin of the illegal drug trade between the United States and Mexico and describes how this illicit business essentially built modern Mexico, affecting everything from agriculture to medicine to economics. He explains the complicated dynamics that drive the current drug war violence and explores corruption on both sides of the border. Although the drug cartels are often blamed as the villains, the economic and political forces driving the enormous drug business are equally significant in both countries. Corrupt politicians play a huge role in protecting and profiting from drug trafficking. Simply put, the problem persists due to the insatiable demand for drugs in the United States and the extensive poverty in Mexico.[35] The government agencies have difficulty solving the widespread problems such as illegal drug operation or human trafficking because they are deeply rooted in humanity's sin. Christians have the ultimate resource to get to the bottom of these issues by eradicating the power of

---

34. CFR.org Editors, "Mexico's Long War," paras. 1–3.
35. Smith, *Dope*.

sin through the gospel. But why should the world hear the gospel from Christians who do not care about their problems?

The attitude of avoidance can form when Christians develop a strong disinterest in this world due to their deep sensitivity of its corruption. It can be found in Christians with strong spiritual and moral values who face insurmountable challenges within corrupt society. In contrast to Christians who believe that much of the world cannot be renewed because its people and institutions are corrupted by sin and evil, secular humanists believe that all worldly problems can be solved through progress in science, reason, and humanism.[36] In Gen 19, Lot lived in a sinful city, representing Christians who are powerless to renew corrupt society. While living in Sodom and Gomorrah, "Lot was a righteous man who was tormented in his soul by the wickedness he saw and heard day after day" (2 Pet 2:8 NLT). Although Lot himself was commended for his righteousness, he was unable to influence society and bring about a renewal. He lived in constant fear of the wicked people in society. This state of powerlessness against the evils of this world applies to many Christians who find comfort in God's promise to save them on the day of his judgment yet lack the courage to face the problems of globalization.

John Stott argues against those Christians who do not see the need to engage the world regarding social issues: "In the end there are only two possible attitudes which Christians can adopt towards the world. One is escape and the other is engagement." He explains that escape means turning our backs on the world in rejection and washing our hands of it. By contrast, engagement means turning our faces toward the world in compassion and getting our hands dirty, sore, and worn in its service.[37] Caleb Kaltenbach is at the forefront of helping Christian organizations and churches develop influence with LGBTQ+ individuals without sacrificing their theological convictions. He says, "Toxic fear always diverts us from Jesus's mission: loving people well. It prevents us from embracing anyone unlike us or engaging in complicated situations. Fear can provoke us to ask unhelpful questions, such as 'What's at stake if we engage?'" He adds that Christians are often focused on "what we might potentially lose instead of what God and others stand to lose. It reveals our fixation on personal loses rather than on what others might gain."[38] Instead, we should ask what refusing to engage might cause us to lose. Jesus answered

36. Pinker, *Enlightenment Now*, 322–453.
37. Stott and Wyatt, *Issues Facing Christians Today*, 26.
38. Kaltenbach, *Messy Truth*, 11–12.

this question by explaining to his disciples that "there will be more joy in heaven over one sinner who repents than over ninety-nine righteous persons who need no repentance" (Luke 15:7). Christians must realize that God's work of creation and redemption is at stake if the world perishes in sin.

Since the beginning of Christianity, the desire to live far away from the world's corruption has led devoted Christians to hide away in the deserts, caves, and monasteries. Today, many Christians may be living in a similar situation by enclosing themselves within their church, ministry, or academia. While these institutions are necessary and beneficial for developing disciples, ministers, and missionaries, Christians must ask themselves if they will be returning to global society with the power to save and heal. Do they have the message of salvation as well as the compassion to heal this world? Can they give the gospel to the world as well as bind people's physical wounds and provide for their material needs? The parable of the good Samaritan told by Jesus teaches the lesson that in order to inherit eternal life, Christians must not avoid looking at their neighbors who are hurting but must instead obey God's commandment of love (Luke 10:25–37). In a globalized world, living in avoidance of sin, corruption, and evil is impossible. Today, the world with all of its problems is coming to the Christians living in the West. The world is coming not only into their neighborhoods and churches, but into their homes through the Internet and smartphones. Thus, Christians have no choice but to engage with the problems of globalization and help the world gain deliverance from sin, corruption, and evil.

CONDEMNATION AND RESISTANCE

The second theological attitude toward globalization is condemnation and resistance. It is based on seeing globalization as being driven by a false ideology, namely, neoliberalism. It judges globalization as a modern phenomenon of capitalist greed that has occurred since the end of the Cold War. This critical view is found among adherents of all religions.[39] Within Christianity, it is widely held by the antiglobalist ecumenical circles that include the World Council of Churches, the World Reformed Alliance, and the Lutheran World Federation.[40] It is also widely held

---

39. Beyer, "Globalization and Religion," 3498.
40. Stackhouse, *Globalization and Grace*, 5.

by the sectarian, pietistic, or monastic communities within the Roman Catholic Church, the Eastern Orthodox Church, and Protestant circles.[41] Their response of criticism and rebuke stems from the belief that economic and social norms associated with globalization are in conflict with the ethical principles of Christ. They recognize globalization as at once a largely economic, imperialistic, and homogenizing process of the secular West. Peruvian liberationist theologian Gustavo Gutiérrez says that "globalization as it is now being carried out exacerbates the unjust inequalities among different sectors of humanity and the social, economic, political, and cultural exclusion of a good portion of the world's population."[42]

This view of criticism against globalization generally understands it to be driven by the spirit of Babel, which means that autonomous humanity has collectively rebelled against its creator. Bauckham explains that humanity's rebellion, which is portrayed in the enigmatic story of the Tower of Babel, pursues economic prosperity at the expense of upholding social justice.[43] By contrast, says Bauckham, "The Bible has one economic preoccupation," which is "the plight of the poorest, the truly destitute."[44] According to Walter Brueggemann, the church has been "mostly silent in the face of a predatory economy that reduces many persons to second-class humanity."[45] David Fraser summarizes the verdict of those who condemn globalization:

> The foundations of global capitalism are irredeemably rooted in humanistic ideals of self-sufficiency. The global village is simply a much larger arena for greed and oppression. The governing dynamic produces gross inequality (within and between nations), sustains high levels of tragic poverty and marginalizes the weak. It embodies the principalities and powers of injustice, self-interest and the hegemony of corporatist agents who are unaccountable for concrete suffering. It offers the allure of abundance while destroying the earthly basis that produces that abundance and sustains all life. It promises life while spreading global arms and war into every corner of the globe.[46]

---

41. Dreher, *Benedict Option*, 7–20; Hunter, *To Change the World*, 150–55.
42. Gutiérrez, "Memory and Prophecy," 32.
43. Bauckham, *Bible in the Contemporary World*, 51, 66–67.
44. Bauckham, *Bible in the Contemporary World*, 68.
45. Brueggemann, *Money and Possessions*, xxi.
46. Fraser, "Globalization," 340.

Throughout Scripture, God's kingdom is characterized by justice, in sharp contrast to the modern world forged by globalization (Deut 16:20; Isa 61:8–9; Zech 7:9; Mic 6:8; Luke 11:42; Heb 10:30). Groody explains that the kingdom of this world has grown rich and powerful at the expense of the poor and weak. He attacks the new world system of globalization previously described by Thomas Friedman, refuting Friedman's promotion of interpreting the world through the framework of globalization, an ultra-competitive winner-takes-all system. To describe the idolatry of globalization, he coins the term *money-theism*:

> Money-theism deals with the idolization of capital, expressed as the worship of the gods of the marketplace, and is often practiced through the rituals of the stock market and the liturgies of global capitalism. In this system people are measured in terms of their net worth, accumulated possessions, and incomes rather than their human worth, the quality of their character, and their spiritual depth.[47]

Groody replaces Friedman's so-called "super-story of globalization" with the larger story of human beings in relationship with God and each other. He challenges those who are ambivalent toward or supportive of globalization to reflect on what it means to be human before God. In contrast to Friedman's framework of globalization, which understands salvation almost exclusively in terms of material and economic progress, human beings are made in the image and likeness of God (Gen 1:26–27). One of the primary tasks of theology is to distinguish the God in whose image and likeness we are made from a god of our own making.[48] Groody asserts that justice is administered when we are rightly related to God and to each other and God's creation. Thus, Christianity must oppose the prioritization of the autonomous individual seen in Western society. Groody affirms that "Christianity sees each human life as profoundly interconnected with others in a series of overlapping relationships. . . . People are embedded into God, into self, into others, and into the natural world. These relationships are central to the process of human fulfillment and global transformation."[49] God's kingdom of justice is founded on right relationships, not on financial profits of opportunistic individuals who take advantage of the globalization system.

---

47. Groody, *Globalization, Spirituality, and Justice*, 24.
48. Groody, *Globalization, Spirituality, and Justice*, 24–25.
49. Groody, *Globalization, Spirituality, and Justice*, 25.

For the theologians who oppose globalization, the worldly kingdom of demonic idolatry is spiritually identified as Babylon, and it is bound to receive God's ultimate judgment of destruction (Rev 18:2–3). They are critical of those Christians in affluent countries who have become comfortable living in a Babylon that defies the reign of Christ. They believe Christian resistance to the lures of Babylon must lead to the formation of a spiritual remnant that chooses to administer God's kingdom of justice on the earth. According to Bolivian theologian Mortimer Arias, this new life of radical commitment leads to "the kingdom evangelization." He explains that the arrival of God's kingdom produces a crisis because the coming of Jesus Christ establishes a new order of God's kingdom that has begun to penetrate this world.[50] There is an unbearable tension in Jesus's proclamation of the kingdom. The kingdom has come—and will come. It is "already" and "not yet."[51] God's new order for this world has begun to confront the old order of humanity. His kingdom is forcing its way through the old order, producing a more intense reaction. The kingdom of God "suffers violence" by the reaction of evil forces (Matt 11:12).[52] Jesus's evangelization was confrontational for he denounced collective, institutional, and structural sin.[53] He called for "total commitment, total renunciation, total subordination of all other values and loyalties—including family, possessions, and life—to the demands of the in-breaking kingdom (Luke 14:25–26, 33; cf. Mark 2:31–35; 1:28–30)."[54] Arias concludes, "The annunciation of the kingdom of God demands the denunciation of the kingdoms of men and of powers, which are destroying human life and exploiting creation."[55] The eschatological community of Christians are called to dream with God to deliver the people of this world from their idols. As Arias asserts, "Our evangelism falls short of the mark if we limit ourselves to naming the personal sins and commending the personal virtues without pointing to collective sins, structural powers, and societal trends."[56] Christian resistance against globalization is an intense spiritual warfare aimed at upholding the ethics of God's kingdom in society.

50. Arias, *Announcing the Reign of God*, 42–43.
51. Arias, *Announcing the Reign of God*, 27.
52. Arias, *Announcing the Reign of God*, 42.
53. Arias, *Announcing the Reign of God*, 45.
54. Arias, *Announcing the Reign of God*, 50–52.
55. Arias, *Announcing the Reign of God*, 117.
56. Arias, *Announcing the Reign of God*, 117.

Postmodern and postliberal theologians who resist globalization reject the universal and utopian vision of cosmopolitans: the idea that all human beings, regardless of their political affiliation, are (or can and should be) citizens in a single community. Instead, they align with a communitarian ethic, which emphasizes the importance of social institutions in the development of individual meaning and identity. For them, moral practice and discourse are always rooted within a boundary of community with its own distinctive form of life. Grenz believes that theology is inherently communitarian, asserting that "a central task of theology is to express communal beliefs and values as well as the meaning of the symbols of the faith community. Theological construction has as its goal that of setting forth an understanding of the mosaic of beliefs that lies at the heart of a particular community."[57] James McClendon defines theology as "the discovery, understanding or interpretation, and transformation of the convictions of a convictional community, including the discovery and critical revision of their relation to one another and to whatever else there is."[58] He claims that this definition emphasizes the pluralistic character of theology, its relation to some historical narrative, its rational or scientific nature, and its praxis-related and self-involving character.[59] Thus, he introduces a new kind of systematic theology that begins with the ethics of a local community, rather than universal doctrines that apply to all believers.

Neo-Anabaptist theologians adhere to the ideal of true and authentic New Testament Christianity and the primitive church of the apostolic age. Although the group is small in number, their intellectual fortitude has influenced progressive Christians significantly. Neo-Anabaptists assess that the American church is caught up in a dual allegiance to both Christ and the political economy of liberal democracy and consumer capitalism.[60] The theology of radical orthodoxy expressed by John Milbank, Graham Ward, and Catherine Pickstock holds that capitalism, liberalism, and secularism grow from the roots of metaphysical nominalism, which severs the world from the transcendent. Without any acknowledgment of God, the nominalist world is construed as an enclosed order of fundamental opposition and violence characterized by unregulated competition in the economic sphere and a mitigated possessive individualism in

---

57. Grenz, *Renewing the Center*, 223.
58. McClendon, *Ethics*, 1:23.
59. McClendon, *Ethics*, 1:24.
60. Hunter, *To Change the World*, 150–51.

the political sphere. The world that champions the individual is further restricted by knowledge, a supposedly neutral realm of secular objectivity that marginalizes and privatizes religious voices and identities.[61] Thus, Christians must reject globalization as it oppresses Christian communities and their ethics.

Stanley Hauerwas is a leading voice in developing Christian ethics for the globalized world, criticizing both Christian fundamentalism and liberal Christianity. Hauerwas aims to "reassert the social significance of the church as a distinct society with an integrity peculiar to itself."[62] For Christians, he believes that "their most important social task is nothing less than to be a community capable of hearing the story of God we find in the scripture and living in a manner that is faithful to that story."[63] Rather than simply merging with the secular culture of liberal democracy, Christians should influence the world by being the visible church with the vision and faith in Christ.[64] Hauerwas is especially outspoken in his criticism of the notion that Christians can employ a neutral public language, on the assumption that terms like *justice* and *peace* are understandable from a variety of worldview perspectives. He insists that Christians cannot give meaning to such terms apart from the life and death of Jesus Christ.[65]

When the theological attitude of condemnation and resistance against globalization takes its last step, the result is separatism. In *The Benedict Option*, Rod Dreher calls Western Christians to rethink how to exist as a community in a post-Christian world. He argues that Christians must face the reality of having lost the culture war: "Christians today may think we stand in opposition to secular culture, but in truth we are as much creatures of our own time as secular people are."[66] The influence of secularism has made Christianity devoid of power and life in large.[67] He asserts that "the forces of dissolution from popular culture are too great for individuals or families to resist on their own. We need to embed ourselves in stable communities of faith."[68]

61. Smith, "Radical Orthodoxy," 726.
62. Hauerwas, *Community of Character*, 1.
63. Hauerwas, *Community of Character*, 1.
64. Hauerwas and Willimon, *Resident Aliens*, 46.
65. Mouw, *Challenge of Cultural Discipleship*, 126–27.
66. Dreher, *Benedict Option*, 44.
67. Dreher, *Benedict Option*, 10–12.
68. Dreher, *Benedict Option*, 50.

Dreher recommends that conservative Christians, including evangelicals, Catholics, and Orthodox, make a strategic withdrawal from the world, and unite to strengthen the institutions that remain, such as schools, universities, and families in accordance with biblical values. He is hopeful that if Christians choose to retreat in order to preserve and strengthen the institutions, they can once again stand strong against the influence of the world, as Saint Benedict's monastic communities once accomplished. Dreher says, "If a defining characteristic of the modern world is disorder, then the most fundamental act of resistance is to establish order. If we don't have internal order, we will be controlled by our human passions and by the powerful outside forces who are in greater control of directing liquid modernity's deep currents."[69] Benedict established a community of resistance by installing his Rule, which includes three distinct vows: obedience, stability (fidelity to the same monastic community until death), and conversion of life (dedication to the lifelong work of deepening repentance). The Rule divides each day into periods of prayer, work, and reading of Scripture and other sacred texts. Benedict taught his followers not only to live apart from the world but also how to treat pilgrims and strangers visiting the monastery.[70] Monasticism flourished throughout the Middle Ages, exercising a powerful influence on Western society and culture. Dreher's vision of Christian seclusion diverges from globalization because the church lacks the power to influence globalization at this time.

Although there are legitimate reasons for condemning and resisting globalization, Christians must accept another reality that is not acknowledged by the critics. Despite its problems, globalization has accomplished much good through the worldwide interconnection of diverse peoples, nations, and civilizations. If Christians do not participate in the process of renewing the political, economic, cultural, and technological domains of globalization, the world will simply rot in sin. However, there is something Christians can do to rescue humanity from self-destruction. They can help the world by demonstrating a better way to pursue globalization so that humanity can be delivered finally from the scourges of poverty and war.

Brent Waters presents two principal reasons to not give up on globalization: First, economic globalization is the only realistic strategy for

---

69. Dreher, *Benedict Option*, 54.
70. Dreher, *Benedict Option*, 50–51.

ameliorating poverty. According to Waters, "Starting with the formation of the World Trade Organization (WTO) in 1995, for instance, in conjunction with liberalized and integrative economic policies, it is estimated that nearly a billion people have escaped abject poverty, and income has risen steadily even with the recent financial crisis and economic downturns."[71] Second, economic globalization helps resist the universal and homogenous state. Waters adds, "Nationalism tends to exacerbate conflict, given contending national interests that are resolved through the threat or implementation of coercive solutions. In short, it is consumers, not politicians, who have much more at stake in preserving a peaceful world of trade and exchange."[72] He envisions a world in which the political ordering of the world would transition from the nation-state to the market-state. In this process, Christians must help the world embrace the creative destructions of global markets in ways that promote widespread prosperity while simultaneously providing sufficient stability for communicative associations to flourish. Christian theological and moral tradition can help humanity conceive a relation between civil society and political ordering that fosters human flourishing within the context of dynamic global markets.[73]

In response to the critics of globalization who call for separating the church from the world to become a distinct society that can influence the world, Scripture indicates that in the age of globalization the church must exist alongside the world with its door open. As Jesus prayed, "I will remain in the world no longer, but they are still in the world, and I am coming to you. Holy Father, protect them by the power of your name. . . . My prayer is not that you take them out of the world but that you protect them from the evil one" (John 17:11, 15 NIV). It is true that globalization is tainted by the existence of evil and poses a dangerous influence on the church. As a result, Christians are now vulnerable to being swallowed up by the corruption of this world. Despite the danger, strategic withdrawal from the world is not the biblical way to respond to globalization. Even though the world is a dangerous place for Christians, Scripture never instructs Christians to live within a safe community protected from worldly evil powers and influences; rather, as Mark 16:15 says, "Go into all the world and proclaim the gospel to the whole creation." In doing so, the disciples are promised that neither serpents nor deadly poison

---

71. Waters, *Just Capitalism*, 3.
72. Waters, *Just Capitalism*, 4.
73. Waters, *Just Capitalism*, 163.

will harm them (Mark 16:18). This promise refers to the same spiritual protection beautifully described in the book of Psalms: "He who dwells in the shelter of the Most High will abide in the shadow of the Almighty.... Because you have made the LORD your dwelling place—the Most High, who is my refuge—no evil shall be allowed to befall you, no plague come near your tent" (Ps 91:1, 5). These Scriptures affirm that Christians living in obedience to God's word and his commandment of love will not be harmed by the evil powers of globalization.

Since believers are called to engage in a spiritual battle, they are exhorted to don the full armor of God, which can protect them from the enemy's weapons (Eph 6:10–18). The belt of truth, helmet of salvation, breastplate of righteousness, shield of faith, and sword of the Spirit are available for the protection of believers. God's word commands believers to face the enemy and run to the battle. The attitude of condemnation and resistance disappears when Christians realize that God's purpose for leaving the church in this world is to send his children of light to be alongside the sinful people of this world. God is for the people of this world, despite all the wrong they have done against him. John 3:17 says, "For God did not send his Son into the world to condemn the world, but in order that the world might be saved through him." The church is the hands and feet of Christ that must touch all domains of globalization and renew them as God has intended from eternity.

CONTROL AND DOMINATION

The third prevailing theological attitude toward globalization is control and domination. This attitude is based on the fact that Christianity is a missionary religion that aims to save individual souls from personal sins and liberate societies from social ills. Many Christians believe the church is the solution to the problems in the world. With missionary enthusiasm, the church looks to the twenty-first century with great optimism about changing culture and society. This attitude reflects the nineteenth-century postmillennial and liberal accounts of the Christian future, with their sense of the imminent arrival of the divine kingdom.[74]

At present, both conservative and liberal circles consider globalization to be aligned with their respective objective of changing society and culture. The globalized world that such conservative Christians envision

---

74. Hall, *End of Christendom*, 21; Fraser, "Globalization," 339.

is achieved by the right ordering of society. They believe the church should simply define biblical truths and create universal beliefs to which everyone in society can conform. Charles Colson and Nancy Pearcey assert that "when we are redeemed, we are not only freed from the sinful motivations that drive us but also restored to fulfill our original purpose, empowered to do what we were created to do: to build societies and create culture—and, in doing so, to restore the created order."[75] They are mainly concerned with moral relativism, which erodes absolute truths. Many liberal Christians, on the other hand, aim to achieve their vision of a globalized world through social justice. Their approach is to accept the cultural realities arising from society and contribute religious support to secular ideals that pursue the common good. They want to cultivate flourishing communities of justice, equality, inclusion, and tolerance, and insist that widespread poverty in the midst of plenty is a moral wrong that cannot be accepted. As Jim Wallis says, "We must learn to judge our social and economic choices by whether they empower the powerless, protect the earth, and foster true democracy."[76] This liberal Christian agenda for social justice extends to the environment, war, women's rights, race, and immigration.

Sociologist James Hunter explains that the confidence of changing culture exhibited in the Christian thinking of both conservative and liberal circles is based on idealism, the Western tradition in metaphysics that reaches back to Plato. Idealism was powerfully articulated by the German Enlightenment, most importantly by philosopher Georg W. F. Hegel. It basically holds that something ideal or nonphysical is the primary reality. Adherents of idealism believe that history is moved by ideas.[77] For Christian idealists, globalization is regarded positively as a continuation of progress, moving humanity toward a flourishing community of justice, freedom, security, and prosperity. This confident attitude emphasizes the immanence of God in the movements of history, thus presenting history as an inevitable progress in accordance with Christian ideas. Hegel believed that God as an entity had not always existed as is but had gradually become a *Weltgeist* (world spirit) containing and uniting all the preceding epochs within it. God's presence in the world pulls human civilization toward the final consummation that unites all creation together in Christ and brings about a renewed world society. Hegel offered "a panentheistic

75. Colson and Pearcey, *How Now Shall We Live?*, 295.
76. Wallis, *Soul of Politics*, xxi.
77. Hunter, *To Change the World*, 24–25.

conception of the divine as the unification of nature and freedom, finite and infinite, and universal and particular."[78] From this perspective, globalization is a dialectical process that unfolds the will of God on earth in the dispensation of time (Eph 1:10). The philosophical influence of Hegel on Western culture and Christianity is profound.

Stackhouse is hopeful that globalization will be the process through which humanity will be saved from many of its social miseries. He believes that globalization is "a potential civilizational shift that involves the growth of a worldwide infrastructure that bears the prospect of a new form of civil society, one that may well comprehend all previous national, ethnic, political, economic or cultural contexts."[79] For ardent supporters of globalization, capitalism and liberal democracy are partial fulfillments of the coming order. In the future world, work and productivity will supply people's needs and affirm their dignity, overcoming the current limitations of poverty, oppressive hierarchies, lack of opportunity, and technological shortcomings.[80] Christians should be engaged in influencing politics, economics, religion, and culture to facilitate a peaceful unification of the world through globalization. The proponents of this view generally hold a "cosmopolitan" ethic of German philosopher Immanuel Kant and the concept of global citizenship. Kant's *Weltbürgerrecht* (cosmopolitan law) states that respect for humanity transcends all borders; therefore, respectful cosmopolitan societies can work together to strengthen universal justice. Today's cosmopolitans, in search of a new universalistic global ethic, believe in secularism's universal and transcultural norms and ideals, and that they should shape the evolving world order.[81] Their universal ethic resonates with liberal Christians who strongly identify with the biblical theme of the coming of God's universal kingdom that transcends gender, ethnic, and class divisions, which have long plagued this world.

Christianity is inherently a dominating religion, attested to by myriad Scriptures in reference to the church's authority and power. In the Gospels, Christ dominated over all forms of evil, including storm, sickness, demons, and death (Matt 28:6; Mark 4:41; Luke 8:26–33; John 12:31). He came to destroy the works of the devil (1 John 3:8) and promised to give the keys of the kingdom of heaven to his church (Matt 16:19).

78. Dorrien, *Kantian Reason and Hegelian Spirit*, 160.
79. Stackhouse, *Globalization and Grace*, 2.
80. Fraser, "Globalization," 340.
81. Raschke, "Globalization and Theology," 643.

After he overcame his death, the disciples expected him to restore the kingdom of Israel, which would dominate the world (Acts 1:6). It was natural for them to come to this conclusion because Scripture promises that God will gather and redeem the remnant of his people from their exile (Isa 52:7–10; Jer 23:3–4), and the Son of Man will rule the entire world with "authority and sovereign power" (Dan 7:13–14). The disciples believed that through the Son of Man, God would establish his dominion over all nations, a dominion that will never pass away or be destroyed. For the disciples, the kingdom of heaven was not separated from the earthly kingdom. Christ had taught them to pray "Your kingdom come, your will be done on earth, as it is in heaven" (Matt 6:10) and told them "whatever you bind on earth shall be bound in heaven, and whatever you loose on earth shall be loosed in heaven" (Matt 18:18). Christians were made into "a kingdom and priests to our God" so that they would "reign on the earth." Even after death, they "came to life and reigned with Christ for a thousand years" (Rev 5:9–10; 20:4). These Scriptures facilitate the conclusion that Jesus wants Christians to join his mission to redeem the world through the union of religion and politics.

The rise of Western culture that dominates the world through globalization is the product of Christendom. Christendom historically refers to the Christian world: Christian states, Christian-majority countries, and the countries in which Christianity dominates or prevails. Public evangelism events targeting a city or region are often referred to as gospel crusades, evoking the crusades launched by the Roman Catholic Church in the medieval period to liberate Jerusalem and its surrounding area from Islamic rule. Modern gospel crusades reflect the hope and dream of mission-minded Christians that a great number of unbelievers will be delivered from the power of sin and death by receiving the gospel. When enough people are converted to Christianity, it will result in "the time of restoration of all things" (Acts 3:19–21 CSB). The vision of Christendom is deeply ingrained in the psyche of many Christians. Hall assesses that Christians, particularly liberals from mainstream denominations, have a long tradition of believing in the progressive triumph of the Christian religion over all obstacles, rivals, and alternatives. Some evangelical Christians have now assumed the same attitude and expect the twenty-first century to be "the Christian Century."[82] They believe that the hope of building a great society of freedom and liberty rests on the

---

82. Hall, *End of Christendom*, 21.

principles of the Judeo-Christian worldview of America.[83] Thus, they have created a new kind of Christendom that has synthesized the values of Jewish and Christian religions. According to historian Jonathan Sarna, promoting the concept of the United States as a Judeo-Christian nation first became a political program in the 1940s, in response to the growth of anti-Semitism in America. The rise of Nazi anti-Semitism in the 1930s led concerned Protestants, Catholics, and Jews to take steps to increase understanding and tolerance.[84]

For those Christians who advocate for Christendom, Constantinianism is seen as the fulfillment of God's promise. Constantinianism is a policy establishing a particular Christian church as the religion of the state. According to this policy, state and church should form a close alliance to achieve mutual objectives. Established by the Roman emperor Constantine I, Christendom continued its existence in the Byzantine Empire (until 1453), the Frankish kingdom, the Holy Roman Empire (962–1806), and numerous European states.[85] Christendom came to an end in the East with the Ottoman conquests of the fourteenth and fifteenth centuries, in the West with the Protestant revolt in the sixteenth century, and with the rise of secularism in the eighteenth and nineteenth centuries. For approximately one thousand years, Christianity had dominated the whole continent of Europe. In the globalized world where democratic governance has proliferated, Constantinianism has manifested itself in a different way. Christians have learned to dominate the world through political mobilization. In the United States, although conservative leaders once gained a tremendous amount of political power during the 1980s and 1990s, their influence peaked in 2004. Since then, they continued to struggle in maintaining the support from their base. On the other hand, the liberal leaders who previously struggled to gain much traction have gained increased political power since 2000.[86] In the twenty-first century, a new generation of evangelicals has risen to challenge the Christian right, preaching social justice and the common good for the society.

Many conservative evangelicals, especially the Reformed circles, adhere to the concept of cultural mandate or creation mandate. At the

---

83. Robison, *Absolutes*, 28.

84. Sarna, *American Judaism*, 266.

85. Hinson, "Constantinianism," 1968. Although Christianity was first legalized by Constantine I in 313, it did not become the state religion until 380 when Theodosius I issued a decree to that effect.

86. Fitzgerald, *Evangelicals*, 585–623.

creation of the world, God tasked Adam and Eve with working and keeping the Garden of Eden (Gen 2:15). He commanded them to cultivate the world by being fruitful, multiplying, filling the earth, and subduing nature, and to have dominion over all living things on the earth (Gen 1:28). This divine mandate is construed as the cultural mandate to cultivate this world with Christian values. In *Earth Restored*, John Barber explains that the cultural mandate is God's instrument to create a flourishing context for the reception of the gospel in the world. It is understood as the means of shaping society to produce the optimum opportunity for people to come to Christ.[87] He describes the relationship between the cultural mandate and the Great Commission:

> In both Genesis 1:28 and 9:1–7, God intends the Cultural Mandate to serve as His directive to redeemed man to maintain the order God placed in His world, better enabling all men to seek the truth. It is in this sense of upholding and conserving the creation in its balance and design, that the Cultural Mandate serves the Great Commission. For where there is lack of order, men are preoccupied with non-order. But where there is peace, men are free to discern the meaning behind their liberty. They are free to both hear and respond to the call of God upon their lives.[88]

How can peaceful social order be established in a society populated by unbelievers? Barber argues that the laws that support God's order in a society must be passed through legislation even if there is a lack of popular support. He is critical of Christian social activists who assert that the laws passed through legislation cannot produce moral transformation for individuals. Barber says that God did not wait for a moral consensus to form among the Israelites before he gave them the Ten Commandments.[89] In other words, social order is established when God's law is enforced on society. Barber's method of cultivating the culture is rooted in the presuppositionalism of the Dutch Reformed theologian Cornelius Van Til. By insisting that the truth of Christianity and the falsity of other systems simply had to be presupposed, Van Til influenced the extreme Christian right thinkers who argued for Christians to impose the dominion of biblical law on secular society.[90] He believed that the realities conceived by autonomous human reason of unbelievers stand diametrically

---

87. Barber, *Earth Restored*, 67.
88. Barber, *Earth Restored*, 68–69.
89. Barber, *Earth Restored*, 225–26.
90. Stanley, *Global Diffusion of Evangelicalism*, 126–27.

opposed to the Christian values derived from the biblical revelation.[91] Following this reasoning, Francis Schaeffer explains that until about 1935, US society maintained a reasonable level of social order because people accepted the presuppositions that were in accord with Christians' own presuppositions. They accepted the possibility of absolutes in knowledge and morals. As secular culture drifted away from the concept of antithesis, it became increasingly difficult to discuss what was true and false, and what was right and wrong.[92] Schaeffer concludes that since the social order was overtaken by secular humanism, Christians now have a duty to turn society back to following Christian presuppositions; consequently, he calls for a political revolution to reclaim Christian rule over society.[93] Although he rejects theocracy, or the linking of church and state, it is not difficult to imagine what kind of world he is advocating. If Christians are locked into a culture war against secular humanists, what can resolve the impasse between the two antithetical ideologies? The logical conclusion is control and domination by the use of force via political action.

Within Reformed circles, there are those who take the idea of cultural mandate to the extreme through a theological system known as Christian Reconstructionism, or theonomy. R. J. Rushdoony argues that the church must completely reconstruct the world's social order by applying biblical law (including Mosaic law) in society.[94] There can be no intellectual common ground between believers and unbelievers.[95] Rushdoony highlights the problem of liberal society that is built without God's law:

> Liberalism dissolves the religious and familial ties of a society and leaves only the rootless individual and the humanistic state. Society then veers between collectivism and individualism. A social order which denies that God is the source of law must of necessity seek its principle of law from within history or from man. The conflict of law, then, is no longer between God's law and man's sin, but it is now the law of some men's ordering, which now makes sinners of all other men who differ. The law also shows then an ambivalence between an aristocracy

---

91. Fitzgerald, *Evangelicals*, 339.
92. Schaeffer, *Complete Works*, 5:6–7.
93. Schaeffer, *Complete Works*, 5:434–37 and 485.
94. Fitzgerald, *Evangelicals*, 342.
95. Fitzgerald, *Evangelicals*, 339.

suppressing the people, and a democracy seeking to suppress the aristocracy.[96]

Rather than a revolution, Rushdoony's strategy was a long-term plan to change society slowly. According to David Chilton, "The Christian goal for the world is the universal development of biblical theocratic republics, in which every area of life is redeemed and placed under the Lordship of Jesus Christ and the rule of God's law."[97] Although the movement has now nearly disappeared, its conception of reconstructing America has left a lasting influence on conservative Christians: it has crystallized the idea that America was founded as a Christian nation, and that Christians must reclaim it politically.[98] In 1979, Jerry Falwell launched the Moral Majority, an organization designed to register conservative Christians to mobilize them into a political force against secular humanism and the moral decay. He declared a holy war against the secular culture; many conservatives followed his lead.[99] Pat Robertson's *The Christian Broadcasting Network* and James Dobson's *Focus on the Family* began to air on television networks and radio stations in the late 1970s and had a tremendous impact throughout the 1980s and the 1990s. American politics were to be determined by the will of the Christian voters who had identified with the Republican Party and Ronald Reagan. The new world order that resulted from the political mobilization of evangelical Christians was called neoliberalism.

In the twenty-first century, another kind of Constantinian movement has risen to dominate culture and society. A significant portion of Pentecostal and charismatic believers hold to dominion, or kingdom theology, which is based on the idea that the world has been under the influence of Satan since the fall of man, and that Christians have the authority as well as the duty to reclaim it for God. Christian dominionists believe that God desires Christians to rise to power through civil systems so that his word might then govern the nation. According to Peter Wagner, the New Apostolic Reformation is a dominionist movement that asserts that God is restoring the lost offices of church governance, namely, the offices of prophet and apostle. He explains that the movement rejects theocracy and instead believes the way to achieve Christian dominion is "to have

---

96. Rushdoony, *Institutes of Biblical Law*, 144.
97. Fitzgerald, *Evangelicals*, 341–42.
98. Worthen, "Chalcedon Problem," 399–437.
99. Fitzgerald, *Evangelicals*, 291.

kingdom-minded people in every one of the Seven Mountains: Religion, Family, Education, Government, Media, Arts and Entertainment, and Business so that they can use their influence to create an environment in which the blessings and prosperity of the Kingdom of God can permeate all areas of society."[100] Political researcher Rachel Tabachnick views dominionism as a Christian belief system that must take control over all the various institutions of society and government, adhering to an unusual concept of spiritual warfare. She interprets the movement as "a religio-political movement" due to the fact that "it has networked across the United States in something that looks like a hybrid between a religious denomination and a political party."[101]

The attitude of control and domination arises when Christians believe themselves to be spiritually and morally superior to others. Many Christian leaders falsely assume that they will not misuse the power to rule over others because they are better than unbelievers. This attitude is akin to that of the elite, the decision makers in society whose power is not subject to control by any other body in society. Recent studies show that Christian leaders are also vulnerable to the structures within the church that allow them to abuse power.[102] Human beings are, by divine intent and their very nature, world-makers with power. Scripture offers a glimpse of what this power can achieve: Adam named all the living creatures in the world, and he and Eve had the ability to take care of nature's welfare, ensuring that the Garden of Eden flourished according to God's will. After the fall, however, this power given to mankind to rule over the creation became corrupt. Sin has corrupted the use of power in society, and Christians also struggle in this aspect.

Genesis 6 alludes that the Nephilim were the first elite to usurp the power given by God to cultivate the world. They were known as "men of renown," implying they ruled the world, shaping culture and society in accordance with their preference (Gen 6:4). Their wrong use of the power corrupted the earth and filled it with violence, resulting in God's judgment of destruction (Gen 6:11). The Hebrew term *Nephilim* should be interpreted as "tyrants" or "oppressors."[103] The context makes it clear that

---

100. Wagner, "New Apostolic Reformation," para. 18.
101. Gross, "Evangelicals Engaged in Spiritual," para. 16.
102. Langberg, *Redeeming Power*; Epp, "Abuses of Religious Power."
103. William Tyndale translated *Nephilim* as "tyrants," thus removing the ambiguity of its meaning. The Authorized Version translated the term as "giants." Modern translations have left the term in the original Hebrew form, causing much speculation

they were the ruling elite of ancient times who caused great wickedness to become prevalent in human civilization. The whole world had submitted to the rule of the Nephilim, who were too strong to be resisted by ordinary people; nevertheless, God held all of humanity responsible for succumbing to the ruling elite. A similar predicament is also told in the Epic of Gilgamesh, recorded on the 4,200-year-old Sumerian tablets. Gilgamesh, the semi-mythic king of Uruk, was a tyrant whose corruption exceeded all bounds. Even as people suffered under his oppression, they submitted to his rule for the benefits he provided: a flourishing city with social order and public services for its inhabitants.[104] This struggle between the ruling elite and the ordinary people would be repeated throughout history as cities and nations were built with the corrupt power of the ruling elite and the compliance of the citizens.[105] When Joshua led Israel into the land of Canaan, God commanded his people to drive out all the nations ruled by wicked kings (Deut 7:1–2). Although Israel was afraid of the people living in the land, namely, the Anakim, Joshua and Caleb drove them out and divided the land as their inheritance (Josh 11:21–23; 14:12–15). The power of the elite was broken in the land of promise, foreshadowing the great ministry of God's children in the world.

How should Christians today claim their inheritance in a globalized world? How should the church realize the coming of God's kingdom on earth? How can the disciples of Jesus carry out God's plan and purpose of redeeming the world in a pluralistic society? They must come to terms with the cultural reality that the world has now become a single and shared space for all people. It may have been possible to punish heretics or drive out those who had different religious beliefs during the Reformation, but that kind of hegemony is not acceptable in a globalized world. Christians now share their city, country, and world with all kinds of people who adhere to different religions, philosophies, ideologies, and lifestyles. When Christians pursue cultural mandate or social justice from the position of dominance, they are following the elite in misusing power.

The elite do not respect the needs of others. Instead, they want to bypass the wishes and needs of the ordinary people and enforce a

---

concerning the identity of Nephilim. The context makes it clear that they were powerful men who caused much wickedness and violence in ancient times.

104. Acemoglu and Robinson, *Narrow Corridor*, xiii–xv.

105. Some historical examples are the Mongol Empire of Genghis Khan, the Japanese Empire of Shogun Tokugawa Ieyasu, the First French Empire of Napoleon, the Nazi Germany of Hitler, and the Communist Soviet Union of Lenin and Stalin.

hegemonic system that satisfies their ideals. With their immense wealth, they can influence politicians to work for their causes rather than those of ordinary citizens. They are proficient in using politics to achieve their agenda. For example, Charles and David Koch—commonly referred to as the Koch brothers—have enormous financial and political influence in the US politics. According to historian Nancy MacLean, their network of operation is on the scale of a national US political party and employs more than three times as many people as the Republican committees. In promoting a libertarian ideology, they use "the tactic of overwhelming the normal political process with schemes to disrupt its functioning."[106] Hunter says that, in the end, "politicization means that the final arbiter within most of social life is the coercive power of the state."[107] He further explains, "The politicization of everything is an indirect measure of the loss of a common culture and, in turn, the competition among factions to dominate others on their own terms."[108] With the strategy and method of politicization, too many Christians have resorted to using the power of the state in order to force their will on others.

Although Christians are called to live a life of service by placing the interest of others before their own (Phil 2:3–4), many have taken on a model of leadership that is based on elitism, ruling over others to serve their own agenda. Even though Jesus warned against operating in the way of the gentiles (Matt 20:25–26), Christians are prone to relying on the same strategies and methods that aim to gain power in order to dominate society. Some theologians advocate that ordinary Christians must aspire to take up the positions of power that are widely held by the elite. A paper presented at the Lausanne Committee for World Evangelization explains how Christians can gain the power to serve their cities:

> One of the most desperately needed aspects of this call to serve the city is the commissioning of Christian professionals (by definition, elites) who will work out the implications of the whole gospel story in realms of economics, politics, science and engineering, the arts, medicine, and the like. It is a fact of our world-historical moment that humanity increasingly relies on such powers in the ordering of its affairs. It is also a fact that these powers have become the reigning idols of the age.[109]

---

106. MacLean, *Democracy in Chains*, xxxi.
107. Hunter, *To Change the World*, 106.
108. Hunter, *To Change the World*, 107.
109. Lausanne Occasional Paper, "Globalization and the Gospel," 58.

Many Christians have aligned with democratic ideals, principles, and reasoning that provide a framework for politicization in public life. In doing so, they are engaging in a culture war. Those who follow this path to power believe that the key to controlling society is by voting for those who possess a biblical or conservative worldview. Among evangelical circles, it is commonly believed that when conservative individuals with the right morals and values are placed in the position of power, they can transform culture. As a result, many Christians have turned to politics to transform this world in accordance with their ideals. The final outcome of this path can only be the destruction of others who do not share Christian beliefs and values.

Only Jesus Christ is the final judge of all peoples, nations, and civilizations. Until the day of judgment, while teaching biblical truths in the public sphere, Christians must learn to walk patiently with those who are different from them. To build a just, free, peaceful, and flourishing society for the twenty-first century, Christians must abide by the Golden Rule. As Jesus says, "So in everything, do to others what you would have them do to you, for this sums up the Law and the Prophets" (Matt 7:12 NIV). This command means that Christians must learn to serve and respect others without compromising their beliefs and values of Scripture. In a globalized world, Christians can learn to dialogue with others, patiently persuading them to believe the gospel and live in accordance with the ethics of God's kingdom. Christians are called not to change the world but to live as faithful witnesses of Christ to their neighbors by teaching them God's word and healing their wounds.

ENGAGEMENT

The fourth theological attitude toward globalization is engagement characterized by mercy and love. This view sees globalization as a rescue operation or an emergency order. It derives from the belief that although the world has fallen into sin, corruption, and evil, it is still God's created order and can be salvaged. Richard Mouw affirms that even in the midst of a fallen world, "God has not given up on restoring the purposes that were at work in God's initial creating activity."[110] Globalization is a messy process, a mixed bag of good and bad that needs to be cared for by all people, especially Christians. The church must engage with globalization

---

110. Mouw, *Challenge of Cultural Discipleship*, 20.

through dialogue and empathy, thus ensuring all people can readily recognize the reign of Christ and accept his plan and purpose of redeeming the world. When the church preaches the gospel and engages in addressing the problems of globalization, it gains plausibility for being faithful witnesses to the reign of Christ.

As God's people who are redeemed by Christ, Christians have a unique role of showing the world what God desires from his creation: Believe in the name of his Son Jesus Christ and love one another (1 John 3:23). Obedience to this command moves globalization toward ushering in the new heaven and earth where "the dwelling place of God is with man" (Rev 21:3). In the Old Testament, God's mission for Israel was expressed in his command: "To do justice, and to love kindness, and to walk humbly with your God" (Mic 6:8). The biblical concept of justice is intricately tied with acting righteously and behaving with mercy, love, kindness, and compassion (Isa 1:17). Israel was chosen to serve as "a people holy to the LORD" and "God's witnesses" among the nations by administering God's justice and mercy in its society (Deut 7:6–8; Isa 43:10). In the New Testament, God has raised up Christians as "a chosen race, a royal priesthood, a holy nation, a people for his own possession" to serve as his witnesses for they have received God's mercy (1 Pet 2:9–12). God is therefore resolved to fill the whole world with his fullness through the body of Christ, the church (Eph 1:23). Grenz expresses the universal nature of the church's ministry for the world in the following manner:

> We seek to be a people who embody God's intention for all humankind. Thus, we view the vision of salvation we proclaim as more than merely the way of life of a specific religious tradition. Rather than huddling together as the "chosen few" who live unto themselves, our desire is to live according to God's will in the midst of, and for the sake of, the many. We long that the many might join with us—become part of "the few" as it were—so as to actualize God's intentions for all humankind.[111]

As kingly priests, God's people must minister to the globalized world so that it can realize Christ's reign on earth (Rev 1:5–6). The church's attitude of engagement leads believers to give thoughtful attention to the development of human civilization toward justice and mercy for all. Since God did not abandon the world to perish in sin but intends to renew it under the reign of Christ, Christians have a public duty to

---

111. Grenz, *Renewing the Center*, 292.

nurture globalization by approving what is good and rejecting what is evil. The twenty-first century has witnessed cultural, religious, and political polarizations, which have led to violent conflicts worldwide. In his book *A Public Faith*, Volf paves a public way of life that is undeniably Christian while maintaining a peaceful relationship with others who are different from us. He builds on the worldly hope of Jürgen Moltmann's eschatology: "The expectation of good things that come as a gift from God—that is hope. And that is love too, projecting itself into our and our world's future. For love always gives gifts and is itself a gift; inversely, every genuine gift is an expression of love. At the heart of the hoped-for future, which comes from the God of love, is the flourishing of individuals, communities, and our whole globe."[112]

Volf asserts that the challenge facing Christians is simply this: "Love God and neighbor rightly so that we may both avoid malfunctions of faith and relate God positively to human flourishing."[113] Malfunctions of faith occur when Christians become discouraged by religious diversity in a pluralistic world, resulting in either an idle faith or a coercive faith. Idle faith involves withdrawal from public life and leaves one's faith idling in all spheres outside their private and church lives. Coercive faith involves engagement with public life but does so by forcing the demands of one's faith on those who embrace other faiths or no faith at all. Volf develops a notion of engaged faith that can dispel the gloom and generate new hope for Christian communities facing new challenges in the twenty-first century.[114] He argues that the most effective way of changing the world is by an "internal difference."[115] It means that Christians must work within culture, adopting what is acceptable and rejecting what violates biblical standards. As a result, according to Volf, "the majority of the elements of a culture will be taken up but transformed from within."[116] In other words, Christian faith that engages with others in the public sphere shapes a renewed understanding of globalization that reflects the common good for society.

The conception of common good was originally given by Christ, who was the first king to show mercy and love for all people, including the poor and outcast of society. Christ appeared in the Roman Empire, which

112. Volf, *Public Faith*, 56.
113. Volf, *Public Faith*, 73.
114. Volf, *Public Faith*, 74–79.
115. Volf, *Public Faith*, 89.
116. Volf, *Public Faith*, 91.

maintained its domination of the Mediterranean world through judicial institutions, legislative systems, property ownership, control of labor, and brute force. As with most societies, the empire developed mechanisms for maintaining multifaceted inequality and promoted justifications that made the inequity seem normal or at least inevitable.[117] Christ did not directly dismantle the unjust system in society. Rather, by preaching the gospel, he dealt with the root of all social problems: the human heart that rebels against God's will and harms others for one's own good. He set people free from their slavery to sin (John 8:34) so they can pursue the good of others rather than their own (1 Cor 10:24). Through his death on the cross, Christ destroyed the dividing wall of hostility between God and mankind (Eph 12:14–16). In doing so, he broke down the wall of hatred and division between the Jew and Greek, the slave and free, the male and female, allowing all believers to become coheirs of God's kingdom (Gal 3:26–29; Rom 8:17). Understanding the universal nature of the gospel, the first Christians in Jerusalem voluntarily shared their possessions and generously provided for the needs of one another (Acts 4:32). The apostle James spoke against partiality and exhorted Christians that it was their religious duty to identify with the poor and oppressed in society (Jas 1:27—2:13). From early on, Christians were learning that other people's suffering was their own suffering because of their common identity and fellowship in Christ.

The Christian ethos of common good made its mark throughout the Roman Empire as Christianity spread. It is estimated that the total number of Christians grew from 7,500 in AD 40 to about 6 million at the beginning of the fourth century.[118] By the time of Constantine, approximately 10 percent of the empire's population was Christian. This rapid growth of the Christian movement despite severe persecutions during the first three centuries indicates that something was deeply attractive to society. According to historian Tom Holland, Christianity had unleashed a moral revolution that shook the world like no other. Before Christianity came, the pagan world was captive to fatalistic belief, resulting in unrestrained exaltation for the rich and strong, and the complete lack of regard for the poor and weak. The pagan world believed that all events in the history of the world, including the actions and incidents which make up the story of each individual life, are determined by fate. This cruel

---

117. Garnsey and Saller, *Roman Empire*, 131–50.

118. Stark, *Rise of Christianity*, 6. The growth of Christianity is calculated at the rate of 40 percent per decade.

pagan world was transformed by Christianity, the religion that cared for all people.[119]

Christianity began as a spiritual and moral movement that aimed to change the human heart and behavior. Throughout history, mistreatment of slaves and women was prevalent in society. Church historian Gerald Bray explains how the apostles taught Christians to resolve the injustices in society:

> The apostles did not advocate slavery as an institution, but they did not claim that emancipation was an obligation enjoined by the gospel either. Instead, they sought to restrict the nature of slave-master relationships in a way that would make the fellowship of believers the determining factor in them. They were not blind to the injustices of slavery, but believed that submission to it was the right way to imitate the example of Christ and the one that was most likely to convict the oppressors of their evil behavior. Above all, they did not seek to abolish the difference between men and women, which went back to the creation, but to transform them. Wives were to submit to their husbands, but husbands were to sacrifice themselves for their wives, and in that way they would achieve the equality of difference.[120]

In God's kingdom, in the hearts of people where Christ reigned, all people had dignity regardless of their social status. This new dynamic in human relationship began to permeate a world ruined by division and strife.

A change of heart and behavior en masse leads to change of institution. When Constantine legalized the church, it became a powerful social institution that transformed Western society. Lesslie Newbigin argues that although the church has regularly fallen into the temptation of worldly power, the Constantinian project had its origins in a creative response to a significant cultural challenge. The wider culture was undergoing spiritual crisis, and people turned to the church as the one institution that could hold a disintegrating world together.[121] When Rome was sacked by the barbarians, this marked the beginning of the medieval period. The fourth kingdom described in Daniel's vision (Dan 7:7) was crumbling, giving way to the kingdom of God, which was now conquering Western society. At this critical juncture in history, Augustine set the course for Western society with his influential treatise *The City of God*. Among many other

---

119. Holland, *Dominion*, 107–36.
120. Bray, *Church*, 59.
121. Newbigin, *Foolishness to the Greeks*, 100–101.

topics, this work addressed how Christians pursuing eternal truths should relate to a world that seeks earthly pleasures. Keith Yandell explains how Augustine resolved the question of value and human life:

> If a person is no more than a biologically sophisticated animal that lives for a few years on earth and then no longer exists, it is not unthinkable that a man's or a woman's life, insofar as it is worthwhile, does consist in the abundance of what he or she possesses—that the whole point of life is one of acquiring and enjoying as many things as one can, of seeking wealth and pleasure and power to the fullest extent available. But if a person's life on this earth is but a small part of his overall existence, and if the purpose of life is fulfilled only if one loves God with all one's heart, soul, mind and strength, and loves others as him or herself, then what Jesus said is appropriate.[122]

After the fall of Rome, Pope Gregory the Great became instrumental in solidifying the Christian church as a pillar of Western society for centuries to come. Although Gregory had practiced rigorous asceticism as a monk, he denied the traditional claim of ascetic writers that the summit of the Christian life is to be found in contemplation alone. Instead, he affirmed that the summit is to be found in service to others.[123] In pursuit of this belief, he took on the title "the servant of the servants of God." During a tumultuous period in which the Lombards invaded and ruled the Italian peninsula, Gregory served as an effective diplomat and administrator. Realizing he could neither defeat the Lombards militarily nor continue a cycle of warfare and ransom, Gregory repeatedly sought peace.[124] To provide charitable relief for the poor who were predominantly refugees from the incursion of the Lombards, he developed permanent ecclesiastical institutions under the authority of the Bishop of Rome. According to Miles Doleac, "In the fall of 590, Bishop Gregory inherited a long tradition of Christian charity, but not a uniform or organized one. Based on the socio-political circumstances of the late sixth century, he also inherited unusually sweeping, temporal powers. He employed these powers to create a permanent infrastructure through

---

122. Yandell, "City of God," para. 10.
123. Demacopoulos, *Gregory the Great*, 60.
124. The Lombards were a Germanic people that invaded Italy and ruled most of the Italian Peninsula from 568 to 774. They were pagans or Arian Christians that increasingly converted to Catholicism.

which Christianity's longstanding directive of care for the poor might be effectively administered."[125]

Gregory's theological writings were extremely influential. They were based on his vision of pastoral care to meet the spiritual and physical needs of the people. In his treatise *Pastoral Care*, he directly confronted the reluctance of ascetics to assume positions of pastoral leadership, arguing that they were given gifts not only for themselves only but also for others: "When these men contemplate their own spiritual advantages and do not consider anyone else, they lose these goods because they desire to keep them for themselves."[126] Gregory wrote that the most fundamental responsibility of the clergy was to preach the good news of Christ. A thoughtful interpretation of the whole of Scripture would inspire the spiritual and moral reform of the congregation.[127] He reminded the clergy to pursue morality, cultivate humility, and maintain contemplative life in the midst of actively serving others.[128] In *Dialogues*, his most popular book, Gregory insisted on the need to soften our hearts and form a disposition of goodwill toward our neighbors.[129] Furthermore, Gregory wrote letters to aristocratic men and women far away from Rome, in which he corrected errant belief, reproved the ways that the wealthy treated their slaves, and encouraged his correspondents to pursue the spiritual rewards through charity.[130] Although the church was far from perfect, it began the extensive work of educating Western society to conform to Christ's reign. Understanding that all people bear the image of God, many began to recognize that all human lives are valuable, and that everyone should be treated with dignity.

After experiencing tremendous growth during the Middle Ages, the church as an institution degenerated into corruption. When the church was exposed for its abuse of power, the Protestant Reformers further improved society's institutions to uphold the reign of Christ. Resisting the pope, who claimed authority over secular rulers, Martin Luther distinguished the spiritual kingdom from the temporal one. He believed there are three God-ordained hierarchies: the home, the government, and the

---

125. Doleac, "Triclinium Pauperum," 9–10.
126. Demacopoulos, *Gregory the Great*, 66.
127. Demacopoulos, *Gregory the Great*, 70–71.
128. Demacopoulos, *Gregory the Great*, 74–78.
129. Moorhead, "Taking Gregory the Great's Dialogues," 210.
130. Demacopoulos, *Gregory the Great*, 76.

church.[131] Remaining true to his monastic roots, Luther was content to focus on the reformation of faith and doctrine. He taught passive obedience in politics and brought the church under the civil authority. James Madison credited Luther for providing a proper distinction between the civil and ecclesiastical spheres, paving the way for the success of liberal democracy in the United States.

In contrast to Luther, Huldrych Zwingli aimed at a social and political, as well as an ecclesiastical, reformation. For Zwingli, being a good citizen and a good Christian coincided. Before being appointed as the *Leutpriester* (people's priest) in Zurich, he was a humanist and a patriot.[132] Bruce Gordon explains, "True religion, the subject of [Zwingli's] most polished theological work, was a narrow path. . . . Zwingli did not reject the world or human bodies. The inner working of the Spirit was expressed in outward acts."[133] He adds, "His goal was to bring the people and society back to God's Word. From an early stage, he adopted the identity of a prophet, bringing scripture to the people, advising political leaders and imagining a new land governed by God's justice."[134] Zwingli envisaged a new church and society in Zurich transformed by Scripture.

Turning away from a millennium-old tradition of preaching according to the lectionary schedule, Zwingli's ministry began with the exposition of the Gospel of Matthew. Zwingli then continued to preach expositional sermons through Acts, Timothy, Galatians, 1 and 2 Peter, Hebrews, the Gospel of John, and the other Pauline letters before turning to the Old Testament. Aiming to teach everything based on Scripture, he was keenly interested in improving the ethical standards of believers.[135] For Zwingli, the primary responsibility of the pastor was preaching the word of God; among the secondary responsibilities was the care of the poor.[136] As Lee Wandel observes, "Zwingli envisioned a true Christian as active, expressing his faith externally, through social and civic engagement."[137] Zwingli's understanding of the preacher's role extended into the realm of politics and economics, with the preacher functioning

---

131. Luther, *Works of Martin Luther*, 5:298–99.
132. Schaff, *History of the Christian Church*, 8:34.
133. Gordon, *Zwingli*, 8.
134. Gordon, *Zwingli*, 9.
135. Schaff, *History of the Christian Church*, 35.
136. Wandel, *Always Among Us*, 39.
137. Wandel, *Always Among Us*, 69.

to strengthen the Christian conscience of leaders and encourage them to oversee the proper use of the community's wealth.[138]

In *The Shepherd*, a publication addressed to pastors, Zwingli argued that the proper use of the wealth traditionally invested in church decoration was the care of the poor:[139] "Whoever does not watch over the poor, lets them be oppressed and burdened, are false shepherds."[140] In his sermons and printed texts, from beginning to end, he preached that the poor were "the true images of God." The Christian community, in reaching out to the poor as "brothers," at once mirrored God's relation to humanity.[141] According to Wandel, "In both spoken and printed word, the poor were given a place within Zwingli's theology, in his construction of Christian ethics."[142] Reflecting his mercy and love for others, Zwingli's pamphlets always printed images of Christ calling beggars and other poor folk to him. Zwingli's attitude toward the poor directly influenced the passing of civil ordinances in Zurich that established categories of poverty, distinguishing the "truly poor" from those who were not genuinely needy and deserving.[143]

Under Zwingli's theological guidance, Zurich became one of the first communities in Europe to reform its religious life and the care of its poor. The influence of Zurich's reform extended to larger cities such as Strasbourg and Augsburg in southwest Germany to Basel and Geneva in Switzerland.[144] The permanence of Zurich's reform is still evident today in European states' extensive welfare system, which provides healthcare, college education, and other social protections for all its citizens. Franz-Xaver Kaufmann affirms the Christian influence on Europe's institutional reform: "The fundamental belief in the equal worth of all human beings is the only basis for understanding the power of those processes that are associated with the idea of increasing inclusion. . . . Thus, a universalistic ethos shattering group and class barriers, as Christianity had laid down from the very beginning, materialized itself institutionally."[145]

---

138. Wandel, *Always Among Us*, 42–43.
139. Wandel, *Always Among Us*, 43.
140. Wandel, *Always Among Us*, 44.
141. Wandel, *Always Among Us*, 75–76.
142. Wandel, *Always Among Us*, 15.
143. Wandel, *Always Among Us*, 77–124.
144. Wandel, *Always Among Us*, 15.
145. Kaufmann, *European Foundations of the Welfare State*, 80.

John Calvin envisaged church and state as a united force that protects the people, each with a distinct purpose. Both were mutually spiritual: the state adjudicated temporal matters under God, while the church adjudicated specifically spiritual matters, with both opposing evil.[146] Calvin made a decisive impact on the economic growth of Western society by declaring that every vocation was "truly respectable" and "deemed highly important in the sight of God," thereby allowing Christians to pursue their trade with dignity.[147] This theological expression set Christians free to pursue the accumulation of wealth by their faithfulness in business enterprise. Waters explains how the need for employment in society prompted Calvin's permissive teaching on charging interest on loans: "He argued that the biblical prohibition against usury reflected an agricultural economy in which interest was used to crush the livelihood of poor farmers. But employment in an increasingly urban context was derived primarily through trade and commercial activities, requiring in turn investment, and sufficient capital could only be generated through borrowing and lending."[148] Merchants, traders, and bankers could now work with dignity since they were no longer looked down upon by society. Calvinism had laid the theological ground for the development of capitalist principles.

The Industrial Revolution dramatically altered Western society, expanding the types of employment available and transforming how people lived. Thus, labor came to be seen as another God-ordained institution. Dietrich Bonhoeffer explains, "It is God's will that there shall be labour, marriage, government, and church in the world; and it is His will that all these, each in its own way, shall be through Christ, directed towards Christ, and in Christ. . . . This means that there can be no retreating from a 'secular' into a 'spiritual' sphere."[149] As with Calvin, Bonhoeffer had expressed that no aspect of society lies outside the realm of Christ. All of society, all of life is bound inextricably with Christ and his reign of the world. Against this overarching view that once governed the Western world, the secularism of modern Western society has pushed Christ from the public realm by separating reason and faith, fact and value. Such separation removed morality and any sense of human purpose into the

---

146. Calvin, *Institutes of the Christian Religion*, 1:779–82.
147. Calvin, *Institutes of the Christian Religion*, 1:791.
148. Waters, *Just Capitalism*, 31.
149. Bonhoeffer, *Ethics*, 204.

subjective realm of personal preference, thereby leaving Western society in an abyss of relativism and despair.[150]

Christ achieves his reign over all the earth through the patient and compassionate engagement of his people with those who are not yet saved by the gospel. Dutch journalist and theologian Abraham Kuyper responded to the institutional pressure of secularism by founding the Anti-Revolutionary Party and Vrije Universiteit (Free University). The *vrijeid* (freedom) of his university was intended as a freedom from both governmental and ecclesial control.[151] He lived in a tumultuous time when secularism had overcome Christendom in the Netherlands. In the late nineteenth century, European monarchies were being replaced by various post-Enlightenment models for government. Kuyper rejected the popular sovereignty of France in which all rights originated with the individual, and the state sovereignty of Germany in which all rights derived from the state. Such models seemed to deny any real rights to intermediate bodies in society. Throughout his life, says Vincent Bacote, "Kuyper argued for the right to bring a revelation-based perspective into public life."[152] Against the secular insistence that Christians should stay out of public life, Kuyper powerfully expressed that Christ is sovereign over "every square inch" of this world.

Kuyper's conception of *sphere sovereignty* differentiated responsibilities that belong to diverse entities of society or life, such as family, church, state, school and academy, recreation and art, business and labor, journalism and media, charitable groups, and medicine. He believed that each sphere has its own identity, its own unique task, its own God-given prerogatives.[153] In other words, these societal structures are not merely instruments of the church or state but God-created entities, each with their own responsibilities.[154] He hoped that all free societal structures would eventually conform to Christ's reign through dialogue and cooperation.

Kuyper was also one of the early writers on the topic of common grace. This concept acknowledges the presence of grace throughout the cosmos, meaning that even though the unbeliever may be mistaken about

---

150. Stanley, *Global Diffusion of Evangelicalism*, 143–44. Stanley comments that this diagnosis of the Western society was drawn by both Lesslie Newbigin and Francis Schaeffer.

151. Mouw, *Challenges of Cultural Discipleship*, 48.

152. Bacote, *Spirit in Public Theology*, 56.

153. Bacote, *Spirit in Public Theology*, 70.

154. Mouw, *Challenges of Cultural Discipleship*, 38.

many things, they can still be correct about other things. He expressed that although all of life is tainted by sin, the methodology for finding the divine ordinances does not require a cessation of the observation of life, nor does it mandate the adoption of Scripture as a code of Christian law for the state.[155] Rather, says Bacote, "Kuyper maintained that the rules of political life are built into the created order and that even non-Christians can articulate approaches to national life that reflect divine principles."[156] Thus, fruitful dialogue can take place between believer and unbeliever. According to James Bratt, Kuyper "proposed for religious believers to bring the full weight of their convictions into public life while fully respecting the rights of others in a pluralistic society under a constitutional government."[157] Drawing from Kuyper's vision of pluralism, Christians in a globalized world can learn to live within the tension between freedom and order, thereby respecting others who hold different views.[158] Christians involved with various institutions of globalization can influence society by attesting biblical truths with mercy and love.

Since there are institutional gaps in the development of emerging global order, Christians must be nuanced and selective in their approach to various aspects of globalization. According to Volf, "We ought neither to demonize nor sacralize the present form of globalization but assess it using a given religion's account of the good life as a measure and advocate for its transformation so that it can contribute to authentic human flourishing and the global common good."[159] He recognizes world religions as part of the dynamics of globalization throughout the entire history of humanity.[160] Volf affirms, "To shape globalization with a view toward the global common good, religions will have to learn how to advocate universalistic visions in a pluralistic world without fomenting violence."[161] From a Christian perspective, he perceives the problem of globalization as rooted in humanity's inability to find the unity between ordinary life

---

155. Bacote, *Spirit in Public Theology*, 58.

156. Bacote, *Spirit in Public Theology*, 59.

157. Bratt, *Abraham Kuyper*, xiii.

158. Bratt, *Abraham Kuyper*, xix. Bratt says that much of Kuyper's legacy has been divided by the twin themes of liberation and order. His conservative heirs have amplified the theme of order, ontological fixedness, suspicions of secularism, and aspersions toward the left. His progressive heirs, on the other hand, have followed his call for fresh thinking, epistemological openness, social justice, and aspersions toward the rich.

159. Volf, *Flourishing*, 45–46.

160. Volf, *Flourishing*, 67.

161. Volf, *Flourishing*, 58.

and transcendent life. Globalization has brought many material benefits but with little meaning. Volf asserts that "globalization needs to be tamed so it will be less likely to rob us of our humanity by making our moral lives subservient to our material wants."[162] Taming and shaping globalization will require the massive collaborative effort of many people, adherents of diverse ideologies with wide-ranging expertise. Humanity can flourish only if Christianity, along with other world religions, takes on the role of providing a spiritual and moral foundation to globalization.[163]

Christian cultural commentator Mark Sayers assesses that the contemporary Western world driving globalization has embraced Gnosticism as the great post-Christian religion of its culture. He says "while the early Gnostics wished to escape the world of matter to enter a purely spiritual plane, the reduced neo-Gnosticism of our day wishes to escape the world of the mundane for the world of the awesome, the stimulating, and the pleasurable."[164] Through its own effort, the contemporary world wishes to overcome all barriers and find happiness by attaining the perfect bodies people see in the imagery all around them.[165] Sayers explains that Gnosticism is not a movement but a temptation, which originated in the Garden of Eden when the serpent promised mankind they could be like God. He describes it as "a term for the trajectory of humans to flee from God, His order, and His authority."[166] Through Gnosticism, globalization fulfills the human desire to rule the world on our terms without God. By contrast, Christians are called to believe the gospel and follow Christ by living a selfless life of serving the needs of others, thereby ruling the world with God.

Can Christians do anything for the people of this world who have rebelled against God's authority and pursued the life of seeking their own happiness? Myers believes globalization is the central missiological challenge of our time. He says "the central failure of globalization is its inability to provide satisfactory answers to the questions of meaning: Who are we? Why are we here? How then should we live?"[167] In a world that has provided abundant material goods with very little meaning, Christians

---

162. Volf, *Flourishing*, 49.
163. Volf, *Flourishing*, 58.
164. Sayers, *Disappearing Church*, 61.
165. Sayers, *Disappearing Church*, 61.
166. Sayers, *Disappearing Church*, 62.
167. Myers, *Engaging Globalization*, 243.

are to be the signs of the coming kingdom of God as faithful witnesses.[168] Myers explains the role of Christians in God's project of redeeming his creation: "We need the faith to believe that the values, processes, and dynamics of globalization are the objects of God's love as well as of God's project of redemption and restoration. Our mission is to become faithful witnesses to Jesus Christ and God's kingdom from within the institutions, structure, and domains of this globalizing world."[169]

Myers adds that Christians are not commanded to be successful; they cannot banish evil, create justice, or redeem globalization. He states that "only God can save the world, and this will happen in fullness only when Jesus comes again."[170] Still, Christians must engage globalization missionally and work to shape it ethically. Myers explains that our engagement has a cumulative effect in the coming of God's kingdom: "While we cannot save the world or transform it into the kingdom of God, every kingdom-like action we take, every prayer we utter, every act of kindness and grace, every correction of a small injustice, all are signs of God's emerging kingdom. Somehow our various humble offerings come together as part of God's global work of grace and justice, and the kingdom comes a little bit closer."[171]

Being faithful witnesses by engaging with globalization requires both affirmation and confrontation with the institutions that direct and manage globalization. First, the elements of goodness must be affirmed and strengthened. Examples of the benefits of globalization are clear: improved living standards, the spread of beneficial technology, access to better medicine, the demise of oppressive political ideologies and hierarchies, and the increase of freedom and democracy. Second, there is an absolute need to confront the many evils of globalization: self-sufficiency, self-aggrandizement, global criminal networks, violent conflicts in developing countries, a growing disparity of wealth in developed countries, abuse of power, ecological destruction, loss of privacy, and flawed anthropology that wrongly defines humanity—to name a few.

Eddie Byun explains why the church must take leadership in confronting the evils of globalization. In 2010, he learned that up to 30 million people were in slavery around the world. Human trafficking is a multibillion-dollar industry that affects every nation in the world. As

---

168. Myers, *Engaging Globalization*, 5.
169. Myers, *Engaging Globalization*, 243.
170. Myers, *Engaging Globalization*, 255.
171. Myers, *Engaging Globalization*, 255.

a pastor, Byun was deeply troubled by his findings and felt convicted to lead his church to do something. When he engaged to confront human trafficking, specifically sex trafficking in South Korea, Byun was faced with unexpected challenges. First, he could not find churches with ministries combating trafficking so that he could get his church on board. Then, a high-ranking government official discouraged his initiative to start the ministry. Furthermore, he received the greatest opposition from evangelical pastors, who accused him of being a social gospel preacher. The attacks and criticisms he received insinuated that the church does not belong in these parts of society.[172] "Sadly," says Byun, "we have outsourced almost every area of vulnerability and justice to NGOs, nonprofits and the government."[173] He believes that while it is important for all people to help end human trafficking, the church has a specific duty to do so. By refusing to address the issue directly and allowing non-Christian groups to do all the work, says Byun, Christians are not meeting God's expectations. As he explains, "If we, the church, are not the primitive leaders in the pursuit of justice in this generation—if we're not leading the way, we're letting the world look more like Jesus than we do."[174]

The first and second greatest commandments are to love God with all your heart and with all that you have and to love your neighbor as yourself (Matt 22:36–40). Engagement with globalization must be carried out by the presence of believers, characterized by love. "For the Christian, if there is a possibility for human flourishing in a world such as ours," explains Hunter, "it begins when God's Word of love becomes flesh in us, is embodied in us, is enacted through us and in doing so, a trust is forged between the word spoken by the church and the reality to which it speaks."[175] Thus, Christians should be fully present and committed as faithful witnesses in their spheres of social influence: their families, neighborhoods, voluntary activities, and places of work.[176] Christians are to strive for cultural change that reflects the kingdom values—fairness, justice, inclusion, truth, transparency, and unity—in whatever social situations or institutions God has placed us.[177]

---

172. Byun, *Justice Awakening*, 14–16, 78–79.
173. Byun, "Time for Justice," 12.
174. Covarrubias, "Eddie Byun Presents," para. 18.
175. Hunter, *To Change the World*, 241.
176. Hunter, *To Change the World*, 247.
177. Hunter, *To Change the World*, 177.

When the people of this world see the kingdom values displayed in the lives of Christians, they can realize that the Christian beliefs and practices are inherently plausible and that their advice is trustworthy. From their earliest days, Christians showed the world how to live together in fairness, transparency, and unity by pursuing the common good. They sought the kingdom of God and his righteousness rather than their own interests (Matt 6:33). Their demonstration of the kingdom values added great power to the apostles who gave their testimony about the resurrection of the Lord Jesus (Acts 4:32–37). According to South African theologian Craig Bartholomew, "Plausibility refers to the personal, communal, and social embodiment of the life of the kingdom so that when Christians do speak they are listened to."[178]

In the twenty-first century, the credibility of the church is falling rapidly and steadily. The Barna Group's 2007 study revealed what Christianity looks like from the outside. The most common reaction to Christianity in society was that Christians no longer represent what Jesus had intended. A survey of non-Christians aged sixteen to twenty-nine found that a high number of unbelievers were disappointed in Christians for being anti-homosexual (91 percent), judgmental (87 percent), hypocritical (85 percent), overly involved in politics (75 percent), and out of touch with reality (72 percent). They had experienced Christians to be insensitive toward their struggles and did not believe that Christians have sincere love for all people.[179] Not much has changed since that landmark study. According to more recent studies, unbelievers are disappointed that Christians in general have not shown sufficient leadership in resolving social problems prevalent in global society, such as poverty, racial discrimination, domestic violence, misogyny, and homophobia.[180] Rather than demonstrating that the church is working toward the common good, some of the most prominent Christian leaders worldwide were exposed in perpetuating the evils of globalization.[181] Their ethical failures are not only personal but also indicative of the church's struggle as a whole to exist as faithful witnesses of Christ's reign. Meanwhile, the

---

178. Bartholomew, *Contours of the Kuyperian Tradition*, 8.

179. Kinnaman and Lyons, *UnChristian*, 28.

180. Earls, "Young Adults See Leadership"; Benton, "White Noise and White Silence."

181. Influential Christian leaders with global leadership who were exposed for sexual abuse or inappropriate behavior toward women in the twenty-first century include Willow Creek Church founder and pastor Bill Hybels, Hillsong Church founder and pastor Brian Houston, and Christian minister and apologist Ravi Zacharias.

social justice movement has taken the lead in showing the world how societal problems should be resolved. Since the church has offered no alternative, a large portion of millennials and Generation Z are following the lead of social activists calling for a revolution in order to create a new world of solidarity.[182]

Throughout history, Christians have shown remarkable leadership by acknowledging the cultural realities of their time empathetically and refining them with biblical truths. These Christians did not abandon the world to decay in sin but, with mercy and love, strived to reform their society by giving spiritual and moral guidance to society's institutions. The cumulative effect of their engagement has healed and strengthened untold number of broken individuals, communities, and nations to make undeniable progress under the reign of Christ. Today, Christians are faced with newly emerging cultural realities that require theological engagement to further expand the reign of Christ in a globalized world. How Christians respond at this juncture of globalization is critical in regaining the credibility of the church as faithful witnesses of the gospel and ambassadors of Jesus Christ.

---

182. Blakemore, "Youth in Revolt"; Meehan, "Next Generation."

6

Theological Engagement with Globalization

THIS FINAL CHAPTER ACKNOWLEDGES the cultural realities that are emerging through globalization and engages with the theological issues raised by a globalized world. The interdisciplinary method incorporates the cultural realities into theology to enhance its efficacy in influencing globalization. The weakness of this method is that it can obscure the gospel in a long, drawn-out dialogue with diverse fields of knowledge. Thus, this chapter offers a theological framework that affirms the gospel in relation to globalization. The first part of the chapter addresses how the gospel can give meaning to humanity's existence as a whole, and how Christians can lead the world in pursuit of the common good. After establishing a theological framework based on the gospel, the second part of the chapter presents a theological response to the issues of globalization.

THEOLOGICAL FRAMEWORK FOR THE RENEWAL OF GLOBALIZATION

The purpose of theology is to make Jesus Christ known as the Savior of humanity and to renew the world by applying the ethical demands of the gospel in every domain of globalization. It engages with various public domains to discover new ways to administer God's grace and peace and promote the common good of global society. Before theology can engage with globalization, its framework must first affirm the core of the gospel that generates God's power of salvation. This theological framework consists of the following themes: (1) power of God for humanity's salvation, (2) existence of evil in society, (3) atoning work of Christ, (4) final judgment of Christ, and (5) good works of the church.

Power of God for Humanity's Salvation

A theological framework for the globalized world begins with soteriology, which has personal, communal, and societal implications.[1] When sinful individuals are saved by the gospel and their lives are united in the love of Christ, they become a holy nation with the power to act collectively to administer God's grace and peace in society for its renewal. The gospel is the power of God that saves humanity—the totality of the human being—from the power of sin and death (John 3:16; Rom 8:1–11). According to B. B. Warfield, "the unity of the human race" is the basis of the entire scheme of restoration devised by divine love for the salvation of a lost race.[2] The gospel is the good news of the kingdom of God disseminated to the poor (i.e., the captive, sick, and oppressed; Luke 4:18–19). According to Jesus, the good news is that God's reign has now come upon this world. He demonstrated God's reign by "preaching the gospel of the kingdom, and healing every disease and every infirmity" (Matt 9:35). Arias says that Jesus's evangelization was not limited to saving souls or performing social services. His gospel reflected "the biblical understanding of the human person as a total unity."[3]

The purpose of individual salvation is to become a part of the holy nation that fills the globalized world with God's love, truth, justice, and righteousness and promotes society's renewal. When corrupt individuals are saved by the gospel, their lives are joined together as the body of Christ to shine the light of God's glory by doing good works for society. The church's ministry of reconciliation sanctifies the world to become

---

1. Society is the result of social interactions between individuals. The term *societal* means relating to society or social relations. The adjective *social* can describe people, whereas the adjective *societal* cannot describe people.

2. Zaspel, *Theology of B. B. Warfield*, 392. Living in a society dominated by racism, Warfield was a forerunner in developing a theological framework for the globalized world. According to Zaspel, Warfield was ahead of his time in the matter of condemning racial pride. As a son of the South, he decried in his own Presbyterian church what he condemned in society at large. Referencing passages such as Jas 2:1–13 and Eph 3:1, he argued against those who were worried about probable intermarriage between the races.

3. Arias, *Announcing the Reign of God*, 3.

ready for the consummation of God's kingdom. This world that is corrupted by sin and evil will pass away, but it will also be renewed as the new creation for Christ's eternal inheritance. Those who are joined with Christ will become coheirs with him, receiving this world as their inheritance (Matt 5:16; Rom 8:17; Eph 2:10; Titus 3:8). This understanding of eternal life that gives purpose and meaning for humanity's existence is largely missing in globalization. According to Paul Tillich, "the ultimate negativity" that requires humanity's salvation is "condemnation or eternal death, the loss of the inner *telos* of one's being, the exclusion from the universal unity of the Kingdom of God, and the exclusion from eternal life."[4] Through separation from God, humankind has lost the meaning of its existence. Accepting the view that no objective meaning for life can be found, many people in Western society have found relief in two highly contradictory ways of life: materialism and social activism. They wish to enjoy the riches and comfort made possible by globalization without making the sacrifice necessary to heal their broken society. Social activism cannot renew society without the power of God's salvation. By contrast, those who are saved by the gospel are commanded to give up their life and take up the cross in following Christ. All Christians are called to serve the world as Christ did.

The primary strength of Protestant teachings is the doctrine of justification by God's grace alone, which enables corrupt individuals to receive the gift of salvation and claim righteousness from God through faith in Jesus Christ (Rom 3:21–24; Eph 2:8–9). Every believer of the gospel can stand firm in the righteousness of Christ and resist the temptation of remaining as a slave to sin (Gal 5:1). Believers are free to say "No" to sin and "Yes" to righteousness, bearing the fruit of sanctification that leads to eternal life (Rom 6:22).[5] These Scriptures teach that Christians should no longer live to please themselves by pursuing the lust of the flesh, but instead they should live to love God and their neighbors by doing good works. The reason why God made human beings in his image, according to Myers, is "to be creative and productive, nurturing God's creation for the well-being of all."[6] By his death on the cross, Christ has redeemed humanity to live as God intended. Those who believe the gospel have the power to resist sin and evil, and act as God's agents in society

---

4. For a brief explanation of how the term *salvation* was understood by various churches in history, see Tillich, *Systematic Theology*, 2:165.

5. Harvey, *Commentary on Romans*, 182.

6. Myers, *Engaging Globalization*, 24.

by administering his grace and peace. As a part of the holy nation, every Christian can overcome the evil one's scheme to destroy humanity.

When God's power of salvation comes upon individual lives through the gospel, and his kingdom of grace and peace permeates throughout society, a new kind of nation emerges in the world. According to Grenz, "When God's rule is present—when God's will is done—community emerges. Or viewed from the opposite direction, in the emergence of community, God's rule is present and God's will is accomplished." This dialectic of kingdom and community develops the concept of "the eschatological community."[7] He affirms, "The final goal of the work of the triune God in salvation history is the establishment of the eschatological community—a redeemed people dwelling in a renewed earth, enjoying reconciliation with their God, fellowship with each other, and harmony with all creation."[8] The people of God, living as the eschatological community, are united in the love of Christ, thereby transcending ethnic identity and allegiance to a single nation (Eph 4:1–6). They assume a new spiritual identity of the holy nation whose allegiance is to Christ and his kingdom. According to Grenz, the church is a community of God's covenant, consisting of those persons who declare individually their loyalty to God by confessing "Jesus is Lord."[9] He further adds, "By establishing the eschatological community of love, the covenant people, God brings into being a new humankind, a people who mirror for all creation the divine character and essence."[10] He concludes that the eschatological community of God reaches its fullness when heaven and earth are renewed after the final judgment of Christ.[11] God saves individuals to raise up the eschatological community, the holy nation that can unleash God's power of salvation in a globalized world for society's healing and renewal.

Existence of Evil in Society

Humankind wishes to flourish and live well together in a globalized world, but apart from being set free from the bondage of sin and being united in the love of Christ, individuals and nations of the world lack the

7. Grenz, *Theology for the Community*, 24.
8. Grenz, *Theology for the Community*, 115.
9. Grenz, *Theology for the Community*, 480.
10. Grenz, *Theology for the Community*, 489.
11. Grenz, *Theology for the Community*, 646.

power to overcome evil structures in society. The existence of evil naturally corrupts all societies, leading them to be overtaken by despotism and filled with crime, warfare, and violence regardless of their ideology. Rather than causing people to love one another, the collective activity of humanity without the power of God's salvation leads to envy, hatred, bitterness, murder, and destruction (Gen 6:5–12; Jas 4:1–2). The final result of hegemonic globalization is war between nations and, ultimately, the annihilation of humankind (Rev 19:19).

The nations of the world are vulnerable to structural corruption in society caused by the existence of evil. Liberal democratic society is no exception. Today, many experts are concerned that liberal democracy is in danger of falling apart.[12] Scott Moore says that "as statecraft, Liberal democracy is unmatched, and it is certainly superior to much of what has preceded it. But as soulcraft, Liberalism is woefully inadequate for the formation of persons who have competing ideas about and practices for obtaining human maturity."[13] The forces of fundamentalism, racism, and nationalism worldwide have revealed that society has not really changed much through human progress. Deep resentment has risen against the hegemonic globalization of the West that imposes a so-called global village, the ideological dream of liberalism that wishes to unite the world as one.[14] The cultural and social conflicts of the twenty-first century have shown that at their core, humans are tribal. In a global society shaped by liberal democracy, the existence of evil causes strife between peoples and leads to division and violence. At worst, society falls into anarchy, insurgency, revolution, civil war, or war against other nations.

Humankind cannot build a world order that can secure permanent peace because war is ingrained in the human condition. The corruption of individuals and society toward violence was evident from the beginning (Gen 2:17). The relationship between the first siblings of humankind deteriorated by envy and hatred, resulting in Cain's senseless murder of his brother Abel (Gen 4:1–8). When the human population multiplied, the

---

12. For an extensive study on how society struggles to maintain its liberty against a despotic state, see Acemoglu and Robinson, *Narrow Corridor*. The authors argue that the only way to prevent the state from growing into despotism is for society to gain more power by the persistent activism of its citizens; also see Cohn, *All Societies Die*. Cohn discusses the problems all societies face and the development of certain characteristics that threaten their survival. The author argues that the death of modern Western society is inevitable, but it is possible to prolong its existence by collective effort.

13. Moore, *Limits of Liberal Democracy*, 104.

14. Porter, *Global Village Myth*, 1–17. Mearsheimer, *Great Delusion*, 1–13.

world became corrupt and filled with violence (Gen 6:11–12). According to Lutheran theologian Adolph Harstad, "every utopian religion or philosophy that has the goal of eliminating all earthly warfare is doomed to fail because it fails to reckon with the total depravity of human nature and the ongoing activity of Satan in this world."[15] Thus, humans have waged war essentially since humanity began. The Thirty Years' War (1618–48) was one of the most destructive wars in European history, causing an estimated 4.5 to 8 million deaths. The current world order is a vestige of the Westphalian Treaty, which recognized the sovereignty of nation-states to minimize wars against one another.

A *nation* is a large group of people united by common ancestry, history, culture, and language. On the other hand, a *state* is a centralized political organization that imposes and enforces rules over a population within a territory. When globalization imposes to unite all nation-states into a single society, they are bound to war against each other. Geopolitical expert Christopher Coker explains that war "has played such a central role in the human story because it is embedded in our cultural evolution."[16] He says that for most of history, poets have inspired young men to take up arms and fight for the honor of their tribe or country. Today, video games and war movies fulfill the same role, enhancing the culture of war.[17] As with religion, war inspires people to believe in and die for something.[18] Arguing against John Mueller, who insists that war is merely a historical human creation and consequently can be simply eliminated as were slavery and dueling, Coker reasons that war is different.[19] Humankind is a story-telling species who developed the culture of war through the process of evolution; war is what makes us human and distinguishes us from other species.[20] Coker concludes that with the advancement of technology and complications of geopolitics, it is likely that humanity will continue to experience the evolution of war.[21]

15. Harstad, *Joshua*, 256.
16. Coker, *Can War Be Eliminated?*, xiv.
17. Coker, *Can War Be Eliminated?*, 18.
18. Coker, *Can War Be Eliminated?*, 24–33. The extremely popular war video game series *Call of Duty* has sold over 400 million copies, becoming the most successful video game franchise created in the United States. In cinema, the popular war movie *Saving Private Ryan* has fulfilled the culture enhancing role of the ancient poem of *The Iliad* and the nineteenth-century novel *War and Peace*.
19. Coker, *Can War Be Eliminated?*, 19–24.
20. Coker, *Can War Be Eliminated?*, 6.
21. Coker, *Can War Be Eliminated?*, 104–9.

War is the ultimate debasement of humanity, resulting from people's inability to settle for peaceful resolutions in cultural or social conflict. Confrontation of powers leads to organized killing, which is a unique feature of the human race. Humans are allowed to kill others with weapons only in a time of war. "The license to kill," according to Oona Hathaway and Scott Shapiro, "is among the strangest rules ever recognized by human beings."[22] The universal code of law for using violence was first introduced by the Dutch theologian Hugo Grotius. His book *The Rights of War and Peace* was a major defense of the rights of states and private persons to use their power to secure themselves and their property. According to Grotius, a declaration of war gives human beings the license to kill for both the just and unjust. Blanket immunity for killing others applied to all sides involved in a war. This law ensured the protection of the just from outsiders who may prosecute them as common criminals.[23] The just war theory and the international law that granted the license to kill in a declared war eventually led to World War I, which was promoted as "the war to end all wars." The war did not end quickly as expected. Instead, humanity began to experience war on an entirely new level. Europe was shocked by the new weapons of destruction that were used in the war against humanity. Shrapnel from mortars; grenades; and, above all, artillery projectile bombs, or shells, would account for an estimated 60 percent of the 9.7 million military fatalities of the war. The term *shell shock* began to be used in medical journals to describe a new type of mental injury emerging among many soldiers who bore no visible wounds.[24]

After World War I brought an end to the golden age of globalization, the leading statesmen of the world devised a plan to outlaw war. On August 27, 1928, the Paris Peace Pact (the Kellogg-Briand Pact) was signed by fifteen nations. This pact was initially proposed by French Minister of Foreign Affairs Aristide Briand to outlaw war between France and the United States. In response, US Secretary of State Frank B. Kellogg suggested that the two nations take the lead in inviting all nations to join them in outlawing wars of aggression. Within the year, almost every nation in the world had joined the pact, which required the signatories to outlaw war as an instrument of national policy and settle their disputes by peaceful

---

22. Hathaway and Shapiro, *Internationalists*, 63.
23. Hathaway and Shapiro, *Internationalists*, 70.
24. Alexander, "Shock of War."

means. For the first time in history, war became illegal.[25] Although the pact was a noble effort, a statement of liberal idealism expressed by the advocates of peace was insufficient to prevent World War II. The worst destruction of humanity in history was caused by the conflict between fascist, communist, and liberal nation-states of the world. Adherents of each political ideology claimed to fight for humanity, but instead, they unleashed weapons of mass destruction against it. The global war took an estimated total of 68 million lives, or about 3 percent of the 1940 world population.[26] Between 35 and 40 million people died in Europe as a direct result of the war. Historian Keith Lowe remarks: "Perhaps the only way to understand what happened is to stop trying to imagine Europe as a place populated by the dead, and to think of it instead as a place characterized by the absence. Almost everyone alive when the war ended had lost friends or relatives to it. Whole villages, whole towns and even whole cities had been effectively erased, and with them their populations."[27]

The trauma caused by the savagery of war remains not only in the West but also in the East. Most of the literatures on World War II depict it as essentially a Western war, minimizing the Chinese and Russian involvements and contributions in defeating the Axis forces. In a globalized world, however, it is important to recognize that the East suffered as much as the West during the war. From China's view, the war began in 1937 with the Rape of Nanjing, the mass murder and defilement of Chinese civilians in the capital city by the Imperial Japanese Army. China was the first of the Allies to fight the Axis power in Asia. As a result of this resistance, from February 18, 1938, to August 23, 1943, the provisional wartime capital of Chongqing suffered massive terror bombing operations by the Japanese military.[28] Within eight years of war, China lost an estimated 14 million lives while taking the brunt of Japanese attacks as

---

25. Hathaway and Shapiro, *Internationalists*, xii–xiii and 101–30. The authors argue that although the Paris Peace Pact did not end war between states, it marked the beginning of the end. The pact inaugurated a new era of human history characterized by the decline of inter-state war as a structuring dynamic of the international system. Between 1816 and 1928 there was on average one military conquest every ten months. After 1945, in very sharp contrast, the number of such conflicts declined to one every four years.

26. Lopez et al., *World War II: Infographics*, 5.

27. Lowe, *Savage Continent*, 16.

28. For a comprehensive history of the war from a Chinese perspective, see Mitter, *Forgotten Ally*.

"the great fourth ally."²⁹ Russia, on the other hand, bore the brunt of the fighting in the Eastern front of Europe, eventually launching massive counteroffensives that drove the Wehrmacht back into Germany, forcing the final surrender.³⁰ At the Battle of Kursk, the German strategic offensive was halted for the first time in the war before it could break through the Russian defense.³¹ Thereafter, Hitler's tank divisions, which had ravaged the whole of Europe, were decimated by the Red Army. The price of victory was staggering. It is now officially recognized that 26.6 million people of the Soviet Union gave their lives to defeat the Nazi fascism in what Russian people call Великая Отечественная война (The Great Patriotic War).³²

Although the West has celebrated May 8, 1945, as the Victory in Europe Day, the true victory in the world was not achieved on that day. Historian Sean McMeekin asserts that the main antagonist against humanity was not Hitler but Stalin. After the defeat of the Third Reich and the end of Auschwitz, the Soviet Empire continually expanded its terror against humanity, absorbing vast waves of forced-labor inmates in Stalin's Gulag camps with Poles, Latvians, Estonians, Lithuanians, Finns, Romanians, Crimean Tatars, Volga Germans, Circassian Muslims, Ukrainians, Balts, and Hungarians. In addition, almost 2 million Germans and nearly one million Japanese, Mongolians, and Koreans suffered in misery. The Soviet communist terror lasted until Stalin's death in 1953.³³ It is important to recognize that the suffering of humanity is beyond the boundaries of Europe. McMeekin reminds the West that under the Truman administration, American military and financial aid to China ended, whereas Stalin continued to provide Mao Zedong with whatever he needed, including new Soviet tanks and artillery. General George C. Marshall was sent to Chongqing in December of 1945 to broker a coalition government between Chiang Kai Shik's Nationalist Party and Mao Zedong's Communist Party, two mortal political enemies. Marshall's plan to form a coalition government failed. By 1947, Mao's Communists had won the Chinese

---

29. Mitter, *Forgotten Ally*, xii.

30. For a comprehensive history of the war from a Russian perspective, see Glantz and House, *When Titans Clashed*.

31. Glantz and House, *When Titans Clashed*, 167. The battle of Kursk counts as the greatest land battle in history. Three million soldiers, 69,000 guns, 13,000 tanks, and 12,000 aircraft were used by both sides.

32. Glantz and House, *When Titans Clashed*, 307.

33. McMeekin, *Stalin's War*, 651–52.

Civil War, which would lead to an untold number of human sufferings in the East.[34] On October 1, 1949, Mao declared China's independence and the creation of the People's Republic of China. His infamous experiment of social engineering, the Great Leap Forward (1958–62), subsequently caused the death of tens of millions.

In its evolution of war, humankind has pursued the path of developing weapons of mass destruction. By the end of World War II, humankind had developed nuclear technology, which could destroy most life on earth. On August 6, 1945, the United States dropped the first atomic bomb on the city of Hiroshima, Japan. Three days later, the second bomb was dropped on Nagasaki. An estimated 200,000 people died in the two cities. Upon hearing the news, Albert Einstein remarked, "Woe is me." Although he had no direct involvement in the Manhattan Project, Einstein had written a letter of warning to US President Franklin D. Roosevelt that the Nazis were working on a new and powerful weapon, an action he later regretted. His response represents humanity's guilty conscience for we were all somehow involved in this terrible project that led to mass murder in a blink of an eye. It is said that more than 130,000 people contributed their skills to the Manhattan Project.[35] In 1945, 85 percent of Americans approved of using the new atomic weapon. By 2015, the approval rating has only dropped to 56 percent.[36] It is a clear indication that humanity has not abandoned the belief that the use of nuclear weapons is sometimes necessary. Today, according to the International Campaign to Abolish Nuclear Weapons, a total of nine nation-states have developed nuclear weapons that are far more destructive than the original one. Detonating just one nuclear weapon over New York would cause an estimated 583,160 fatalities. Together, the United States, Russia, China, the United Kingdom, France, Israel, India, Pakistan, and North Korea possess 12,700 nuclear weapons, of which 9,400 are in active military stockpiles.[37] Even though it possesses enough power to destroy the planet many times over, humankind refuses to do what is sensible and end the nuclear arms race.[38] Humankind has also developed biotechnology that threatens planetary life through genetic engineering and synthetic

---

34. McMeekin, *Stalin's War*, 654.
35. Rhodes, "Why Robert Oppenheimer's Atomic Bomb."
36. Stokes, "70 Years after Hiroshima."
37. International Campaign to Abolish Nuclear Weapons, "Which Countries Have."
38. Rhodes, *Twilight of the Bombs*.

biology.[39] While many people idealistically think biotechnology could be used solely for the benefit of humanity, they underestimate the evil that exists in society and the potential development of new biological weapons.[40]

The reality of war and the development of weapons of mass destruction are the ultimate proof of the existence of evil. They accentuate the desperate need for humanity's salvation, which comes from God's judgment against evil. Although the promotion of peace initiated by leading statesmen, humanitarians, and spiritual figures seems laudable, from a biblical perspective, such efforts of humanity give the world nothing but false hope. According to the prophet Jeremiah, those who proclaimed peace without God's commission were false prophets who spoke of "false visions, divinations, idolatries and the delusions of their own minds" (Jer 14:13–14). The dream of achieving world peace without Christ is an idolatrous and delusional vision of liberalism.[41] There is, however, true hope of peace for those who look to the Savior. As Ps 46:8–9 says, "Come and see the works of the Lord, the desolations he has brought on the earth. He makes wars cease to the ends of the earth; he breaks the bow and shatters the spear, he burns the shields with fire." Christ fulfills this messianic prophecy by ending all wars between nations and eliminating all weapons of mass destruction. He has given his peace to those who believe in him (John 14:27; Rom 5:1). Thus, peace among nations is only possible when Christians act as "peacemakers" by ministering to all people in the world to be reconciled with God and with each other in Christ (Matt 5:9).

The presence of evil in society prevents humankind from pursuing God's kingdom of righteousness and peace. Globalization led by the West

---

39. Biotechnology refers to the application of scientific and engineering principles to the processing of materials by biological agents to provide goods and services. Genetic engineering is the process of using recombinant DNA (rDNA) technology to alter the genetic makeup of an organism. Genetic engineering involves the direct manipulation of one or more genes. Most often, a gene from another species is added to an organism's genome to give it a desired phenotype. Synthetic biology is the design and construction of new biological parts, devices, and systems, and the re-design of existing, natural biological systems for useful purposes.

40. Langer and Sharma, "Blessing and Curse of Biotechnology."

41. Mearsheimer, *Great Delusion*, 194–99. According to the proponents of democratic peace theory, nations that adopt liberal democracy do not go to war with each other. Mearsheimer, however, argues that there were at least four cases in the modern era where democracies waged war against each other: World War I, the Boer War between Britain and South Africa, the Spanish-American War, and the Kargil War between India and Pakistan.

cannot save humanity when it is driven by the collective activity of human hubris, which imagines itself as a creator and not a creature. According to Tillich, the word *hubris* "is most distinctly expressed in the serpent's promise to Eve that eating from the tree of knowledge will make man equal to God. *Hubris* is the self-elevation of man into the sphere of the divine. . . . It is universally human. . . . *Hubris* is not one form of sin beside others. It is sin in its total form." He adds, "All men have the hidden desire to be like God, and they act accordingly in their self-evaluation and self-affirmation."[42] Knowing the potential danger of humankind's collective activity driven by hubris, God frustrated the people who gathered in Shinar to build a city with the tower of Babel (Gen 11:1–9). This enigmatic story of the Old Testament serves as an important allegory of humanity's self-reliance and failure to save themselves without God's power of salvation. The New Testament also affirms that "God opposes the proud but gives grace to the humble" (1 Pet 5:5). God's grace is displayed in the world by the preaching of the gospel, which is "the power of God for salvation to everyone who believes" (Rom 1:16). The gospel frees humanity from the power of sin and death, and enables humanity to pursue God's kingdom of righteousness and peace (Rom 6:4–11).

It is through the proclamation of the gospel that God has planned to release his power of salvation for humanity. Those who acknowledge the corruption of individuals and society can humbly turn to Christ, the Savior of humanity who alone has the power to save individuals and raise up the holy nation that can heal social ills or evil structures in society. In the West, the existence of evil and human misery through war have caused many in the intellectual circles to doubt God's existence or sovereignty. By contrast, Nkansah-Obrempong explains that most African cultures do not see the presence of evil and suffering in the world as sufficient reason to deny the existence of God. In these cultures, God is the most powerful reality. Rather than focusing on the reality of evil, they choose to see God's presence, his providential care and love manifesting in the midst of the many evils present in their communities.[43] Nkansah-Obrempong argues that the problem of evil should not remain as an academic debate but rather must challenge humanity to take action against evil through means within one's power and sphere of influence.[44] He adds, "Since God hates evil, so must all who love him. Human communities should make

42. Tillich, *Systematic Theology*, 2:50–51.
43. Nkansah-Obrempong, "Problem of Evil," 301.
44. Nkansah-Obrempong, "Problem of Evil," 302–3.

sure they do something about the moral evil in societies by destroying evil structures and systems that have been put in place to nurture and promote evil in those societies."[45] When individuals are saved by the gospel and become a part of the eschatological community that is united in the love of Christ, they receive the power of God's salvation, which can overcome the evil structures in society. While preaching the gospel, the church can teach nations to lay down their weapons of war and destruction against humanity.

Atoning Work of Christ

Humanity is saved from the existence of evil by the power of God's salvation, which is generated by the atoning work of Christ. Atonement is the saving work of Christ that has reconciled humanity to God, thereby uniting individuals from diverse nations as one in Christ and making them into a "holy nation" (1 Pet 2:9). The atoning work of Christ eradicates the stains and effects of sin in individuals and raises them up as the church, "holy and blameless" children of God who can bring healing and renewal to broken society (Eph 1:3–6). Atonement is a multi-layered work that includes victorious (Satanward), substitutionary (Godward), and transformative (humanward) aspects. In Rev 11:15, the seventh angel proclaimed, "The kingdom of the world has become the kingdom of our Lord and of his Christ, and he shall reign forever and ever." This proclamation signaled that a monumental event had taken place in the course of history. According to James Hamilton, "the death and resurrection of Jesus of Nazareth is the definitive moment when the glory of God is displayed in salvation through judgment."[46] He adds, "The four Gospels all proclaim that salvation has come through the judgment that fell on Jesus."[47]

For the first thousand years after the death and resurrection of Christ, atonement was seen as Christ's cosmic victory over sin (John 8:34–36), death (Rom 6:23), and Satan and his demonic hosts (Luke 13:10–16). It was seen as Christ's act of delivering humankind from the enslaving powers by giving himself as a ransom (Matt 20:28). According to Swedish theologian Gustaf Aulén, the central theme of the classic view or the

---

45. Nkansah-Obrempong, "Problem of Evil," 302–3.
46. Hamilton, *God's Glory in Salvation*, 399.
47. Hamilton, *God's Glory in Salvation*, 439.

ransom theory "is the idea of the Atonement as a divine conflict and victory; Christ—Christus Victor—fights against and triumphs over the evil powers of the world, the 'tyrants' under which mankind is in bondage and suffering, and in Him God reconciles the world to Himself."[48] This classic view originated from Irenaeus, who described Christ's work as recapitulation. Summing up the life of humanity, Christ reconciled all things to himself by being born, living, dying, and resurrecting as a human being. As the Second Adam, Christ lived a perfect human life and triumphed at every stage over the power of evil, thereby reversing the effects of sin caused by the First Adam and restoring humanity's fellowship with God (1 Cor 14:45). The redemption or ransom was made not only by the death of Christ, but also through the entire life of Christ that was lived in this world. Following John Chrysostom's interpretation of Paul's directions for practical Christian living, the Eastern Orthodox Church has consistently held the classic view of atonement. Its theological emphasis is on the individual believer's union with Christ, taking seriously the promise of becoming "participants of the divine nature" (2 Pet 1:4).[49] Within the Western church, the Anabaptist tradition has kept the *Christus Victor* paradigm as a centerpiece of its approach to the atonement. Thomas Finger says, "Jesus the Victor locates struggle against evil at the heart of the Christian life—and the joyful assurance that evil will never prevail because it has already been decisively defeated."[50] Following Christ who overcame the evil powers of the world, Christians can live victoriously in the world, thereby influencing all peoples, nations, and civilizations.

After the Reformation, when Western society matured in its understanding of the Roman legal aspect of life, the substitutionary aspect of atonement became prominent. Christ's death on the cross was regarded as a legal penal transaction between God and Christ for the salvific benefit of humanity. It was the supreme sacrifice of love that appeased God's wrath toward sinners, upholding his holiness. When Christ was crucified on the cross, he became the propitiation for ὅλου τοῦ κόσμου, "all the world." God's wrath against humanity's sin was poured on him, thereby making the atoning sacrifice for all people (1 John 2:2, 4:10). The significance of Christ's self-sacrifice was that those who were far away from God "have been brought near by the blood of Christ" (Eph 2:13). Humanity was reconciled to God. According to William Tyndale,

48. Aulén, *Christus Victor*, 4.
49. Tibbs, "Eastern Orthodox Theology," 245.
50. Finger, *Contemporary Anabaptist Theology*, 364.

the blood of Christ was shed to forge the eternal covenant between God and mankind, to forgive the sin of mankind, and to enable mankind to obey God's law (Matt 26:28; Rom 12:1–2; Heb 9:22, 13:20–21).[51] In other words, God has promised to save humanity in Christ's blood; he has purchased humanity from the captivity of sin and death with Christ's blood; and he has liberated humanity for righteous living by Christ's blood. The atoning sacrifice of Christ makes it possible for all people who believe in him to conform to God's holiness.

In the age of globalization, Christ's work of atonement is transformative. By dying for the sin of humanity, he was given the authority to rule over this world (Matt 28:18). When Christ was raised from the dead, he overcame the power of death and became the Savior of the world (Rom 6:9). Hebrews 1:3 says, "After making purification for sin, he sat down at the right hand of the Majesty on high." Since then, metaphorically speaking, Christ is conquering this world by judging the nations and making war against them in his righteousness (Rev 19:11–16). The result of atonement is that Christ is saving the world by removing all that is evil in society and turning it into the kingdom of God. This work is done by God's people who choose to follow the moral example of Christ and suffer for his sake (1 Pet 2:21). The power of God's salvation extends to society at large when saved individuals learn to live in moral excellence and sincere love by taking interest in the affairs of others in society (John 13:34; Acts 4:32–35; 1 Cor 12:12–26; Eph 2:19; Phil 2:4). The moral excellence of Jesus and his example of love have established the ethics of the gospel by which God's kingdom can first be realized within the church and subsequently permeate society. In other words, God saves and heals the world by the power that flows from Christ through the ministry of the church. When Christians follow Christ and take up their cross by dying to self, evil structures in society can be conquered and destroyed (Rom 16:19–20; Rev 12:11). The church is the fullness of Christ, who "fills everything in every way" (Eph 1:22–23 NIV). Paul's declaration that God has installed Christ as the head "over everything" pertains to Christ's

---

51. Werrell, *Blood of Christ*, 12–13, 39–56, 95–98. According to Werrell, Tyndale's theology of covenant centered on the power of the blood of Christ, differing from Luther's theology of the cross and forensic justification. He emphasized the renewing and transforming work of the Holy Spirit within a person by the sprinkling of Christ's blood. Whereas Luther's justification of faith emphasized believers' deliverance from the condemnation of sin, Tyndale's justification of faith emphasized believers' re-creation by the blood of Christ and how this blood enables one to love God's law, to love one's neighbor, and to do God's will by one's good works.

supremacy over the principalities and powers of this world.[52] Through his work of atonement, Christ has raised up a holy nation that possesses the power to drive out evil from society, sanctifying the world to become ready for the consummation of God's kingdom.

Final Judgment of Christ

The completion of humanity's salvation comes through the final judgment of Christ upon all nations. When Christ returns in his glory after the tribulations of globalization, the world will be united as one, becoming the kingdom of God. As explained in the first chapter, from a biblical perspective, globalization has a purpose and meaning that is determined by God and carried out by humanity. Globalization can be defined as the divinely ordained process of creation, multiplication, dispersion, separation, redemption, integration, and sanctification of humanity in preparation for the consummation of God's kingdom. Many people will fall away from God, but at the same time, it is possible that a far greater number will return to him. When the nations of the world undergo the entire process of globalization, they will be ready for the final judgment of Christ, which would reveal the children of God and complete humanity's salvation (1 Cor 4:5; Rev 20:12). The biblical revelation regarding the final judgment of Christ accentuates humanity's need to be sanctified, through salvation as individuals and through renewal as society, for the consummation of God's kingdom.[53]

The final judgment of Christ is the way through which God saves humanity by eradicating those who are evil and preserving those who are good in the world (Matt 13:24–30, 36–43). When Christ returns, all the dead will rise to be judged according to their actions (Rev 20:11–15). Abraham affirms that God is the Judge who separates the righteous from the wicked (Gen 18:25). God's judgment of the nations would finally resolve the discordance of humanity caused by personal and social sin. Without the judgment that can remove all evil elements from the individuals and society, humanity would perish by being separated from the eternal presence of God's holiness. Until the return of Christ, the world remains corrupt by immorality and injustice, filled with violent conflict

---

52. Arnold, *Ephesians*, 115.

53. For a detailed exposition of humanity's need for salvation, see Demarest, *Cross and Salvation*, 28–31.

between peoples, nations, and civilizations. The Preacher observes that unfathomable evil and human sufferings exist under the sun. Thus, he declares, "Vanity of vanities! All is vanity" (Eccl 1:1–2). From a secular perspective, in his book *Being and Nothingness*, French philosopher Jean-Paul Sartre views the world to be absurd: human life has no sense, purpose, or explanation. He concludes that every individual must create meaning in one's own life by committing to social, political, and moral beliefs. He rejects Christian morality based on religion for surrendering humanity's problem to God and withdrawing from personal engagement.[54] Without resolving the discordance of the individuals and society, however, globalization fails to give meaning to humanity's existence. In contrast to Sartre's emphasis on the individual's choice of making a commitment, the Preacher concludes that the meaning of life can be found by those who trust in God by fearing him and keeping his commandments. He offers these last words of wisdom for the enlightenment of humanity: "For God will bring every deed into judgment, with every secret thing, whether good or evil" (Eccl 12:13–14). He is pointing toward the final judgment of Christ, which would fulfill God's promise to save humanity by separating those who are good from those who are evil. God, not the individual, is the Judge of humanity.

The final judgment of Christ entails eternal punishment against all who are evil and eternal life for all who are righteous (Matt 25:31–46). In the New Testament, Jesus and the apostles explain that the essential nature of the punishment is one's separation from God's holiness and exclusion from his kingdom of righteousness. Jesus lamented the sinful and unbelieving state of humanity, saying "when the Son of Man comes, will he find faith on the earth?" (Luke 18:8). Paul foretells the perilous time in which many people will depart from faith and the world will degenerate further into wickedness: "People will be lovers of themselves, lovers of money, boastful, proud, abusive, disobedient to their parents, ungrateful, unholy, without love, unforgiving, slanderous, without self-control, brutal, not lovers of the good, treacherous, rash, conceited, lovers of pleasure rather than lovers of God—having a form of godliness but denying its power. Have nothing to do with such people" (2 Tim 3:1–5). Paul also speaks about the revealing of the man of lawlessness and the rebellion of humanity against God before the day of the Lord comes (2 Thess 2:3). After removing those who participate in this rebellion, John reveals that

---

54. Sartre, *Being and Nothingness*.

the consummation of God's kingdom will bring forth the new heaven and earth, which are ruled by Christ and his saints. The new creation will be a dwelling place of God's holiness in which wicked individuals cannot exist (Rev 21:1–8).

Although the world remains corrupt, and God's judgment is impending against all who do evil, the gospel provides the way for sinners to be included in God's kingdom. According to Paul, those who "repent toward God" and "believe in Christ" are justified by the faithfulness of Christ (Acts 20:21; Gal 2:16).[55] The gospel invites and welcomes all sinners into God's kingdom of righteousness, but their admission requires repentance and faith (Matt 22:1–14). Those who believe the gospel are credited with God's righteousness and identified as God's people, Abraham's descendants and heirs of the promise (Gen 13:14–15; Rom 4:13; Gal 3:29). According to Peter, believers are "a chosen race, a royal priesthood, a holy nation, a people for his possession." Believers were once separated from God as a people, but now they have received his mercy (1 Pet 2:9–10). Knowing that they were once considered as God's enemies, Christians cannot refuse to show mercy toward those who sin against humanity (Matt 18:21–35). James elaborates further, stating that "judgment is without mercy to one who has shown no mercy. Mercy triumphs over judgment" (Jas 2:13).

The final judgment of Christ gives hope to those who believe in God's promise to deliver humanity from the oppression and injustice of globalization. Without the power of God's salvation, the nations of the world have failed to mobilize and work together in bringing justice, freedom, security, and prosperity for humanity. The United Nations is an intergovernmental organization made up of 193 member states to achieve international cooperation and be a center for harmonizing actions of nations. Since 1948, the organization has pursued its "peacekeeping," "peacemaking," and "peacebuilding" policies and operations worldwide. Despite the efforts of the member states, the United Nations could not achieve "peace and security" for humanity.[56] Chris McGreal offers a disturbing assessment of the leading institution in charge of global governance:

---

55. Schnabel, "Repentance in Paul's Letters," 159–86. The author argues that although Paul rarely uses the terms μετάνοια/μετανοεῖν, he uses other terms and phrases in order to express the need to change mind and heart, outlook and behavior.

56. United Nations, "Maintain International Peace and Security."

> In its 70 years, the United Nations may have been hailed as the great hope for the future of mankind—but it has also been dismissed as a shameful den of dictatorships. It has infuriated with its numbing bureaucracy, its institutional cover-ups of corruption and the undemocratic politics of its security council. It goes to war in the name of peace but has been a bystander through genocide. It has spent more than half a trillion dollars in 70 years.[57]

In his book *The Failure of the United Nations Development Programs for Africa*, Madagascan political scientist Adrien Ratsimbaharison gives a thorough appraisal of the politics of development within the United Nations that hindered rather than aided the growth of poorer countries. His study reveals that the United Nations has been much more about ideologically charged politics than about sound economics. He explains how the two major UN development programs for Africa in the 1980s and 1990s (UNPAAERD and UNNADAF) failed to promote economic and social development on the continent.[58]

According to Scripture, when the nations come together, they conspire to attack Christ and the church. Psalm 2:1–2 says that the nations rage and peoples plot in vain, and the kings and rulers of the earth conspire against the Lord and his Anointed. Revelation 20:7–8 says that Satan will deceive the nations and gather them for battle against the saints and the beloved city. These metaphors imply that the enemy will use the nations and world leaders to undermine the gospel and build evil structures in society that oppress the church from unleashing the power of God's salvation for humanity. Systemic persecution against Christ's disciples is the natural state of a world that remains corrupt (Matt 5:11; Luke 12:4–5; John 15:18; 1 Pet 4:12–14). Until the day of judgment, the tribulations of globalization continue to intensify the effects of evil structures in the world. The trials and temptations of globalization, however, sanctify God's people to be "perfect and complete, lacking in nothing" (Jas 1:2–4).

At the coming of Christ, God's kingdom of righteousness will consume this world, thereby completely replacing the institutions of globalization that have failed to administer justice and mercy for humanity. In the end, the nations will see the fruit of good works by the church, which would cause humanity to flourish. As a result, they will give glory to God by giving their allegiance to Christ. The saints, the holy ones

---

57. McGreal, "70 Years," para. 5.
58. Ratsimbaharison, *Failure of the United Nations*, 147–54.

who overcome the power of evil in the world, will inherit the nations of the world as the coheirs with Christ (Rom 8:17; Heb 1:2; 1 Pet 1:3–4; Rev 21:22–27). Pannenberg affirms that hope for the end-time kingdom of God "carries with it as such the thought of the reconciliation of the individuals and society."[59] He explains that God's kingdom demands all members of society to overcome the power of sin, thereby resolving the problem of governmental institutions that impose laws for all but cannot be free from injustice:[60]

> In keeping with the promise of Jer. 31:33–34 it demands that the righteous will of God be living and active in all human hearts. This means, however, that God himself must take control in human hearts so that we may accept one another, forgive one another, and help one another. Then it would no longer be necessary to enforce the legal claims of some against others. Then the rule of some over others would be superfluous, and the associated injustices would no longer be unavoidable.[61]

In Rev 18, Babylon is described as a global city that kills prophets and saints while seducing all the nations into corruption. It represents an all-powerful world system of a wicked society existing throughout history that opposes the gospel, corrodes the faith of individuals, and prevents the power of salvation from being unleashed through God's people. Thus, it must fall under the severe judgment of God. By contrast, Rev 21 describes the New Jerusalem as the Holy City coming down out of heaven from God. It is a renewed society consisting of all nations, built by the faithfulness of Christ that is actualized by the deeds of all God's people throughout history, culminating in a truly globalized world. Every single act of faith exercised by the human race would add up together and be realized in the new creation to make up a renewed society, becoming the kingdom of God (Mark 9:41; Heb 11:1–2, 39–40). Progressing toward such a glorious end, all nations are being tried and tested by globalization. Pannenberg affirms, "Eternity is judgment. . . . Eternity brings the truth about earthly life to light (4 Ezra 6:28) when the concept of truth is also characterized by the unity and harmony of everything that is true."[62] He explains that God's judgment removes everything that causes dissonance

---

59. Pannenberg, *Systematic Theology*, 3:584.
60. Pannenberg, *Systematic Theology*, 3:583–84.
61. Pannenberg, *Systematic Theology*, 3:584.
62. Pannenberg, *Systematic Theology*, 3:610.

in his kingdom.⁶³ Thus, he adds, "the judgment is simply that sinners are left to the consequences of their own deeds. When that takes place, their lives necessarily perish of the inner contradictions of their existence."⁶⁴ Consequently, after the final judgment of Christ, "the cowards, the unbelieving, the vile, the murderers, the sexually immoral, those who practice magic arts, the idolaters, and all liars" are excluded from God's kingdom and perish by "the second death" (Rev 21:8 NIV).

The final judgment of Christ is the full execution of God's justice in accordance with his ordinance, thereby sanctifying humanity to prepare for the consummation of God's kingdom. In the Old Testament, the Hebrew word מִשְׁפָּט (*mishpat*) means judgment, justice, or ordinance. These meanings are interrelated, reflecting God as the "Judge of all the earth" who loves "justice" and gives his "ordinance" (Gen 18:25, 37:28; Deut 6:1–5, 10:18; Eccl 12:14; Pss 50:6, 94:2). Understanding God's judgment in the light of these three unified concepts leads to humanity's sanctification by being saved as individuals and renewed as society. God does not want to destroy the nations but heal them by removing the evil elements from society through his צְדָקָה (*tsedeqah*), which means righteousness. As Isa 56:1 says, "Maintain justice and do righteousness, because my salvation is about to come, and my righteousness be revealed." When justice (*mishpat*) and righteousness (*tsedeqah*) are used in parallelism, God's חֶסֶד (*checed*, mercy, love, and kindness) emerges. In Scripture, God's justice is always accompanied by his act of righteousness that extends his mercy, love, and kindness to save humanity. This holy partnership between God's *mishpat* and *tsedeqah*, resulting in *checed*, means that the biblical concept of "justice and mercy" differs from the popular notion of justice in the world. Justice in our societies often takes on a punitive drive and comes to mean punishing those who do wrong or who do not conform to established societal standards. By contrast, biblical justice calls forth compassionate and delivering action for those who are downtrodden or cast out in society (Isa 58:6–7). Thus, in a globalized world, Christians are responsible for upholding God's "delivering justice" for the poor and helpless by extending God's mercy toward all who are suffering in sin, shame, and poverty because society has abandoned them.⁶⁵ When corrupt individuals are transformed into a holy nation that collectively

---

63. Pannenberg, *Systematic Theology*, 3:610–11.
64. Pannenberg, *Systematic Theology*, 3:611.
65. Choge and Stassen, "Social Ethics," 834.

rises to extend justice and mercy, God's glory would shine in society (Isa 60:1). The salvation of individual souls and the healing of broken society give meaning to humanity in a globalized world. The result is that at the renewal of creation, the nations of this world will not be destroyed but healed to become the inheritance for Christ and God's children (Ps 2:8–12; Ezek 47:12; Hos 6:1).

All people are God's children in the sense that they were created by God. In the sense of redemption, however, there exists the children of God and those of the enemy. God wants all people to be saved from the condemnation of sin, but only those who believe the gospel are spiritually born again as God's children to enter the kingdom (John 1:10–13, 3:3–18). Since God loves all people, Christians must possess his heart and act on his behalf by loving all people regardless of their class, gender, age, ethnicity, religion, or lifestyle. Globalization tests Christians in their response to those who suffer without partiality. According to Tyndale, Christians must love all people "because God hath created them unto his likeness, and Christ hath redeemed them and bought them with his blood."[66] He emphasizes that Christians must love all people because they do not know who God's elect is. Similarly, Jesus explains through a parable that at the end of the age, the angels will weed out of God's kingdom the children of the evil one, removing all causes of sin and all lawbreakers (Matt 13:36–43). Using the analogy of the vine and branch, Jesus affirms that it is the fruit of one's life that proves the genuineness of one's discipleship (John 15:1–8). Thus, God withholds his final judgment until the individual's fruit of life is fully displayed at the end of the age. Paul affirms it is premature for believers to pass judgment on others until the day when all individuals would have to stand before the judgment seat of God (Rom 14:10–12). Until the final judgment of Christ, all people should be treated and respected as God's children.

God is holy and love. Thus, he judges and loves all people without partiality, and his love is steadfast or unfailing. Today, God's love is often misconstrued with the expression "unconditional love." It distorts the nature of God's covenantal love by implying the false reality that God will receive all people into his kingdom of righteousness regardless of what they have done.[67] Such tolerance of sin by God would create an-

---

66. Tyndale, *Works of William Tyndale*, 1:470.

67. Gentry and Wellum, *Kingdom through Covenant*, 527–80. According to the authors, God's covenant cannot be understood as either conditional or unconditional. There exists a tension between the commitment of God to his promises and a call for

other unjust society, which would benefit no one. According to Edward Welch, God's love is deeper than abstract and ambiguous unconditional love. He explains, "God's love has an immense condition. It is bought at an astoundingly great price."[68] In the act of sending his only begotten Son to die on the cross, God's unfailing love has met the condition of his holiness and transcended his wrath against humanity's sin. Christ has demonstrated God's steadfast love upon all sinners, and accordingly, he calls all believers to stop living as God's enemies and start the new life of seeking God's kingdom and his righteousness (John 8:11; Col 3:1–3). By sending his Holy Spirit, God has enabled all his children to overcome evil by faith and deed. Those who succumb to evil by resisting all righteousness are the children of the devil (John 8:44; Acts 13:10; 1 John 3:10). God's judgment against evil, which brings forth salvation for his people, is the central theme that runs across Scripture (Gen 6:5–9; Deut 7:9–10; Ps 7:8–10; Isa 56:1), culminating with the day of judgment (Matt 24:36; Rev 20:11–13). Thus, Hamilton proposes that the center of biblical theology is "the glory of God in salvation through judgment."[69] He explains that God's salvation of his people always comes through judgment of their enemies:

> Salvation for the nation of Israel at the Exodus came through the judgment of Egypt, and this pattern is repeated throughout the Old Testament, becoming paradigmatic even into the New. When God saves his people, he delivers them by bringing judgment on their enemies. This is not limited to Old Testament enemies such as the Philistines. At the cross, the ruler of this world was cast out (John 12:31). At the consummation, Jesus will come to afflict those who afflict his people (2 Thess. 1:6, cf. 6–10).[70]

In Rev 6:9–11, those who died for the Word of God as his witnesses are seen standing around the throne of Jesus and crying out for justice: "O Sovereign Lord, holy and true, how long before you will judge and avenge our blood on those who dwell on the earth?" In response, the martyrs are each given a white robe and told to rest a little longer. Their cry for justice implies their salvation will be complete when God's judgment is made against their enemies. While those who loved Christ and suffered

---

obedience that affects how covenants are realized.

68. Welch, *Addictions*, 145.
69. Hamilton, *God's Glory in Salvation*, 39.
70. Hamilton, *God's Glory in Salvation*, 57.

for the gospel are saved, those who hated Christ and killed his witnesses are judged; they are excluded from the kingdom of God because they rejected Christ's ambassadors who speak for him (Luke 20:9–16; 2 Cor 5:19–20). When Scripture speaks of "the poor and meek" and "the least of these," it is primarily referencing the disciples of Christ who have accepted their lowly position as miserable sinners in this world and followed him by carrying the cross (Matt 5:3–12; 18:2–6, 10; 25:45).[71] George Ladd affirms, "The final destiny of individuals will be determined by the way they react to these representatives of Jesus. To receive them is to receive the Lord who sent them."[72] God's salvation for humanity comes through his judgment of the nations in their response to the gospel and treatment of those who bear witness to the gospel. It will be complete when the discordance between the individuals and society is resolved by the last judgment of Christ, uniting all nations of this world as one through the good works springing forth from the gospel.

Good Works of the Church

Good works of the church emanate from the gospel of true religion, demonstrating God's power of salvation for humanity in a globalized world. The gospel affirms that all believers are saved by God's grace, through faith which is the gift of God. Salvation is given freely apart from any good works of individuals so that no one can boast (Eph 2:8–10). As a result, all believers are joined together as the body of Christ to do the good works prepared by God (Rom 12:4–5; 1 Cor 12:12–14). God is glorified on the day of judgment when the world recognizes believers' good works that align with human "institution" ($\kappa\tau i\sigma\iota\varsigma$), which promotes justice and order in society (1 Pet 2:11–17).[73] Saved individuals, however, do not naturally know how to do good works that would benefit society. While believers are often convicted of turning from personal sins, they may remain oblivious to the social ills and structural evils perpetuated

---

71. Carson, "Matthew," 520.

72. Ladd, *Theology of the New Testament*, 117.

73. The biblical term *institution* ($\kappa\tau i\sigma\iota\varsigma$) refers to creation or the act of creating (Rom 1:20). Since humankind is made in God's image and represents God on earth, they are able to create institutions or ordinances to rule society. Both Peter and Paul taught Christians to submit to human institutions (1 Pet 2:13) or governing authorities (Rom 13:1). Jesus also affirmed Caesar's institution over the Roman society, namely the taxation of its citizens (Luke 20:25).

in society. As Fraser says, "Gaps exist in the institutions that facilitate globalization and moderate the ill effects of globalization. At the same time, theological and Christian ethical reflection has yet to catch up to the dramatic changes brought about by globalization."[74] Thus, the church must be educated and equipped to take social action collectively, having regard for the marginalized people affected by globalization (Ps 41:1). Through the gospel, which saves individuals from the power of sin, and the good works of the church that press the institutions of globalization, evil structures in society can begin to disintegrate.

Although the fruit of good works is not required for one's salvation, it is fully expected to be produced in the life of a believer (John 15:1–8). The constitution of the Missionary Church affirms that "a living faith must express itself in a life of loving obedience to God and in loving service to others. Genuine faith will inevitably produce good works, which are born out of gratitude for salvation and ultimately done for God's glory."[75] According to Paul, God's power of salvation is working in us "to will and to work for his good pleasure." The result is that our lives would be "blameless and innocent," without any blemish, making us "shine as lights in the world" (Phil 2:12–16). Doing good works for society is simply the proper outcome that stems from the gospel. According to James, faith and deeds are not the same thing but are inseparable (Jas 2:14). According to Ronald Sider, "Evangelism and social action are not identical. They are distinct, albeit closely related, activities. To insist on a distinction between evangelism and social action is not, however, to draw that distinction exclusively at the point of verbal proclamation versus visible demonstration. Both Jesus's actions and his words were central to his announcement of the kingdom."[76] Jesus's preaching was invariably accompanied by his ministry of healing, feeding, and comforting the helpless (Matt 9:36). Accordingly, the New Testament repeatedly exhorts the church to do good works (Titus 3:8). Believers were bought by the blood of Christ to live for God (1 Cor 7:22–23). The very purpose of their salvation is to serve others in society and thus bring glory to God (Matt 5:16; Mark 10:42–45).

Good works involve serving the poor, sick, and outcast in society by including them in the flourishing of humanity. Sadly, humanity's effort to build a just and orderly society through globalization has fallen short

74. Fraser, "Globalization," 342.
75. Missionary Church, *Constitution of the Missionary Church*, 7.
76. Sider, *Good News and Good Works*, 162–63.

by perpetuating social, economic, political, and cultural exclusion of the marginalized. The migration and refugee crisis, which has intensified in the last three decades, embodies the consequence of globalization: the rise of market-states has enabled opportunistic moguls, corporations, and investors to prosper immensely at the demise of nation-states and the breakdown of national communities.[77] According to a study by World Bank Group, "By the end of 2017, the world had witnessed its highest recorded number of forcibly displaced people worldwide to date at 68.5 million persons, including 3.1 million asylum-seekers and 25.4 million refugees."[78] These people are the losers of global capitalism. The great injustice and chaos resulting from globalization have now become evident, yet evangelical Christians in large have turned a blind eye to the evil structures that have caused suffering among the poor and powerless worldwide.[79] Many Christians in the West have supported global capitalism with its shortcomings while neglecting justice and mercy ministry for the poor. Waters argues that "if humans are to flourish, then economic exchange is a necessary but not sufficient condition."[80] Although he accepts economic globalization as the only viable option for alleviating poverty and promoting prosperity, he rejects the argument that Christians should ignore or gloss over the obvious problems of globalization.[81] He advocates that Christian moral theology should inform ethical and ecclesial leadership in a time when the globalized world is transitioning from nation-state to market-state.[82] Good works of the church entail standing against evil structures and developing new institutions of globalization that can allow humanity to flourish without exclusion.

From a biblical perspective, the great injustice and chaos of globalization are rooted in the "wickedness of man" that corrupts everything in society (Gen 6:5). It is Adam's sin, the original sin of humankind that has caused the corruption of society. The root of all problems in society

77. Waters, *Just Capitalism*, 60–79; Roberts and Lamp, *Six Faces of Globalization*, 55–77; Dasgupta, "Demise of the Nation State."

78. Devictor et al., "Globalization of Refugee Flows," 2.

79. For an overview of the structural and cultural critiques of modern worldviews and a proposal for solving the problems of globalization, see Goudzwaard and Bartholomew, *Beyond the Modern Age*, 37–56, 217–45. For a brief synopsis of the refugee crisis and theological approach to the crisis, see Măcelaru, "Christianity and the Refugee Crisis," 69–76.

80. Waters, *Just Capitalism*, 15.

81. Waters, *Just Capitalism*, 16.

82. Waters, *Just Capitalism*, 9.

lies in the heart of the individual. To resolve the human problem, Christ has commissioned the church to preach the gospel for the salvation of sinful individuals so they can do good works for the renewal of corrupt society. The Great Commission specifies that all nations should be made into Christ's disciples by "baptizing them" and "teaching them" to do all that Christ commanded (Matt 28:19-20). When Christians turn away from indulging in sin and begin to do good works for society, this action draws their respective nation closer to God by warming people's hearts that have turned cold toward others (Matt 24:12; 2 Tim 3:1-4). Good works afford the common ground between unbelievers and believers, whereby they can recognize God's power of salvation for individuals and his broader work of societal renewal. Augustine says, "A people is the association of a multitude of rational beings united by a common agreement on the objects of their love."[83] When individuals are saved by the gospel, and society is pressed by good works of the church, all nations in the world must choose between love of God and love of self. The great ministry of the church is to evangelize and teach nations how to seek God's kingdom and his righteousness by converging on the common ground of human flourishing. To serve the poor and powerless in a globalized world, the church must collaborate with nation-states to end militarism and improve political order, market economy, and sustainable environment. When unbelievers and believers work together for the common good, this action builds solidarity among peoples, nations, and civilizations, thereby preparing humanity to accept God's kingdom of grace and peace at the coming of Christ.

The gospel redefines what a society ought to be and paves the way for social action of the church. According to Singaporean theologian Michael Poon, since the early days of Christianity, becoming a disciple of Christ was never a private affair. Disciples had to redefine their lives and reinterpret their worlds. For the first Christians living in the Roman Empire, their confession of faith in Christ was an act of refusal to accede ultimate loyalty to Caesar. For instance, they found military service problematic because the military oath might compromise their allegiance to Christ.[84] Poon says, "Christian reflection on discipleship led necessarily to discussion on public matters and eventually on the nature of the society. As Christians began to define their 'Christian' boundaries, the

---

83. Augustine, *City of God against the Pagans*, 960.
84. Poon, "Patristic Theology," 630-31.

question, What should a society be? naturally followed."[85] Thus, the church maintained an ongoing dialogue with the world to address the problems rooted in the evil structures of society. The church's engagement with society opened up the opportunities for Christians to become its agents of change. Poon adds that "doctrinal, missiological and ecclesiological reflections were coordinated within a more fundamental reflection of what the gospel of Jesus Christ meant for human society.... Ecclesial life itself was formulating the necessary public frameworks that would eventually bring forth the birth of the Western world out of the ruins of the Roman Empire."[86]

Sider identifies three categories of social action: relief, development, and structural change. In relief, we seek to provide immediate material needs to victims in society. In development, we seek to help individuals, families, and communities obtain appropriate tools, skills, and knowledge and thus care for themselves. In structural change, we seek to demolish the abusive powers of society's elites, who take advantage of the poor and weak.[87] According to Sider, "Politics is one of the important ways to change the basic societal structures to create greater freedom, democracy, economic justice, and environmental sustainability."[88] Political works of the church in this world are not about taking sides or identifying with a political party, but about persuading and uniting people to take the right social action in building a just and orderly society. Jesus authorized political engagement of the church when he pronounced to Peter, "I will give you the keys of the kingdom of heaven; whatever you bind on earth will be bound in heaven, and whatever you loose on earth will be loosed in heaven" (Matt 16:19).[89] The church has always been the custodian of God's kingdom, which consists of both the spiritual and political realms. Until the return of Christ, the church has the keys to open or shut the door to those who wish to enter the realm of God's blessings on earth. The gospel opens the door in the private sphere, while social action opens the door in the public sphere.

Jonathan Leeman states that "the activities of the public square are always undergirded by some spiritual or religious worldview and that everything taught inside a church building has political meaning because

85. Poon, "Patristic Theology," 631.
86. Poon, "Patristic Theology," 631.
87. Sider, *Good News and Good Works*, 138–39.
88. Sider, *Good News and Good Works*, 139.
89. Leeman, *Political Church*, 22.

the church is a political assembly."[90] Although the church and the state are separate institutions, Leeman believes they are partially overlapping in religious and political circles of realities,[91] adding that "we must not confuse separation of church and state with the separation of religion and politics."[92] Contrary to secularists who insist that religion should be kept out of the public square, the founding fathers of the United States never intended for Christians to have no political influence in society. In Great Britain and the United States, the institution of slavery was finally abolished by political means, which were strengthened by the religious convictions based on Scripture.[93] The biblical teachings, persistent prayers, and social actions of Christians prevailed against the evil structure within human institution that excluded black slaves from participating in a liberal democratic society. The issue of racial conflict, however, remains unresolved in US society as the church has largely withdrawn from taking social action in the public square, thereby closing the door to the kingdom of heaven.

The work of healing a broken society is a privilege delegated to the church. Finger asserts that the church is the eschatological sacrament, embodying God's desire for the world and calling people toward them.[94] The church is the model of God's kingdom, his chosen instrument to heal a distressed and wounded society. Meanwhile, governmental and nongovernmental agencies exist to complement the church by providing necessary assistance, such as passing new laws, conducting research, and engaging in international cooperation. Unlike the gospel, laws do not change people's hearts. God did not empower the United Nations or the nation-states to alleviate the misery of the poor and powerless. In the early twentieth century, the church at large made a critical error by not preaching about justice or God's concern for the poor in society.[95] This overreaction against the heretical aspect of social gospel diverged from

---

90. Leeman, *Political Church*, 94.

91. Leeman, *Political Church*, 94.

92. Leeman, *Political Church*, 95.

93. Shaw, *Churches, Revolutions and Empires*, 139–62. The abolition campaign in Britain was led by those who believed that Britain had been providentially set apart to take a moral lead on the issue. They succeeded in persuading a large section of society to oppose slavery. Among Christians, Quakers stressed the universal brotherhood of mankind by using Acts 17:26. William Wilberforce relied on Exod 21:16 and 1 Tim 1:9–10 as a basis for opposition to slave trading.

94. Finger, *Contemporary Anabaptist Theology*, 256.

95. Sider, *Good News and Good Works*, 35.

the preaching and good works of the Old Testament prophets, Jesus, the early church, and the Reformers.[96] By neglecting its ministry of justice and mercy, the church has allowed governmental and nongovernmental agencies to usurp its sacred role given by God, thereby leading globalization to become corrupted by injustice and disrupted by chaos. Thus, the separation of church and state is no longer a viable solution to solve the problems of globalization. To reclaim its sacred role of healing all nations, the church must preach the gospel to save individuals and take the necessary social actions to renew all domains of globalization.

The good works that God expects from the church are to make this world a place where God's holiness can dwell: a renewed society of love, truth, justice, and righteousness, where God's people would turn from evil and seek good (Amos 5:6–24). Volf and Croasmun affirm that "the purpose of theological endeavor is to discern, articulate, and commend visions of flourishing life in light of Jesus Christ in a given time and place,"[97] referring to the world in which God would dwell with humanity. They explain that the kingdom of God refers to both God's rule and realm. Without the realm, God would rule over nothing. Inversely, without the rule, the realm would not be God's, and God would not be God in it. Thus, God became the king when he created the world. Volf and Croasmun assert that the kingdom of God Jesus proclaimed and enacted is a particular kind of *dynamic relation* between God and the world; it is "the world-with-God" and "God-with-the world." Human beings and the world come to fulfillment when they become what God always intended, when God comes to dwell in the world and the world has become and experiences itself as being God's home.[98] The new creation is, therefore, a transformed world in which God's holy presence is with humanity. The purpose of creation and redemption is the sanctification of humanity. God's people are liberated from sin so that they can act with the power of God to build the

---

96. Daniel, "Three Fallacies." In the early twentieth century, the social gospel movement falsely believed that the Second Coming of Christ could not happen until humanity rid itself of all social evils by human effort. Walter Rauschenbusch and his followers tended to blame sin on societal structures rather than human nature. They applied Christian ethics to social justice issues, especially as it related to economic policy. They also believed that the gospel was centered on cultural movement, over-emphasizing cultural restoration and minimizing Christ as agent of cultural transformation. Finally, redemption was seen to be achieved collectively, by means of unified social and political activism.

97. Volf and Croasmun, *For the Life*, 61.

98. Volf and Croasmun, *For the Life*, 66–71.

world as a home for Christ. In this new world, where heaven and earth are merged, they will reign with Christ forever (Rev 22:5).

THEOLOGICAL RESPONSE TO THE ISSUES OF GLOBALIZATION

This second section introduces the theology of True Globalization. It aims to educate and equip the church to respond to the issues of social justice, religious pluralism and ethics, and the missional method. When individual human beings are regenerated and their hearts transformed by God's word, they can be educated and equipped to serve humanity as ambassadors for the reign of Christ in all domains of this world.

True Globalization

The era of contemporary globalization is coming to an end, thereby making way for God to manifest his grace and peace more fully than in previous times in history through True Globalization. The term *True Globalization* refers to the fulfillment of God's own globalization through which he brings all things in heaven and on earth under the lordship of Jesus Christ in accordance with Eph 1:10.[99] It first began at Pentecost when the church received the power of the Holy Spirit to be the witnesses for Christ. The first Christians all spoke in other tongues to praise God in unison, signifying that the gospel was now bringing diverse peoples, nations, and civilizations of this world into complete unity in Christ (Acts 1:4–11). Aligning with God's eternal purpose of bringing the whole world under the lordship of Jesus Christ, a truly globalized world is characterized by the church's engagement with all domains of globalization in preparation for the consummation of God's kingdom in the world (Isa 2:2–4, 9:7).

When the gospel spreads throughout the world, the power of God's salvation transforms not only individuals but also their respective society. In the past, all societies were separated by languages, cultures, political borders, and distance; therefore, Christians were only able to

---

99. The conception of *True Globalization* in this book was inspired by the "Letter to the Churches of the North" written by the participants of the WCC-WARC-CCA-CCT-ACFOD Symposium on the Consequences of Economic Globalization (November 12–15, 1999, Bangkok, Thailand). This letter is reprinted in Andringa and Goudzwaard, *Globalization and Christian Hope*, 23–25.

influence their local community, city, or state. Today, almost all societies are joined together by economic integration, ease of international travel, the Internet, and homogenizing cultural forces. In this universal environment, the gospel can spread faster and wider than at any other time in history, and Christians can have a global influence. If the gospel can save and change the lives of individuals but cannot transform the world at large, the power of God's salvation would seem quite limited. According to Jesus, the "light" of believers displays the glory of God to unbelievers and prepares the world for Christ's return. The imagery of light refers to good works that Christians do in the world (Matt 5:14–16). In the age of True Globalization, Christians have the power to do what is good and instill the ethics of God's kingdom in all domains of globalization, thereby sanctifying humanity to come under the reign of Christ on earth. Through the preaching of the gospel and the doing of good works, God's kingdom of righteousness is displayed for all to see.

According to Jesus, the kingdom of God expands to cover the whole world as time passes (Matt 13:31–32; Mark 4:30–32; Luke 13:18–19). Before he ascended into heaven, he commissioned his disciples to go into the world and make disciples of all nations by teaching them to obey all that he has commanded. In his letter to the Ephesians, the apostle Paul affirmed that God's incomparably great power, the same mighty strength that was exerted to raise Christ from the dead, is available for those who believe the gospel (Eph 1:19–20). In the Old Testament, God showed the prophet Ezekiel that he is able to raise up "an exceedingly great army" of Israel among the dry bones in the valley (Ezek 37:10). In the New Testament, God revealed to the apostle Paul that "the Israel of God" refers to people of faith, consisting of both the Jews and the gentiles (Gal 6:16). In the apostle John's vision, "the armies of heaven" are raised up to wage the most intense spiritual warfare against the evils in this world. They follow Christ, who sits on a white horse while clothed in fine linen, white and clean (Rev 19:14). The color white symbolizes the purity of God's holiness, wisdom, love, and righteousness. The armies of heaven are Christians who are given the mandate to make the full preparation for the day of the Lord by preaching the gospel and showing the world how to live according to God's holy statutes.

True Globalization does not refer to the Christianization of the world. Christianity is not a synonym for the gospel. Netland explains that every form of religion includes the social, cultural, and historical patterns of distinct religious communities; therefore, believers of the gospel should acknowledge that the same limitation applies to Christianity.[100] In a pluralistic society, all believers must learn to hold dialogue with secularists and other religious adherents for the common good of humanity, as the relation between Christians and others is not one of division and conflict. This approach should not become a compromise with secularists or interfaith worship with other religious adherents. Christians must talk with others without succumbing to relativism. Respecting other people's traditions and values should not prevent them from speaking clearly about the gospel and displaying the ethics of God's kingdom. There are, however, certain things beyond the gospel that Christians can learn from interaction with others. The plausibility of the gospel will rest on the way the church demonstrates its faith with action. Christians not only believe in the power of Christ's blood that washes away their sin but also display his virtue of moral excellence. The power of true religion is the spiritual and moral strength of Christ, which is displayed by Christians living in a globalized world. The ministry of the church is to awaken the world spiritually and morally to prepare it for the coming of Christ. In a parable, Jesus describes the church as the servants who are ready and keep the lamps burning while waiting for their master to return from a wedding banquet, so that when he comes and knocks, they can immediately open the door for him (Luke 12:35–59). When Christians are united in their collective ministry of administering God's grace and peace to the world, this leads to the sanctification of humanity by naturally curbing social, class, gender, and ethnic oppression and discrimination worldwide (Isa 58:5–7; Jas 2:1–13).

Temple of God's Dwelling

The age of True Globalization bears the first fruits of what is to come at the renewal of creation upon the return of Christ, bringing closer unity among believers in Christ to serve as faithful witnesses of the gospel (Ps 133:1; John 17:21). The eschatological community consists of all believers in Christ throughout the history of globalization. Contrary to popular understanding, Christians are not to be simply taken up to live in ethereal heaven but are to exist as God's temple in the world by coming down from heaven to earth (Rev 21:2).[101] By believing the gospel and living in

---

100. Netland, *Christianity and Religious Diversity*, 165–67.
101. See Beale, *New Testament Biblical Theology*, 751–52, 759–60. Beale argues that

obedience to God's command of love, all God's children would become the temple of God's dwelling.

The church's great ministry is to prepare humanity for the day of the Lord, upon which heaven and earth would be fully integrated as the new creation. Since this world is the church's inheritance in Christ, believers have the responsibility to administer God's grace and peace to all people. Scripture promises that God's power working through his children will destroy the rulers, authorities, and cosmic powers of this dark world, and the spiritual forces of evil in the heavenly realms (Eph 6:10–12). Removal of evil requires repentance from sin. This biblical understanding of upholding God's love, truth, justice, and righteousness is entirely absent from secular institutions promoting liberal democracy, human rights, and social justice. Although unbelievers claim to pursue justice, freedom, security, and prosperity for all people, they are in actuality attempting to build a world that falls short of God's glory. Without becoming reconciled with God and with each other through Christ, globalization cannot bring forth human flourishing in the world. Without receiving the gospel and living in obedience to Christ, humanity lacks the power to change society.

Christians need to reassess how the church should interact with the social justice movement of the world. When contemplating social justice, if the term *justice* is understood in the biblical sense of making right, it is not an option for Christians, who are commanded to be righteous. As Tim Dearborn writes, "Justice is a relational term—*people living in right relationship with God, one another and the natural creation*."[102] He adds, "For Christians, pursuit of social justice for the poor is the decisive mark of being people who submit to the will and way of God."[103] Since the 2010s, however, the meaning of social justice has changed drastically. According to Thaddeus Williams, "social justice is one of the most epic and age-defining controversies facing the twenty-first-century church."[104] The term *social justice* has now become ubiquitous, permeating every area of global society. In the past, it was mainly understood as a religious conception,

---

Eden was a garden sanctuary and Adam was its high priest. Adam was a divine image-bearer whose task was to fill the world with God's glory by expanding the garden's territory. This divine purpose is finally fulfilled when God's faithful people become the temple-city that would widen to cover the whole world.

102. Dearborn, *Reflection on Advocacy*, 16.
103. Dearborn, *Reflection on Advocacy*, 21.
104. Williams, *Confronting Injustice without Compromising*, 1.

arising from Scripture's commands to "do justice and righteousness" and "seek justice" for the poor and outcast of society (Mic 6:8; Isa 1:17). Williams explains how this Christian understanding of social justice has been altered today to reflect different values:

> In the last few years, social justice has taken on an extremely charged political meaning. It became a waving banner over movements like Antifa, which sees physical violence against those who think differently as "both ethically justifiable and strategically effective" and celebrates its underreported "righteous beatings." Social justice is the banner waved by a disproportionate ratio of professors in universities around the nation where the "oppressor vs. oppressed" narrative of Antonio Gramsci and the Frankfurt School, the deconstructionism of Michel Foucault and Jacques Derrida, and the gender and queer theory of Judith Butler have been injected into the very definition of the term. This ideological definition of social justice has been enshrined in many minds not as *a* way but as *the* way to think about injustice.[105]

When the concept of social justice removes its roots from God's power of salvation for humanity, it becomes a dangerous entity or movement of social activism that aims to destroy society. Secularists Helen Pluckrose and James Lindsay argue that postmodernism has led to the development of a social philosophy called theory. Postmodernism applies its cynical theories to deconstruct conventional religions such as Christianity, secular ideologies such as Marxism, and cohesive modern systems such as science, philosophical liberalism, and progress. Postmodernism then replaces them with a new religion of its own, called social justice.[106] According to Pluckrose and Lindsay, the scholarship undertaken under the broad banner of social justice took shape within a new, third phase in the postmodern project.[107] They explain how social justice scholarship and its activists now drive theory, a new meta-narrative that defines society as consisting of only the oppressed and the oppressors:

> The postmodern knowledge principle and the postmodern political principle were used primarily for deconstructive purposes in the first phase (roughly 1965–1990) and made applicable for reconstruction during the second phase in the form of applied

---

105. Williams, *Confronting Injustice without Compromising*, 4–5.
106. Pluckrose and Lindsay, *Cynical Theories*, 17–18.
107. Pluckrose and Lindsay, *Cynical Theories*, 181.

postmodernism (roughly 1990–2010), yet they were confined principally to specific academic fields and activist circles. In this third phase of postmodernism, these principles are treated as fundamental truths both within these two settings and beyond. After decades of being treated like knowns within sectors of academia and activism, the principles, themes, and assertions of Theory became *known-knowns*—idea taken for granted as true statements about the world that people "just know" are true. The result is that the belief that society is structured of specific but largely invisible identity-based systems of power and privilege that construct knowledge via ways of talking about things is now considered by social justice scholars and activists to be an objectively true statement about the organizing principle of society.[108]

Although Christians have a long tradition of providing charitable relief to the poor and outcast of society, the church no longer controls or influences the definition of what constitutes social justice. According to Michael Novak, the term *social justice* was originally a Catholic term, first used in circa 1840 to denote a new kind of virtue necessary for post-agrarian societies. Social justice was once understood as the capacity to organize with others to accomplish ends that benefited the whole community. It was a virtue or habit necessary in building free societies. Today, the meaning of social justice is determined by the academics, affirming the idea of "uniform state distribution of society's advantages and disadvantages."[109] The *Oxford English Dictionary* defines social justice as "Chiefly *Politics* and *Philosophy*. Justice at the level of a society or state as regards the possession of wealth, commodities, opportunities, and privileges."[110] Dictionary.com, a popular online dictionary for ordinary people, defines social justice as "fair treatment of all people in a society, including respect for the rights of minorities and equitable distribution of resources among members of a community."[111] Social justice is now commonly understood as equal or equitable distribution of wealth, opportunities, and privileges. Under the current definition of social justice, evangelical Christians are struggling to make a meaningful stand with those who are suffering from the consequence of globalization: the widening disparity of wealth. As the temple of God's dwelling in this world,

---

108. Pluckrose and Lindsay, *Cynical Theories*, 182.
109. Novak, "Social Justice," para. 1.
110. *Oxford English Dictionary*, s.v. "Social Justice."
111. Dictionary.com, s.v. "Social Justice."

Christians must reclaim the biblical definition of social justice and take decisive action.

Most Christians associate social justice with charitable work that provides relief to and saves the lives of the marginalized and disadvantaged in society. As social scientist Allan Ornstein says, "The notion of social justice is based on the Christian doctrine of helping less fortunate people—the weak, sickly, and oppressed."[112] Jesus cared deeply about people. Following in his footsteps, an untold number of Christians went out of their way to eradicate societal injustices. Greek and Roman society, like all the previous ancient societies, were built on the backs of slaves, and only a minority of Greeks and Romans enjoyed the rights and privileges. Most people ignore the fact that both civilizations believed in a government run by the well-educated and property class—what later would be called the European nobility. The idea of a social contract between government and the people, or that people had natural rights and could live a decent life with access to opportunities for improving their condition, was considered illogical and contrary to the norms of society. This attitude began to change in the United States, spearheaded by political leaders influenced by the humanitarian ideas of the Age of Enlightenment.[113]

Since the 1920s, social democratic governments in Western Europe have reinforced the view that all citizens should be treated equally. This means that income and wealth should be redistributed to ensure greater opportunity and equality, and thus more justice, among the populace. In the United States, association with Europe's social democracy was avoided; therefore, the word *liberalism* was used in lieu of socialism. When *liberal* became a derogatory word, the same ideas were expressed as "progressive." In 1971, John Rawls's book was influential in determining that justice must be conceived in terms of fairness and basic moral principles. Eventually, the notion of justice was fused into the US civil rights movement, emphasizing the rights of all people and the moral principles of justice.[114]

According to John Stott, in the twentieth century, evangelicals reacted against the so-called social gospel that theological liberals were developing at the time. The aim of the social gospel was to bring about a Christian society by social and political action. Theologians such as Walter Rauschenbusch criticized capitalism and advocated a simple kind

---

112. Ornstein, "Social Justice," 545.
113. Ornstein, "Social Justice," 546–49.
114. Ornstein, "Social Justice," 550.

of "communism" or Christian socialism. Rauschenbusch's main error was in identifying the kingdom of God with "a reconstruction of society on a Christian basis." He also erred by implying that human beings can establish the divine kingdom by themselves.[115] Against the wrongful approach of the social gospel, Stott explains how God's kingdom is built through the gospel: "The kingdom of God is not Christianized society. It is the divine rule in the lives of those who acknowledge Christ. It has to be 'received', 'entered' or 'inherited' by humble and penitent faith in him. God's new society is called to exhibit the ideals of his rule in the world and so to present the world with an alternative social reality."[116]

In reacting against the social gospel, evangelical Christians have largely shunned the ministry of alleviating social ills until recent times. They have often used the Scripture, which says "the poor you will always have with you" (Matt 26:11), to reinforce the idea that it is not God's will to eradicate poverty in the world. Many evangelicals solely understood their mission as preaching the gospel. It was widely believed that Christian involvement with social work would be a slippery slope to joining with the liberals, who were linked with Marxist ideals and collectivism. By reacting against the social gospel, they allowed most of the social work for justice to be done by those who were outside the church. By separating the Christian mission from meaningful enterprise in social reform, the church often fell short of taking decisive actions that would give plausibility to the gospel.

Since social justice is not actually a part of the gospel, many evangelical Christians have not integrated it into their ministry. The mission of the church, however, is not simply propositional proclamation of the gospel. If this were so, Christ would not have fed the thousands of hungry people who followed him; however, when preaching the gospel, he healed and comforted those who were abandoned in society. Christians can only accomplish God's mission when they begin to feel the suffering of the world by walking closely with its people. The Christian mission is to plant the gospel message in the hearts of people by showing God's love and compassion. If so, is there any common ground between the mission of the church and the objectives of the social justice movement? There are certainly some overlapping areas between the two approaches. For example, American churches cannot put off racial reconciliation any

---

115. Stott and Wyatt, *Issues Facing Christians Today*, 29.
116. Stott and Wyatt, *Issues Facing Christians Today*, 29.

longer by simply posting official statements against racism. If Christians do not want to march with social activists in the street, they can earn their trust and respect other ways. Denominations need to simply end racial segregation on Sunday mornings by organizing their churches to meet together as one body of Christ, regardless of how their members respond. Scripture clearly indicates that division in church grieves the Holy Spirit. There is no reason why denominational leadership cannot give practical guidance toward the path of unity. American Christians cherish personal freedom of choice, but there are times when God's people need to unite for a greater purpose. If Christians can lead the United States to eliminate racism from society, they would become powerful witnesses in the eyes of the world. Today, Christians who have received the divine rule over their lives are called to model the kingdom of God in global society so that the world can easily recognize and accept the reality of Christ's reign on earth.

Prince of Peace

According to Scripture, Jesus Christ is the Prince of Peace. The prophet Isaiah prophesied that "the government will be on his shoulders" (Isa 9:6). He came into this world to dispense God's grace and peace for humanity's flourishing (Luke 2:14; John 14:27). To accomplish this mission, he defeated Satan and cast him out of the heavenly realms so he could draw all people to himself through the gospel (John 12:32). Satan, the prince of this world and the enemy of God, leads the whole world astray by deceiving its people to reject the Word of God (Rev 12:9). Nations that resist Christ and his gospel are described as being at war against him (Ps 2:1–3). Christ is the King of kings and Lord of lords, who strikes down the nations of this world with a "sharp sword" and rules them with an "iron scepter" (Ps 2:8–9; Rev 19:15–16). These metaphors indicate that Christ rules over this world with power and authority, judging all the nations. By the preaching of the gospel, his kingdom of grace and peace has already taken root in this age and will keep growing larger and stronger toward the age to come (Matt 28:18–20; Acts 1:8; 1 Tim 2:1–4). In this age, God does not want his people to engage in militaristic or cultural warfare; rather, he wants the church to seek peaceful relationship with the people of this world without compromising the gospel (Heb 12:14; Rom 12:17–18). In other words, he wants his people to engage in a "spiritual warfare," which involves the ministry of praying for unbelievers and bringing them closer to becoming reconciled with God (Eph 6:12; Matt 5:43-48; Luke 6:27). God's purpose of globalization is to draw many people to him and prepare humanity for the consummation of his kingdom.

The Church's Ministry of Reconciliation

The age of True Globalization marks the time in which World Christians are fulfilling the church's ministry of reconciliation. They are called to lead and serve the globalized world by acting as Christ's ambassadors to the unbelieving world (2 Cor 5:18-20). This is the ministry of preaching the gospel and helping people turn away from sinful lives that offend God and cause corruption and injustice in global society. Those who believe the gospel are granted the power of God's salvation (Rom 1:16-17). This means that all who believe the gospel can turn away from living in sin and live according to the Spirit (Rom 8:1-4).[117] Believers can offer their lives to God as a living sacrifice, which is their spiritual service of worship as his priests (Rom 12:1). If more and more people worldwide were saved by the ministry of reconciliation, God's power would naturally transform global society to discover the kingdom of grace and peace. Those who were once far away from God will be brought near to him by the blood of Christ that was shed on the cross (Heb 9:22). As a result, all the people who were formerly enemies of God could live together in harmony and solidarity (Eph 2:14-16). God has reconciled all things in heaven and earth to himself through Christ, in whom God's fullness dwells (Col 1:19-20).

Contemporary globalization has led the world toward cultural or moral relativism, rejecting the exclusive claim of the gospel for humanity's salvation in the public sphere. It has resisted God's will for all people to come to the saving knowledge of his Son who has risen from the grave. Only the gospel can save humankind from perishing in sin. While theological engagement with globalization recognizes the cultural reality of pluralism, it remains faithful to the universal gospel by training Christians to serve as "mediators" between diverse cultures of the world.[118] Evangelical missiologist Paul Hiebert views pluralism as a critical issue of the twenty-first century. He assesses that the new context of globalization

---

117. For various interpretations of salvation, see Demarest, *Cross and Salvation*, 31-36.

118. Hiebert, "Missionary as Mediator," 288-308.

requires missionaries to take on the new role of mediator, building bridges between different cultures, and explains this role as follows:

> Globalization raises profound questions regarding the need for and limits to contextualization. It is here that missionaries can first add much to the dialogue on the mediation between gospel and human cultures because, through their encounters with other cultures, they are deeply aware of cultures and their differences and of ways to study cultures. The dangers are to undercontextualize and to overcontextualize the gospel and the church. Global discussions on contextualization need missionaries and global leaders who understand both the gospel and human cultures well and who can bridge between them. In this, missionaries must not speak only to the world from the church but also for the world to the church. Most churches know little about their own neighborhoods, let alone people in other parts of the world. Missionaries must help their sending churches understand, identify with, and love people around them, and around the world. For example, they need to help Western churches understand the great ethnic, cultural, and religious diversity that is increasingly found in their own communities.[119]

In the age of True Globalization, the Christian mission is a two-way street. All nations must learn God's truth from one another. If Western culture were truly transformed by the gospel, it would be reasonable to conclude that the Christian mission should continue to flow in one direction as it did in the past. Although the West has come to understand certain aspects of God's truth, and its society has advanced greatly from knowing the gospel, its society has also been corrupted by certain deficiencies. God is therefore using all the cultures of humanity to make the church more holistic so that it can complete the mission of rescuing the world from perishing by its corruption. Christians from the Majority World are given much wisdom and insight from God, and those who live in the West must be open to learning and growing into greater spiritual and moral maturity in following Christ. Thus, John Franke introduces the intercultural model and explains the task of theology by a missional church:

> In the intercultural model, witness does not consist in the delivery of pre-established conceptions of the gospel and Christian teaching, in which the recipients of the message are treated as

---

119. Hiebert, "Missionary as Mediator," 297–98.

the objects of the one proclaiming the message and also are expected to receive the message just as presented if they are to benefit from its promises. Such an approach leads to the message functioning like the introduction of an alien ideology that, if accepted, undermines and subverts the ecosystem of the existing culture and has detrimental effects on its participants. Rather, intercultural understanding involves genuine, loving concern for others and for the cultural settings that shape their identity. Applied to the task of theology, the discipline becomes an enterprise in mutual understanding in which all of the partners provide crucial and necessary elements to the discourse.[120]

The theology of the West has lacked in one major area: the healing of individuals and society from infirmities and diseases which cause suffering and pain. Many Western churches do not emphasize God's power of healing and deliverance for humanity although it is abundantly evident throughout Scripture. According to Isa 53:4, Christ has "borne our griefs and carried our sorrows." This prophecy refers to spiritual, emotional, and physical healing of humanity's wounds in Christ. From a biblical perspective, God's salvation for humanity has personal, communal, and societal implications. First, Christ liberates individuals from sin and corruption, while healing them from all kinds of infirmities and diseases (Matt 5:9); second, he baptizes them with the Holy Spirit and unites them into a community of love (Acts 2:38, 3:42–47); and third, he sends them out into the world to spread the gospel and heal broken homes, villages, and cities (Mark 6:7–13; Matt 10:1–15; Acts 5:12–16). God has joined individuals together as the body of Christ, the holy temple of his presence through which Christ's power of regeneration and healing flows into the world for its renewal. Finnish Pentecostal theologian Veli-Matti Kärkkäinen notes that unlike proclamation and evangelism, healing has not been the hallmark of Christian mission for a long time, nor does healing occupy any place in standard theological discussion. In contrast to Western theology, adds Kärkkäinen, "Jesus was not merely a gospel preacher but was first and foremost an itinerant healer and exorcist in whose proclamation of the kingdom of God healings and deliverances—alongside the pronouncement of sins—were enacted as 'signs' of the approaching righteous rule of God."[121] The manifestation of healing is widespread in the Majority World and is often an integral aspect of the gospel that draws

---

120. Franke, *Missional Theology*, 66.
121. Kärkkäinen, *Hope and Community*, 350–51.

many unbelievers to Christ. Together, they dream of living in a world that is healed by the power of Christ.

The theological response to the social ills of globalization is that all Christians can heal broken society by renewing the institutions of globalization toward human flourishing (Eph 2:10). In the twentieth century, the church resisted getting involved with social work, fearing this would cause it to eventually drift away from the mission of preaching the gospel. In the twenty-first century, however, the church must lead the way in lifting the poor and helpless out of their misery. Furthermore, it must show the world how to end racism, misogyny, discrimination, and war. These problems still exist in the world because most people are not living in obedience to the gospel. When Christians repent and live in obedience to the gospel, the fruit of their repentance is displayed in the public sphere by the church's complete unity in loving God and serving others (John 17:20–23; Phil 2:1–4). The ethics of God's kingdom demonstrated by the church redefine what a global society ought to be and pave the way for social action.

The Ethics of God's Kingdom

The theology of True Globalization focuses on the gospel and its ethics. Humanity is sanctified in this world by struggling against evil to meet the ethical demands of God. Jesus taught the ethics of God's kingdom most clearly in his Sermon on the Mount (Matt 5–7). Today, many evangelical Christians neglect Jesus's emphasis on the ethical requirement for all believers to "surpass" the righteousness of the Pharisees and the teachers of the law (Matt 5:17–20). Relying on Luther's doctrine of justification by faith, evangelical theology upholds that the righteousness of Christ imputed in believers is sufficient for their salvation. Although this important doctrinal concept resists the false doctrine of salvation by works, it does not address the spiritual and moral problem of allowing sin to exist continually in a believer's life. While having the assurance of salvation, Christians must also realize the gravity of sin and its ultimate outcome. Jesus clearly explained that sin chokes the lives of people who believe in God's word and prohibits the maturing of good fruit in their life (Luke 8:14). Living in sin is a clear indication that one is not living by the truth and does not have fellowship with Christ (1 John 1:5–7).

If professing believers continue to live in sin, they cannot fulfill God's mission in this world.

There is no question that Luther did immense service by restoring the biblical understanding of justification. He was fighting against the contemporary practice of the church regarding indulgences, which became part of the economy of salvation. Today, however, the main theological problem is uncommitted and slothful faith. While Christians should uphold the doctrine that salvation is attained by faith alone, they should not dismiss Scripture's exhortation to "work out your salvation with fear and trembling" (Phil 2:12). The term κατεργάζομαι (*katergazomai*), "to work out," means to bring about, produce, or do. Working out one's salvation with humility is not legalism but the natural way of living by the ethics of God's kingdom. Those who believe the doctrinal proposition of the gospel cannot live carelessly in regard to sin. Jesus did not condemn the woman who was caught in the act of adultery, but he also did instruct her to "go and sin no more" (John 8:11). Jesus closed his Sermon on the Mount with this famous saying: "Therefore everyone who hears these words of mine and puts them into practice is like a wise man who built his house on the rock" (Matt 7:24 NIV). Scripture therefore speaks of salvation in three tenses: past, present, and future. In Christ, believers are "saved" in the past (Eph 2:8–9), "being saved" in the present (1 Cor 1:18), and "will be saved" in the future (Rom 5:9). In the age of True Globalization, the church must address its weakness and be focused on meeting the ethical demands of Christ in the present.

In his original exposition of Scripture, William Tyndale clarifies what Christian ethics entail. He explains that understanding of the law and the promise (the gospel) is the key to unlocking all Scriptures. With true salvation comes a God-given love for the law and the power to follow the law. Such a love is a natural outgrowth of believing the promise, receiving the life-giving Spirit, and being justified in the blood of Christ from all condemnation.[122] According to Tyndale, the law and the gospel may never be separate:

> I must therefore have always the law in my sight, that I may be meek in the spirit, and give God all the laud and praise, ascribing to him all righteousness, and to myself all unrighteousness and sin. I must also have the promises before mine eyes, that I despair not; in which promises I see the mercy, favour, and good-will of God upon me in the blood of his Son Christ, which

---

122. Tyndale, *Works of William Tyndale*, 1:11.

hath made satisfaction for mine unperfectness, and fulfilled for me that which I could not do.[123]

Donald Smeeton writes, "Tyndale refused Luther's strong distinction between the Law and the Gospel, maintaining, in contrast, that justification by faith enabled man to fulfill the Law."[124] Luther taught that the divine law had nothing to do with the salvation of sinner, affirming that it only exposes the inability of sinners to fulfill the law. Tyndale, on the other hand, taught that believers' commitment to pursuing God's law and their failure to reach perfection constantly remind them that they are always at God's mercy. It is only the perfect and full righteousness of Christ that saves believers. Tyndale understood that "the law requireth love from the bottom of the heart [and that love only is the fulfilling of the law.] If they did, they would not condemn their neighbors."[125] He clarifies that "by faith are we saved only, in believing the promises. And though faith be never without love and good works, yet is our saving imputed neither to love nor unto good works, but unto faith only."[126] Tyndale therefore exhorts readers of the Scriptures to seek after "the covenants made between God and us" by living in obedience to God's law and commandments, which would lead to receiving God's promise of mercy.[127] The theology of True Globalization appropriates Tyndale's emphasis to fulfill the covenants made with God, which is to love our neighbors from the bottom of our hearts.

True Globalization fulfills God's new covenant with humanity, which is made with his people through the gospel. God's law is put within those who believe God's promise and inscribed on the believer's heart (Jer 31:33). Christ taught us to pray "your kingdom come, your will be done, on earth as it is heaven" (Matt 6:10). This prayer reflects people's longing to live in a world in which everyone obeys God's law of love with a renewed heart. Christ has set humanity free from the bondage of sin so all God's children can live in obedience to his Spirit who lives in them. Christ alone has the power and authority to rule over this world by giving his commands for his people to live righteously. They were promised to receive material blessings if they sought after God's kingdom and his

---

123. Tyndale, *Works of William Tyndale*, 1:11.
124. Smeeton, *Lollard Themes in the Reformation*, 24.
125. Tyndale, *Works of William Tyndale*, 1:12.
126. Tyndale, *Works of William Tyndale*, 1:15.
127. Tyndale, *Works of William Tyndale*, 1:403.

righteousness (Matt 6:33), and to see "the Son of Man coming in the kingdom" before they die (Matt 16:28). Christ cast out demons by the Spirit of God, signaling that the kingdom of God has come upon them at a local level (Matt 12:28). Christ provided relief to those who were "harassed and helpless" (Matt 9:16). Christ has reigned over the whole world ever since he was raised from the dead and seated at the right hand of God in the heavenly places (Eph 1:20–21). Upon Christ's ascension, his power and authority became universal. His spiritual blessings became available for all who would believe in his name, no matter where they lived (Eph 1:3). For two thousand years, the universal reign of Christ over this world has brought "righteousness, peace, and joy" for many individuals living in the Holy Spirit (Rom 14:17). During this time, God's word was planted in the hearts of people, transforming corrupt individuals and societies worldwide. The gospel has brought forth the first fruits of love, truth, justice, and righteousness so that God's glory can be seen over all the earth.

Human Flourishing under the Reign of Christ

Scripture reveals that those who take delight in God's law and find refuge in Christ are blessed abundantly. God's children who believe the gospel and obey Jesus's command of love will flourish in this life and afterlife (Pss 1:1; 2:12; Matt 5:44–45; Luke 21:36; John 14:15). In the twenty-first century, the conception of "human flourishing" has become ubiquitous in global society. In contrast to the nihilistic attitude of the twentieth century, many experts are now using the terms *progress* and *flourish* to express their belief in humanity to achieve the state of abundance.[128] This belief competes with Jesus's claim that he is the Christ who can give the living water to those who thirst in this world. In a globalized world, Christians must be able to testify that Jesus Christ is the way toward human flourishing. Jonathan Pennington explains that human flourishing is the direct evidence of God's work of redemption in this world:

> The Bible certainly speaks to the issue of human flourishing in very significant ways. But this is not unique among other ancient or current philosophies, religions, or worldviews. What is unique and what is revelational and authoritative for the Christian is that Holy Scripture understands human flourishing to be a function of God's redemptive work in the world, the very core

128. Norberg, *Progress*; Seligman, *Flourish*; Diamandis and Kotler, *Abundance*.

of his relation toward his creatures. Throughout both the Old and New Testaments, God is at work redeeming his broken, sinful, and rebellious creatures. From the promise of redemption in Genesis 3:15 through the climactic vision at the end of the book of Revelation, God reveals himself to be actively and graciously redeeming his people, saving them from oppression, forgiving their disobedience and dishonoring acts, and leading them into a time and place of his full presence. The biggest metaphor or image to describe this work is God's kingdom or reign.[129]

If that is so, what Christians must do in this world is ensure every human being can flourish by living in obedience to God's command of love in global society.

Neil Messer says, "To flourish as a human creature is to fulfill the goods, goals, and ends that belong to this kind of creaturely life."[130] In this respect, Swiss Reformed theologian Karl Barth offers an account of Christian ethics in terms of "the command of God the Creator." This is God's gracious call or summons, which set us free to be the creatures God has made us to be. To understand ethics in terms of God's command is unique to the Christian faith and religion, contrasting with globalization's humanistic ethics expressed by the United Nations Universal Declaration of Human Rights. Living out such a life includes "freedom before God" (relationship with God), "freedom in fellowship" (relationships with others), "freedom for life" (living a physically embodied and integrated life), and "freedom in limitation" (living out a particular vocation in a particular place and time).[131] Barth's ethical framework is based on the belief that God's people will discover what they should do by hearing the command of God.[132] What God does is right, and therefore, he calls humanity to obedience (Gen 2:16–17). God's command that leads to the sanctification of humanity is now expressed as the gospel of repentance (Acts 2:38; 3:22–26). By contrast, the ethical framework of globalization is rooted in humanism, which defines its own laws in a sinful self-isolation from God. The result is that more than 150 countries (out of 193 countries that belong to the UN) still engage in torture. The nations of this world have neither the will nor the power to live by the ethics they impose upon themselves. American legal scholar Eric Posner presents

---

129. Pennington, "Biblical Theology of Human Flourishing," 16.
130. Messer, "Human Flourishing," 289.
131. Messer, "Human Flourishing," 289.
132. Messer, "Human Flourishing," 289.

the following verdict on humanity's futile attempt to enforce its own law upon the nations:

> The truth is that human rights law has failed to accomplish its objectives. There is little evidence that human rights treaties, on the whole, have improved the wellbeing of people. The reason is that human rights were never as universal as people hoped, and the belief that they could be forced upon countries as a matter of international law was shot through with misguided assumptions from the very beginning. The human rights movement shares something in common with the hubris of development economics, which in previous decades tried (and failed) to alleviate poverty by imposing top-down solutions on developing countries. But where development economists have reformed their approach, the human rights movement has yet to acknowledge its failures. It is time for a reckoning.[133]

Posner explains the underlying reasons for the human rights movement's failure:

> The weaknesses that would go on to undermine human rights law were there from the start. The universal declaration was not a treaty in the formal sense: no one at the time believed that it created legally binding obligations. It was not ratified by nations but approved by the general assembly, and the UN charter did not give the general assembly the power to make international law. Moreover, the rights were described in vague, aspirational terms, which could be interpreted in multiple ways, and national governments—even the liberal democracies—were wary of binding legal obligations. The US did not commit itself to eliminating racial segregation, and Britain and France did not commit themselves to liberating the subject populations in their colonies.[134]

God's command of love frees humanity from the bondage of sin and brings its existence into the powerful and peaceful existence of God. Faith in Christ leads to a personal growth of spiritual and moral excellence (Phil 2:12–15), empowering God's children to exercise the love, truth, justice, and righteousness in society (1 Cor 6:2–3). When God's people live in obedience to his command of love, their community prospers (Acts 4:34). Humanity flourishes when it discovers God's grace and peace by knowing Christ as the Savior and King. Jesus said, "Peace I leave

---

133. Posner, "Case against Human Rights," para. 6.
134. Posner, "Case against Human Rights," para. 8.

with you; my peace I give you. I do not give to you as the world gives. Do not let your hearts be troubled and do not be afraid" (John 14:27 NIV). In God's kingdom, the private and public spheres of life are intertwined, held together as one in Christ (Col 1:17). Although God's kingdom is fully established at the coming of Christ, much of the work is to be done by Christians in the age of True Globalization. Christ promised that "whoever believes in me will do the works I have been doing, and they will do even greater things than these" (John 14:12 NIV). God did not plan to do all the work of establishing his kingdom on earth. Instead, he decreed that the work of serving the world is to be done by his children, so that they can receive their eternal inheritance in Christ (Eph 2:10; 1 Pet 1:3–5). The church must mobilize to fulfill God's purpose of globalization. Grenz explains how this eschatological hope leads Christians to actively wait for God's future:

> We wait for the Lord's return, of course, but ours is an active waiting. Because we are certain that God will bring his plan to completion, we become actively involved in that program. In this way, hopeful living means living hopefully. Motivated by hope of the final consummation, we seek to fulfill our divinely given mandate in the world, proclaiming in word and action by the power of the Holy Spirit the good news about God's activity in the world.[135]

God's love, truth, righteousness, and justice flow from his throne (Ps 89:14), and Christians are the channels of God's blessing for the world (Matt 28:18–20; Acts 1:8). Thus, God has assigned the church the mission of engaging with all domains of globalization through the gospel, which has the power to transform not only the human heart but also society. Nkansah-Obrempong believes the church has a mission to transform society:

> The church is God's agent for bringing economic, political, spiritual, moral, and social transformation in society. This implies Christian communities must live their lives in society to influence society so they will glorify God. This sets forth the church's mission, as well as the kind of mission it should engage: namely, a "transformative mission."[136]

---

135. Grenz, *Theology for the Community*, 656.
136. Nkansah-Obrempong, "Africa's Contextual Realities," 283.

He explains that the church has three roles. Its primary role is spiritual, carrying a priestly function: to bring God's word to people and present them before God. Its second role is missionary: to guide others to God through the preaching of the word, and to address the existential needs of humanity and care for God's creation. Its third role is to maintain the moral order of society, by challenging the "status quo" and dealing with issues of injustice, exploitation, human rights abuses, and lack of respect for human dignity and the sanctity of human life.[137] Through this mission, God's power of salvation flows into this world like a mighty river, which is metaphorically described as the living water (Ezek 47:1–12; Rev 22:1–5). From his earthly throne within the temple made of his children, Christ uses his church to fill this world with his abundant blessings. To fulfill their mission, Christians are to approach the throne of God's grace with confidence, with "faith" (Heb 4:16, 11:6). The result is that they would receive Christ's righteousness as a free gift, and they would administer Christ's grace and peace for the world. Since Christians are saved by God's grace and not by their deeds (Eph 2:8–9), they are responsible for understanding the problems of globalization with empathy and helping the world find renewal through biblical truths. Accepting the role of priesthood in Christ, Christians can serve in step with the high priest who showed empathy toward their own weakness (Heb 4:14–16).

In the age of True Globalization, the church can connect God's kingdom with all domains of this world. From a theological perspective, globalization cannot be completed by secular institutions and their efforts alone: it needs the church, which possesses "the keys of the kingdom of heaven" (Matt 16:19). The keys represent the church's authority and power given by God to open the door of blessing for all domains of globalization. Only the church can preach the gospel to set individuals free from the bondage of sin. In a globalized world of inclusivity and solidarity, secular institutions and church are no longer separated but bound together. Today, a new philosophical thinking accepts the reality of intersection between religion, politics, economics, and technology in a pluralistic society. According to Jürgen Habermas, one of the most influential philosophers and social theorists of our time, "religion and the secular world always stand in a reciprocal relation."[138] He argues that we have entered into a "post-secular" age in which liberal democracies must

---

137. Nkansah-Obrempong, "Africa's Contextual Realities," 284.
138. Habermas et al., *Awareness of What*, 5.

address the claims of religion in a more serious manner than before.[139] Habermas speaks on behalf of modern, secular reason, which he admits is now aware that something is sorely missing from its philosophically enlightened view of the world. Recent developments in biotechnology and genetic research are raising complex ethical questions concerning the legitimate scope and limits of genetic intervention. Habermas says that secular reason is aware of "the defeatism lurking within it" and is "threatening to spin out of control."[140] After resisting any discussion of religion for several decades, Habermas now describes it as an important moral resource for addressing urgent social questions such as bioethics.[141] He states, "Religious citizens have special access to a potential for justifying moral questions. Its meaning-endowing function provides a moral basis for public discourse and thereby plays an important role in the public sphere."[142]

When people from diverse cultures, backgrounds, and lifestyles join institutional religions in a democratic society, social and political issues are inevitable. In a pluralistic society, personal faith and piety rooted in religion are combined with social and political activity. The interlinkage of the two cannot return to Christendom because there are now several world religions competing in the public sphere. The problem is particularly acute in Africa and Asia, where Christians and Muslims are engaged in violent conflicts.[143] Berger says, "Arguably the two most dynamic religious movements in the contemporary world are resurgent Islam and popular Protestantism, the latter principally in the form of the Pentecostal movement. Both are truly global phenomena."[144] These two religious movements have successfully defied modern societies in which religion is largely relegated to the private sphere. For example, in the highly secularized society of Sweden, Muslims can be seen praying on their knees in public spaces. Meanwhile, Pentecostals openly express their belief in God's miraculous healing of any disease, even raising of the dead. Adherents of these groups include doctors, lawyers, and scientists. Through globalization, the religious lifestyles of these two groups

139. Habermas et al., *Awareness of What*, 15.

140. Habermas et al., *Awareness of What*, 18.

141. For an excellent synopsis of Habermas's critical hermeneutics, see Porter and Robinson, *Hermeneutics*, 131–52.

142. Habermas et al., *Awareness of What*, 5.

143. Griswold, *Tenth Parallel*.

144. Berger, "Toward a Theory."

are being witnessed worldwide on a massive scale through globalization. Berger explains that we are now living in a pluralistic world with "multiple modernities," where each modernized nation is creatively preserving its own religious way of life despite its technological and economic advances. He affirms that secularization did not remove religious elements from modernized societies.[145] The theology of True Globalization combines personal faith with political, economic, and technological issues. The biblical mandate for the church is to communicate the gospel while bridging the gap between church and secular society, thereby reconciling the world with God.

There is still much hope for this world even though it is greatly corrupted by sin. Paul prayed for Christians to "abound in hope" (Rom 15:13). When Christians are full of hope, it is then possible to take the step of faith by demonstrating what they hope for (Heb 11:1). The gospel empowers humanity to overcome much evil in this world. Ladd says, "The power of the Kingdom of God has invaded the realm of Satan—the present evil Age. The activity of this power to deliver men from satanic rule was evidenced in the exorcism of demons. Thereby, Satan was bound; he was cast down from his position of power."[146] If the power of the gospel is truly great, it must be able to curb great evils in social and political realms. Armed with the gospel, Christians have an important duty in using it to administer God's grace and peace to all nations of this world. Christians must not look back to the time of Christendom and aim for a political union with the state but rather move toward the future by preparing the whole world to accept the reign of Christ upon his return. Until the day of his revealing, the church must strive to bring unity in the midst of the plurality wrought by globalization. Such unity cannot be accomplished by following the ways of this world, which demonizes and knocks others down for their way of political thinking. The church must distance itself from the toxic political culture that has lost the ability to hold civil discourse. Rather, it must participate in politics by setting an example for the world to follow. Seeking to win the culture war through political dominance is not conducive for spreading the gospel. In the present age of globalization, willingness to compromise and find solutions through sincere dialogue is the only viable option for Christians who participate

---

145. Berger, *Many Altars of Modernity*, 68–78; Berger, "Good of Religious Pluralism," 39–43.

146. Ladd, *Gospel of the Kingdom*, 50.

in politics. Kristen Johnson explains how Augustine's ontology informs the church to make a theological turn of political theory:

> Augustine's ontology suggests that it is only in the *polis* of the Heavenly City that differences can come together in loving harmony through participation in the Triune God. Citizens of the Heavenly City come from all nations, speak all languages, adorn different dress and adhere to different manners of life, they are unrestrained by conformity of customs, laws, and institutions, and are free to have "their innumerable variety of desires and thoughts and everything else which makes human beings different from one another." And yet they are unified through Jesus Christ, bound together in a fellowship of love.[147]

Since different peoples, nations, and civilizations can be united only in the Heavenly City, the only viable theory that can avert violence and war in this world is pluralism. This moment of subjectivity and uncertainty is an opportunity for God's children to bring the gospel into the public realm. The biblical mandate for the church in the twenty-first century is to serve as a bridge between all people and help humanity build new societal structures. By reconciling humanity with God and with each other in Christ, the church can fully administer God's grace and peace in this world. There are myriad ways for human civilization to exist together until the coming of Christ. God has promised to give his wisdom and insight to the church so that humanity can flourish through Christ's love, truth, justice, and righteousness. In the age of True Globalization, the church's ministry is to lead and serve the globalized world to know God's only begotten Son Jesus Christ. In Scripture, the Preacher says that there is "a time to love, and a time to hate; a time for war and a time for peace" (Eccl 3:8). Humanity has suffered many tribulations throughout history, and it is the church's responsibility to heal and unite the fragmented world in Christ. Living in this time of great turmoil and uncertainty, Christians must believe in God's promise to use them as peacemakers who can help all people to be reconciled with God and with each other. The hope of human flourishing can be realized in the world when humanity comes under the reign of Christ.

---

147. Johnson, *Theology, Political Theory*, 25.

Conclusion

THIS BOOK HAS ADDRESSED the problems of theological engagement with globalization. My claim is that the power of true religion becomes evident when all Christians engage with globalization to reconcile humanity with God and with each other in preparation for the consummation of God's kingdom. The gospel, which is "the power of God for the salvation of everyone who believes" (Rom 1:16), brings forth human flourishing in society when the church is leading and serving all people to renew globalization (Isa 2:2-4). In the twenty-first century, people are increasingly coming together as a single society, yet humanity still lacks the power to overcome the existence of evil that perpetuates injustice in the world. While being entrusted with the gospel and authority of Christ, which are "the keys of the kingdom of heaven" (Matt 16:19), the church has not been able to lead and serve the world in resolving the problems arising from globalization. Today, however, the paradoxical influence of globalization through its unitary and fragmentary movements provides a creative tension, which the church can exploit to reclaim its God-given role of ministering to all people for the salvation of the individual and the renewal of society. God has not given up on humanity; rather, he intends to redeem and heal the world by the preaching of the gospel and the doing of good works by the church. He has given his power to the church for the mission of making Christ known and administering God's grace and peace in a globalized world that has now imploded.

In addressing the central question of how globalization influences theology and how the church should approach globalization, this book has considered the three theological issues raised by the globalized world: social justice, religious pluralism and ethics, and the church's missional method. The following is a summary of the main conclusions drawn from studying these issues.

SOCIAL JUSTICE

First, our interconnected world presses theology to give religious guidance to humanity's existence as a single society, and to address how the church should lead the development of globalization spiritually and morally for the common good of humanity. The church has a responsibility to ameliorate the social ills of this world because God created humankind to represent him on the earth by working together to build a just, harmonious, and prosperous world for his glory. As Christians wait for the consummation of God's kingdom that would bring forth the new creation, they are responsible for engaging with the contemporary globalization that has been forging the world without the gospel. Globalization is now in a state of great turmoil and uncertainty due to the sin that entered the world through one man and corrupted the entire creation. Humanity perishes when it rejects the gospel and attempts to save itself. It is not, however, God's desire for the world to remain corrupt and be destroyed by his wrath. God is our Savior "who wants all people to be saved and come to the knowledge of the truth" (1 Tim 2:4). When Christians preach the gospel and exercise biblical love, truth, justice, and righteousness for all, God's grace and peace are administered to humanity for its salvation and flourishing.

There is hope for this world, although it is passing away. Corruption in global society can be reformed by God's people, who are liberated from sin, led by the Holy Spirit, and united in the love of Christ. The emergence of an eschatological community spreads the gospel in the world, bringing forth healing and renewal for the global society. Christians can lead and serve all humanity by expanding God's kingdom on the earth because they are "a chosen people, a royal priesthood, a holy nation" (1 Pet 2:9). The church is God's instrument for renewing globalization toward humanity's sanctification in preparation for the return of Christ. Although the world will not become perfect in the present age, Christians can minister in global society with hope in the knowledge that all things will be made new. The church's obedience to do good works in this world correlates with the final outcome in the new creation. God's purpose for creating this world is to establish his everlasting peace in the New Jerusalem, the eschatological city of God in which all the people who are saved by the gospel and judged as righteous will live together under the reign of Christ (Ps 122:6–8; Matt 5:9; John 14:27; Rev 21:2–8). The dwelling place of God with humanity emerges, grows, and strengthens in the globalized world, but it will fully manifest itself when Christ returns to claim his church and fills the new earth with his presence.

God has placed Christians in the world not only because individuals need to be saved by the gospel, but also because global society needs to be renewed by those who are saved. Many evangelical Christians mistakenly believe Christ will return to resolve all problems in the world, and that it is therefore not their responsibility to repair society. Although Scripture says believers are called to preach the gospel rather than change the world, the church's work of overcoming the manifestations of evil in society is an expression of the gospel. The repeated exhortation in the New Testament for those who are being saved by God's word is to do good works for others who are suffering under the oppression of evil. Christ has not returned even after two thousand years because Christians are still engaged in a war against the enemy whose goal is to destroy humanity through sin. Christians must understand that God's purpose for creating, multiplying, dispersing, separating, integrating, and sanctifying humanity through globalization has not yet been fulfilled. Through the ministry of the church, God desires to demonstrate his power of salvation by enabling individuals to do his will in this world. To accomplish his purpose, the gospel of Jesus Christ and his kingdom of grace and peace must expand in the world through engagement of the church with globalization. Biblically speaking, just as Joshua once led the people of Israel in conquering the land of Canaan to claim their inheritance, Christ is now leading the church in renewing all domains of globalization that were corrupted by the existence of evil (Josh 11:23; Rom 16:17–20). The gospel not only saves souls but also enables Christians to administer God's grace and peace in society, renewing the globalized world, which would become our eternal inheritance in the new creation (Matt 25:14–30; 1 Pet 1:3–9).

RELIGIOUS PLURALISM AND ETHICS

Second, the ongoing integration of diverse cultures in a globalized world presses theology to answer the question of what it means to be both disciples of Jesus Christ and good citizens in a pluralistic society. For the gospel to be recognized as the exclusive path to salvation and the universal ethics for humanity, the world must recognize that Christians are working in partnership with all people to alleviate the problems inherent to globalization. The work of renewing the domains of politics, economics, and technology cannot be done by Christians alone; therefore, the church must learn to interact with secularists and adherents of world religions in an inclusive society. This book has identified the contemporary conception of globalization as a false religion. It promises that humanity can save itself by building a world that is just, free, peaceful, and prosperous. While claiming that all nations can unite and flourish together without any spiritual and moral foundation, the hegemonic globalization of the West has driven humanity to the brink of annihilation through political, economic, and technological disasters. Although the world is now facing the tribulations of globalization, Christians can transform this turmoil into opportunity by demonstrating that Jesus Christ and the gospel alone can save and heal humanity (1 Tim 2:1–6).

For Christians, living in a highly pluralistic society may not seem ideal; nevertheless, it provides new avenues for reaching unbelievers. More than ever, secularists and adherents of other religions are willing to enter into dialogue with Christians for the sake of resolving global issues, including poverty, migration, pandemic, nuclear war, and climate change. In a globalized world, Christians have an unprecedented opening to make disciples of all nations because humanity is now in need of universal ethics as never before. The people of this world need the church to guide them in protecting humanity and the planet Earth. The attempts of secularists to establish universal ethics through human rights and environmental movements have turned out to be acts of hubris rather than justice. As a result, they have been unsuccessful in protecting human lives and the environment. A growing number of people are realizing that globalization has failed because it lacks the spiritual and moral foundation that stems from deeply held religious beliefs, values, and commitments. The catastrophic failure of the hegemonic globalization of the West is finally allowing World Christians, especially those from the Majority World, to present a new future based on true religion. Now is the time for the church to regain its lost confidence in showing the world how to live by the ethics of God's kingdom. Christ has given us his authority and power to teach all nations to live together in God's grace and peace (John 17:15–21).

The contemporary globalization dominated by Western secular culture is coming to an end, making way for True Globalization. Rather than aiming to revive Christendom, the church must lead the world toward completing God's own globalization, which began at the creation of this world. True Globalization is characterized by Christian engagement with globalization in preparation for the consummation of God's kingdom. In this final stage of globalization, the role of giving spiritual and moral foundation to human civilization is shared by all world religions. Scripture says that God's love is patient. It does not insist on its own way; it bears all things and endures all things (1 Cor 13:4–7). Thus, interaction with religious others must be dialogical and mutual rather than argumentative and divisive. All religions do not lead to the same God; therefore, the goal of interaction with religious others is not to become interfaith by praying, worshiping, or joining together spiritually, but to make Christ known to all peoples, nations, and civilizations by demonstrating the love of God through service for the common good of humanity. Christians can make the most compelling case for the gospel when they live in accordance with the ethics of God's kingdom while engaging with all people in the public arena. When Christians are actively serving humanity by exercising biblical love, truth, justice, and righteousness, unbelievers living in a globalized world can recognize God's power of saving individuals and renewing society, thereby giving glory to God (Matt 5:14–16).

THE CHURCH'S MISSIONAL METHOD

Third, the formation of global consciousness presses theology to redefine the biblical mandate for God's people in the twenty-first century. The cultural reality of a globalized world is that Christians are now living in a single space consisting of diverse cultures that can influence each other. It requires all peoples, nations, and civilizations to maintain an open dialogue and determine our future together. World Christians must learn to complete the mission of God in this new context of inclusivity. The globalized world requires a missional method that aims to make the gospel known to all people by effectively communicating that humankind is created, redeemed, and sanctified by Christ. Since the beginning of its history, humankind was divided into ethnic clans, tribes, peoples, and nations possessing a shared cultural identity. One of the consequences of Adam's sin was that humankind succumbed to the fleshly works of "enmity, strife, fits of anger, rivalries, divisions, and envy" (Gal 5:19–21). Since ancient times, the wickedness of people has increased greatly under the oppression of the ruling elite, and the earth has become filled with violence and oppression (Gen 6:5–12). Many people, including Christians, have struggled to overcome the corrupt way of their flesh.

In a globalized world, however, God's eternal purpose of redeeming humanity in Christ is reaching its fulfillment. Diverse peoples, nations, and civilizations are now coming to terms with the gospel story of reconciliation (Eph 1:3–10). All over the world, people know that poverty, racism, misogyny, discrimination, hatred, division, and war are wrong. More and more people are realizing that they are all related to one another regardless of their ethnic, religious, and cultural differences. Thus, the biblical mandate for the church in a globalized world is to be "peacemakers" by ministering to all people to be reconciled with God and with each other in Christ (Matt 5:9; Heb 12:14; Rom 12:17–19).

Globalization has brought the mission field very close to the church, requiring all Christians to live as a new kind of missionaries. Christians must become ready to preach the gospel and thereby save individual souls as well as facilitate renewal in global society. Aligning with the eschatological vision of all things holding together in Christ to glorify God on earth (Col 1:17), the task of theology is to educate and equip the church for the ministry of reconciliation in a globalized world (2 Cor 5:18). The church should not withdraw into cultural seclusion, engage in cultural warfare, or fall into cultural relativism. Rather, it must lead all people with the truth and love of Christ to accomplish God's mission of saving and healing the world (John 17:20–23). The missional method must reflect the reciprocal relationship between the church and the world: the world needs the church, and the church needs the world. Without the church, the world cannot know the gospel. Without the world, the church cannot have its inheritance as coheirs with Christ. In the age of globalization, the church must proclaim the gospel while leading all people to pursue the common good of humanity. The biblical mandate for the church is to lead and serve all people to build this world in accordance with God's plan and purpose of globalization. When the church fulfills its mission of preparing this world for the consummation of God's kingdom, it will reign with Christ. When all things are made new by the coming of Christ, this world will merge with the heaven and become the New Jerusalem. The world will finally become a beautiful and magnificent city in which all nations will flourish together in peace and walk by the light of God's glory. All of humanity's achievements and triumphs accomplished by the power of Christ through "the kings of the earth" will be displayed throughout the new heaven and earth (Rev 21:1–5, 22–27). All God's children fulfilling his mission of making Christ known and uniting humanity under his reign will be the kingly priests of this world.

This book has demonstrated that humanity exists together, and that humanity can be saved and renewed together. It has defined globalization as God's work of creation, multiplication, dispersion, separation, redemption, integration, and sanctification of humanity for the consummation of his kingdom. According to Scripture, all human activities will ultimately fulfill God's purpose for the creation. As the Preacher says, "He has made everything beautiful in its time. He has also set eternity in the human heart; yet no one can fathom what God has done from beginning to end" (Eccl 3:11 NIV). In Christ, ordinary human beings can become "living stones" built into God's dwelling place in this world (1 Pet 2:5). As globalization comes closer to its completion, God is saving his wayward children who were lost in sin and scattered in the world as stones. Scripture is clear that all people will be judged to either enter God's kingdom or be excluded from God's kingdom. "The creation waits in eager expectation for the children of God to be revealed" (Rom 8:10). The biblical revelation regarding the final judgment of Christ accentuates humanity's need to be sanctified through salvation as individuals and renewal as society for the consummation of God's kingdom. Therefore, every Christian should contribute to God's mission of rescuing and healing humanity while anticipating the coming of Christ. The significance of this book is the message that all Christians can become agents of renewal for globalization by administering God's grace and peace for humanity. I have written this book with the hope that the church will pursue the ministry of reconciling diverse peoples, nations, and civilizations as one in Christ and unleash the full potential of humanity to glorify God in this world. May the light of God's glory shine over all the earth through all his children.

Bibliography

Acemoglu, Daron, and James A. Robinson. *The Narrow Corridor: States, Societies, and the Fate of Liberty*. New York: Penguin, 2019.
Addison, Meeke. "The Stated Goals of Black Lives Matter Are Anti-Christian." *Decision*, July 1, 2020. https://decisionmagazine.com/the-stated-goals-of-black-lives-matter-are-anti-christian/.
AIB Spiritual Journey. "The Spiritual Journey of Rev. Dr. Syngman Rhee." YouTube video, Apr. 14, 2015. https://www.youtube.com/watch?v=mQoY-jShF6s.
Alesina, Alberto, et al. "Fractionalization." *Journal of Economic Growth* 8 (2003) 155–94.
Alexander, Caroline. "The Shock of War." *Smithsonian*, Sept. 2010. https://www.smithsonianmag.com/history/the-shock-of-war-55376701/.
Al-Khalili, Jim. *The House of Wisdom: How Arabic Science Saved Ancient Knowledge and Gave Us the Renaissance*. New York: Penguin, 2011.
Al-Rodhan, Nayef R. F., and Gérard Stoudmann. "Definitions of Globalization: A Comprehensive Overview and a Proposed Definition." *Program on the Geopolitical Implications of Globalization and Transnational Security* (June 19, 2006) 1–21.
American Society of Human Genetics Perspective. "ASHG Denounces Attempts to Link Genetics and Racial Supremacy." *American Society of Human Genetics* 103 (2018) 636.
Andringa, Leo, and Bob Goudzwaard. *Globalization and Christian Hope: Economy in the Service of Life*. Translated by Mark Vander Vennen. Toronto: Citizens for Public Justice, 2003.
Appadurai, Arjun. *Modernity at Large: Cultural Dimensions of Globalization*. Minneapolis: University of Minnesota Press, 1996.
Arias, Mortimer. *Announcing the Reign of God: Evangelization and the Subversive Memory of Jesus*. Eugene, OR: Wipf & Stock, 1984.
Arnold, Clinton E. *Ephesians*. Exegetical Commentary on the New Testament 10. Grand Rapids: Zondervan, 2010.
Augustine. *The City of God against the Pagans*. Edited by R. W. Dyson. Cambridge: Cambridge University Press, 1998.
Aulén, Gustaf. *Christus Victor: A Historical Study of the Three Main Types of the Idea of Atonement*. Translated by A. G. Hebert. Eugene, OR: Wipf & Stock, 2003.
Bacote, Vincent E. *The Spirit in Public Theology: Appropriating the Legacy of Abraham Kuyper*. Eugene, OR: Wipf & Stock, 2010.
Barber, John. *Earth Restored: Calling the Church to a New Christian Activism*. Rev. ed. Fearn, Scot.: Christian Focus, 2002.

Bartholomew, Craig G. *Contours of the Kuyperian Tradition*. Downers Grove, IL: IVP Academic, 2017.
Bauckham, Richard. *The Bible in the Contemporary World: Hermeneutical Ventures*. Grand Rapids: Eerdmans, 2015.
Beale, G. K. *A New Testament Biblical Theology: The Unfolding of the Old Testament in the New*. Grand Rapids: Baker Academic, 2011.
Beck, Julie. "The New Age of Astrology." *Atlantic*, Jan. 16, 2018. https://www.theatlantic.com/health/archive/2018/01/the-new-age-of-astrology/550034/.
Bediako, Kwame. "African Theology as a Challenge for Western Theology." In *Christian Identity in Cross-Cultural Perspective*, edited by Martien E. Brinkman and Dirk van Keulen, 52–67. Leiden: Brill, 2003.
Benson, Charles D., and William Barnaby Faherty. *Moonport: A History of Apollo Launch Facilities and Operations*. Washington, DC: NASA Special Publication-4204, 1978.
Benton, Matthew A. "White Noise and White Silence: Evangelicals and Race." *Marginalia*, Dec. 4, 2020. https://themarginaliareview.com/white-noise-and-white-silence-evangelicals-and-race/.
Berger, Peter L. "The Good of Religious Pluralism." *First Things* 262 (Apr. 2016) 39–43.
———. *The Many Altars of Modernity: Toward a Paradigm for Religion in a Pluralist Age*. Berlin: de Gruyter, 2014.
———. "Toward a Theory of Religious Pluralism." Lecture, Berkeley Center for Religion, Peace and World Affairs at Georgetown University, Washington DC, February 5, 2013.
Beyer, Peter. "Globalization and Religion." In *ER* 5:3497–98.
———. *Religion in the Context of Globalization*. New York: Routledge, 2013.
Blain, Keisha N. "Civil Rights International." *Foreign Affairs* 99 (Sept./Oct. 2020) 176–81.
Blakemore, Erin. "Youth in Revolt: Five Revolutions Started by Young Activists." *National Geographic*, Mar. 23, 2018. https://www.nationalgeographic.com/culture/article/youth-activism-young-protesters-historic-movements.
Bobinac, Una. "The Disintegration of Yugoslavia: An Analysis of Globalization Effects on Union and Disintegration of Yugoslavia." *International ResearchScape Journal* 1 (2014) 1–10.
Boff, Leonardo. *Global Civilization: Challenges to Society and to Christianity*. Translated by Alexandre Guilherme. New York: Routledge, 2014.
Bolger, Daniel P. *Why We Lost: A General's Inside Account of the Iraq and Afghanistan Wars*. New York: Houghton Mifflin Harcourt, 2014.
Bonhoeffer, Dietrich. *Ethics*. Edited by Eberhard Bethge. Translated by Neville Horton Smith. New York: Touchstone, 1995.
Bottéro, Jean. *Religion in Ancient Mesopotamia*. Translated by Teresa Lavender Fagan. Chicago: University of Chicago Press, 2004.
Bottéro, Jean, et al. *Ancestor of the West: Writing, Reasoning, and Religion in Mesopotamia, Elam, and Greece*. Translated by Teresa Lavender Fagan. Chicago: University of Chicago Press, 2000.
Bourke, Stephen. *The Middle East: The Cradle of Civilization Revealed*. New York: Metro, 2008.
Bratt, James D. *Abraham Kuyper: Modern Calvinist, Christian Democrat*. Grand Rapids: Eerdmans, 2013.

Bray, Gerald. *The Church: A Theological and Historical Account*. Grand Rapids: Baker Academic, 2016.
Bridgeman, Tess, and Brianna Rosen. "Still at War: The United States in Syria." *Just Security*, Apr. 29, 2022. https://www.justsecurity.org/81313/still-at-war-the-united-states-in-syria/.
Briney, Amanda. "The History of Cartography." *ThoughtCo*, Oct. 7, 2019. https://www.thoughtco.com/the-history-of-cartography-1435696.
Brown, Joe David. *India*. New York: Time Incorporated, 1961.
Brueggemann, Walter. *Money and Possessions*. Louisville, KY: Westminster John Knox, 2016.
Buckle, Anne. "Time Zone History of the United Kingdom." Time and Date. Accessed April 1, 2024. https://www.timeanddate.com/time/uk/time-zone-background.html.
Byun, Eddie. *Justice Awakening: How You and Your Church Can Help End Human Trafficking*. Downers Grove, IL: InterVarsity, 2014.
———. "A Time for Justice." *Talbot* 5 (2021) 10–12.
Calvin, John. *Institutes of the Christian Religion*. Vol. 1. Translated by John Allen. Grand Rapids: Eerdmans, 1949.
Carl, Noah. "CSI Brexit 4: People's Stated Reasons for Voting Leave or Remain." Centre for Social Investigation, Apr. 24, 2018. https://media.ukandeu.ac.uk/wp-content/uploads/2018/07/CSI-Brexit-4-People%E2%80%99s-Stated-Reasons-for-Voting-Leave.pdf.
Carroll, Sean. *The Big Picture: On the Origins of Life, Meaning, and the Universe Itself*. New York: Penguin, 2016.
Carson, D. A. "Matthew." In *Matthew, Mark, and Luke*, edited by Frank E. Gæbelein, 205–573. The Expositor's Bible Commentary with the New International Version 8. Grand Rapids: Zondervan, 1984.
Casanova, José. "Globalization and the Growing Church." Faith and Leadership, Apr. 8, 2013. https://faithandleadership.com/jose-casanova-globalization-and-the-growing-church.
———. *Public Religions in the Modern World*. Chicago: University of Chicago Press, 1994.
Caselli, Francesco, and John Coleman. "On the Theory of Ethnic Conflict." *Journal of the European Economic Association* 11 (2013) 161–92.
Cetorelli, Valeria, and Sareta Ashraph. *A Demographic Documentation of ISIS's Attack on the Yazidi Village of Kocho*. London School of Economics Middle East Centre, June 2019. http://eprints.lse.ac.uk/101098/.
CFR.org Editors. "Mexico's Long War: Drugs, Crime, and the Cartels." Council on Foreign Relations, Feb. 26, 2021. https://www.cfr.org/backgrounder/mexicos-long-war-drugs-crime-and-cartels.
Chanda, Nayan. *Bound Together: How Traders, Preachers, Adventurers, and Warriors Shaped Globalization*. New Haven, CT: Yale University Press, 2007.
Chang, Kenneth. "SpaceX Wins NASA $2.9 Billion Contract to Build Moon Lander." *New York Times*, Oct. 22, 2021. https://www.nytimes.com/2021/04/16/science/spacex-moon-nasa.html.
Chang, Taiping. "Three Millennia of Writings—A Brief History of Chinese Literature." *OUPblog*, Dec. 8, 2017. https://blog.oup.com/2017/12/chinese-literature-history-writings/.

Chibber, Vivek. *Confronting Capitalism: How the World Works and How to Change It.* New York: Verso, 2022.
Choge, Emily J., and Glen H. Stassen. "Social Ethics." In *GDT* 827–37.
Choi, Jae-hee. "S. Korea among Unhappiest Countries in OECD." *Korea Herald*, May 19, 2021. https://www.koreaherald.com/view.php?ud=20210519000126.
Clouser, Roy A. *The Myth of Religious Neutrality: An Essay on the Hidden Role of Religious Belief in Theories.* Rev. ed. Notre Dame, IN: University of Notre Dame, 2005.
Cohen, Jon. "As Creator of 'CRISPR Babies' Nears Release from Prison, Where Does Embryo Editing Stand?" *Science*, Mar. 21, 2022. https://www.science.org/content/article/creator-crispr-babies-nears-release-prison-where-does-embryo-editing-stand.
Cohn, Nate, and Kevin Quealy. "How Public Opinion Has Moved on Black Lives Matter." *New York Times*, June 10, 2020. https://www.nytimes.com/interactive/2020/06/10/upshot/black-lives-matter-attitudes.html.
Cohn, Samuel. *All Societies Die: How to Keep Hope Alive.* New York: Cornell University Press, 2021.
Coker, Christopher. *Can War Be Eliminated?* Cambridge: Polity, 2014.
Colson, Charles, and Nancy Pearcey. *How Now Shall We Live?* Wheaton, IL: Tyndale House, 1999.
Commins, David. *The Wahhabi Mission and Saudi Arabia.* New York: I.B. Tauris, 2006.
Connolly, William E. *Pluralism.* Durham, NC: Duke University Press, 2005.
Covarrubias, Brenda. "Eddie Byun Presents on Human Trafficking in Chapel." *Zu Media*, Feb. 20, 2020. https://zunews.com/2020/02/eddie-byun-presents-on-human-trafficking-in-chapel/.
Curry, Andrew. "Ancient DNA Pioneer Svante Pääbo Wins Nobel Prize in Physiology or Medicine." *Science*, Oct. 3, 2022. https://www.science.org/content/article/nobel-prize-physiology-or-medicine-2022.
Curry, Patrick. "Astrology." In *The Oxford Illustrated Companion to the History of Modern Science*, edited by J. L. Heilbron, 24. New York: Tess, 2008.
Daalder, Ivo H. "Decision to Intervene: How the War in Bosnia Ended." Brookings, Dec. 1, 1998. https://www.brookings.edu/articles/decision-to-intervene-how-the-war-in-bosnia-ended/.
Daniel, Elise. "Three Fallacies of the Social Gospel." Institute for Faith, Work and Economics, Oct. 19, 2012. https://tifwe.org/three-fallacies-of-the-social-gospel/.
Dasgupta, Rana. "The Demise of the Nation State." *Guardian*, Apr. 5, 2018. https://www.theguardian.com/news/2018/apr/05/demise-of-the-nation-state-rana-dasgupta.
Dawson, Stephen. "The Religious Resurgence and International Relations Theory." *Religious Studies Review* 39 (2013) 201–21.
Dearborn, Tim. *Reflection on Advocacy and Justice.* Monrovia, CA: World Vision International, 2009.
Deconstructed. "France and the Myth of the Colorblind Society." *The Intercept*, Feb. 26, 2021. https://theintercept.com/2021/02/26/deconstructed-france-race-color blind-myth/.
Deen, Thalif. "Staff Surveys Reveal Widespread Racism at the United Nations." *Inter Press Service*, Aug. 21, 2020. http://www.ipsnews.net/2020/08/staff-surveys-reveal-widespread-racism-united-nations/.

Demacopoulos, George E. *Gregory the Great: Ascetic, Pastor, and First Man of Rome.* Notre Dame, IN: University of Notre Dame Press, 2015.
Demarest, Bruce. *The Cross and Salvation: The Doctrine of Salvation.* Foundations of Evangelical Theology. Wheaton, IL: Crossway, 1997.
Deneen, Patrick J. *Why Liberalism Failed.* New Haven, CT: Yale University Press, 2018.
Devictor, Xavier, et al. "The Globalization of Refugee Flows." World Bank Group, Jan. 2021. https://openknowledge.worldbank.org/bitstream/handle/10986/33580/The-Globalization-of-Refugee-Flows.pdf?sequence=5&isAllowed=y.
Dhand, Arti. "The Dharma of Ethics, the Ethics of Dharma: Quizzing the Ideals of Hinduism." *Journal of Religious Ethics* 30 (2002) 347–72.
Diamandis, Peter H., and Steven Kotler. *Abundance.* New York: Free Press, 2014.
Dictionary.com. s.v. "Social Justice." Accessed April 1, 2024. https://www.dictionary.com/browse/social%20justice.
Dodman, Benjamin. "The Year Charlie Hebdo Was Loved, Hated and Misunderstood." *France 24*, July 1, 2016. https://www.france24.com/en/20160107-charlie-hebdo-islam-racism-press-freedom-rushdie-satire-liberals.
Doleac, Miles. "Triclinium Pauperum: Poverty, Charity and Papacy in the Time of Gregory the Great." PhD diss., Tulane University, 2013.
Dooyeweerd, Herman. *Roots of Western Culture: Pagan, Secular, and Christian Options.* Edited by D. F. M. Strauss. Translated by John Kraay. Grand Rapids: Paideia, 2012.
Dorrien, Gary. *Kantian Reason and Hegelian Spirit.* Sussex, UK: Wiley-Blackwell, 2012.
Dreher, Rod. *The Benedict Option: A Strategy for Christians in a Post-Christian Nation.* New York: Sentinel, 2017.
Dugin, Alexander. *The Theory of a Multipolar World.* Translated by Michael Millerman. London: Arktos, 2020.
Earls, Aaron. "Young Adults See Leadership Crisis in Society, Lack of Opportunities at Church." Lifeway Research, Dec. 12, 2019. https://lifewayresearch.com/2019/12/12/young-adults-see-leadership-crisis-in-society-lack-of-opportunities-at-church/.
Eisinger, Jesse, et al. "The Secret IRS Files: Trove of Never-Before-Seen Records Reveal How the Wealthiest Avoid Income Tax." *ProPublica*, June 8, 2021. https://www.propublica.org/article/the-secret-irs-files-trove-of-never-before-seen-records-reveal-how-the-wealthiest-avoid-income-tax.
Elliott, Larry. "Ireland's Austerity Measures Show Us How Not to Do It." *Guardian*, Sept. 23, 2010. https://www.theguardian.com/business/2010/sep/23/ireland-austerity-budgets-comment.
Elzarka, Mohamed. "The Role of Religion in the Yugoslav War." *Aisthesis* 9 (2018) 29–35.
Epp, Susannah. "Abuses of Religious Power: Why Do They Happen and What Can We Do about It?" *Chimes*, Mar. 18, 2021. https://calvinchimes.org/2021/03/18/abuses-of-religious-power-why-do-they-happen-and-what-can-we-do-about-it/.
Esmark, Anders. *The New Technocracy.* Bristol, UK: Bristol University Press, 2020.
Esposito, John L. *The Oxford History of Islam.* Oxford: Oxford University Press, 2000.
Evans, Tony. "Kingdom Race Theology." Recorded at Oak Cliff Bible Fellowship, Dallas, Texas, July 14, 2021. https://sundaytosaturday.com/2021/09/01/sermon-kingdom-race-theology/.
Fadaee, Simin. "Hamburg G20 Protests and Alternative Futures." *Open Democracy*, July 18, 2017. https://opendemocracy.net/en/hamburg-g20-protests-and-alternative-futures/.

Ferris, Jaquelle Crowe. "Gen Z, Let's Prioritize the Gospel as We Pursue Justice." *The Gospel Coalition*, May 7, 2018. https://www.thegospelcoalition.org/article/generation-z-social-justice-prioritize-gospel/.

Fields, David P. *Foreign Friends: Syngman Rhee, American Exceptionalism, and the Division of Korea*. Lexington: University Press of Kentucky, 2019.

Finger, Thomas N. *A Contemporary Anabaptist Theology: Biblical, Historical, Constructive*. Downers Grove, IL: InterVarsity, 2004.

Fisch, Yesica, et al. "Brazil's Bolsonaro Assumes Presidency, Promises Big Changes." *CTV News*, Jan. 1, 2019. https://www.ctvnews.ca/world/brazil-s-bolsonaro-assumes-presidency-promises-big-changes-1.4236927.

Fitzgerald, Frances. *The Evangelicals: The Struggle to Shape America*. New York: Simon and Schuster, 2017.

Flood, Gavin. *An Introduction to Hinduism*. Cambridge: Cambridge University Press, 1996.

Frank, Mark R. "A Brief History of the Great Clock at Westminster Palace." 2008. http://www.my-time-machines.net/Big_Ben_paper_web_05-15-14.pdf.

Franke, John R. *Missional Theology: An Introduction*. Grand Rapids: Baker Academic, 2020.

Fraser, David. "Globalization." In *GDT* 336–43.

Freiden, Jeffrey. "The Modern Capitalist World Economy: A Historical Overview." In *The Oxford Handbook of Capitalism*, edited by Dennis C. Mueller, 17–37. New York: Oxford University Press, 2012.

French, David. "In Defense of the Iraq War." *National Review*, Mar. 20, 2019. https://www.nationalreview.com/corner/iraq-war-just-cause-saddam-hussein-threat-stability/.

Friedman, George. "Nationalism Is Rising, Not Fascism." *Geopolitical Futures*, May 31, 2016. https://geopoliticalfutures.com/nationalism-is-rising-not-fascism/.

Friedman, Thomas L. *The Lexus and the Olive Tree: Understanding Globalization*. New York: Picador, 1999.

Frum, David. "Take It from an Iraq War Supporter—War with Iran Would Be a Disaster." *Atlantic*, May 15, 2019. https://www.theatlantic.com/ideas/archive/2019/05/the-iraq-war-was-a-failurewar-with-iran-would-be-worse/589534/.

Fukuyama, Francis. *Liberalism and Its Discontents*. New York: Farrar, Straus and Giroux, 2022.

Galadima, Bulus. "Religion and the Future of Christianity in the Global Village." In *One World or Many? The Impact of Globalisation on Mission*, edited by Richard Tiplady, 292. Pasadena, CA: William Carey Library, 2003.

Gallo, Ernesto. "Three Varieties of Authoritarian Neoliberalism: Rule by the Experts, the People, the Leader." *Competition and Change* 26 (2022) 554–74.

Gardiner, Marilyn. "Led by the Global South." *A Life Overseas*, Oct. 12, 2021. https://www.alifeoverseas.com/led-by-the-global-south/.

Garnsey, Peter, and Richard Saller. *The Roman Empire: Economy, Society, and Culture*. 2nd ed. Berkeley: University of California Press, 2015.

Garrison, Justin. "A Covenant with All Mankind: Ronald Reagan's Idyllic Vision of America in the World." *Humanitas* 21 (2008) 34–63.

Gentry, Peter J., and Stephen J. Wellum. *Kingdom through Covenant: A Biblical-Theological Understanding of the Covenants*. 2nd ed. Wheaton, IL: Crossway, 2018.

Giddens, Anthony. *The Consequences of Modernity*. Stanford, CA: Stanford University Press, 1990.
Giridharadas, Anand. *Winners Take All: The Elite Charade of Changing the World*. New York: Knopf, 2018.
Glantz, David M., and Jonathan Mallory House. *When Titans Clashed: How the Red Army Stopped Hitler*. Rev. and exp. ed. Lawrence: University Press of Kansas, 2015.
Global Solidarity Summit. "The Alternative to the G20 Summit in Hamburg—Global Solidarity Summit." Degrowth, May 4, 2017. https://www.degrowth.info/en/blog/the-alternative-to-the-g20-summit-in-hamburg-global-solidarity-summit.
Goff, Kerby. "Globalplus: Missionary Trends." The Association of Religion Data Archives, Nov. 20, 2020. https://www.thearda.com/categories/ahead-of-the-trend/missionary-trends.
Goheen, Michael W. *The Church and Its Vocation: Lesslie Newbigin's Missionary Ecclesiology*. Grand Rapids: Baker Academic, 2018.
Goossaert, Vincent, and David A. Palmer. *The Religious Question in Modern China*. Chicago: University of Chicago Press, 2011.
Gordon, Bruce. *Zwingli: God's Armed Prophet*. New Haven, CT: Yale University Press, 2021.
Gorman, Robert F. *What's Wrong with Global Governance?* Grand Rapids: Action Institute, 2016.
Goudzwaard, Bob, and Craig G. Bartholomew. *Beyond the Modern Age: An Archaeology of Contemporary Culture*. Downers Grove, IL: InterVarsity, 2017.
Green, Eric. "The Human Genome Sequence Is Now Complete." National Human Genome Research Institute, Apr, 7, 2022. https://www.genome.gov/about-nhgri/Director/genomics-landscape/april-7-2022-the-human-genome-sequence-is-now-complete.
Greenwald, Glenn. "The Untouchables: How the Obama Administration Protected Wall Street from Prosecutions." *Guardian*, Jan. 23, 2013. https://www.theguardian.com/commentisfree/2013/jan/23/untouchables-wall-street-prosecutions-obama.
Grenz, Stanley J. *A Primer on Postmodernism*. Grand Rapids: Eerdmans, 1996.
———. *Renewing the Center: Evangelical Theology in a Post-Theological Era*. 2nd ed. Grand Rapids: Baker Academic, 2006.
———. *Theology for the Community of God*. Grand Rapids: Eerdmans, 2000.
Griffin, Cailey. "Why Has France's Islamist Separatism Bill Caused Such Controversy?" *Foreign Policy*, Feb. 23, 2021. https://foreignpolicy.com/2021/02/23/why-france-islamist-separatism-bill-controversy-extremism/.
Griswold, Eliza. "How Black Lives Matter Is Changing the Church." *New Yorker*, Aug. 30, 2020. https://www.newyorker.com/news/on-religion/how-black-lives-matter-is-changing-the-church.
———. *The Tenth Parallel: Dispatches from the Fault Line between Christianity and Islam*. New York: Farrar, Straus and Giroux, 2010.
Groody, Daniel G. *Globalization, Spirituality, and Justice: Navigating the Path to Peace*. Rev. ed. Maryknoll, NY: Orbis, 2015.
Gross, Terry. "The Evangelicals Engaged in Spiritual Warfare." NPR, Aug. 19, 2011. https://www.npr.org/transcripts/139781021.
Gutiérrez, Gustavo. "Memory and Prophecy." In *The Option for the Poor in Christian Theology*, edited by Daniel G. Groody, 17–40. Notre Dame, IN: University of Notre Dame Press, 2007.

Habermas, Jürgen, et al. *An Awareness of What Is Missing: Faith and Reason in a Post-Secular Age.* Cambridge: Polity, 2010.

Hagopian, Amy, et al. "Mortality in Iraq Associated with the 2003-2011 War and Occupation: Findings from a National Cluster Sample Survey by the University Collaborative Iraq Mortality Study." *PLOS Medicine* 10 (Oct. 15, 2013). https://doi.org/10.1371/journal.pmed.1001533.

Halberstam, David. *War in a Time of Peace: Bush, Clinton, and the Generals.* New York: Scribner, 2001.

Hall, Douglas John. *The End of Christendom and the Future of Christianity.* Valley Forge, PA: Trinity, 1997.

Hamilton, James M., Jr. *God's Glory in Salvation through Judgment: A Biblical Theology.* Wheaton, IL: Crossway, 2010.

Hanciles, Jehu. *Beyond Christendom: Globalization, African Migration, and the Transformation of the West.* Maryknoll, NY: Orbis, 2008.

Harari, Yuval Noah. *Homo Deus: A Brief History of Tomorrow.* New York: HarperCollins, 2017.

Harrington, Daniel J. *The Maccabean Revolt: Anatomy of a Biblical Revolution.* Eugene, OR: Wipf & Stock, 1988.

Harstad, Adolph L. *Joshua.* Concordia Commentary. St. Louis, MO: Concordia, 2004.

Harvard Gazette. "Remarks of Chinese Premier Wen Jiabao." Dec. 11, 2003. https://news.harvard.edu/gazette/story/2003/12/harvard-gazette-remarks-of-chinese-premier-wen-jiabao/.

Harvey, John D. *A Commentary on Romans.* Kregel Exegetical Library. Grand Rapids: Kregel Academic, 2019.

Hathaway, Oona A., and Scott J. Shapiro. *The Internationalists: How a Radical Plan to Outlaw War Remade the World.* New York: Simon and Schuster, 2017.

Hauerwas, Stanley. *A Community of Character: Toward a Constructive Christian Social Ethic.* Notre Dame, IN: University of Notre Dame Press, 1981.

Hauerwas, Stanley, and William H. Willimon. *Resident Aliens.* Nashville: Abingdon, 1989.

Hayden, Robert M. "Yugoslavia's Collapse: National Suicide with Foreign Assistance." *Economic and Political Weekly* 27 (1992) 1377-82.

Held, David. *Global Covenant: The Social Democratic Alternative to the Washington Consensus.* Malden, MA: Polity, 2004.

Held, David, and Anthony McGrew. *The Global Transformations Reader.* 2nd ed. Cambridge: Polity, 2003.

Henderson, Mark. "Human Genome Sequencing: The Real Ethical Dilemmas." *Guardian*, Sept. 9, 2013. https://www.theguardian.com/science/2013/sep/09/genetics-ethics-human-gene-sequencing.

Henley, Jon. "How Mitterrand Sought Advice from Astrologer." *Guardian*, June 24, 2000. https://www.theguardian.com/world/2000/jun/25/jonhenley.theobserver2.

Hennig, Benjamin D. "Remapping Geography: Using Cartograms to Change Our View of the World." *Geography* 104 (2019) 71-80.

Hickman, Louise. "The Good, the True and the Beautiful: Imagining an Ethico-Political Future for the Philosophy of Religion." *Palgrave Communications* 4 (2018) 1-10.

Hiebert, Paul G. "The Missionary as Mediator of Global Theologizing." In *Globalizing Theology*, edited by Craig Ott and Harold A. Netland, 288-308. Grand Rapids: Baker Academic, 2006.

Hinson, E. Glenn. "Constantinianism." In *ER* 3:1968.
Hiro, Dilip. *After Empire: The Birth of a Multipolar World.* New York: Bold Type, 2010.
Holland, Tom. *Dominion: How the Christian Revolution Remade the World.* New York: Basic, 2019.
Hollingham, Richard. "The NASA Mission That Broadcast to a Billion People." BBC, Dec. 21, 2018. https://www.bbc.com/future/article/20181220-the-nasa-mission-that-broadcast-to-a-billion-people.
Hublin, Jean-Jacques, et al. "New Fossils from Jebel Irhoud, Morocco and the Pan-African Origin of Homo Sapiens." *Nature* 546 (2017) 289–92.
Hudson, Robert, and Glenn Bowman, eds. *After Yugoslavia: Identities and Politics within the Successor States.* New York: Palgrave, 2011.
Hummel, Horace D. *Ezekiel 21–48.* Concordia Commentary. Saint Louis, MO: Concordia, 2007.
Hunt, Mary E., and Diann L. Neu, eds. *New Feminist Christianity: Many Voices, Many Views.* Woodstock, VT: SkyLight Paths, 2010.
Hunter, James Davison. *To Change the World: The Irony, Tragedy, and Possibility of Christianity in the Late Modern World.* New York: Oxford University Press, 2010.
Huntington, Samuel P. "Dead Souls: The Denationalization of the American Elite." *The National Interest* 75 (Mar. 1, 2004) 5–18.
Ibn Ishaq. *The Life of Muhammad.* Translated by Alfred Guillaume. New York: Oxford University Press, 1998.
Ifanti, Amalia A., et al. "Financial Crisis and Austerity Measures in Greece: Their Impact on Health Promotion Policies and Public Health Care." *Health Policy* 113 (2013) 8–12.
Ilich, Bobby. "The United States after 9/11: How Many Major Terrorist Attacks Have There Been in America since 2001?" *International Business Times*, Sept. 9, 2016. https://www.ibtimes.com/united-states-after-911-how-many-major-terrorist-attacks-have-there-been-america-2001-2414070.
Imbua, David Lishilinimle. "Robbing Others to Pay Mary Slessor: Unearthing the Authentic Heroes and Heroines of the Abolition of Twin-Killing in Calabar." *African Economic History* 41 (2013) 139–58.
Institute for Economics and Peace. "Global Peace Index 2022: Measuring Peace in a Complex World." June 2023. https://www.visionofhumanity.org/wp-content/uploads/2022/06/GPI-2022-web.pdf.
International Campaign to Abolish Nuclear Weapons. "Which Countries Have Nuclear Weapons?" Accessed April 5, 2024. https://www.icanw.org/nuclear_arsenals.
International Telecommunication Union. "2.9 Billion People Still Offline." Nov. 30, 2021. https://www.itu.int/en/mediacentre/Pages/PR-2021-11-29-FactsFigures.aspx.
Jablonski, Nina G. "Skin Color and Race." *American Journal of Physical Anthropology* 175 (2021) 437–47.
James, Harold. "Deutsche Bank Isn't Deutsch Anymore." *Foreign Policy*, Feb. 24, 2016. https://foreignpolicy.com/2016/02/24/deutsche-bank-uber-alles/.
Jo, Yongmie Nicola, and Robert Walker. "Social Isolation and Poverty in South Korea: A Manifestation of the Poverty-Shame Nexus." In *Poverty and Shame: Global Experiences*, edited by Elaine Chase and Grace Bantebya-Kyomuhendo, 175–87. Oxford: Oxford University Press, 2015.
Johnson, Ian. *The Souls of China: The Return of Religion after Mao.* New York: Pantheon, 2017.

Johnson, Kristen Deede. *Theology, Political Theory, and Pluralism: Beyond Tolerance and Difference.* Cambridge Studies in Christian Doctrine 15. Cambridge: Cambridge University Press, 2007.

Joshua Project. "How Many People Groups Are There?" Accessed April 1, 2024. https://joshuaproject.net/resources/articles/how_many_people_groups_are_there.

Kaltenbach, Caleb. *Messy Truth: How to Foster Community without Sacrificing Conviction.* New York: Waterbrook, 2021.

Kärkkäinen, Veli-Matti. *Hope and Community.* Grand Rapids: Eerdmans, 2017.

Kaufmann, Franz-Xaver. *European Foundations of the Welfare State.* Translated by John Veit-Wilson. New York: Berghahn, 2012.

Keller, Timothy. *The Reason for God: Belief in an Age of Skepticism.* New York: Penguin, 2008.

Khanna, Parag. "America's 'Deep State' Is Not Nearly Deep Enough." *Fast Company*, Feb. 10, 2021. https://www.fastcompany.com/90595835/americas-deep-state-is-not-nearly-deep-enough.

Khwaja, Jamal. *The Call of Modernity and Islam.* Los Angeles: Alhamd, 2014.

Kim, Grace Ji-Sun. *Embracing the Other: The Transformative Spirit of Love.* Grand Rapids: Eerdmans, 2015.

Kim, Sebastian. "The Future Shape of Christianity from an Asian Perspective." In *Global Christianity: Contested Claims*, edited by Frans Wijsen and Robert J. Schreiter, 69–94. Amsterdam: Rodopi, 2007.

———. *Theology in the Public Sphere: Public Theology as a Catalyst for Open Debate.* London: SCM, 2011.

Kim, Sebastian, and Kirsteen Kim. *A History of Korean Christianity.* New York: Cambridge University Press, 2014.

Kim, Youna, ed. *Routledge Handbook of Korean Culture and Society.* New York: Routledge, 2017.

Kinnaman, David, and Gabe Lyons. *Unchristian.* Grand Rapids: Baker, 2007.

Klett, Leah MarieAnn. "Evangelical Seminary Condemns Black Lives Matter Movement, 'Wokeness' Ideology." *Christian Post*, Aug. 20, 2020. https://www.christianpost.com/news/evangelical-seminary-condemns-black-lives-matter-movement-wokeness-ideology.html.

Knickmeyer, Ellen. "Costs of the Afghanistan War in Lives and Dollars." AP News, Aug. 17, 2021. https://apnews.com/article/middle-east-business-afghanistan-43d8f53b35e80ec18c130cd683e1a38f.

Kovacs, Gyula. "The Human Genome Project and the Question of Ethicality." *University of Western Ontario Journal of Anthropology* 7 (1999) 1–6.

Kuhn, Dieter. *The Age of Confucian Rule: The Song Transformation of China.* Cambridge: Harvard University Press, 2011.

Kumar, Aditi, and Ric Rosenbach. "The Truth about the Dark Web." IMF, Sept. 2019. https://www.imf.org/en/Publications/fandd/issues/2019/09/the-truth-about-the-dark-web-kumar.

Küng, Hans, and K. J. Kuschel, eds. *Global Responsibility: In Search of a New World Ethic.* New York: Continuum, 1991.

Kuperman, Alan J. "The Moral Hazard of Humanitarian Intervention: Lessons from the Balkans." *International Studies Quarterly* 52 (Mar. 2008) 49–80.

Ladd, George Eldon. *The Gospel of the Kingdom.* Grand Rapids: Eerdmans, 1959.

———. *A Theology of the New Testament.* Rev. ed. Grand Rapids: Eerdmans, 1993.

Langberg, Diane. *Redeeming Power: Understanding Authority and Abuse in the Church*. Grand Rapids: Brazos, 2020.
Langer, Ronit, and Shruti Sharma. "The Blessing and Curse of Biotechnology: A Primer on Biosafety and Biosecurity." Carnegie Endowment for International Peace, Nov. 20, 2020. https://carnegieendowment.org/2020/11/20/blessing-and-curse-of-biotechnology-primer-on-biosafety-and-biosecurity-pub-83252.
Launius, Roger D. *Apollo's Legacy: Perspectives on the Moon Landings*. Washington, DC: Smithsonian Institution, 2019.
Lausanne Occasional Paper. "Globalization and the Gospel: Rethinking Mission in the Contemporary World (LOP 30)." Pattaya, Thailand: 2004.
Lecler, Romain. "What Makes Globalization Really New? Sociological Views on Our Current Globalization." *Journal of Global History* 14 (2019) 355–73.
Lee, Barbara. "Why I Opposed the Resolution to Authorize Force." *SFGATE*, Sept. 23, 2001.
Lee, Claire. "Fewer Koreans Feel Responsible for Aging Parents." *Korea Herald*, May 8, 2016. http://www.koreaherald.com/view.php?ud=20160508000359.
Lee, Sang Hyun. *The Philosophical Theology of Jonathan Edwards*. Rev. ed. Princeton: Princeton University Press, 1988.
Lee, Sue-Im. "We Are Not the World: Global Village, Universalism, and Karen Tei Yamashita's Tropic of Orange." *Modern Fiction Studies* 53 (2007) 501–27.
Lee, Young-Hoon. "Korean Pentecost: The Great Revival of 1907." *Asian Journal of Pentecostal Studies* 4 (2001) 73–83.
Leeman, Jonathan. *Political Church: The Local Assembly as Embassy of Christ's Rule*. Downers Grove, IL: InterVarsity, 2016.
Leffler, Melvyn P. *Confronting Saddam Hussein: George W. Bush and the Invasion of Iraq*. New York: Oxford University Press, 2023.
Legutko, Ryszard. *The Demon in Democracy*. New York: Encounter, 2018.
Lloyd, Cathie. "Race and Ethnicity." In *Modern France: Society in Transition*, edited by Malcolm Cook and Grace Davie, 34–52. New York: Routledge, 1999.
Locke, Larry G. "The Promise of CRISPR for Human Germline Editing and the Perils of 'Playing God.'" *CRISPR Journal* 3 (2020) 27–31.
Lopez, Jean, et al. *World War II: Infographics*. New York: Thames & Hudson, 2021.
Lopez, Mark Hugo, et al. "More Latinos Have Serious Concerns about Their Place in America under Trump." Pew Research Center, Oct. 25, 2018. https://www.pewresearch.org/hispanic/2018/10/25/latinos-and-discrimination/.
López-Alves, Fernando, and Diane E. Johnson, eds. *Globalization and Uncertainty in Latin America*. New York: Palgrave Macmillan, 2007.
Lowe, Keith. *Savage Continent: Europe in the Aftermath of World War II*. New York: St. Martin's, 2012.
Luo, Guanzhong. *Three Kingdoms*. Translated by Moss Roberts. Oakland: University of California Press, 2020.
Luther, Martin. *Works of Martin Luther*. Vol. 5. Philadelphia: A. J. Holman Company and the Castle, 1931.
Lyotard, Jean-François. *The Postmodern Explained: Correspondence, 1982–1985*. Translated by Don Barry. Minneapolis: University of Minnesota Press, 1993.
Macedo, Donaldo, and Panayota Gounari, eds. *Globalization of Racism*. New York: Routledge, 2016.

Măcelaru, Marcel V. "Christianity and the Refugee Crisis." *Transformation* 35 (2018) 69–76.

———. "Theology Encounters Globalization." *European Journal of Science and Theology* 10 (Feb. 2014) 67–78.

MacLean, Nancy. *Democracy in Chains*. New York: Viking, 2017.

Maguire, Sarah. "How the Moon Landing Changed the World." *The Lighthouse*, July 17, 2019. https://lighthouse.mq.edu.au/article/july-2019/how-the-moon-landing-changed-the-world.

Makooi, Bahar. "'The Violence Shook Me Profoundly': Teachers, Students Remember Samuel Paty's Murder." *France 24*, Oct. 15, 2021. https://www.france24.com/en/france/20211015-the-violence-shook-me-profoundly-teachers-students-remember-samuel-paty-s-murder.

Malkasian, Carter. *The American War in Afghanistan: A History*. New York: Oxford University Press, 2021.

Mandelbaum, Michael. "A Perfect Failure: NATO's War against Yugoslavia." *Foreign Affairs* 78 (Sept./Oct. 1999) 2–8.

Mao, Frances. "South Korea Records World's Lowest Fertility Rate Again." BBC, Aug. 25, 2022. https://www.bbc.com/news/world-asia-62670717.

Mavelli, Luca. "Neoliberalism as Religion: Sacralization of the Market and Post-Truth Politics." *International Political Sociology* 14 (Mar. 2020) 57–76.

McClendon, James William. *Ethics: Systematic Theology*. Vol. 1. 2nd ed. Nashville: Abingdon, 2002.

McCurry, Justin. "South Korea's Inequality Paradox: Long Life, Good Health and Poverty." *Guardian*, Aug. 2, 2017. https://www.theguardian.com/inequality/2017/aug/02/south-koreas-inequality-paradox-long-life-good-health-and-poverty.

McGreal, Chris. "70 Years and Half a Trillion Dollars Later: What Has the UN Achieved?" *Guardian*, Sept. 7, 2015. https://www.theguardian.com/world/2015/sep/07/what-has-the-un-achieved-united-nations.

McLaren, Brian. "Brian McLaren Extended Interview." *PBS Religion and Ethics*, July 15, 2005. https://www.pbs.org/wnet/religionandethics/2005/07/15/july-15-2005-brian-mclaren-extended-interview/11774/.

McMeekin, Sean. *Stalin's War: A New History of World War II*. New York: Basic, 2021.

Mearsheimer, John J. *The Great Delusion: Liberal Dreams and International Realities*. New Haven, CT: Yale University Press, 2018.

Meehan, Mary. "The Next Generation: What Matters to Gen We." *Forbes*, Aug. 11, 2016. https://www.forbes.com/sites/marymeehan/2016/08/11/the-next-generation-what-matters-to-gen-we/?sh=7d73bbb47350.

Mellow, David. "Iraq: A Morally Justified Resort to War." *Journal of Applied Philosophy* 23 (2006) 293–310.

Meloni, Giorgia. "God, Homeland, Family." Speech at National Conservatism Conference, Rome, Italy, Feb. 3, 2020. nationalconservatism.org/natcon-rome-2020/presenters/giorgia-meloni.

Messer, Neil G. "Human Flourishing: A Christian Theological Perspective." In *Measuring Well-Being: Interdisciplinary Perspectives from the Social Sciences and the Humanities*, edited by Matthew T. Lee et al., 285–305. New York: Oxford University Press, 2021.

Metz, Johannes. *Theology of the World*. Translated by W. Glen-Doepel. New York: Herder, 1971.

Milanović, Branko. *Capitalism, Alone: The Future of the System That Rules the World.* Cambridge: Belknap, 2019.

Miller, Paul D., et al. "Is Christianity Compatible with Liberal Democracy?" *Providence*, Nov. 5, 2018. https://providencemag.com/2018/11/christianity-compatible-liberal-democracy/.

Missionary Church. *Constitution of the Missionary Church.* Fort Wayne, IN: Missionary Church Inc., 2021. https://mcusa.org/constitutionaldocs.

Mitter, Rana. *Forgotten Ally: China's World War II.* Boston: Houghton Mifflin Harcourt, 2013.

Momani, Bessma. "The Human Cost of the Iraq War Outweighs All Other." Brookings, Mar. 20, 2013. https://www.brookings.edu/opinions/the-human-cost-of-the-iraq-war-outweighs-all-others/.

Moore, Scott H. *The Limits of Liberal Democracy: Politics and Religion at the End of Modernity.* Downers Grove, IL: IVP Academic, 2009.

Moorhead, John. "Taking Gregory the Great's Dialogues Seriously." *Downside Review* 121 (2003) 197–210.

Mouw, Richard J. *The Challenges of Cultural Discipleship: Essays in the Line of Abraham Kuyper.* Grand Rapids: Eerdmans, 2012.

Mullen, Ruby. "The Shocking Speed of the Taliban's Advance: A Visual Timeline." *Washington Post*, Aug. 16, 2021. https://www.washingtonpost.com/world/2021/08/16/taliban-timeline/.

Müller, Retief. "Christianity and Globalisation: An Alternative Ethical Response." *HTS Teologiese Studies/Theological Studies* 67 (2011) 1–7.

Myers, Bryant L. *Engaging Globalization: The Poor, Christian Mission, and Our Hyperconnected World.* Grand Rapids: Baker Academic, 2017.

Nanda, Meera. *The God Market: How Globalization Is Making India More Hindu.* New York: Monthly Review, 2011.

NASA Earth Observatory. "All of You on the Good Earth." Accessed April 1, 2024. https://earthobservatory.nasa.gov/images/144427/all-of-you-on-the-good-earth.

National Human Genome Research Institute. "Human Genome Project: Fact Sheet." Accessed April 1, 2024. https://www.genome.gov/about-genomics/educational-resources/fact-sheets/human-genome-project.

Netland, Harold A. *Christianity and Religious Diversity: Clarifying Christian Commitments in a Globalizing Age.* Grand Rapids: Baker Academic, 2015.

Newbigin, Lesslie. *Foolishness to the Greeks: The Gospel and Western Culture.* Grand Rapids: Eerdmans, 1986.

New Encyclopædia Britannica: Macropædia. 15th ed. Chicago: University of Chicago, 1986.

New York Times. "At Home and Abroad." Apr. 16, 1961.

———. "Man in Space." Apr. 16, 1961.

Nkansah-Obrempong, James. "Africa's Contextual Realities: Foundation for the Church's Holistic Mission." *International Review of Mission* 106 (Dec. 2017) 280–94.

———. "The Problem of Evil." In *GDT* 300–303.

Norberg, Johan. *In Defense of Global Capitalism.* Translated by Roger Tanner with Julian Sanchez. Washington, DC: Cato Institute, 2003.

———. *Progress: The Reasons to Look Forward to the Future.* London: Oneworld, 2017.

Norberg-Hodge, Helena. "How Globalization Fuels Terrorism and Fundamentalism." *Films for Action*, Nov. 12, 2015. https://www.filmsforaction.org/articles/globalization-and-terror.

Novak, Michael. "Social Justice: Not What You Think It Is." The Heritage Foundation, Dec. 29, 2009. https://www.heritage.org/poverty-and-inequality/report/social-justice-not-what-you-think-it.

Nurullah, Abu Sadat. "Globalisation as a Challenge to Islamic Cultural Identity." *International Journal of Interdisciplinary Social Sciences: Annual Review* 3 (2008) 45–52.

Obenchain, Diane B. "The Study of Religion and the Coming of Global Generation." In *Christ and the Dominions of Civilization*, edited by Max Stackhouse and Diane B. Obenchain, 59–109. Harrisburg, PA: Trinity, 2002.

O'Brian, Matthew. "Sorry, Latvia Is No Austerity Success Story." *Atlantic*, Jan. 3, 2013. https://www.theatlantic.com/business/archive/2013/01/sorry-latvia-is-no-austerity-success-story/266774/.

O'Connell, Gerard. "Giorgia Meloni Is a Christian and a Right-Wing Nationalist. How Will She Relate to Pope Francis?" *America* 227 (2022) 14–15.

Oden, Thomas C. *How Africa Shaped the Christian Mind*. Downers Grove, IL: InterVarsity, 2010.

O'Ferrall, Fergus. "The Flourishing Society: Introduction." TASC, Oct. 2011. https://www.tasc.ie/assets/files/pdf/the_flourishing_society_introduction_a5.pdf.

Ogle, Vanessa. *The Global Transformation of Time: 1870–1950*. Cambridge, MA: Harvard University Press, 2015.

Orji, Cyril. *A Science-Theology Rapprochement: Pannenberg, Peirce, and Lonergan in Conversation*. Newcastle upon Tyne, UK: Cambridge Scholars, 2018.

Ornstein, Allan C. "Social Justice: History, Purpose and Meaning." *Society* 54 (2017) 541–50.

Ott, Craig, and Harold A. Netland, eds. *Globalizing Theology: Belief and Practice in an Era of World Christianity*. Grand Rapids: Baker Academic, 2006.

Oxford English Dictionary. s.v. "Social Justice." Accessed April 1, 2024. https://www.oed.com/search/dictionary/?scope=Entries&q=social+justice.

Pagden, Anthony, ed. *The Idea of Europe: From Antiquity to the European Union*. Cambridge: Cambridge University Press, 2002.

Pannenberg, Wolfhart. *Systematic Theology*. Vol. 3. Translated by Geoffrey W. Bromiley. Grand Rapids: Eerdmans, 1998.

Pape, Robert A. "It's the Occupation, Stupid." *Foreign Policy*, Oct. 18, 2010. https://foreignpolicy.com/2010/10/18/its-the-occupation-stupid/.

Partzsch, Lena. "Powerful Individuals in a Globalized World." *Global Policy* 8 (Feb. 7, 2017) 5–13.

Pennington, Jonathan T. "A Biblical Theology of Human Flourishing." Institute for Faith, Work and Economics, Mar. 4, 2015. https://tifwe.org/wp-content/uploads/2015/03/A-Biblical-Theology-of-Human-Flourishing-Pennington.pdf.

Pew Research Center. "Christianity and Conflict in Latin America." Apr. 6, 2006. https://www.pewresearch.org/religion/2006/04/06/christianity-and-conflict-in-latin-america/.

Philosophy Talk. "Move Over Letterman: A Philosophical Top 10 List for the 21st Century." Dec. 17, 2009. https://www.philosophytalk.org/blog/move-over-letterman-philosophical-top-10-list-21st-century.

Piketty, Thomas. *Time for Socialism: Dispatches from a World on Fire, 2016–2021*. New Haven, CT: Yale University Press, 2021.
Piketty, Thomas, et al. "Distributional National Accounts: Methods and Estimates for the United States." *Quarterly Journal of Economics* 133 (May 2018) 553–609.
Pinker, Steven. *Enlightenment Now: The Case for Reason, Science, Humanism, and Progress*. New York: Penguin, 2018.
Pluckrose, Helen, and James A. Lindsay. *Cynical Theories: How Activist Scholarship Made Everything about Race, Gender, and Identity*. Durham, NC: Pitchstone, 2020.
Poggioli, Sylvia. "Giorgia Meloni Is Italy's First Female Prime Minister." NPR, Oct. 25, 2022. https://www.npr.org/2022/10/25/1131449415/giorgia-meloni-is-italys-first-female-prime-minister.
Poon, Michael N. C. "Patristic Theology." In *GDT* 628–37.
Porter, Patrick. *The Global Village Myth*. Washington, DC: Georgetown University Press, 2015.
Porter, Stanley E., and Jason C. Robinson. *Hermeneutics: An Introduction to Interpretative Theory*. Grand Rapids: Eerdmans, 2011.
Posner, Eric. "The Case against Human Rights." *Guardian*, Dec. 4, 2014. https://www.theguardian.com/news/2014/dec/04/-sp-case-against-human-rights.
Prontzos, Peter G. "The Concept of 'Race' Is a Lie." *Scientific American*, May 14, 2019. https://blogs.scientificamerican.com/observations/the-concept-of-race-is-a-lie/#.
Qiu, Jane. "How China Is Rewriting the Book on Human Origins." *Nature* 535 (2016) 218–20.
Rajashekar, J. Paul. "Theological Education in an Era of Globalization." *Journal of Lutheran Ethics* 15 (Jan. 2015). https://learn.elca.org/jle/theological-education-in-an-era-of-globalization-some-critical-issues/.
Raschke, Carl. "Globalization and Theology." *Religion Compass* 5 (Nov. 2011) 638–45.
Ratsimbaharison, Adrien M. *The Failure of the United Nations Development Programs for Africa*. Lanham, MD: University Press of America, 2003.
Reich, David. *Who We Are and How We Got Here*. New York: Oxford University Press, 2018.
Rhodes, Richard. *Twilight of the Bombs: Recent Challenges, New Dangers, and the Prospects for a World without Nuclear Weapons*. New York: Vintage, 2011.
———. "Why Robert Oppenheimer's Atomic Bomb Still Haunts Us." *Newsweek*, May 15, 2013. https://www.newsweek.com/2013/05/15/why-robert-oppenheimers-atomic-bomb-still-haunts-us-237382.html.
Roberts, Anthea, and Nicolas Lamp. *Six Faces of Globalization*. Cambridge, MA: Harvard University Press, 2021.
Robertson, Roland. "Globalization and the Future of Traditional Religion." In *Religion and the Powers of the Common Life*, edited by Max Stackhouse and Peter J. Paris, 53–68. New York: T&T Clark, 2000.
———. *Globalization: Social Theory and Global Culture*. London: Sage, 1992.
Robinson, William I. *Latin America and Global Capitalism: A Critical Globalization Perspective*. Baltimore, MD: Johns Hopkins University Press, 2008.
Robison, James. *The Absolutes: Freedom's Only Hope*. Wheaton, IL: Trinity House, 2002.
Rodrik, Dani. *The Globalization Paradox: Democracy and the Future of the World Economy*. New York: Norton, 2011.

Romero, Luis Gómez. "López Obrador Takes On Corruption and Poverty in Mexico through Austerity." *Pacific Standard*, Feb. 8, 2019. https://psmag.com/economics/combatting-corruption-in-mexico-through-austerity.

Ross, Hugh. "A Beginner's—and Expert's—Guide to the Big Bang: Separating Fact from Fiction." *Journal of the International Society of Christian Apologetics* 4 (2011) 1–27.

Rushdoony, R. J. *The Institutes of Biblical Law*. Nutley, NJ: Craig, 1973.

Rutland, Peter. "Racism and Nationalism." *Nationalities Papers* 50 (Dec. 2, 2021) 629–42.

Sachs, Jeffrey D. *The Ages of Globalization: Geography, Technology, and Institutions*. New York: Columbia University Press, 2020.

Saey, Tina Hesman. "We Finally Have a Fully Complete Human Genome." *Science News*, Mar. 31, 2022. https://www.sciencenews.org/article/human-genome-complete-dna-genetics.

Salaün, Tangi. "Charlie Hebdo Attackers Killed to Avenge Prophet Mohammad, French Court Hears." Sept. 1, 2020. https://www.reuters.com/article/us-france-charliehebdo-trial/charlie-hebdo-attackers-killed-to-avenge-prophet-mohammad-french-court-hears-idUSKBN25S6AZ.

Sample, Ian. "Earthrise: How the Iconic Image Changed the World." *Guardian*, Dec. 24, 2018. https://www.theguardian.com/science/2018/dec/24/earthrise-how-the-iconic-image-changed-the-world.

Sandel, Michael J. *Justice*. New York: Farrar, Straus and Giroux, 2009.

Sanks, T. Howland. "Globalization and the Church's Social Mission." *Theological Studies* 60 (Dec. 1999) 625–51.

Sarna, Jonathan D. *American Judaism*. New Haven, CT: Yale University Press, 2004.

Sartre, Jean-Paul. *Being and Nothingness: An Essay in Phenomenological Ontology*. Translated by Sarah Richmond. New York: Washington Square, 2018.

Saval, Nikil. "Globalisation: The Rise and Fall of an Idea That Swept the World." *Guardian*, July 14, 2017. https://www.theguardian.com/world/2017/jul/14/globalisation-the-rise-and-fall-of-an-idea-that-swept-the-world.

Sayers, Mark. *Disappearing Church: From Cultural Relevance to Gospel Resilience*. Chicago: Moody, 2016.

Schaeffer, Francis A. *The Complete Works of Francis A. Schaeffer*. 5 vols. Wheaton, IL: Crossway, 1985.

Schaff, Philip. *History of the Christian Church*. Vol. 8. Grand Rapids: Eerdmans, 1910.

Schnabel, Eckhard J. "Repentance in Paul's Letters." *Novum Testamentum* 57 (2015) 159–86.

Schwartz, Stephen. "Shariah in the West." In *New Threats to Freedom*, edited by Adam Bellow, 248–58. Conshohocken, PA: Templeton, 2010.

Segal, Troy. "Enron Scandal: The Fall of a Wall Street Darling." *Investopedia*, Apr. 5, 2023. https://www.investopedia.com/updates/enron-scandal-summary/.

Seligman, Martin E. P. *Flourish*. New York: Atria, 2011.

Selk, Avi, et al. "'They Showed His Photo, and My Stomach Just Dropped': Neighbors Recall Synagogue Massacre Suspect as a Loner." *Washington Post*, Oct. 28, 2018. https://www.washingtonpost.com/nation/2018/10/28/victims-expected-be-named-after-killed-deadliest-attack-jews-us-history/.

Shaw, Ian J. *Churches, Revolutions, and Empires: 1789–1914*. Geanies House, Scot.: Christian Focus, 2012.

Sherwood, Harriet. "Religion: Why Faith Is Becoming More and More Popular." *Guardian*, Aug. 27, 2018. https://www.theguardian.com/news/2018/aug/27/religion-why-is-faith-growing-and-what-happens-next.

Sider, Ronald J. *Good News and Good Works: A Theology for the Whole Gospel*. Grand Rapids: Baker, 1993.

Siekmeier, James. "Nationalism and Globalization in Latin America." *Current History* 114 (2015) 68–72.

Singh, Manoj. "The 2007–2008 Financial Crisis in Review." *Investopedia*, Sept. 18, 2022. https://www.investopedia.com/articles/economics/09/financial-crisis-review.asp.

Singh, Mrinal. "Top 10 Biggest Issues in the World Today." The Borgen Project, Aug. 21, 2018. https://borgenproject.org/biggest-issues-in-the-world/.

Singh, Upinder. *A History of Ancient and Early Medieval India: From the Stone Age to the 12th Century*. Delhi: Pearson, 2009.

Smallwood, Christine. "Astrology in the Age of Uncertainty." *New Yorker*, Oct. 21, 2019. https://www.newyorker.com/magazine/2019/10/28/astrology-in-the-age-of-uncertainty.

Smeeton, Donald Dean. *Lollard Themes in the Reformation Theology of William Tyndale*. Sixteenth Century Essays and Studies 6. Kirksville, MO: Sixteenth Century Journal, 1986.

Smith, Benjamin T. *The Dope: The Real History of the Mexican Drug Trade*. New York: Norton, 2021.

Smith, James K. A. "Radical Orthodoxy." In *GDT* 724–27.

Smith, Noah. "The Dark Side of Globalization: Why Seattle's 1999 Protesters Were Right." *Atlantic*, Jan. 6, 2014. https://www.theatlantic.com/business/archive/2014/01/the-dark-side-of-globalization-why-seattles-1999-protesters-were-right/282831/.

Soelle, Dorothee. *Suffering*. Translated by E. Kalin. Philadelphia: Fortress, 1975.

Song, Young Sub. "The Cultural Context of Globalization and 'Globalizing Theology' as a Christian Response to the Globalization Process." *Korean Journal of Christian Studies* 81 (2012) 243–63.

Southern Evangelical Seminary and Bible College. "Racism and Social Justice." Accessed April 1, 2024. https://ses.edu/about-ses/racism-and-social-justice/.

Sozek, Jonathan. "Osama Bin Laden's Global Islamism and Wahhabi Islam." *Middle Eastern Studies* 42 (Nov. 2006) 33–52.

Stackhouse, Max L. *Globalization and Grace*. God and Globalization 4. New York: Continuum, 2007.

Stackhouse, Max L., and Diane B. Obenchain, eds. *Christ and the Dominions of Civilization*. God and Globalization 3. Harrisburg, PA: Trinity, 2002.

Stackhouse, Max L., and Peter J. Paris, eds. *Religion and the Powers of the Common Life*. God and Globalization 1. New York: T&T Clark, 2000.

Stanley, Brian. *The Global Diffusion of Evangelicalism: The Age of Billy Graham and John Stott*. Downers Grove, IL: InterVarsity, 2013.

Stark, Rodney. *The Rise of Christianity*. Princeton: Princeton University Press, 2023.

Steger, Manfred B. *Globalization: A Very Short Introduction*. 5th ed. New York: Oxford University Press, 2020.

Steger, Manfred B., and Paul James. *Globalization Matters: Engaging the Global in Unsettled Times*. Cambridge: Cambridge University Press, 2019.

Steinmann, Andrew. *Daniel*. St. Louis, MO: Concordia, 2008.

Stiglitz, Joseph E. "Moving beyond Market Fundamentalism to a More Balanced Economy." *Annals of Public and Cooperative Economics* 80 (2009) 345–60.

Stiver, Dan R. *Theology after Ricoeur: New Directions in Hermeneutical Theology.* Louisville, KY: Westminster John Knox, 2001.

Stokes, Bruce. "70 Years after Hiroshima, Opinions Have Shifted on Use of Atomic Bomb." Pew Research Center, Aug. 4, 2015. https://www.pewresearch.org/short-reads/2015/08/04/70-years-after-hiroshima-opinions-have-shifted-on-use-of-atomic-bomb/.

Stop AAPI Hate. "2023 Impact Report." Accessed April 1, 2024. https://stopaapihate.org/2024/03/19/2023-impact-report/.

Stott, John, and John Wyatt. *Issues Facing Christians Today.* Edited by Roy McCloughry. 4th ed. Grand Rapids: Zondervan, 2006.

Sullivan, Dylan, and Jason Hickel. "How British Colonialism Killed 100 Million Indians in 40 Years." Aljazeera, Dec. 2, 2022. https://www.aljazeera.com/opinions/2022/12/2/how-british-colonial-policy-killed-100-million-indians.

Talbot, Karen. "The Real Reasons for War in Yugoslavia: Backing Up Globalization with Military Might." *Social Justice* 27 (2000) 94–116.

Taylor, Alan. "Six Million Displaced by War in Syria." *Atlantic*, Sept. 9, 2013. https://www.theatlantic.com/photo/2013/09/six-million-displaced-by-war-in-syria/100587/.

Taylor, Charles. *A Secular Age.* Cambridge: Belknap, 2007.

Tedlow, Richard S. "What Titans Can Teach Us." *Harvard Business Review* 19 (Dec. 2001) 70–79.

Tennent, Timothy C. *Theology in the Context of World Christianity.* Grand Rapids: Zondervan, 2007.

Thomas, Deja, and Juliana Menasce Horowitz. "Support for Black Lives Matter Has Decreased since June but Remains Strong among Black Americans." Pew Research Center, Sept. 6, 2020. https://www.pewresearch.org/fact-tank/2020/09/16/support-for-black-lives-matter-has-decreased-since-june-but-remains-strong-among-black-americans/.

Tibbs, E. M. "Eastern Orthodox Theology." In *GDT* 245–51.

Tillich, Paul. *Systematic Theology.* Vol. 2. Chicago: University of Chicago Press, 1957.

Tomlinson, John. *Globalization and Culture.* Chicago: University of Chicago Press, 1999.

Tracy, David. "Public Theology, Hope, and the Mass Media." In *Religion and the Powers of the Common Life*, edited by Max Stackhouse and Peter J. Paris, 231–54. New York: T&T Clark, 2000.

Tseng, Shao Kai. "The Theological Foundations of Natural Science." *Christianity Today*, Nov. 29, 2022. https://www.christianitytoday.com/ct/2022/november-web-only/science-christian-worldview-theology-apologetics.html.

Tyndale, William. *Works of William Tyndale.* 2 vols. East Peoria, IL: Versa, 2010.

Tyson, Alec, et al. "Gen Z, Millennials Stand Out for Climate Change Activism, Social Media Engagement with Issue." Pew Research Center, May 26, 2021. https://www.pewresearch.org/science/2021/05/26/gen-z-millennials-stand-out-for-climate-change-activism-social-media-engagement-with-issue/.

Ugbam, Ogechukwu C., et al. "The Effects of Globalization on African Culture: The Nigerian Perspective." *Journal of Business and Management* 16 (2014) 62–71.

United Nations. "Maintain International Peace and Security." Accessed January 10, 2023. https://www.un.org/en/our-work/maintain-international-peace-and-security.

United States Environmental Protection Agency. "Volkswagen Clean Air Act Civil Settlement." Accessed April 1, 2024. https://www.epa.gov/enforcement/volkswagen-clean-air-act-civil-settlement.

Urnov, Fyodor. "We Can Cure Disease by Editing a Person's DNA. Why Aren't We?" *New York Times*, Dec. 9, 2022. https://www.nytimes.com/2022/12/09/opinion/crispr-gene-editing-cures.html.

Van der Valk, Ineke. "Racism, a Threat to Global Peace." *International Journal of Peace Studies* 8 (Autumn/Winter 2003) 45–66.

Vanhoozer, Kevin J. *The Drama of Doctrine*. Louisville, KY: Westminster John Knox, 2005.

Volf, Miroslav. "After the Grave in the Air." *Christianity Today*, Sept. 1, 2001. https://www.christianitytoday.com/ct/2001/septemberweb-only/9-17-54.0.html.

———. *Flourishing: Why We Need Religion in a Globalized World*. New Haven, CT: Yale University Press, 2016.

———. *A Public Faith: How Followers of Christ Should Serve the Common Good*. Grand Rapids: Brazos, 2011.

Volf, Miroslav, and Matthew Croasmun. *For the Life of the World: Theology for the Life of the World*. Grand Rapids: Brazos, 2019.

Voon, Tania. "Pointing the Finger: Civilian Casualties of NATO Bombing in the Kosovo Conflict." *American University International Law Review* 16 (2001) 1083–113.

Wagner, Peter. "The New Apostolic Reformation Is Not a Cult." *Charisma News*, Aug. 24, 2011. https://www.charismanews.com/opinion/-the-new-apostolic-reformation-is-not-a-cult.

Walker, Stephen. *Beyond: The Astonishing Story of the First Human to Leave Our Planet and Journey into Space*. New York: HarperCollins, 2021.

Walker, William A., III. *A Theology of the Drug War: Globalization, Violence, and Salvation*. London: Fortress Academic, 2019.

Wallis, Jim. *The Soul of Politics*. New York: New Press, 1995.

Wandel, Lee Palmer. *Always Among Us: Images of the Poor in Zwingli's Zurich*. Cambridge: Cambridge University Press, 1990.

Waters, Brent. *Just Capitalism: A Christian Ethic of Economic Globalization*. Louisville, KY: Westminster John Knox, 2016.

Waters, Malcolm. *Globalization*. New York: Routledge, 2001.

Wattles, Jackie. "First Space Station Tourism in Ten Years Docks at ISS." CNN, Dec. 9, 2021. https://www.cnn.com/2021/12/07/tech/space-tourism-maezawa-soyuz-scn/index.html.

Welch, Edward T. *Addictions: A Banquet in the Grave*. Phillipsburg, NJ: P&R, 2001.

Wells, Spencer. *The Journey of Man: A Genetic Odyssey*. Princeton: Princeton University Press, 2002.

Werrell, Ralph S. *The Blood of Christ in the Theology of William Tyndale*. Cambridge: James Clarke, 2015.

Wilkins, Charlotte. "'Revival of the Occult': French Youth Turn to Tarot, Astrology during COVID-19." *France 24*, May 22, 2021. https://www.france24.com/en/france/20210522-revival-of-the-occult-french-youth-turn-to-tarot-astrology-during-covid-19.

Williams, Thaddeus J. *Confronting Injustice without Compromising Truth: 12 Questions Christians Should Ask about Social Justice*. Grand Rapids: Zondervan Academic, 2020.

Winant, Howard. "The Dark Matter: Race and Racism in the 21st Century." *Critical Sociology* 41 (2015) 313–24.
Wood, Michael. *The Story of China: The Epic History of a World Power from the Middle Kingdom to Mao and the China Dream.* New York: St. Martin's, 2020.
World Population Review. "Religion by Country 2024." Accessed April 1, 2024. https://worldpopulationreview.com/country-rankings/religion-by-country.
Worthen, Molly. "The Chalcedon Problem: Rousas John Rushdoony and the Origins of Christian Reconstructionism." *Church History* 77 (June 2008) 399–437.
Wunderlich, Jens-Uwe, and Meera Warrier. *A Dictionary of Globalization.* London: Routledge, 2010.
Wycliffe Global Alliance. "2023 Global Scripture Access." Sept. 2023. https://www.wycliffe.net/resources/statistics/.
Xinhua. "Cultural China: Ancient Chinese Concept of Harmony Continues to Influence Modern Life." *Guangming*, Oct. 15, 2021. https://en.gmw.cn/2021-10/15/content_35236462.htm.
Yandell, Keith E. "The City of God: Augustine's Timeless Classic about the Timeless City." *Christian History Institute* 15 (1987) 30–33. https://christianhistoryinstitute.org/magazine/article/city-of-god-augustines-timeless-classic.
Yankuzo, Kabiru Ibrahim. "Impact of Globalization on the Traditional African Cultures." *Journal of Educational and Social Research* 3 (2013) 43–49.
Yeung, Jessie. "She Was Attacked in the Street for Being Asian. Her Community Still Lives in Fear." CNN, Jan. 30, 2022. https://www.cnn.com/2022/01/29/us/asian-american-attacks-aftermath-intl-hnk-dst/index.html.
Zaspel, Fred G. *The Theology of B. B. Warfield.* Wheaton, IL: Crossway, 2010.
Zauzmer, Julie. "Meet the Astrologer Who Brought the Cosmos into the Reagan White House." *Washington Post*, Mar. 11, 2016. https://www.washingtonpost.com/news/acts-of-faith/wp/2016/03/11/meet-the-astrologer-who-brought-the-cosmos-into-the-reagan-white-house/.
Zimmerman, Yvonne C. "Christianity and Human Trafficking." *Religion Compass* 5 (2011) 567–78.
Zinkina, Julia, et al. *A Big History of Globalization: The Emergence of a Global World System.* Cham, Switz.: Springer International, 2019.
Zivanovic, Maja, and Serbeze Haxhiaj. "78 Days of Fear: Remembering NATO's Bombing of Yugoslavia." *BalkanInsight*, Mar. 22, 2019. https://balkaninsight.com/2019/03/22/78-days-of-fear-remembering-natos-bombing-of-yugoslavia/.

www.ingramcontent.com/pod-product-compliance
Lightning Source LLC
Chambersburg PA
CBHW071236230426
43668CB00011B/1461